Still Lifting, Still Climbing

Still Lifting, Still Climbing

Contemporary African American Women's Activism

EDITED BY

Kimberly Springer

PREFACE BY
Beverly Guy-Sheftall

EPILOGUE BY
Loretta J. Ross

New York University Press

NEW YORK AND LONDON

NEW YORK UNIVERSITY PRESS
New York and London

Library of Congress Cataloging-in-Publication Data
Still lifting, still climbing : contemporary African American
women's activism / edited by Kimberly Springer.
p. cm.
Includes bibliographical references (p.) and index.
ISBN 0-8147-8124-1 (alk. paper)
ISBN 0-8147-8125-X (pbk. : alk. paper)
1. Afro-American women—Political activity. 2. Afro-American
women—Social conditions.   I. Springer, Kimberly, 1970–
E185.86 .S766 1999
305.48'896073—dc21   99-6173
CIP

New York University Press books are printed on acid-free paper,
and their binding materials are chosen for strength and durability.

Manufactured in the United States of America

10 9 8 7 6 5 4 3 2 1

For Skylar
A little girl with the future in her eyes

Contents

Acknowledgments

The editing of this volume was, at least in spirit, a collective effort. Thanks to Jennifer Hammer of New York University Press for encouraging the project to fruition. The contributors made editing this volume a rich, educational, and inspiring endeavor. Many thanks to them for enduring my nudging and editorial suggestions. I appreciate the institutional support of Emory University's Institute for Women's Studies. And, of course, much gratitude to Lee Ann Lloyd and Susan Maxwell for tolerating my intrusion into their work space. John Howard, Matthew Papa, and Neil King provided invaluable publishing advice and encouragement for this project from its inception to its publication. Many thanks to my sisters in struggle Meredith Raimondo, Andrea Heiss, Vanessa Jackson, Linda Calloway, Aaronette White, Patti Duncan, Ami Mattison, Angela Cotten, Maria Bevacqua, Jennifer Stocking, and Deborah Grayson for intellectual and spiritual support. Without their conversations about everything from how Black women relate to one another to money-making inventions, this project surely would have never been completed. Additional gratitude to Marion Moffitt, Terry Burks, Wendy Simonds, Randy Malamud, and Ben and Jakey Simonds-Malamud for familial sustenance. Lastly, a wellspring of gratitude to Sandra and Fitzpatrick Springer for teaching me what it means to be a Black woman activist and about dogged persistence, respectively.

Contributors

Receiving her doctorate from Syracuse University in 1997, *Kristin Anderson-Bricker* is an assistant professor teaching U.S. history at Loras College in Dubuque, Iowa. Her current research focuses on grassroots communities working to end racism through chapters of the Congress of Racial Equality.

Angela Ards is an academic turned writer who received her bachelor of arts in English from the University of North Carolina at Chapel Hill, and her master of arts in Afro-American Studies from UCLA. For more than four years, she was a senior editor and writer at *The Village Voice*, where she covered African American arts and culture, race politics, and social affairs. Angela is currently the 1998–1999 Haywood Burns Fellow at the Nation Institute, a nonprofit arm of the *Nation* magazine. Her work has appeared in *The Village Voice*, *The Nation*, *The Voice Literary Supplement*, and various journals.

Patricia Bell-Scott, professor of child and family development, women's studies, and psychology at the University of Georgia, is contributing editor of *Ms. Magazine*. A cofounding editor of *Sage: A Scholarly Journal on Black Women*, she is coeditor of *But Some of Us Are Brave: Black Women's Studies* (1981), the first textbook in Black women's studies and the award-winning *Double-Stitch: Black Mothers Write about Mothers and Daughters* (1993). She recently edited *Life Notes: Personal Writings by Contemporary Black Women* (1995) and *Flat-Footed Truths: Telling Black Women's Lives* (1998).

Dionne Bensonsmith is a doctoral candidate in the Department of Political Science at Syracuse University's Maxwell School of Citizenship and Public Affairs. Her dissertation, which she is currently writing, examines the job education portion of the 1996 welfare reform bill, the Personal Responsibility and Work Opportunity Act.

Lynn M. Eckert is a doctoral candidate in the Department of Political Science at Syracuse University's Maxwell School of Citizenship and Public Affairs. She is currently working on her dissertation, which concerns the free-speech issues around the recent passage of New York's Sex Shop Zoning Law.

Frances Gateward is a doctoral candidate at the University of Maryland-College Park, where she is completing a dissertation on Black American women filmmakers. She has published essays in such publications as *The Paper Channel, Women Filmmakers and Their Films,* and *Angels.* An accomplished independent film and video maker, her works have been screened throughout the United States and in Buenos Aires, Prague, and London. She is currently involved in preproduction for *Need,* a film based on the Audre Lorde poem *Need: A Chorale of Black Women's Voices.*

Deborah R. Grayson is assistant professor in the School of Literature, Communication and Culture at the Georgia Institute of Technology. Her book, currently titled *The Hyper(in)Visible Woman: Constructing the Black Female Body in Medicine and Science,* is forthcoming from Duke University Press. Grayson is also working on a project on contemporary Black women's health activism, from which her chapter comes.

Beverly Guy-Sheftall is Anna Julia Cooper Professor of English and women's studies at Spelman College and founding director of the Women's Research and Resource Center. She is cofounding editor of *Sage: A Scholarly Journal on Black Women.* Her publications include *Daughters of Sorrow: Attitudes Toward Black Women, 1880–1920; Double-Stitch: Black Mothers Write about Mothers and Daughters* (coeditor); *Sturdy Black Bridges: Visions of Black Women in Literature* (coeditor); and *Words of Fire: An Anthology of African American Feminist Thought* (editor).

M. Bahati Kuumba, Ph.D., currently holds the position of assistant professor of sociology at Buffalo State College, where she is also coordinator of African and African American Studies. Her scholarship and activism are focused in the areas of African and African diasporan women, gender and social resistance movements, reproductive liberation, and race/class/gender theory. She has published numerous articles and book chapters on these topics and is currently working on a book-length manuscript titled *Revolution Engendered: The Gender Dialectics in Social Change Movements* (forthcoming, Sage Publications). M. Bahati Kuumba has been involved in the Pan-African, International Women's, and Cuban solidarity movements. She is also a single mother of daughter Tendayi.

Kristin Myers finished her doctorate in sociology from North Carolina State University in 1996. She is currently an assistant professor of sociology at Northern Illinois University. Her teaching and research are committed to the eradication of racial, gender, and class inequalities in society.

Margo V. Perkins, Ph.D., is assistant professor of English and American studies at Trinity College in Hartford, Connecticut. Her essay, "Inside Our Dangerous Ranks," is excerpted from a book in progress on the autobiographies of Angela Davis, Assata Shakur, and Elaine Brown. The book, tentatively titled *Autobiography as Activism: African American Women Writing Resistance*, is forthcoming from the University Press of Mississippi.

Loretta J. Ross is the founder and executive director of the Center for Human Rights Education (CHRE) in Atlanta. CHRE is a training and resource center for grassroots activists on using human rights to address social injustices in the United States. She is an expert on human rights, women's issues, diversity issues, and hate groups and bias crimes. She is a political commentator for Pacifica News Service, and has appeared as a political commentator on *Good Morning America, The Donahue Show, The Charlie Rose Show,* CNN, and BET. She was one of the first African American women to direct a rape crisis center in the 1970s. Ms. Ross is currently writing a book on reproductive rights entitled *Black Abortion* for release in 1999.

Benita Roth is an assistant professor in the Department of Sociology at Binghamton University. Her research is primarily in the area of women and social movement activism, and women and work. Her dissertation, "On Their Own and For Their Own: African American, Chicana and White Feminist Movements in the 1960s and 1970s," analyzes the emergence of feminist politics among African American, Chicana and white women in the second wave.

Jennifer E. Smith is a writer and an activist. Her reviews, essays, fiction and poetry have appeared in more than 50 publications, including *Black Renaissance/Renaissance Noire, Adam of Ife, Fast Talk: Full Volume, African American Review, Without Halos, Moving Out, Black Books Bulletin, Obsidian II, The Bridge, Black Male Research,* and *Essence.* She is a cofounder of the African American Feminist Forum in Washington, D.C., and former editor and publisher of *Black Arts Bulletin.*

Wendy G. Smooth is a doctoral candidate in the Department of Government and Politics at the University of Maryland. Her dissertation examines the roles of women in state legislatures and deals with the gendered nature of these institutions. She is also a member of the research staff at the Center for Women Policy Studies in Washington, D.C.

Kimberly Springer is a doctoral candidate in Emory University's Institute for Women's Studies. Her teaching and research interests focus on women and social movements, women-of-color feminisms, and the implementation of theory and activism. Her dissertation, "Our Politics Was Black Women," analyzes the history of five Black feminist organizations from 1968 to 1980.

Vanessa Tait is a doctoral candidate in sociology at the University of California, Santa Cruz, writing a dissertation on the involvement of community and social movement organizations in U.S. labor organizing since the 1960s. Her interests include the history of left movements; race, gender and class theories; urban social movements; and the culture of activism. She is also a radio and print journalist, and active in the Bay Area labor movement.

Tamelyn Tucker is a doctoral candidate in the Department of Government and Politics at the University of Maryland. Her dissertation research focuses on Black megachurches and their involvement in community development activities in metropolitan areas. She also researches gender and political economy.

Aaronette M. White is a social psychologist who received her doctorate from Washington University in St. Louis. She is currently a Bunting Institute Fellow at Radcliffe College and a research associate at Wilberforce University. She is also currently studying African American feminist identity development and has an ongoing interest in rape prevention and reproductive rights education in African American communities. She is a socialist feminist and espouses scholar-activism.

Sharon D. Wright is assistant professor of political science and Black studies at the University of Missouri at Columbia. Her main teaching and research interests are in African American urban political and electoral behavior. She is also the author of the forthcoming text *Race, Power, and Political Emergence in Memphis.*

Preface

Beverly Guy-Sheftall

> I want to suggest . . . that we link our grassroots orga-
> nizing, our essential involvement in electoral politics,
> and our involvement as activists in mass struggles to the
> long-range goal of fundamentally transforming the so-
> cioeconomic conditions that generate and persistently
> nourish the various forms of oppression we suffer.
> —Angela Davis, *Women, Culture, & Politics*

> We who believe in freedom cannot rest.
> —"Ella's Song," Sweet Honey in the Rock

Despite intense interest in contemporary women's activism on the part of
scholars, *Still Lifting, Still Climbing* challenges narrow conceptions of the
nature of women's political struggles over the past four decades. To be
sure, the history of African American women's activism, in particular, has
been grossly ignored or distorted in scholarly narratives of both the civil
rights and second-wave feminist movements. Several correctives to these
erasures have occurred over the past decade, however. They include the
first book-length treatment of the critical role of Black women in the political struggles of the post–World War II era—*Women in the Civil Rights
Movement: Trailblazers and Torchbearers, 1941–1965*, edited by Vicki
Crawford, Jacqueline Rouse, and Barbara Woods (Brooklyn, N.Y.: Carlson Publishing, 1990)—and more recently, Belinda Robnett's *How Long?
How Long? African-American Women in the Struggle for Civil Rights*
(New York: Oxford University Press, 1997); biographies/monographs of

important figures in the civil rights struggles of the '50s and '60s;[1] and writings by activist women.[2]

From the abolitionist movement in the nineteenth century to the recent welfare- and prison-reform crusades, African American women have been engaged in a broad range of public, organized political activities in diverse institutional contexts—community-based Black organizations, multiracial coalitions, grassroots and professional groups, feminist associations.[3] Representing divergent ideological perspectives, they have organized as students, workers, trade unionists, welfare recipients, politicians, educators, prison reformers, writers, sharecroppers, domestic workers, civil rights leaders, attorneys, Black nationalists, and feminist activists.

Still Lifting, Still Climbing is significant in many ways. It is the first collection of critical essays that examines the broad range of political activities on the part of African American women over the past four decades. It includes their more familiar involvement and leadership in civil rights, Black nationalist, and feminist organizations, as well as their struggles for political representation, reproductive rights, welfare and prison reform, and their resistance to poverty, intracommunity sexism, violence against women, demeaning media images, and poor health. Their resistance to a wide range of injustices occurs within very different organizational contexts: the Women's Political Council, NAACP, Student Nonviolent Coordinating Committee (SNCC), Southern Christian Leadership Conference (SCLC), Black Panther Party, Third World Women's Alliance, National Welfare Rights Organization (NWRO), Association of Community Organizations for Reform Now, National Organization for Women, National Black Feminist Organization, All African Women's Revolutionary Union, African American Women in Defense of Ourselves, Republic of New Afrika, National Black Women's Health Project, and Critical Resistance. This retelling of group struggles will enable us to reimagine the political history of Black women because it moves the discussion beyond the narrow confines of the '60s civil rights movement, while reminding us still of the ways in which that history continues to be male-focused. When we think of Black leaders and activists, women such as Ella Baker, Ruby Doris Smith Robinson, Patricia Robinson, Jo Anne Robinson, Frances Beal, and Assata Shakur will more easily come to mind. This anthology will also broaden the discourse on social movement theory that has been insensitive to the political activism of women of color. Appealing to both academic and nonacademic audiences, this long overdue anthology will also enable us to reconstruct a more complex, gender-sensitive history of contemporary Black America.

As a professor of Black women's history and feminist theory, I am especially pleased about the publication of this anthology because of its value in the classroom. I am also happy to be writing a preface for its editor, Kimberly Springer, whom I taught in graduate women's studies classes at Emory University, and for a collection that includes an essay by Professor Margo Perkins, a former undergraduate student of mine at Spelman College during my early teaching days. Equally as gratifying is the presence of other young scholars whose commitment to the field of Black women's studies (which contributors Barbara Smith and Patricia Bell-Scott helped to establish) will ensure its continued development and presence within the mainstream academy.

Rereading Alice Walker's *Anything We Love Can Be Saved: A Writer's Activism*, I was reminded of the truth of Patricia Hill Collins's assertion about the importance of Black women's culture of resistance (which our mothers and grandmothers embody) in assessing our more public acts of courageous rebellion. In her acknowledgments, Alice, the quintessential writer/activist, thanks her great-great-great-grandmother, May Poole, and her mother (among others) for her own belief in activism and her adult life of cultural, political, and spiritual activism, which her most recent collection of essays illuminates. Alice Walker also reveals the profoundly personal dimensions of one's commitment to activism. In her case, a hatred of domestic violence began when she was thirteen and witnessed the body of a woman whose husband had shot half her face off. In educator Anna Julia Cooper's case, her sensitivity to sexism and commitment to gender equity began when she was prohibited from enrolling in a male-only Greek class as a young girl at St. Augustine's Normal School in Raleigh, North Carolina, in the 1870s.[4] In civil rights activist Pauli Murray's case, it was hearing sexist remarks from her male law professor at Howard University in 1941, which illuminated for her the connections between racism and sexism.[5] For countless other African American women, it was humiliating and sometimes dangerous racist situations in white America such as having to sit on the back of the bus, being forced to drink from "colored only" water fountains, having to send their children to segregated, inferior schools, or earning meager wages as servants in white households. In NAACP leader Daisy Bates's case, we learn from her autobiography about her first encounter with racism, at age eight, when she had to wait to be served by a white grocer until all the whites had been served, and around the same age learning that her biological mother had been raped and killed by three white men.

While the narrative of Black women's activism that emerges here has been largely buried, *Still Lifting, Still Climbing* reminds us that there remains an enormous amount of excavation work to be done for a more comprehensive examination of this extraordinary activist tradition among contemporary African American women. The work of all the contributors here certainly points us in the right direction.

Beverly Guy-Sheftall
Spelman College, 1998

NOTES

1. See Kay Mills, *This Little Light of Mine: The Life of Fannie Lou Hamer* (New York: Dutton, 1993); Lorraine Nelson Spritzer and Jean B. Bergmark, *Grace Towns Hamilton and the Politics of Southern Change* (Athens: University of Georgia Press, 1997); Joanne Grant, *Ella Baker: Freedom Bound* (Somerset, N.J.: John Wiley & Sons, 1998); Cynthia Griggs Fleming, *Soon We Will Not Cry: The Liberation of Ruby Doris Smith Robinson* (Lanham, Md., Rowman & Littlefield Publishers, 1998); Joy James, *Race, Women and Revolution: Black Female Militancy and the Praxis of Ella Baker* (Lanham, Md.: Rowman & Littlefield, 1999).

2. Daisy Bates, *The Long Shadow of Little Rock* (New York: Van Rees, 1962); Anna Arnold Hedgeman, *The Trumpet Sounds: A Memoir of Negro Leadership* (New York: Holt, Rinehart & Winston, 1964); Anne Moody, *Coming of Age in Mississippi* (New York: Dial Press, 1968); Shirley Chisholm, *Unbought and Unbossed* (New York: Avon, 1970), and *The Good Fight* (New York: Harper & Row, 1973); Flo Kennedy, *Color Me Flo: My Hard Life and Good Times* (Englewood Cliffs, N.J.: Prentice-Hall, 1976); Septima Clark, *Ready from Within: Septima Clark and the Civil Rights Movement*, edited by Cynthia Stokes Brown (Navarro, Calif.: Wild Trees Press, 1986); June Jordan, *Civil Wars* (Boston: Beacon Press, 1981), and *On Call: Political Essays* (Boston: South End Press, 1985); Angela Davis, *An Autobiography* (New York: Random House, 1974), and *Women, Culture, and Politics* (New York: Random House, 1984); Pauli Murray, *Song in a Weary Throat: An American Pilgrimage* (New York: Harper and Row, 1987); *The Montgomery Bus Boycott and the Women Who Started It: The Memoir of Jo Ann Gibson Robinson*, edited by David Garrow (Knoxville: University of Tennessee Press, 1987); Audre Lorde, *Sister Outsider: Essays and Speeches* (Trumansberg, N.Y.: Crossing Press, 1984); Elaine Brown, *A Taste of Power: A Black Woman's Story* (New York: Pantheon Books, 1992); Assata Shakur, *Assata:*

An Autobiography (Westport, Conn.: Lawrence Hill, 1987); Barbara Omolade, *The Rising Song of African American Women* (New York: Routledge, 1994); Faith Ringgold, *We Flew Over the Bridge: The Memoirs of Faith Ringgold* (Boston: Little, Brown, 1995); Alice Walker, *Anything We Love Can Be Saved: A Writer's Activism* (New York: Random House, 1997); Barbara Smith, *The Truth That Never Hurts: Writings on Race, Gender, and Freedom* (New Brunswick: Rutgers University Press, 1998); Toni Cade Bambara, *Deep Sightings, and Rescue Missions: Fiction, Essays, and Conversations,* edited by Erroll McDonald (Pantheon Books, 1996).

See Evelyn White, ed., *The Black Women's Health Book: Speaking for Ourselves* (Seattle: Seal Press, 1990), for writings about Black women's health activism around a broad range of issues.

3. See Patricia Hill Collins, *Black Feminist Thought* (Boston: Unwin Hyman, 1990), for a compelling analysis of Black women's activist tradition, which she argues includes the struggle for group survival, which often takes place outside the realm of formal, organized political activity and institutional transformation.

4. See *A Voice from the South* (New York: Oxford University Press, 1988), 76–79. Originally published by Aldine Printing House, Xenia, Ohio, 1892.

5. See Pauli Murray, *Song in a Weary Throat*, 183–184.

Introduction

African American Women Redefining Activism for the Millennium

Kimberly Springer

Over the past thirty years, interest and scholarly production in Black women's history increased significantly. Scholars and activists concerned with the intersections of race, class, gender, and sexual orientation examined Black women's political agency in their communities, in the public sphere, and in their personal lives. Our areas of activism are, historically, wide-ranging. Researchers continue to document African American women's resistance during slavery to show that enslaved women did not passively accept forced labor, sexual assault, and reproduction.[1] Our work to abolish slavery and gain the vote put Black women in the center of public life, yielding public intellectuals such as Sojourner Truth.[2] The Black women's club movement, under the rubric of racial uplift, tackled gender and class concerns.[3] Black women's activism in the African American church demonstrates the connections between the physical and the spiritual dimensions of the fight against racist oppression.[4] Recent scholarship has focused on African American women's behind-the-scenes activism in the civil rights movement.[5] Robnett notes, in her history of African American women's leadership in the civil rights movement, "African American women have been at the forefront of movement activism, from the ill-fated days on the slave ships to the peak of the civil rights movement. So what has happened? Why has the Black woman's invisibility once again been required?"[6] To the contrary, this volume tells the story of the visibility and continuity of African American women's activism. This volume brings the sociohistorical narrative up-to-date.

The motto of the National Association of Colored Women (NACW), one of the largest Black women's clubs of the late nineteenth century, used as its motto "Lifting As We Climb." Giddings notes that when the NACW was founded, "all Black women were perceived in the light of those who had the fewest resources and the least opportunity."[7] Hence, African American clubwomen worked to improve economic and educational opportunities for the entire Black community.

The title of this volume, *Still Lifting, Still Climbing,* emphasizes the idea of historical continuity between African American women of the past, present, and future. The struggle is never over as long as social inequality (e.g., AIDS, sexism, institutional racism, drug abuse, poverty, homophobia, to name a few) continues to plague any member of the African American nation. And while women are the focus of this volume, tellingly, a number of the essays illustrate the joint efforts of African American women and men. Undoubtedly, there are other explicit examples of men and women working together to improve the conditions in our community.

Themes of the Volume

Defining Activism. Activism, in this volume, is broadly defined to encompass the myriad tactics African American women employ to confront sexism, classism, heterosexism, and racism. The contributors to this volume analyze African American women's activism for the ways it is often circumscribed by social constructions of Black womanhood. African American women, as noted in several essays, often step outside the bounds of accepted behavior. For example, the statement by African American Women in Defense of Ourselves in defense of Anita Hill violates strictures in the Black community of not "airing dirty laundry."

Also, changes in political opportunity structures in the past thirty years have redefined African American women's activist options. Black women, such as Myrlie Evers, have assumed leadership positions once the exclusive province of Black men. Wright, in "Black Women in Congress," provides evidence of the racism Black women legislators experience on Capitol Hill. Yet, they persevere in the interest of legislating on behalf of the Black community.

African American women's activism takes the form of "direct action" or activism involving face-to-face interaction with members of the community. Direct action discussed in this volume includes the provision of social services, running for public office, self-help health activism, organizing prison ministries, gender-integrated organizational work, unionization, and paid work in social movement organizations. Activism that might be considered intellectual and, hence, removed from street-level direct action includes writing as resistance, political education, consciousness-raising, autobiography as "political witnessing," public statements in major U.S. newspapers, and filing lawsuits.

Far from establishing a hierarchy of activism ("this way is better than that way"), the contributors to this volume evaluate differing forms of activism for their effectiveness in furthering the overall cause of social justice. African American women's acts of "everyday resistance" and intellectual work coexist to create positive, lasting change in the lives of African Americans.[8]

Grassroots to National Levels of Activism. The essays in this volume cover African American women's activism on varying levels in U.S. society. On the local, grassroots level African American women attempt to tackle issues affecting our lives on a day-to-day basis. Contrary to government-created and media-perpetuated images, African American women actively seek to provide for their families, often in conjunction with African American men. African American women are also active on the national level, running for public office and influencing public policy. As this volume demonstrates, grassroots activism and national politics are not mutually exclusive categories.

African American women's activism necessarily transverses constructed boundaries between the local and national levels. Additionally, African American women's local activism has reverberations on a national scale, affecting not only the Black community but also the continuing dialogue on race relations in North America. The essays in the volume explore a range of topics, which include coalitional politics across sexual orientations; film/video activism; the antirape movement; the Black women's health care movement; workfare unionization; local social service organizations; African American women in the Black feminist, Black Nationalist, the Pan-African, and the Million Man March movements; the anti–mass incarceration movement, and the U.S. Congress. Several of these movements were initiated on the local level and replicated across the United States in African American communities.

Historical Continuity. The essays included here, as a whole and in-dividually, demonstrate the continuity of African American women's activism since the civil rights movement. Each contributor has taken care to situate her particular topic in the historical framework of how race and gender influenced the activism of contemporary African American women leaders. Activism does not emerge from a vacuum but is, instead, part of a complex system of institutions, economics, and personal beliefs. For readers unfamiliar with nineteenth-century leaders, such as Eloyce Patrick Gist, or influential 1970s organizations, such as the National Welfare Rights Organization, the essays confirm the historical basis for Black women's activism in the 1970s, '80s and '90s.

Additionally, as with all movements for social change, lessons from the past are brought to bear on the present. For example, though Ida Wells-Barnett did anticipate the rise in intraracial rape in her campaigns against the lynching of Black men and women in the South, her words echo in the ears of Black women in the antirape movement as they remain vigilant in regards to the "myth of the Black rapist"[9] while confronting the Black community on the realities of sexual abuse.

Organizing Strategies. African American women use a wide range of strategies to change the reality of their lives. Women involved in planning and executing the Million Man March repeated the role of women in the 1950s and '60s civil rights movement who organized behind-the-scenes but were nonetheless instrumental in the success of the event. Numerous women included in this volume choose the power of their words, in print and in speeches, as their weapon. And still other African American women opt to approach people in the streets, in churches, in prisons, in beauty salons, in their homes, and through their televisions to spread the word that the time for change is now. The contributors to this volume offer an analysis of these strategies in an effort to further the movement for the empowerment of the African American community. It is left up to the reader to decide, given the goals of the movement and available po-litical opportunity structures, which strategies are most effective and which need refinement.

Diversity of Organizational Structure. The majority of the essays in this volume explore African American women's activism within organiza-tions. The structures of these organizations vary from small, local groups of Black women to interracial organizations to national mobilizations of people across lines of race, class, gender, and sexual orientation. This diversity of organizational structure speaks to the ways activists define issues, mobilize supporters, and speak to the needs of constituents. The case studies included in this volume also provide an opportunity to examine historical actors interacting with institutions larger than themselves and the institutions they create for the betterment of their situation. For activists, this discussion of organizational structure is appealing because it offers several models for comparing their own organizations and the opportunity to critique a variety of strategies.

Methods of Analysis. The contributors to this volume employed a wide range of theoretical models and methodologies to tell the story of African American women's contemporary activism. Interviews with activists, textual analyses of creative works, content analysis of organizational documents, and personal experience are all used to balance human agency with the historical moment and structural factors. The essays included here demonstrate the uses of experiential, historical, and social science methods as they interact to form a cohesive narrative.

Feminist Activism/Women's Activism. It is up to the reader to evaluate and decide which forms of activism contained in this volume constitute Black feminist activism and which constitute strictly *activism by women.* Is all activism by women necessarily feminist? Some case studies in this volume (e.g., Roth, Anderson-Bricker, Bell-Scott, Ards, Eckert and Bensonsmith, and White) demonstrate the explicit connections between gender and race oppression, necessitating the need for Black feminist activism. Other essayists (e.g., Kuumba, Tait, Gateward, Smooth and Tucker, Grayson, Myers, and Perkins), while illuminating the connections between race and gender oppression, make no overt claims to a Black feminist consciousness on behalf of the women that they study.

I would like to suggest several questions to assist the reader in distinguishing specifically Black feminist activism from general activism by Black women. Why is it important to answer this question in the first place? How does the answer to this dilemma shift the reader's perception of the activism described? Does the reader place more or less value on African American women's activism if it is considered feminist?

Also, key to this issue is the position of gender oppression vis-à-vis racial oppression. For example, do the women described in Smooth and Tucker's essay on the Million Man March privilege combating racism over the fight against male supremacy? Is it, as Black feminists have maintained, impossible to separate racism from sexism in Black women's lives and, therefore, politically detrimental to do so? My interest in these questions lies in determining how African American women, with a diversity of political opinions and expressions, can build coalitions for a stronger movement.

Volume Layout

The volume is divided into three parts. Part One, "African American Women's Political Voices," is devoted to personal narratives of Black women's activism. In line with the feminist edict of the personal as political, the writings in this section show us the connections between Black women's personal responsibility to ourselves and how those responsibilities translate into dedication to the entire Black community. Surprisingly, Black women are still struggling to show that concern for the well-being of Black women does not eschew political and personal connection to Black men and children.

Patricia Bell-Scott's essay, "A Home Girl with a Mission," is a personal interview with longtime activist and writer Barbara Smith. In this conversation, reminiscent of so many talks between "sister-friends," Smith "describes the origins, rewards, and consequences of an activist life." Too often we discuss the successes and failures of activist projects, but we do not consider the costs to those doing the work. Though this is a very personal account of one woman's sacrifice for her beliefs, it is also exemplary of the principle of self-care, something activists of all persuasions often forget in the pursuit of social justice.

The next essay, "To Be Young, Female, and Black," first appeared in a *Village Voice* issue that featured Black feminism. Angela Ards, a New York-based writer, explains the difficulties she encountered bringing her Black feminist praxis to her work as a career/vocation counselor for homeless, teenage mothers. She not only brought a Black feminist analysis to her work but constantly questioned and reevaluated how that analysis concretely applied to the lives of young, African American women outside the towers of academia.

Chapter 3 consists of political statements by African American women. In the past, and even still in the present, white men, white women, and African American men have spoken on behalf of African

American women out of thinly veiled racist concern, universalizing claims of woman/sisterhood, and paternalism, respectively. I consider the four statements included in this section radical because they are the voices of African American women. They declare that no longer will anyone else dictate the terms of our lives or purport to know what is in our best interest. The National Black Women's Health Project (NBWHP) Vision Statement speaks to the mission of this national organization and defines health as "not merely the absence of illness, but the active promotion of physical, spiritual, mental and emotional wellness of this and future generations." The next statement, "We Remember," comes from a pamphlet in circulation since the late 1980s. It is one of the few written statements on African American women and reproductive rights. Recognizing a diversity of opinion among African American women, the statement reframes the concept of "choice," above and beyond the issue of abortion, within the context of African American's historical quest for freedom.

The impact of the Clarence Thomas Senate Judiciary Committee hearings upon the entire country, but specifically the Black community, is documented in several academic and popular volumes.[10] One statement to be occasioned by those hearings, "African American Women in Defense of Ourselves," was a full-page ad in the *New York Times*.[11] This statement, signed by 1600 African American women, came to the defense of Anita Hill and declared war on stereotypes of African American women, which affect public policy. The advertisement served as a direct challenge to those in the Black community who would rather dismiss serious charges of the sexual abuse of a Black woman in favor of securing a place in the polity—that is, the Supreme Court—that most likely would not serve their best interests.

The final statement, the resolution of the 1994 "Black Women in the Academy: Defending Our Name" conference is one of the few collective statements by Black women in the academy and highlights higher education as a site of activism. The outgrowth of the largest gathering of Black feminist/womanist scholars and activists to date, the conference resolution called on President Bill Clinton to examine the political and economic needs of African American women, the U.S. Black community, and international issues related to the African diaspora.

Section Two, "Our Continuous Struggle," documents activism born of the 1960s era. These essays provide concrete links to the civil rights movement of the 1950s and '60s. Following the fall of government-sanctioned barriers to access to equal education, employment, and housing, the civil rights struggle splintered into several different movements. The essays in this part provide concrete examples of the opportunities for political advancement wrought by the civil rights movement and leaders, such as Fannie Lou Hamer, Ella Baker, John Lewis, Ruby Doris Smith, and Dr. Martin Luther King, Jr.

Kristin Anderson-Bricker's "Triple Jeopardy" examines the little-known growth of feminist consciousness among Black women in the Student Nonviolent Coordinating Committee (SNCC). Previous studies often discuss the emerging feminist consciousness of white women in SNCC, but assume that Black women were hostile to these developments due to the rise of the Black Power movement. Anderson-Bricker explores the development of the Third World Women's Alliance, an organization fostered by Black feminist activism in SNCC and created to struggle for the elimination of economic, racist, and sexist exploitation.

In "The Making of the Vanguard Center," Benita Roth offers revisions to the historical record on Black feminism. First, she argues that we need to reframe our discussion of the emergence of second-wave feminism in terms of a plurality of *feminisms*. Based solely on numbers, Black feminists were not considered a forceful presence in second-wave feminist organizations. Yet, Roth continues, Black feminism emerged at the same time as white feminist consciousness and, in fact, furthered the agenda of the feminist movement as a whole by critiquing its class bias. Roth also argues that Black feminists challenged the Black liberation movement on its sexism as well as its tendency toward patriarchal, class-based notions of sex roles.

Margo Perkins discusses the tensions arising for Black women between feminist and nationalist desires in "Inside Our Dangerous Ranks." These competing ideologies, Perkins shows, have valuable pedagogical implications for how we assess the overall achievements and shortcomings of the Black liberation movement. She uses the autobiography of former Black Panther leader Elaine Brown as "political witnessing": to document not just the objective fact of sexism as a problem within the Black nationalist movement, but the truth of sexism's material and psychological impact on Black women. Sadomasochism, as Perkins's theoretical framework, exposes power within the party as alternately oppressive or empowering, depending on the subject's position.

"Racial Unity in the Grass Roots?" is Kristin Myer's case study of a southern women's social service organization. Founded by a wealthy African American woman in 1968, the organization sought to end racist violence by mediating between their southern community and local, elite policy makers. Though the twelve white and twelve African American women united in a period of intense racial divisions, the organization persists into the 1990s. Myers situates her examination within the context of race, class, and gender pressures experienced by the women internally and externally to the organization. Most important, Myers demonstrates the complexity of the role of economically empowered African American women and their influence as community role models in challenging the white elite. Yet, she ultimately questions how programs instigated by an elite class, regardless of race, can be truly far-reaching.

"Recognizing that achieving good health is still a central component within the struggle for civil rights, Black women activists work to make the health needs of Black people a central political concern in the national arena," asserts Deborah Grayson in "Necessity Was the Midwife to Our Politics," an examination of local and grassroots organizing around the issues of Black women's physical and mental health. To buttress this assertion, she highlights individual and group efforts to establish the tradition of self-help around AIDS, breast cancer, and the overall well-being of the Black community. Spotlighting the work of such figures as Byllye Avery of the National Black Women's Health Project and Zora Kramer Brown of Rise Sister Rise, Grayson documents the work of Black women's health activists from 1970 to the present.

What gains have Black women made in the higher echelons of United States government? Do Black women in Congress face a double disadvantage because of race and gender factors? Sharon Wright, in "Black Women in Congress during the Post–Civil Rights Movement Era," answers these questions through an analysis of the history of Black women's election to Congress. She compares and contrasts the campaign strategies and agendas for Black women elected in the 1980s and 1990s with those elected in the 1960s and 1970s. Through this methodology, Wright determines whether more recently elected Black women have less difficulty obtaining campaign funds, crossover votes, and endorsements. Wright's essay is a compelling look at the predictors for the success of Black female candidates and their future in U.S. government.

Part Three of this volume, "Contemporary African American Women's Activism," brings us into the 1980s and '90s. The 1970s were a time of reflection upon the gains of the 1960s and, some would maintain, the erosion of many of those gains. The essayists in this part of *Still Lifting, Still Climbing* reexamine the ideology and strategies of the civil rights movement and divergence from past organizing. The part is most of all about the reverberations of the not-so-distant past. What has been the impact of the gay and lesbian, Pan-African, feminist, and socialist movements on African American women's activism? How have African American women, and the entire Black community, responded to the government backlash against the poor and working classes? How have African American women artists/political activists used technology, specifically the media, in response to government repression and white supremacy?

M. Bahati Kuumba continues the exploration of the role of women in 1960s and '70s nationalist struggles into the 1980s and '90s in "Engendering the Pan-African Movement: Field Notes from the All-African Women's Revolutionary Union." She explores the formulation and implementation of race/class/gender praxis in the All-African People's Revolutionary Party (AAPRP) and the All-African Women's Revolutionary Union (AAWRU), the women's wing of AAPRP established in 1980. She chronicles the dialectical struggle between African nationalism, women's liberation, and class struggle. While demonstrating the importance of a gendered voice in this particular Pan-African organization, she also warns against the "double-shift" AAWRU women were subjected to in the interest of a woman-centered reevaluation of the Pan-Africanist movement.

"Talking Black, Talking Feminist," analyzes the gendered micromobilization processes in a collective protest against rape. Aaronette White describes the collective action of a coalition of Black women and men in St. Louis, Missouri, against the valorization of professional boxer Mike Tyson following his 1992 rape conviction. The protest questioned the "Free Mike Tyson" actions, which turned a blind eye to sexual assault against Black women and girls as a crime against the entire Black community. White aptly reconstructs how Black nationalist–civil rights and feminist social movement frames joined to replace "gutter wisdom" about rape with facts about how this crime impacts African American women and men.

Writer and activist Jennifer Smith traces the history of African American women's fight against the disproportionate imprisonment of African Americans in "ONAMOVE: African American Women Confronting the Prison Crisis." Noting the historical legacy of Ida Wells-Barnett, anti-lynching crusader, she explores the work of contemporary Black women activists such as Safiya Bukhari-Alston, Angela Davis, Ramona Africa, and Evelyn Williams. These women, drawn into the anti–mass incarceration movement often because of personal political persecution, are on the frontlines of a struggle that includes protests in behalf of political prisoners, lobbying for changes in sentencing guidelines, working with legislatures, and educating the public. These activities on the national level and the initiation of crime prevention programs on the local level demonstrate a range of political tactics from radical to moderate in the criminal justice reform movement.

An estimated one million men gathered in Washington, D.C., on October 16, 1995, to profess their acceptance of responsibility for their families and communities. In "Behind But Not Forgotten," Wendy Smooth and Tamelyn Tucker tease apart the complexities of the role of African American women in the organization and execution of this momentous community action. Contrasting the role of Black women in the Civil Rights March on Washington to the Million Man March, Smooth and Tucker ask how much progress has been made in the ways women's roles are viewed by the Black community. One side of the debate expressed incredulity that again, in the 1990s, Black women were, as in 1970s Black nationalist rhetoric, being asked to walk behind Black men. Others argued that the importance of the march for the empowerment of Black men far exceeded the significance of women's equal participation and inclusion. Smooth and Tucker engage this debate through secondary source materials and interviews with participants in the organizing of the march.

In "Crossing Lines," Lynn M. Eckert and Dionne Bensonsmith investigate the role of Mandy Carter, a self-described Black lesbian feminist, in the founding of North Carolina Mobilization '96 and its role in the Jesse Helms/Harvey Gantt Senate race. *Mobilization '96*, which united different identity-based minority groups sharing a desire to elect Gantt, forecasted the future of identity-based politics. Eckert and Bensonsmith explore the role of the coalition in the 1996 Senate race but also highlight Carter's enactment of third-wave feminist politics with a focus on understanding the nature of identity in its multiple aspects.

Frances Gateward's "Documenting the Struggle" examines the continued use of the media by African American women as a tool for change. Noting the precedence of nineteenth-century African American women media producers, such as Maria Stewart and Eloyce Patrick Gist, Gateward outlines the challenges faced by contemporary African American media activists. She highlights the compelling work of Madeline Anderson, Portia Cobb, and Cyrille Phipps as exemplary of the power of the media to influence "not only . . . how we think of others, but also ourselves." Their artistry as directors, as well as the influence of their work on the Black community, models direct action that seeks to raise consciousness around issues such as police brutality, health care, employment equity, and poverty.

Situating her argument in the past struggles of African American women in the National Welfare Rights Organization (NWRO), Vanessa Tait examines how the labor organizing of African American women, welfare rights activism of the 1970s, and coalitional politics merged in response to conservative ideologies around welfare "reform" in the 1990s. Using New York City's Work Experience Program (WEP) as a case study, Tait argues in "Workers Just Like Anyone Else," that though workfare organizing is multiracial and multiethnic, African American women are at the helm of this movement and leading the way in building a broader, more egalitarian labor movement. These women are redefining welfare in terms of economic justice, or the right to decent jobs at a livable wage. This redefinition warns unions that they must reckon with the number of women of color demanding representation and, at the same time, the growing gulf between the haves and have-nots in our society.

Still Lifting, Still Climbing represents another weapon in the arsenal of African American struggle: documentation. Throughout African American history, members of the community exhorted one another to "tell it like it is," "testify," and "preach the truth." Without documenting the activism of African American women, who struggle on behalf of the Black community, we are left to wonder, "What happened to the movement?"

The contributors to this volume join with community activists to answer this question. In this respect, the contributors to this volume are activists; they document the activism of African American women, so that our history is not lost. They also analyze our gains and losses since the end of the 1960s, lighting the pathway to future struggles. *Still Lifting, Still Climbing* serves as homage to our African American predecessors and as a drum call to future generations. Our present activism would be missing its purpose without knowledge of past efforts and hopes for continuing the struggle.

NOTES

1. Beverly Guy-Sheftall, *Words of fire: An anthology of African American feminist thought* (New York: New Press, 1995); Deborah Gray White, *Ar'n't I a*

woman?: Female slaves in the plantation South (New York: Norton, 1985); Angela Davis, "Reflections on the Black Woman's Role in the Community of Slaves," *Black Scholar* 3 (December 1971): 2–5.

2. See for example, Harriet A. Jacobs, *Incidents in the life of a slave girl* (Cambridge: Harvard University Press, 1987), and Rosalyn Terborg-Penn, *African American women in the struggle for the vote, 1850 to 1920* (Bloomington: Indiana University Press, 1998).

3. Paula Giddings, *When and where I enter: the impact of Black women on race and sex in America* (New York: William Morrow, 1984).

4. Exemplary works on African American women's religious activism include Evelyn Brooks Higginbotham, *Righteous discontent: The women's movement in the Black Baptist church, 1880–1920* (Cambridge: Harvard University Press, 1993), and Judith Weisenfeld, *African American women and Christian activism: New York's Black YWCA, 1905–1945* (Cambridge: Harvard University Press, 1997).

5. For more on the role of African American women in the civil rights movement, please see Belinda Robnett, *How long? How long? African American women in the struggle for civil rights* (Oxford: Oxford University Press, 1997); Vicki L. Crawford, Jacqueline Anne Rouse, and Barbara Woods, *Women in the civil rights movement: Trailblazers and torchbearers, 1941–1965* (Brooklyn, N.Y.: Carlson Pub., 1990); Charles M. Payne, *I've got the light of freedom: The organizing tradition and the Mississippi freedom struggle* (Berkeley: University of California Press, 1995); and Joanne Grant, *Ella Baker: Freedom bound* (New York: Wiley, 1998).

6. Robnett, *How long? How long?*: 203.

7. Giddings, *When and where I enter*: 97–8.

8. Patricia Hill Collins, *Black feminist thought: Knowledge, consciousness, and the politics of empowerment* (Boston: Unwin Hyman, 1990).

9. Angela Y. Davis, "Rape, Racism and the Myth of the Black Rapist," in *Women, race and class* (New York: Random House, 1981), pp. 172–207.

10. Toni Morrison, ed., *Race-ing justice, en-gendering power: Essays on Anita Hill, Clarence Thomas, and the construction of social reality* (New York: Pantheon Books, 1992); Robert Chrisman and Robert L. Allen, eds., *Court of appeal: the Black community speaks out on the racial and sexual politics of Clarence Thomas vs. Anita Hill* (New York: Ballantine Books, 1992); Geneva Smitherman, *African American women speak out on Anita Hill–Clarence Thomas* (Detroit: Wayne State University Press, 1995); and Anita Faye Hill and Emma Coleman Jordan, eds., *Race, gender, and power in America: The legacy of the Hill-Thomas hearings* (New York: Oxford University Press, 1995).

11. "African American Women in Defense of Ourselves," *New York Times,* November 17, 1991, p. A53.

Part I

African American Women's Political Voices

Chapter One

Barbara Smith
A Home Girl with a Mission

Patricia Bell-Scott

Introduction

Writer-activist Barbara Smith was born in 1946 and reared with her twin sister, Beverly, by a grandmother and aunt after the death of their mother. From womanfolk Barbara inherited a love of African American cultural traditions, as well as a commitment to social change. This commitment is reflected in her politics and in a lifetime of advocacy on behalf of people of color, women's, and lesbian/gay issues.

Although known primarily for her activism, Barbara is first of all a writer. She has written numerous essays, poems, and short stories. She is also editor of several major works including All the Women Are White, All the Blacks Are Men, But Some of Us Are Brave: Black Women's Studies *(with Akasha Hull and Patricia Bell-Scott),* Home Girls: A Black Feminist Anthology, *and* The Reader's Companion to U.S. Women's History *(with Wilma Mankiller; Gwendolyn Mink, Marysa Navarro, and Gloria Steinem) and is cofounder of Kitchen Table: Women of Color Press. Her current project is the first history of African American lesbians and gays in the United States.*

In this conversation, she describes the origins, rewards, and consequences of an activist life, as well as the marginalization of African American lesbians and gays by conventional Black, women, and lesbian and gay organizations. She also reflects on her personal journey toward self-acceptance.

Letters from Home

There has been a tragic occurrence! I've lost my favorite watermelon pin. It was enamel, beautifully done in red and glazed like pottery. Small, very nice, no more than an inch. And it looked just like a slice of watermelon. You know, I could tell a lot about people by how they reacted to my watermelon pin. Those who were obviously down with me would laugh and say, "Oh, that's so wonderful." Then there were other people who couldn't laugh and they'd ask, "What is that for? What does it represent?" So I'd think of little answers like I belong to an organization where we eat watermelon once every month, even when it's out of season. Occasionally some Black person would say, "Well, don't you think that's racist?" I'd say, "No, it's not racist; watermelon is a fruit! Now if I had a White person up here on my lapel, then we could say that that was an embodiment or a depiction of someone or something that could be potentially racist."

I have many watermelon things in my home. To me, they are the perfect food. Many of my friends know that I love them, so I am constantly acquiring representations. When I went to visit the Black woman filmmaker Michelle Parkerson and she too had a house full of watermelons, I thought, Great minds run together. I also have an article by Vertamae Grosvenor titled "A Watermelon Fan Comes Out of the Closet," which I send to people on occasion. In this piece, Vertamae writes about her love of watermelons as an evocation of Black culture. I also see them as a symbol of Black culture generally and perhaps even Black female culture. My aunt who raised me and my sister in Cleveland, Ohio, told us that they called watermelons letters from home. They were precious.

Family Legacies

The people I was raised by worked really, really hard, mostly as domestics. We were one of those respectable Black families, where people did what they were supposed to do—went to work, took care of their children, stayed clear of illegal activities, and refrained from becoming a public nuisance. We were the kind of ordinary Black family that many White folks do not believe existed. And we were like everyone else we knew.

Even though there wasn't a huge amount open to them, people in our family valued education highly. A couple of great-aunts, my grandmother's sisters, went to Spelman in the early 1900s. Once while I was looking through the college archives, I found a penny postcard from my aunt Rosa, whom I grew up with. She had taken normal school courses there. Another great-aunt who died before I was born spoke on the emancipation of Turkish women at her graduation from the Spelman high school division. Now that explains to me in part why I'm such a staunch feminist. I come by it honestly from family.

My twin sister, Beverly, and I were raised by our grandmother and aunts. Our mother, who was a single parent and worked outside the home, died in 1956, when we were only nine. Our grandmother was like the Black women generals Alice Walker describes in some of her writings. Rules were strictly enforced, and there was none of this positive reinforcement so popular today. There was no raving or pay for grades. Are you kidding? When we brought home straight-A report cards, our family would say, "That's nice." Excellence was simply expected. At this point in my life, I think that I have put my grandmother's ways into perspective and have come to appreciate many of the things she taught me. Besides usable skills like sewing, she taught me self-discipline, which is very important. There was never any sense of day-to-day uncertainty in our lives. Whatever grown people said, whatever the plan was, whatever was supposed to happen, happened.

My mother, Hilda, was the youngest of my grandmother's three children and the only one to finish college. She tried to get certified to teach in the Cleveland public school system, but because the conditions in the ghetto schools were so demoralizing, she returned to her job as head cashier at a local supermarket. Before that, she had been a nurse's aide. I will never forget telling a White woman therapist about my mother being a college graduate and the kinds of jobs she had and having this therapist tell me that my mother obviously had a self-image problem. The diagnosis was that I had a similar problem—no self-confidence. What this White woman did not understand was that there had been generations of Black college-educated people, men and women, who were denied jobs that their education had prepared them for. And maybe my mother did have a self-image problem—after all, she was a Black single mother in the 1940s with two little children and she had to take any damn job she could find! In her day, there were Black folks with Ph.D.'s working in the U.S. postal service because they couldn't get jobs elsewhere. That's just the way that was.

A Natural Calling

I'm kind of a natural activist. It's a tendency or capacity that probably would have found an outlet eventually—but because I came of age in the civil rights era, I had a vehicle for channeling my justifiable anger at the circumstances under which I saw my community living. By the time I was eight I noticed that things were not fair—that mostly Brown people lived in tenements and only White people lived in mansions. I also had an endless list of questions like, Why were there Black people and why were there White people? Why didn't any White people live in our neighborhood? Why were there only White people on television? Why were all of our teachers White but all of the children Black? Why, when a White person knocked on our door—though this almost never happened and then it was an insurance salesman or someone like that—was there anxiety in the air that my sister and I could grasp? Why was the tension so strong when my aunt went to a department store to buy stockings? And why did the clerks ignore her? I wanted to know why about all of this.

The first demonstration I ever went to was in the early 1960s, when I was in high school. Bruce Klunder, a White minister, was killed protesting the building of a new elementary school that would be segregated. He lay down in a ditch in front of some construction equipment, and by accident or design, the workers rolled over him. I remember going to protest rallies after that. My sister and I also stayed home on the Monday of the school boycott, going instead to a Freedom School that had been set up in a neighborhood church. I think my family was basically supportive of our participation in these demonstrations because they were race women. They supported the NAACP and my grandmother always worked at the polls. They also had migrated from the South, so they knew even better than I did the horrors of U.S. apartheid that the movement was working to change.

I began my activism early, and eventually I came to identify as a Black feminist, a lesbian, and a Socialist. I also believe that the Combahee Collective—of which I was a cofounder and which functioned from 1974 to 1981 in Boston—was one of the most significant groups to come out of any movement. The collective had a series of retreats that brought together Black women artists and activists who were committed to feminism and political organizing. We made a conscious effort to look at how systems of oppression were connected to each other. We understood that dealing with sexual politics didn't mean that you weren't a race woman, and that speaking out about homophobia didn't mean that you didn't want to end poverty.

A lifetime of activism has had several major consequences for me. It has meant being outside of the academy, but despite my love of teaching I never really envisioned a traditional academic career. Needless to say, it has meant working hard for long hours and for little, if any, pay. It has also meant sometimes putting my writing on hold, particularly the fiction. However, I wasn't raised to think that everything was about me. Black feminism meant to me that I had a responsibility to help build and provide resources for other women of color, and a commitment to struggle requires certain sacrifices. Now, I'm not saying that you have to take a vow of poverty, but I do not think that you can vacation on the Riviera every summer and still be about struggle.

There are tangible rewards to the activist life. I've seen a lot of change in my lifetime. When I was born into segregation in 1946, most Black people in this country could not vote; those who did or tried to vote did so on pain of death. And the women in my family could not try on a hat in a southern department store—and that included Washington, D.C. I never bend over a public water fountain without realizing that once this would have been a revolutionary act. I know these things seem small, particularly to young people who have never lived the other way. We still have a long way to go, but I know that it took revolutionary commitment to get to this point.

An Invisible Sister

Despite all my years of activism on behalf of Black, women's, and lesbian and gay issues, there are times when I really feel like a stranger. At the twenty-fifth anniversary of Stonewall, the underrepresentation of people of color was demoralizing. It reminded me of Ralph Ellison's brilliant book *The Invisible Man*, which captures an experience that almost every person of color can identify with. Very few lesbian and gay men of color, including myself, are ever invited to the leadership summits called by White gay leaders. Being omitted from a meeting or invitation list might seem at first thought like a small thing; the larger issue is about the disenfranchisement of women and men of color within the movement.

I'm convinced that our disempowerment at this moment in history is directly related to a push to mainstream the lesbian and gay movement in the United States. Bruce Bawer's book, *A Place at the Table*, comes out of this mainstreaming effort, which is problematic for me because I really have no interest in reinforcing or dealing with the establishment. As a radical, I want to see it destroyed. I want a nonhierarchical, nonexploitative society in which profit is not the sole motivation for every single decision made by the government or individuals. And if the lesbian and gay movement's motto becomes "A place at the table" in the present system, I have to ask, what am I as a Black woman going to be doing at this table—carrying a tray? Handing someone a dish? A place at the table? Not likely. It really doesn't work for me.

Black women's organizations should be at the forefront of the fight against homophobia in the Black community. They need to indicate their support of all Black women, regardless of sexual orientation. Unfortunately, many of them are afraid to stand publicly in support of gay and lesbian issues. They fear the inevitable charge that they are just a bunch of lesbians, which has been said about all women's groups.

One painful experience that I have over and over again is when prominent Black women leaders who are closeted pull me aside at a conference or some gathering to say, "Barbara, I'm so glad you're doing what you're doing. You're doing wonderful work, girl, and you just go on and do it! Go on, sister, I'm right behind you." Yet they are not about to say on the stage or anywhere publicly, "As a lesbian I'm so proud that Barbara's a lesbian, too. She has helped me be proud as a lesbian." They're not able or willing to do that. These encounters always remind me of the title of Audre Lorde's book *Sister Outsider*. It's an oxymoron because a sister is obviously someone inside the family, close, a home girl. But the sister with the lesbian feminist politics like Audre's or mine is also an outsider.

Writing as Empowerment

I wanted to be a writer as soon as I found out that you could be one. James Baldwin was key in that. I was first introduced to him through *Go Tell It on the Mountain*, thanks to Aunt LaRue, who worked at the Cleveland Public Library as a clerk-typist. She would bring home shopping bags full of books, and my sister and I would devour them. When I read *Go Tell It on the Mountain*, I was thunderstruck. Here was a book that described a little guy, a main character, who was so much like me. He was shy; he liked to write; he was not happy; and he saw so many things. Until

I read Baldwin I never knew that one could write about being Black and poor and get published. I assumed that the only way you could write a book or be a novelist was to write about well-off White people. I thought to myself, This is incredible writing. Maybe I could do that, too. After I read Baldwin, that was it.

Of all my writings, the essay "Toward a Black Feminist Literary Criticism" (1978) continues to hold a special place for me. I think that there are probably moments in every artist's life where you feel that you didn't necessarily create what was there but were instead the vehicle for it to be manifested. Looking back, I feel that way about this essay. It defined a moment, a feeling, a new field, and possibilities. It was a piece after which other things could be written on the topic. And it is still the subject of debate and dialogue. It also fascinates me when men and women who are not of African origin tell me what this essay has meant to them. That says something to me, not because I seek validation from people who are unlike me but because that piece is very Black, very female, and very lesbian.

With the increased acceptance of research and writing about Black women, I sometimes reflect on the introduction to our book *All the Women Are White, All the Blacks Are Men, But Some of Us Are Brave: Black Women's Studies.* In that piece we said that the goal of Black women's studies is to save Black women's lives. We didn't say it was to get tenure, a book contract, or a certain salary. We said it was about saving lives, and we meant every Black woman—not just those lucky enough to get higher education and do college or university teaching or research. We meant the Black woman who's never going to read any of our damn books.

I am writing the first book on the history of African American lesbians and gays. I hope, with this project, to give us back to ourselves and to empower people. Almost all of my writing has been about empowerment and about trying to say to people of color, to women, and to lesbians and gay men that you are really worth something, you are important, you have a history to be proud of. There is no reason to be ashamed.

Coming Home

For me, moving into midlife has had advantages. One of these is a more balanced perspective on life—or maybe even sometimes wisdom. This new perspective has given me a clear vision of what my limits and priorities are, as well as the relative unimportance of what most people think of me. The older I get and the longer I'm here, the more adjusted I become to being a human being on this planet.

I have developed an appreciation for simple acts of self-care—like a daytime nap, eating on time, and sitting quietly after a bout of running around. Self-acceptance is another thing that has come to me. I'm having the time of my life doing the work I love. I'm not saying that my life has been perfect or that I have no regrets, because there have been mistakes and disappointments. But midlife teaches that I don't have to repeat those experiences again, and that is a comforting thought. After all these years of hard work, I'm coming home to me. And the feeling is good. Really good.

NOTE

Reprinted by permission of *Ms. Magazine,* © 1995.

Chapter Two

To Be Young, Female, and Black

Angela Ards

Fifteen students and one teacher, we met Monday through Thursday, 12:30 to 2:00, the fall of 1994, in a closet of a space with one skinny window overlooking 83d Street and West End Avenue on Manhattan's Upper West Side. The class, which I'd designed, was "Passport to Independence," a work-skills/self-esteem course for teenage mothers living with their children at the West End Intergenerational Residence (WIR—part homeless shelter, part adult-education center, part job-training program).

Recently out of grad school and, at 25, only about six years their senior, I felt my students had more real-world smarts than I might ever have, that they knew a side of Black womanhood that I would never get reading bell hooks or Michele Wallace or Alice Walker. And yet, all semester, in room 507, around four card tables laid head-to-head, I led them in desultory conversations about "the myths and realities of independence": of going from welfare to work, from dropouts to graduates, from living in a shelter to making a living in society. When there were no sick babies, WIC appointments, clinic visits, or unexcused absences, and the class was full, to make room I would vacate my spot at the makeshift table and sit on the window sill, shoes propped on the busted radiator. There, at the head of the class, I looked more like the teacher than I wanted to.

Generally, my students had come from inner-city neighborhoods with tough-sounding names and reputations to match: Do or Die Bed-Stuy, Never Ran Never Will Brownsville, the Boogie Down Bronx, Harlem. More specifically, they'd come from an Emergency Assistance Unit, or another homeless shelter, or a foster home, or a friend's home, maybe even their parents' (usually their mother's), for reasons I never really knew, though I sometimes heard tales of abuse-sexual, physical, substance. What I did know was that they were all young, poor, single mothers, mainly of color, with a few hard skills to trade an employer for a living wage. My class was intended to help them turn all that around.

A year before, in November 1993, on a whim, a personal dare, I'd come to New York seeking fame and fortune as a writer. Fresh out of school with a degree better for the soul than for solvency, I landed a copyediting gig paying dirt and decided it was a "sign" to go for broke pursuing a dream. Come April, color my parachute bust and me, looking for a job.

As far as job-search techniques go, the want ads are a long shot. Networking, it's said, is your best bet: you tell two friends, and they tell two friends, and so on. But at the time, as a newcomer to the city, my net didn't feel so big.

In the *New York Times* classifieds, under EDUCATION, an ad sought a career/vocational specialist to develop internships and self-esteem workshops for adolescent women of color at the West End Intergenerational Residence. I'd never heard of a "career/vocational specialist," but for the salary offered, I'd be one. So I pieced together my resume, boasting of my experience with internship placements (I'd codesigned a field study seminar one quarter); "at-risk youth" (I'd tutored GED students in Watts one year); and social issues affecting women of color (my graduate studies focused on Black feminist theory). This would be a chance, I told myself, to put all my ivory-tower knowledge to some real-world use.

I went for an interview with the social service director of WIR. A middle-aged white woman, who seemed to be waiting for retirement, welcomed me into her office, an expanse of dingy yellow with faux-Impressionist paintings seemingly on every wall. A photographic history called *The African Americans* was pointedly placed on a file cabinet. On the cover was a Black woman with textured natural hair, chin cradled in one palm. With my resume inert on her desk, the director asked few questions about my skills and experience, just smiling blankly at my Black face, my short 'fro blooming beyond its borders into the coils of baby dreads. Clearly, I was being hired to be a real live walking talking African American role model. But, I thought, who better than me, a Black feminist with a sense of righteousness and advocacy, for the job?

When I told my family and friends I'd be teaching work skills to teen moms in a homeless shelter, if not tactfully asking, why a *shelter*? *why you*?, they warned *alto voce* that working with welfare recipients would be a thankless task. "You *know* you don't know what you're getting into," my aunt Cat said the week before I was to start. I'd gone home for a little family support and we were in her East Texas barbershop, me getting a trim, she holding forth among her regular patrons and Dallas relations paying an overdue visit. She'd been chatting and clipping all afternoon but stopped to let this comment hover. Mercifully, the mirror in front of us mediated a look telling she feared me a young fool.

"You think?" I asked, more out of respectful acknowledgment than any real interest in her response. By then I'd grown weary of the belly-of-the-beast cautionary tales. When she handed me Ken Auletta's *The Underclass,* mumbling too loudly that I would sure need it, I was stone-faced except for a little tight smile of thanks that slit my eyes. And when she whisked me into the house of her friend Edwardlene, who gave me stacks of vocational curriculum materials that I had the good sense to know I really did need, I was inwardly chanting, "I'm only one but I am one" and "If not me, who?" determined to help break the cycle of poverty, albeit in one small corner of the world. Aunt Cat and Miss Edwardlene waved me along back to New York with little tight smiles of their own.

West End Intergenerational Residence, except for the shabby blue scaffolding buckling under the weight of too many seasons, blends in with its middle-class surroundings. Walking by, on your way to Zabar's, or Barnes & Noble, or the Gap, you'd never know that inside is a homeless shelter for 54 single mothers on public assistance, ages 17 to 21, and their preschool-aged children; they stay anywhere from three months to a year. You might not notice the stream of Black and brown women pushing baby strollers toward Broadway, sometimes veering off to Riverside Park—they're a common enough sight on the Upper West Side. What tells is that the women are so young, and the babies they're caring for in the middle of the day are their own.

At WIR, "independent living" is stressed, with the young women residing in private single rooms, responsible for their own meals, [all] their transportation, and their children. While waiting for a low-income apartment to become available, they participate in a battery of programs designed to keep them from being homeless again, including GED classes, parenting and life-skills workshops, and the career-guidance program.

Using a collage of influences, I eagerly set about creating a two-part curriculum stressing both personal and career development. My sistagirl

Terri loaned me a self-help pamphlet borrowed from her aunt. Called "Self-Esteem Passport," it provided me with the course's name and its guiding metaphor: a journey to self-awareness and independence, achieved with the help of certain essential visas—values, dreams, goals, networking. Miss Edwardlene's vocational materials let me know what a job-readiness course should look like. Then I threw in some material of my own, written works and music with a woman-centered sensibility that ranged from Billie Holiday to Salt-N-Pepa, Nikki Giovanni to Pearl Cleage.

I wasn't so idealistic as to believe that my students and I would automatically connect because of our race and sex. Though a fundamental tenet of Black feminism is that we experience "interlocking systems" and "simultaneity" of oppressions, I was aware of the tendency to oversimplify the differing effects of race, sex, and class on each Black woman's life. I first acknowledged this diversity of Black sisterhood when I sought out the one Black and female like me, thinking she could relate to my "issues"—she could not. Yet, in America, all Black women are affected by the same image whether they're manipulated by the "Contract on America" or mutilated in BET/MTV videos. Which is why I thought that, in some way, our common blackness and femaleness could collapse differences—of teacher and student, education and class—into a circle of sisterhood.

For Week One on my syllabus, the primary objective is "to create a comfortable and safe environment for discussion and sharing." I try to break the ice with the usual describe-yourself-with-the-first-initial-of-your-name games. Like that Jackie, who *will* not let the class proceed until I note on my roster, in pen, the new spelling of her name ("Jacqué"), is joyful. (All the names in this piece have been changed.) And that Elayne, who I can now admit was a favorite, is "evil, because everybody says I am." At first Phylicia—who is soon known as Leese—can't think of an adjective to describe herself. A few moments pass with her looking at the floor, us looking at her, and then Monica ("mellow, 'cause I got Jesus") offers "patient." "Yes, ummph, she is pa-tient," Phylicia's classmates chorus, citing instances of her parental equanimity in the face of a tyrannical toddler. Except for the one young woman who wants to be called Ms. Stanley (she has a two year-old son nicknamed Daddy), I plan for us to be on a first-name basis. Call me Angela, I insist; I don't really see myself as an authority figure. When they opt, instead, to call me Miss Angela, I realize that they do.

In their travels through the social welfare system, these young women had taken many "world of work" training courses that eventually, like this one, segued into a discussion on the pros and cons of welfare reform. Earlier that June, 19 months after winning the '92 presidential election with a campaign promise "to end welfare as we know it," Bill Clinton at last announced his plan: two-year time limits for welfare recipients, workfare programs, child support enforcement. Everyone in my class gave ready approval.

Melissa, an 18-year-old mother of two, who dreams of saving a younger brother from the streets after she earns her GED and becomes a nurse, commends the work requirements as "a good start" in getting welfare recipients "off their butt" rather than simply "waiting around for the checks to come. "It does make you lazy," she concedes.

Others applaud Clinton's intention to reduce the number of teenage births, though no one is more vocal than Sheila, 19 and pregnant with her second child. "To me the Clinton plan is a big change in welfare because a lot of girls have babies to get more money." Affirmative nods ricochet around the room. "I think it is a good thing," Sheila continues, "and I'm with it 100 percent."

And so on for the remainder of the period. "Why would you make a baby if you can't be ready?" asks Aiesha, blasting deadbeat parents and, inadvertently, herself. But in the ultimate irony, Dionica, homeless like all her classmates, says of the preliminary proposals to deny benefits women under 18: "And some teen mothers should stay home."

These were not the responses I'd been expecting. I'd culled from the *New York Times*, the United Way, Homes for the Homeless, and welfare-rights advocate Frances Fox Piven a list of statistics to debunk myths of welfare queens, of cheats and frauds sittin' on the stoop smokin' spliffs and drinkin' forties, of lazy, promiscuous women causing the downfall of the nation as they passed on their degenerate values to their children. When my class agreed that welfare encourages teen pregnancy and poverty, I pointed out that other countries have higher benefits but a fraction of the teen births, suggesting that early parenting is more a function of poverty than poor relief. When they parroted arguments that welfare reform should be aimed at teenage mothers, I informed them that a high percentage of teen mothers have a history of sexual abuse, and that two-thirds of all teen pregnancies involve adult men over 20, suggesting an epidemic of statutory rape rather than promiscuity. But every time I attacked a "myth," my students earnestly confirmed another.

I don't know if they had internalized these popular images of Black women or if they were telling me what they thought they should, but by the end of the semester I knew for a fact that the myths were just that. Melissa, who told me welfare "does make you lazy," proved to be the hardest-working student in my class, meeting me repeatedly during office hours to find a nurse's aide training program she could attend after completing her GED. And Sheila, the 19-year-old mother pregnant with her second child, seemed far more preoccupied with worry than thoughts of a windfall. But it took me a while to sort out when they were being themselves and when I was being treated like an authority figure with whom they had to wear the mask.

WIR began as a joint venture of the New York Archdiocese, the New York Foundling Hospital, and Fordham University. More than a way station on the road to a Section 8 apartment, it aims to help the young women achieve the tools for self-sufficiency—and often succeeds. But after six months as the career/vocational specialist, the gauntlet of educational and employment programs required in order to get housing began to look like hazing: a bunch of hoops to jump in order to be recognized as citizens entitled to government services. In the name of "discipline" and "structure," the head of all the caseworkers—a nun with the demeanor of a pledge master—revoked weekend passes, WIR's equivalent of furlough, for the slightest breach of house rules. She was also the housing specialist, whose favor one did well to court because she could determine whether you were placed in a roach/drug/violence-infested tenement or a renovated development.

WIR's program seemed to subscribe, perhaps unwittingly, to a school of thought that some defect in character, family history, or ethnic heritage causes poverty. Staff members struggled assiduously against calling the young women "mothers," as if it were a dirty word that might be a bad influence; as if poverty were a state of mind and that, simply by transforming their thoughts, the women might transcend the structural inequalities of the inner city. Administrators would proudly tout the affluent ambiance of the Upper West Side as a key component of the WIR program. "They need exposure to different environments, to see another side of life," the executive director was fond of saying.

"They need social graces and etiquette," my supervisor had said during my initial job interview, explaining the self-esteem classes I was to conduct. Once, she recalled while on a field trip to a swanky restaurant, the women went for the roasted chicken with the salad fork, embarrassing the staff and, consequently, themselves. "They need realistic goals," she said, explaining what the aims of my world-of-work program should be. Many young mothers, she said, came in with dreams of being lawyers and doctors, "and we shouldn't set them up for lots of disappointment."

Truth to tell, I wasn't the best candidate to teach anyone about proper behavior for anything, especially the world of work. My corporate drag was piecemeal; I came in late most days; and was increasingly sullen, almost insubordinate, around my supervisor. But I tried. From the *Mind Your Manners* book Miss Edwardlene had given me, I brushed up on "business etiquette" and "workplace expectations." I found the information so enlightening that I compiled a world-of-work handbook for the women. With easy reference headings like "Dress Code/Self-Presentation," "Attendance/Absences/Tardiness," "Calling-In," and "Supervision," my pamphlet emphasized the importance of a strong attendance record, of punctuality, and of a professional presentation in getting and keeping a job.

My first duty as the career/vocational specialist was to coordinate the annual summer program, in which the young women volunteered at various nonprofits and private businesses for six weeks. The internship program, overseen by an advisory panel, was ostensibly to teach the young women work skills that could result in a real job. During a week of orientation, I explained what would be expected of them. I also told them what they could expect: a learning experience that would enhance their skills and career contacts and, at the very least, offer self-respect for a job well done.

Like interns the world over, of course, they were given menial tasks, all the grunt work staff members didn't want to do: stamping dates on labels, reinforcing three-hole binding, filing, serving, gofering. Which would have been fine if WIR, and then I, hadn't promised that these experiences were going to be meaningful. But essentially, beggars can't be choosers, and the young women were expected to do the meanest work and smile about it. When they expressed dissatisfaction, acknowledging that their needs had not been met, they were reprimanded for having "attitude" and "no respect for authority." Initially, I arranged one-on-one meetings weekly with them, ranting from my handbook about insubordination and the need for flexibility. But then I learned that, at one site, a supervisor was harassing my students, calling them lazy welfare queens looking for a free ride. When I read one student's evaluation of the summer program—"No more volunteer work. Jobs with pay. We need money"—I began to think, like writer Jill Nelson, "Can we talk about volunteer slavery?"

Just how much this program and the system it mirrors, was about control, not discipline or work ethics or achieving self-respect, became evident in my own interaction with Tanesha. She was the free spirit of WIR, the kind of woman people gossip about because they find her so unique, and early on we struck up a friendship. She would come by my office almost every day to talk about whatever, and I loaned her books. A favorite was a book of poetry, *We Are the Young Magicians*, a bold proclamation of 21st-century Black womanhood, by my sistafriend Ruth Forman.

For the summer program, Tanesha is assigned to work in the pharmacy at a hospital. But it's a rather mismatched placement, since she's interested in social work and doesn't like going down into a basement every day in the middle of the summer. And I wouldn't either. But like a good career/vocational specialist, I call her into the office about her absences. She always, always has a barrage of suspect, though gracious, excuses that I moderately chew her out about. But one day, tired of our ritual, I guess, she explains her behavior with a flip, "I guess I have summer fever and just didn't feel like going." Before, during our marathon talks, I'd encouraged her to talk freely and honestly with me. But that day I would have rather that she lied. Before I knew it, I'd restricted her weekend pass.

In fact, every day I was feeling more and more like Miss Angela. Once a week, I scheduled career-development workshops in the evening with the New York Junior League. Bearing "door prizes" and bedecked in jewels, the NYJL volunteers presented fun, engaging workshops on how to use the want ads, find job-training programs, give an interview. But in an effort to get more women of color to volunteer, I arranged for Dreams Into Action, professional women of color committed to mentoring teenage girls, to present a minifair. Evening workshops tried the patience of my students, who, after a full day of classes, had to pick up their children, fix dinner, and then put their babies to bed. So participation would be grudging but usually forthcoming after great cooing, prodding, and insistence from me. But during the DIA workshop, young ladies who gave the NYJL their undivided attention whispered back and forth to each other, laughed out loud, spoke out of turn, slouched, and looked as if they really could not care less. At first I thought it was because the DIA presentations lacked the polish and glitz of the NYJL's. But the tension in the room was far more than disappointment, it was resentment.

After a veteran social worker gave her spiel, Jacqué (formerly Jackie), who'd sought me out to develop a five-year plan that would put her on the path to being a social worker, essentially told the DIA that no one had said anything about anything relevant to her goals. And it was true. More accustomed to advising college-bound seniors, they'd talked about SATs and entry-level jobs requiring four-year college degrees. And my students, unaccustomed to people who looked like them having obvious wealth, had no patience. As the usual eight o'clock cutoff point approached, while a mentor was still presenting, Cicely, an exceptionally bright young woman whose demand for answers about everything both inspired and exasperated me, yelled out, "Miss Angela, what time is it? Isn't it time to go?" Our eyes locked and I hoped her retinas burned. I then rolled mine with a vengeance.

The next day in class, I was the one chastised. I was told my eye rolling was most unprofessional, my ignoring their obvious dissatisfaction with the irrelevancy of this workshop rude. I tried to regain the upper hand by lecturing from the handbook, but after my behavior the day before, the point was moot. After I finished, Aeisha raised her hand as we'd agreed to do in the class contract, to ask if I would let them go early. I had the equivalent of a core meltdown and not only dismissed class early but canceled it for the rest of the week—out sick.

The summer program finally ended in a flurry of ceremonies and a rooftop party with a theater theme. I designed the invitations one morning at home after I'd called in to say that I'd be late—lying about waiting for the plumber to come fix a clogged toilet. Over a clapboard graphic, the invite cover read, "It's the Final Act of the 1994 WIR Summer Program." Inside, the "starring" cast of interns and their various assignments were listed like credits on ticker tape with a trailer of "Hope to see you on the 'scene.' Curtain Call's Tuesday, August 16, 12 noon." I threw in some black, swirly borders for flair. Corny, I thought, but cute.

Everyone who completed the summer program, which was everybody, got a certificate of achievement. They had ribbonlike borders in pastel pink and blue, with festive, confetti-looking dots of purple sprinkled across the face. I signed my name on the designated line, tight above the "Career/Vocational Specialist" title I'd typed in.

For those who I thought best exemplified "work maturity skills" I gave special awards, soap and lotion sets in exotic fruit scents, donated by Bath & Body Works: "Best Attendance," "Most Flexible," "Most Professional Attire," "Most Outstanding," "Most Improved," et cetera. As I was bagging up the extra certificates and gifts for the no-shows, Sharee, a nursing-home intern whose evaluation summed her up as "always bright and cheerful," with an "excellent job performance when she was here," approached me about not getting an award.

"Miss Angela, why you didn't represent me?" What could be mistaken for an edge in her voice was more a brace against its breaking. "Why didn't you get a gift for me?"

Her incredulousness was catching because was I was thinking, yeah, Miss Angela, why? As I searched for an answer that would satisfy us both, in carefully modulated tones I acknowledged that, yes, she'd worked extremely well with a great attitude but had spotty attendance. I reminded her that her evaluation reported that she needed to "Focus on being a little more disciplined about coming to work."

The lightning should have struck. Me, whose sense of time is more intuitive than empirical, who takes every supervisor's directive with a grain of salt, telling someone about being a traditional worker in the world of work. Sure, she had missed eight days, which, for a six-week program, is a lot, but it's not like she was getting paid or had truly volunteered to do "the vital but at times menial tasks of a volunteer" (from the handbook). Lord knows, under far better living and working conditions I had taken enough mental health days to give Sybill peace of mind. Besides, a few of Sharee's days were because of doctor's appointments for her child. And for all I know, one day she just might have had a clogged toilet. I don't remember what I said to save face, but I do know that I reached into my bag and gave girlfriend a mango-scented toiletry set. There should have been a "Best Attitude" award anyway.

When the fall semester finally arrived and we were cooped up in room 507 around those card tables, I'd had enough of WIR but felt obligated to my students. Kara, whom I was helping to find a nurse's training program for fall, had written on her summer-program evaluation, "Angela is very important to me. We have plans, about my future, to make together." And with them still mouthing myths about themselves, I felt I still had work to do.

I began sharing womanist icons important to our history. around the walls, I hung posters from the Bread and Roses project series that cruised the subways that summer. Pictures of Maya Angelou, Ruby Dee, Alice Walker, Mae Jemison, Marion Wright Edelman, the Delaney Sisters, Fannie Lou Hamer, and Ida B. Wells skirted the walls like family portraits over the stairwell, or your mother's bedroom bureau. In the company of other Black women, I felt my role-model burden lift a tad.

To lift it even further, I suggested that we create posters of our own "to help the students identify themselves as people with positive futures," the syllabus objective read. Called the Woman That I Am, a title from a book of literature by women of color by my mentor-friend Soyini, our series hung alongside the Women of Hope. In between Ida and Fannie and Mae, our beautiful Black, female faces emerged. At least figuratively, it was that circle of sisterhood that I'd been hoping for.

But in reality, those posters highlighted just how different we were. I'd been warned about encouraging unrealistic goals for the young women, but I pushed them to go ahead and dream. For "dream jobs" people listed social worker, computer operator, recording engineer. On my poster, I wrote writer, as absurd and unrealistic as that felt. However, with resources that I could tap into at will—family support, great friends, education—I knew that I could be almost anything I wanted. But could they?

I did my best to give them tools to fulfill those dreams that had to do with the sometimes arcane "world of work." On resumes, with strokes of pen and fanciful phrases—similar to the ones that got me this job—I made them into highly skilled workers. Informal baby-sitting jobs I glibly transformed into Child Care Provider. Under SKILLS I suggested they include "Head of Household." They seemed as gratified as I was to identify qualities and resources they had to share with their family, friends, and communities.

It isn't lack of ability that will stop them. They were eager to explore their possibilities and how to achieve them. But months after I left WIR, people were still looking for their chance. Inquisitive Cicely had applied for and been offered a hotel internship but was still waiting for the program head to call her back. I don't know what happened to Renee, a quick wit and leader among her peers who sabotaged plans we made for job-training programs, fearing success as much as failure. Once she returned from a weekend pass visibly bruised, and I began to understand what might be getting in her way. And she and her classmates won't be helped by the welfare reform proposals festering in Congress, most re-pugnantly concerned only with how many children it would be cost-ef-fective to throw off the rolls, with less regard for their mothers, who will fall deeper into poverty, scrambling for jobs that aren't there.

Against the odds society has given them, some do make it. One year after the summer program I ran into Tanesha up in Harlem, rushing to work. After the pharmacy debacle, we'd arranged a peer-counseling in-ternship that had resulted in a position at a West Harlem community-based organization. I was covering a story about Mike Tyson and vio-lence against women, and had flagged her down for a quote. "That's a sensitive issue," she said, "women's rights, Black women's rights." At 21, her budding womanist consciousness was broad enough to wish Tyson a second chance within the Black community along with a greater aware-ness of Black women's needs. "It's a lot of violence. If it's not in the music, it's in the way we're portrayed. It's a big problem, and I think it needs to be fought on all levels, just like a lot of other problems we have."

Then, for a good while, we just talked outside the Apollo, giving girl-friend updates. She and her gorgeous, you-should-be-in-pictures-if-they-weren't-so-sexist baby were fine. Her job she loved. And a few weeks be-fore she'd bought a copy of Ruth's book of poetry—being hawked on 125th Street—and was now sharing it with all her friends. I gave her my number at the paper and told her to call, whenever. Shortly thereafter, she did. The community organization for which she was putting in mad hours—her summer fever now cured—was inviting all of New York to a family field day in honor of the group's founder and anniversary. Could I finagle some publicity? I did everything short of putting out an APB. More than a role model, I was able to be a resource, and at that moment, I felt both our nets grow all the wider.

NOTE

Reprinted by kind permission from Angela Ards, "To Be Young, Female and Black," *The Village Voice*, February 13, 1996, 27–31.

Chapter Three

Four Mission Statements

Vision Statement

National Black Women's Health Project

Editor's Note: The National Black Women's Health Project (NBWHP), established in 1984, provides strength, guidance, and vision in the quest for well-being among African American women and the Black community as a whole. The following Vision Statement[1] outlines the organization's purpose. Also included in this volume is an essay by Deborah Grayson ("Necessity Was the Midwife to Our Politics") that provides a narrative account of the NBWHP and its place in the Black women's health movement.

The National Black Women's Health Project (NBWHP) is committed to defining, promoting and maintaining the physical, spiritual, mental and emotional well-being of Black women.

We seek to enable Black women to become aware of the nature of physical and mental health and the relationship between the two, and to enable Black women to take control and become active participants in their health maintenance. It is through a broadened concept of health and an active program to promote healthy lifestyles that Black women can live, love and work in new and more authentic ways. For us, health is not merely the absence of illness, but the active promotion of the physical, spiritual, mental and emotional wellness of this and future generations. Such wellness is impossible without individual and group empowerment, which is essential to the redefining and reinterpretation of who Black women are, were and can become.

We Remember

African American Women Are for Reproductive Freedom

Editor's Note: The following statement, "We Remember," is a testament to the resurgence in reproductive rights activism in the late 1980s and early 1990s. Government restrictions on abortion, such as the 1976 Hyde Amendment and Webster v. Reproductive Services, *severely curtailed access to legal abortion, particularly for poor women and women of color (who are disproportionately among the poor in the United States). Written in the late 1980s, this statement was unique because the authors pushed to expand the definition of reproductive freedom beyond the mainstream women's movement calls for "Safe, Legal Abortion." Important to the reproductive lives of African American women, and all women of color, is the right to choose to* have *children, as well as the right to decide when is the best time to do so.*

Choice is the essence of freedom. It's what we African Americans have struggled for all these years. The right to choose where we would sit on a bus. The right to vote. The right for each of us to select our own paths, to dream and reach for our dreams. The right to choose how we would or would not live our lives.

This freedom—to choose and to exercise our choices—is what we've fought and died for. Brought here in chains, worked like mules, bred like beasts, whipped one day, sold the next—for 244 years we were held in bondage. Somebody said that we were less than human and not fit for freedom. Somebody said we were like children and could not be trusted to think for ourselves. Somebody owned our flesh, and decided if and when and with whom and how our bodies were to be used. Somebody said that Black women could be raped, held in concubinage, forced to bear children year in and year out, but often not raise them. Oh yes, we have known how painful it is to be without choice in this land.

Those of us who remember the bad old days when Jim Crow ruled and segregation was the way of things, know the hardships and indignities we faced. We were free, but few or none were our choices. Somebody said where we could live and couldn't, where we could work, what schools we could go to, where we could eat, how we could travel. Somebody prevented us from voting. Somebody said we could be paid less than other workers. Somebody burned crosses, harassed and terrorized us in order to keep us down.

Now once again somebody is trying to say that we can't handle the freedom of choice. Only this time they're saying African American women can't think for themselves and, therefore, can't be allowed to make serious decisions. Somebody's saying that we should not have the freedom to take charge of our personal lives and protect our health, that we only have limited rights over our bodies. Somebody's once again forcing women to acts of desperation, because somebody's saying that if women have unintended pregnancies, it's too bad, but they must pay the price.

Somebody's saying that we must have babies whether we choose to or not. Doesn't matter what we say, doesn't matter how we feel. Some say that abortion under any circumstance is wrong, others that rape and incest and danger to the life of the woman are the only exceptions. Doesn't matter that nobody's saying who decides if it was rape or incest; if a woman's word is good enough; if she must go into court and prove it. Doesn't matter that she may not be able to take care of a baby; that the problem also affects girls barely out of adolescence; that our children are having children. Doesn't matter if you're poor and pregnant—go on welfare, or walk away.

What does matter is that we know abortions will still be done, legal or not. We know the consequences when women are forced to make choices without protection—the coat hangers and knitting needles that punctured the wombs of women forced to seek back-alley abortions on kitchen tables at the hands of butchers. The women who died screaming in agony, awash in their own blood. The women who were made sterile. All the women who endured the pain of makeshift surgery with no anesthetics, risked fatal infection.

We understand why African American women risked their lives then, and why they seek safe legal abortion now. It's been a matter of survival. Hunger and homelessness. Inadequate housing and income to properly provide for themselves and their children. Family instability. Rape. Incest. Abuse. Too young, too old, too sick, too tired. Emotional, physical, mental, economic, social—the reasons for not carrying a pregnancy to term are endless and varied, personal, urgent and private. And for all these pressing reasons, African American women once again will be among the first forced to risk their lives if abortion is made illegal.

There have always been those who have stood in the way of our exercising our rights, who tried to restrict our choices. There probably always will be. But we who have been oppressed should not be swayed in our opposition to tyranny, of any kind, especially attempts to take away our reproductive freedom. You may believe abortion is wrong. We respect your belief and we will do all in our power to protect that choice for you. You may decide that abortion is not an option you would choose. Reproductive freedom guarantees your right not to. All that we ask is that no one deny another human being the right to make her own choice. That no one condemn her to exercising her choices in ways that endanger her health, her life. And that no one prevent others from creating safe, affordable, legal conditions to accommodate women, whatever the choices they make. Reproductive freedom gives each of us the right to make our own choices, and guarantees us a safe, legal, affordable support system. It's the right to choose.

We are still an embattled people beset with life and death issues. Black America is under siege. Drugs, the scourge of our community, are wiping out one, two, three generations. We are killing ourselves and each other. Rape and other unspeakable acts of violence are becoming sickeningly commonplace. Babies linger on death's door; at risk at birth: born addicted to crack and cocaine; born underweight and undernourished; born AIDS-infected. An ever-growing number of our children are being abandoned, being mentally, physically, spiritually abused. Homelessness, hunger, unemployment run rife. Poverty grows. Our people cry out in desperation, anger, and need.

MEANWHILE, those somebodies who claim they're "pro-life" aren't moved to help the living. They're not out there fighting to break the stranglehold of drugs and violence in our communities, trying to save our children, or moving to provide infant and maternal nutrition and health programs.

Eradicating our poverty isn't on their agenda. No—somebody's too busy picketing, vandalizing and sometimes bombing family-planning clinics, harassing women, and denying funds to poor women seeking abortions.

So when somebody denouncing abortion claims that they're "pro-life," remind them of an old saying that our grandmothers often used: "It's not important what people say, it's what they do." And remember who we are, remember our history, our continuing struggle for freedom. Remember to tell them that We Remember!

REPRODUCTIVE FREEDOM MEANS:

1. The right to comprehensive, age-appropriate information about sexuality and reproduction.
2. The right to choose to have a child.
3. The right to good, affordable health care to assure a safe pregnancy and delivery.
4. The right to health services to help the infertile achieve pregnancy.
5. The right to choose not to have a child.
6. The right to the full range of contraceptive services and appropriate information about reproduction.
7. The right to choose to end an unwanted pregnancy.
8. The right to safe, legal, affordable abortion services.
9. The right to make informed choices.
10. The right to easily accessible health care that is proven to be safe and effective.
11. The right to reproductive health and to make our own reproductive choices.

Originally compiled and published by:

Byllye Avery

Reverend Willie Barrow

Donna Brazile

Shirley Chisholm

Representative Cardiss Collins

Romona Edelin

Jacqui Gates

Marcia Ann Gillespie

Dorothy Height

Jewel Jackson McCabe

Julianne Malveaux

Eleanor Holmes Norton

C. Delores Tucker

Patricia Tyson

Maxine Waters

Faye Wattleton

African American Women in Defense of Ourselves

Editor's Note: This statement,[2] expressing solidarity with Anita Hill following her appearance before the Senate Judiciary Committee, appeared as a full-page advertisement in the New York Times *on November 17, 1991. Signed by 1,603 women of African descent, the statement boldly challenged the acceptance of sexual harassment and sexism in the Black community. The statement also reaffirmed the dual oppression of African American women based on race and gender, refusing to separate one from the other. The statement's authors are Elsa Barkley Brown, Deborah King, and Barbara Ransby.*

As WOMEN OF AFRICAN DESCENT, we are deeply troubled by the recent nomination, confirmation, and seating of Clarence Thomas as an Associate Justice of the U.S. Supreme Court. We know that the presence of Clarence Thomas on the Court will be continually used to divert attention from historic struggles for social justice through suggestions that the presence of a Black man on the Supreme Court constitutes an assurance that the rights of African Americans will be protected. Clarence Thomas's public record is ample evidence this will not be true. Further, the consolidation of a conservative majority on the Supreme Court seriously endangers the rights of all women, poor and working class people and the elderly. The seating of Clarence Thomas is an affront not only to African American women and men, but to all people concerned with social justice.

We are particularly outraged by the racist and sexist treatment of Professor Anita Hill, an African American woman who was maligned and castigated for daring to speak publicly of her own experience of sexual abuse. The malicious defamation of Professor Hill insulted all women of African descent and sent a dangerous message to any woman who might contemplate a sexual harassment complaint.

We speak here because we recognize that the media are now portraying the Black community as prepared to tolerate both the dismantling of affirmative action and the evil of sexual harassment in order to have any Black man on the Supreme Court. We want to make clear that the media have ignored or distorted many African American voices. We will not be silenced.

Many have erroneously portrayed the allegations against Clarence Thomas as an issue of either gender or race. As women of African descent, we understand sexual harassment as both. We further understand that Clarence Thomas outrageously manipulated the legacy of lynching in order to shelter himself from Anita Hill's allegations. To deflect attention away from the reality of sexual abuse in African American women's lives, he trivialized and misrepresented this painful part of African American people's history. This country, which has a long legacy of racism and sexism, has never taken the sexual abuse of Black women seriously. Throughout U.S. history Black women have been sexually stereotyped as immoral, insatiable, perverse; the initiators in all sexual contacts—abusive or otherwise. The common assumption in legal proceedings as well as in the larger society has been that Black women cannot be raped or otherwise sexually abused. As Anita Hill's experience demonstrates, Black women who speak of these matters are not likely to be believed.

In 1991, we cannot tolerate this type of dismissal of any one Black woman's experience or this attack upon our collective character without protest, outrage, and resistance.

As women of African descent, we express our vehement opposition to the policies represented by the placement of Clarence Thomas on the Supreme Court. The Bush administration, having obstructed the passage of civil rights legislation, impeded the extension of unemployment compensation, cut student aid and dismantled social welfare programs, has continually demonstrated that it is not operating in our best interests. Nor is this appointee. We pledge ourselves to continue to speak out in defense of one another, in defense of the African American community and against those who are hostile to social justice, no matter what color they are. No one will speak for us but ourselves.

M.I.T. Conference: Final Resolution

Black Women in the Academy

Editor's Note: The following resolution[3] was drafted at the conference "Black Women in the Academy: Defending Our Name, 1894–1994," held January 13–15, 1994. Participants in the conference gathered to discuss the role and experiences of Black women in the professoriate. This resolution was signed by the participants and sent to President Clinton, partly in response to White House interest in the conference.[4]

Evident from the content of the resolution is a commitment on the part of African American women to intellectual thought as yet another form of activism.

Dear Mr. President:

Eighty-six percent (86%) of African American women who voted, voted for the Democratic Party ticket which brought you and Hillary Rodham Clinton to the White House and a Democratic Congress to Washington in 1992. This was the largest proportion of any constituency to vote for your administration. We, the 2,010 registered participants in the conference "Black Women in the Academy: Defending Our Name, 1894–1994," overwhelmingly comprise a representative segment of this constituency.

Mr. President, this gathering brought together a wide diversity of African American, Asian, Latina, and other women of color. All together, we agreed that for the academy, as well as for the nation this is a crucial moment of challenge and opportunity for learning as well as in public policy. We want to seize this moment to help make public your vision and ours to begin again. Indeed, to begin again means for us to begin on new terms. For example, we fully recognize the complexity of social categories such as race, class, gender, and sexual orientation Necessarily then our responses need mirror these ever-changing realities. We need to respond to both the old and the new forms of social injuries; for example, environmental racism in communities of color and the continuing inability of women, and especially women of color to exercise effective control over our bodies.

Mr. President, we stand ready to work with you to implement meaningful change. Our community is resplendent with talent and preparedness to serve.

We call on you, Mr. President, to undertake the following:

1. To commission a new kind of Blue Ribbon panel on race relations in the United States of America today. This commission will build on the 1968 Kerner Report, which predicted the emergence of two Americas—one Black, one white. The new commission will examine the status of this prediction, and its 1988 review. This new panel must be cognizant of the myriad new realities of race in America, and must present recommendations to alleviate the continuing injuries of racism, sexism, and homophobia.

2. To promote Black women's research which underscores and promotes the overall well-being of the African American community and of their other research subjects and to extend the mandate of the Glass-Ceiling Commission to explore issues of career advancement for women of color in higher education: non-tenure, tenure-track, administrators and staff and in all other sectors of the academy.

3. To substantially increase funding for multi-faceted community-based social service organizations for poor Black families and others in need. We stress the need to extend economic empowerment and development programs, support services, health care, housing, child care and education. Women in prison, those with AIDS, and in crisis need special attention. Critical aspects of this new public policy initiative must center on economic independence, not just welfare reform; the non-demonization of Black youth in the anti-crime bill and elsewhere, and youth upliftment programs.

4. To end the destructive anti-democratic covert actions against Haiti, and to immediately implement your stated Democratic Party policy: the restoration of President Jean-Bertrand Aristide to the Presidency in Haiti. The United Nations Governor's Island Accord is the place to begin through non-military intervention. Aristide's election, with sixty-seven percent of the vote, and seven-month administration, were overwhelmingly supported by Haitian women, some of whom are in attendance at this conference. In response to your administration's respect for the power of African American women, we, sisters of the suffering Haitian people, call on you to support justice and democracy in Haiti now. Your new policy on Haiti, Mr. President, will begin a much needed shift in U.S. Caribbean policy beginning with ending the 30-year embargo on Cuba.

5. To continue to support the democratic process itself in South and Southern Africa by providing meaningful material aid and support to the post-apartheid government. Such aid, which would include support for Somalia, is necessary for the survival of the Black population and the rejuvenation of the entire continent.

Cambridge, Massachusetts
January 15, 1994,
celebrating the 65th birthday of
the Rev. Dr. Martin Luther King, Jr.

NOTES

1. Reprinted by kind permission of the National Black Women's Health Project.

2. Reprinted by kind permission of Barbara Ransby.

3. Reprinted by kind permission of Evelynn Hammonds.

4. Chalis Johnson, "All I'm Askin' Is a Little Respect: Black Women in the Academy," *Black Scholar 24,* 1: 2–3, 5–6.

Part II

Our Continuous Struggle
Activism Born of the 1960s Era

Chapter Four

"Triple Jeopardy"

Black Women and the Growth of Feminist Consciousness in SNCC, 1964–1975

Kristin Anderson-Bricker

Concerning feminism in the Student Nonviolent Coordinating Committee (SNCC), one of the major civil rights organizations active between 1960 and 1972, historians of women primarily think of the feminist manifestos of Mary King and Casey Hayden in 1964 and 1965, along with Stokely Carmichael's often repeated retort, "The position of women in SNCC is prone!"[1] Although well known, these events characterize the development of feminism among white SNCC women only. Historians lack a greater understanding of feminism in SNCC because the historiography lacks a synthesis of women's experience, an analysis of the evolution of feminism among both Black and white women in the organization and an attempt to place women in the larger context of SNCC's historical development.

An analysis of women's experience in SNCC reveals the correlation between the ideology of the organization and the evolution of feminism among white and Black female activists. SNCC experienced two periods during which a comprehensive ideology shaped the orientation of SNCC members. This multidimensional belief system provided a context conducive to the evolution of feminist consciousness and action among Black and white women. Female members of SNCC became aware of their identity as women and mobilized against gender discrimination when their ideology embraced a wide range of concerns and recognized many problems in society as targets of reform. Therefore, white and

49

Black women became feminists at different times and as a result of different catalysts.

White women adopted feminism in 1964 and 1965, when SNCC moved from an environment of ideological openness and diversity to the single-issue orientation of Black nationalism. Black women, increasingly defining themselves solely on the basis of their identity as African Americans, rejected white women's concern with gender discrimination and conceptualization of feminism in 1964 and 1965. By 1968 the meaning of Black nationalism expanded beyond Black identity and racism to encompass a larger critique of American society and a third world perspective. This return to a comprehensive ideological environment stimulated African American female activists in SNCC to form the Black Women's Liberation Committee (BWLC) that later evolved into an independent feminist organization, the Third World Women's Alliance (TWWA). Establishing the development of feminism in SNCC not only integrates the experience of women into the history of the organization, it also reveals the feminism of Black women as an important legacy of SNCC.

SNCC emerged in April 1960 as a result of Ella Baker's efforts to unify and extend the South-wide student sit-in movement that erupted in February 1960 to desegregate public accommodations. Although initially a committee to coordinate the efforts of local student protest groups, beginning in 1961 members shaped SNCC into an organization, creating a distinct organizing style and community.[2] SNCC activists used grassroots organizing to build local community movements across the South. They concentrated on developing indigenous leadership and identifying local concerns by living, working, eating, sleeping and worshipping with the people, by listening and talking to them and by gaining their trust. Ultimately SNCC field secretaries hoped to build a South-wide "people's movement" that would stand independently of SNCC and its staff.[3]

During the course of these organizing efforts, between 1960 and 1964, members of SNCC developed the "beloved community," a multifaceted belief system characterized by nonhierarchical leadership, community-centered organizing and ideological openness. In SNCC, individuals adhered to the Ghandian principle of nonviolence either as a way of life or a tactic. They attempted to maintain an interracial world that revealed that Blacks and whites could work and live together. They also operated by consensus, adhering to group-centered, decentralized leadership. Devoid of a leadership hierarchy, individuals in SNCC acted on the basis of their own decisions and instincts, and excluded no one on the grounds of their ideology, opinions or beliefs. Despite this diversity, SNCC organizers felt bound to one another as a community because of a common sacrifice, belief in equality and commitment to change.[4]

In the fall of 1964 SNCC members began debating the ideology and structure of the organization and over the next two years they redefined the nature of SNCC. Racial tensions, the growth of the organization and gender discrimination resulting from the Mississippi Freedom Summer Project of 1964 initiated these changes. Following Freedom Summer, SNCC staff members debated organizational structure, decision making, ideology, racial composition and programs.[5] This debate divided SNCC into two opposing camps. Although not all SNCC activists took sides, those vocal in the debate fell into either the nonstructure or structure faction.

Those taking the nonstructure view wanted SNCC to retain the ideals of the beloved community. Decision making needed to rest with each individual, they believed, since each individual must act on his or her beliefs. The nonstructure faction, primarily composed of whites and northern, college-educated Blacks, believed SNCC needed to be a loose, nonhierarchical, confederated structure, with decision making and accountability at the local level. Despite this decentralized arrangement and heterogeneous belief system, they thought SNCC would continue, as in the early 1960s, because of common ideals and goals.[6]

The SNCC executive secretary, James Forman, symbolized the position of the structure faction. This group, comprised primarily of southern and less-educated Blacks, valued SNCC as an organization and advocated the need for a stronger, centralized, more hierarchical structure to gain concrete accomplishments and build power. They supported a strong Executive Committee to make decisions and decide policy between Coordinating Committee meetings and wanted the staff to be more accountable to the central office. Structure advocates felt that everyone needed to accept some amount of discipline and that only through a tighter organization would many problems be solved.[7]

While this debate over decision making, identity and program polarized the group, Black SNCC members—both men and women—moved steadily closer to adopting the ideology of Black nationalism. After Freedom Summer these activists focused on developing black consciousness and increasingly questioned the role of whites in SNCC. The ideas of people and events occurring outside SNCC encouraged the group's members to focus on generating Black consciousness among themselves and in the

Black community. SNCC staff member Edward Brown remembered that particularly in 1965 "everybody was talking about the need for Black consciousness."[8] As SNCC advisor Ella Baker later explained, the growth of Black organizing and solidarity in ghetto areas, the emerging popularity and influence of Malcolm X, the work of Franz Fanon and "the rising independence of Black people in Africa and other parts of the world" contributed to SNCC personnel's development of Black consciousness and therefore nationalism in 1964 and 1965.[9] SNCC workers' identification with African Blacks and the strengthening of a pan-Africanist perspective resulted from a September 1964 trip to Guinea taken by ten staff persons. Through this trip SNCC people realized the ties their organization needed with the Blacks of Africa, the importance of Africa to Black people in the United States and the existence of links between Africans and African Americans simply based on race.[10]

These outside elements combined with activists' experiences to promote Black consciousness. This growing definition of identity based on African American heritage intensified the debate over the role of whites in the Student Nonviolent Coordinating Committee. Freedom Summer had exacerbated racial tensions in SNCC, and many staff members began to question more intently the role of whites in organizing Black communities and the continuation of SNCC as an interracial organization. Staff members debated whether to hire the large number of white volunteers remaining on projects after the close of Freedom Summer.[11] During a November 1964 conference, Alabama State Project Director Silas Norman argued that an "ethnic relationship" existed between the Black community and the Black staff. Since this relationship could not be entered into by whites, he questioned the effectiveness of white organizing in Black communities.[12] Even Chairman John Lewis, a strong advocate of interracialism, identified the growing racial identity of Black women and men in SNCC and the changing role of whites in the organization. Speaking early in 1965, Lewis identified the important relationship existing among Blacks and the need for the movement to be "Black-controlled, dominated, and led." He asked white staff people to understand that Black people were "caught up with a sense of destiny with the vast majority of colored people all over the world who are becoming conscious of their power and the role they must play in the world."[13]

As SNCC moved away from the ideological openness and loose structure of the beloved community to a more centralized organization based on Black nationalism, feminism developed among a small group of predominately white women in SNCC. As part of the debate over structure, Mary King and Casey Hayden drafted the 1964 "Position Paper" and, in 1965, "A Kind of Memo" as a reaction to growing Black nationalism and an attempt to return SNCC to the ideals of the beloved community. King and Hayden wanted SNCC activists to maintain the individualism, heterogeneity and diversity of SNCC's past.

King and Hayden drafted the 1964 "Position Paper" for the November 1964 Waveland Conference, the first open confrontation between structure and nonstructure factions. This paper represented the first overt critique of gender inequality in SNCC and presented examples of the lack of women in leadership positions, the assignment of women to traditional female roles and the unacknowledged assumption of male superiority.[14] King and Hayden called for a discussion of discrimination and a beginning to "the slow process of changing values and beliefs" so that everyone would come "to understand that this is no more a man's world than it is a white world."[15]

Standing alone, the 1964 "Position Paper" on women that identifies gender discrimination in SNCC does not appear to be part of the internal dissension and crisis plaguing SNCC in the fall of 1964. But when viewed in context, through the perceptions of King and Hayden, the Position Paper assumes a deeper meaning. Both King and Hayden later identified it as part of the structure debate.[16] It was written as a nonstructure argument, supporting the need to return SNCC to "the basic values of the early sit-ins and SNCC's original concept of leadership."[17]

In her autobiography, King writes that her concern in the fall of 1964 was not only how to structure SNCC but also whether there would be room in the movement for a variety of political and social concerns, including those of women, and issues such as poverty and war.[18] The "Position Paper" represented an example of an issue compatible with the past ideals of SNCC. In the eyes of those in the nonstructure group, SNCC needed to enable individuals to act on their own beliefs and to support diversity in the movement.[19]

One year after the first paper, King and Hayden authored a second paper revealing the gender discrimination in SNCC, their motivation and critique again based on nonstructure group ideals. In November 1965 the two white staff members mailed "A Kind of Memo" to forty women activists across the country. It went to female Black activists in SNCC and to white and Black women in other progressive organizations, such as Students for a Democratic Society, National Student Association,

Northern Student Movement, and the Student Peace Union.[20] This manifesto marked their reaction to the worsening crisis in SNCC. By late 1965 the ideas of the structure group began to gain ascendancy in the organization and racial tensions worsened. As SNCC steadily moved toward Black nationalism and separatism and became increasingly structured, white staff members, particularly those struggling to return SNCC to the ideals of the beloved community, such as King and Hayden, felt their role in SNCC threatened.

"A Kind of Memo" was another attempt by King and Hayden to halt SNCC's move toward structure and Black nationalism and to return the organization to the early values and vision of SNCC.[21] Mary King later remembered, "[We] were asking whether we would be able to act out our beliefs and make decisions based on our convictions, beliefs grounded in our definition of freedom and self-determination as women," and "whether there would be room in the civil rights movement for differing political and social concerns, as various groups, and, in our case, women defined them." King and Hayden believed that the organizational structure they supported, one of decentralization, democracy and autonomous local movements, allowed for ideological openness, diverse belief systems, women's equality and personal freedom.[22] In a 1977 interview with Clayborne Carson, Stokely Carmichael also linked the "Position Paper" and "A Kind of Memo" to the ideological transformation occurring in SNCC during 1964 and 1965, particularly the rising strength of Black nationalism in SNCC. Carmichael explained to Carson that white women raised the issue of gender discrimination in SNCC "to stop the movement from going toward Black nationalism, because they thought they were going to be put out of the movement."[23]

"A Kind of Memo" went beyond identifying instances of gender discrimination in SNCC. It focused on an analysis of the "sexual-caste system," or set of rules, that dictated women's roles inside and outside the movement. The determination of these roles was based on assumed subordination. This entrenched "common law caste system," they believed, influenced women's work assignments and personal relationships. In the manifesto, King and Hayden called into question the institutions that reinforced this system, the men who ignored or reacted negatively to questions of gender inequality and the lack of discussion, writing and organizing among women in the New Left movements about their similar experiences of gender inequality. Although the authors doubted that a movement based upon the liberation of women would come about, they sent "A Kind of Memo" to "provoke the reaction of a selected group of women" and to facilitate the creation of a women's support network.[24]

As King and Hayden feared, the overwhelming response to the issue of gender inequality in SNCC and the question of the position of women in the movement was ridicule, criticism or lack of interest.[25] Only a few people responded directly and positively to King and Hayden at the Waveland Conference. Overwhelmingly, these Black and white individuals were members of the nonstructure faction, those sharing a similar philosophy about SNCC with the paper's authors.[26] The response of Black women to the questions raised by King and Hayden diminished in 1965. Not one Black female friend of theirs in SNCC who received "A Kind of Memo" responded to it.[27]

Black women ignored or reacted negatively to "A Kind of Memo" because Black activists increasingly defined themselves and SNCC as part of the African American community. As the ideas of Black nationalism and separatism gained strength in SNCC, and Black men and women focused more intently on race, Black women concentrated on achieving Black consciousness and the elimination of racism. Cynthia Washington later explained that Black women's "single-minded focus on the issues of racial discrimination and the Black struggle for equality blinded us to other issues."[28] Blacks involved in SNCC increasingly concentrated on racism, while many white staff members and volunteers continued to view other injustices as important to struggle against as well.[29]

Along with this emphasis on Black consciousness, Black women consciously chose to disassociate themselves from King and Hayden's ideas of feminism because of the enmity and lack of understanding that existed between Black and white women. To Black women, the problem they experienced was much different from that of white women. Washington recalled that Black women did not understand many of the concerns raised by white women because many female Black staffers had more authority, respect and responsibility than their white counterparts. Those Black women who ran projects, such as Washington, did not see their role limited to office work and believed they already had much of the independence white women craved. Rather, Black women's anger focused on their treatment "as one of the boys." Their skills and abilities seemed to place them in a category other than female to Black men and therefore Black men developed relationships with white women.[30] The sexual relationships between white female Freedom Summer volunteers and Black men enhanced the racial tensions already existing in SNCC. Most Black women were openly hostile toward white women following Freedom Summer, and their anger, in combination with Black nationalist ideas, led them to support separatism and, along with males, to help to purge whites from SNCC.[31] The barrier to sisterhood that evolved out of Freedom Summer combined with an ideology emphasizing Black consciousness to prevent Black women from supporting the concerns about gender equality raised by white women.

By 1966 and 1967, the Black nationalist ideology of most Black women and men in SNCC continued to emphasize racism as the cause of Black oppression and the centrality of Black consciousness in mobilizing the Black community against it. Understanding that the belief system of African American women—like that of African American men—focused on developing Black identity to fight racism provides an explanation as to why African American women did not join with white women in SNCC to develop a feminist analysis in 1964 and 1965. These SNCC activists based membership in the organization on African American heritage, openly espoused Black Power, expelled whites from the organization and defined the central reason for Blacks' oppression as racism.[32] To SNCC members, Black Power essentially meant uniting Black people and building social, economic and political institutions to gain power. By building bases of power, Blacks would gain control of their communities and be able to initiate change from a position of strength, rather than weakness.[33] To achieve these goals, SNCC field workers believed they needed to develop Black consciousness in Black communities. Therefore, at a meeting in May 1966 a majority of staff members decided that white people must organize in white communities since they did not, and could not, possess Black consciousness.[34] Although this decision did not expel whites from SNCC, Betita Martinez, a Mexican-American staff member, indicated later that the decision foreshadowed the expulsion of whites that would soon follow in May 1967. She wrote, "Since SNCC wasn't organizing in the white community, nor [was it] really serious about doing so, the decision in effect signaled: get out."[35] Staff members decided to expel whites from the organization at a meeting in December 1966; the SNCC Central Committee carried out the decision in May 1967 by asking all non-Black staff members to resign.[36]

Writing in his autobiography, *The Making of Black Revolutionaries*, SNCC executive secretary James Forman identified 1966 and 1967 as a period when most SNCC members saw the whole struggle as a "racial thing."[37] In fact he believed that ideological debate among SNCC militants occurred at a low intellectual level because only a few individuals in the organization understood other ideas that could expand the meaning of Black nationalism, such as capitalism, imperialism, class struggle, colonialism and revolutionary nationalism.[38] Forman began to talk about these ideas during 1967 and to influence the staff members in New York City, particularly those involved with the International Affairs Commission, a committee that generated international contacts for SNCC.[39]

As a result, an internal debate arose between two factions in SNCC, one led by Stokely Carmichael, the other congregating around the ideas of Forman. The two groups debated whether a race or class analysis should determine SNCC's principles.[40] Most SNCC activists adhered to the ideas represented by Carmichael. He stressed the overriding importance of the racial, rather than class, roots of oppression. This faction strengthened its racial separatist stance by discounting future Black and white alliances and endorsing pan-Africanism. Under this ideology, SNCC members de-emphasized a class analysis and socialism.[41] Conversely, the group led by Forman argued that Black inequality resulted from both class position and race. Forman believed that the problems facing Blacks resulted not only from racism but also from economic exploitation and class structure. This group kept open the possibility of future alliances with radical and working-class whites.[42]

Although the ideology of SNCC militants remained focused on Black consciousness and racism throughout 1967, the meaning of Black nationalism to SNCC activists continued to evolve and by 1968 the environment in SNCC again resembled the ideological diversity of the beloved community. By 1968 SNCC activists again broadened their critique of society and their perception of the problems of African Americans. In the late 1960s SNCC staff still adhered to Black nationalism but identified the fight against racism and development of Black consciousness as only part of the Black struggle. They believed that in addition to racism, capitalism and imperialism resulted in Black inequality. They recognized the connection between Black Americans and third world peoples and nations around the globe.[43] Like the beloved community, this multifaceted belief system created a comprehensive orientation in SNCC that provided the context necessary for feminism to develop among Black female activists. Understanding Black nationalism in its international context and rooting Black inequality in racism, capitalism and imperialism provided the intellectual environment necessary for Black women in

SNCC to identify themselves not only as Blacks but also as women and workers.

Between 1966 and 1972 the size, stability and programs of SNCC declined as a result of internal debates over ideology, external repression and a lack of community organizing.[44] Despite the overall decline, a few individuals tried to spearhead programs. In December 1968 Frances Beal founded the Black Women's Liberation Committee(BWLC) of SNCC. Although small and centered in New York City, this group of Black female SNCC activists concentrated on eliminating the triple oppression of Black women as Blacks, workers and women.[45]

The women in SNCC's New York City office who founded the BWLC adhered to the ideas expressed by James Forman, the Director of the International Affairs Commission. Like him, they saw the oppression of Blacks as rooted not only in racism but also in capitalism, and they held an international perspective. It is clear that Forman's ideas had bearing on their thinking; he had a strong influence in the New York City office and the group's leader, Frances Beal, worked closely with him. Beal began with SNCC in 1966 in the New York Communications Department and later worked with Forman in the International Affairs Commission.[46] The expanded ideology of SNCC as represented by Forman provided the organizational and ideological conditions necessary for SNCC female activists to form a Black women's group.

Beal, Gwen Patton and the other women involved with the Black Women's Liberation Committee came to believe that the Black movement did not address the specific needs of Black women. These activists thought Black women needed a forum to talk about their unique problems, their relationships with men and children and their role in the Black struggle. The BWLC maintained that the Black community needed to deal with women's inequality while struggling for Black liberation because without the complete equality of women, Black people could not achieve liberation since half of the community would remain unequal and unfree.[47]

Although concerned with all Black women, the founders of the BWLC of SNCC initially focused on their own encounters with inequality in the organization. By 1968 they had discerned that male SNCC members confined them to secretarial or supportive roles beyond which they were never able to move regardless of their capabilities and skills.[48] Kathleen Cleaver, a Black militant who began working for SNCC in 1966 and later became the communications secretary of the Black Panther Party for Self-

Defense (BPP), found that although women in the organization carried out most of the basic responsibilities and daily work, few achieved any significant position of power.[49]

The Black female activists organized by Beal expanded their reasons for creating the BWLC beyond their personal experiences of gender discrimination in SNCC to include a critique of the male chauvinism characterizing Black nationalism. To BWLC women, Black nationalism in the late 1960s symbolized a rise in sexism among Black militant men because such men adhered to several myths faulting Black women for Black male oppression and narrowly defined the role of Black women in the Black community and the struggle for Black liberation.[50]

According to the women of the BWLC, Black nationalist men accepted discriminatory notions such as the matriarchy myth and used the Black liberation struggle to search for manhood and to assert their masculinity.[51] Although these men rejected white culture, values and norms, they applied the white conception of womanhood to Black women.[52] According to Beal, Black men based their definition of the role of Black women in the movement and society on "the pages of the *Ladies Home Journal*."[53] Many believed that women should step back and take a supportive, nonpolitical role in the Black struggle or strengthen the family and become "breeders" to provide an army for the revolution.[54]

Beal and the other members of the BWLC thought that men who advocated these roles for women in order to assert their manhood were "assuming a counterrevolutionary position." They thought that in order for Black men to be strong, Black women did not need to be weak. The BWLC argued that Black women must define their own role in society and educate the Black community to understand that Black women needed to participate fully in the revolution for Black liberation. According to Beal, "We need our whole army out there dealing with the enemy, not half an army."[55]

The early efforts of the BWLC to change attitudes in the Black community, to end gender discrimination by Black nationalists and to achieve women's liberation involved group study and community education programs. In particular, BWLC militants analyzed liberation movements, looking at the role of women in other revolutionary struggles. From their study they concluded, "[U]nless the woman in any oppressed nation is completely liberated, then a revolution cannot really be called a revolution."[56] BWLC activists urged community members to reconceptualize their ideas about relationships, persuaded men to accept women as equals and opened heritage houses in New York City to teach Black youth the truth about Black history.[57]

Through this intense study and concentration on education, the Black women of SNCC who had been meeting throughout 1969 as the Black Women's Liberation Committee decided to expand the membership of the organization to include all Black women, rather than just those in SNCC. Early in 1970 the BWLC moved forward to create the Black Women's Alliance (BWA), a radical Black women's organization that drew on all Black women from single mothers to community workers to campus radicals.[58] Still a component of SNCC, the female activists envisioned the BWA as both a think tank and an action-oriented organization, designed to "improve the conditions of Black people and particularly the condition of the Black female."[59] The BWA proposed to do this by promoting educational, cultural, economic, social and political unity and sisterhood among Black women. They also strove "to collect, interpret, disseminate and preserve information about the Black Community" and to use this knowledge in educational programs. Ultimately, they wanted to eliminate "any and all forms of oppression based upon race, economic status, or sex."[60]

Although the BWLC and BWA focused on the triple oppression of Black women as Blacks, workers and women, their main emphasis remained the liberation of all Black people.[61] As the women of the BWA continued discussion and study in 1969 and 1970, they increasingly concentrated on the economic basis of Black oppression. Although concerned with racism and sexism, they "became convinced that capitalism and imperialism were our main enemies."[62] With their ideology rooted in an economic critique of the United States government, capitalism and imperialism, they realized the need for third world solidarity. They began to see that third world women, such as Asians, Puerto Ricans, African Americans, Chicanas and Native Americans, experienced similar exploitation from a common oppressor. Therefore, they concluded that the BWA would be more effective by becoming a third world women's organization. During the summer of 1970 the group expanded to include all third world women, calling itself the Third World Women's Alliance (TWWA).[63]

By November 1970, the New York City membership of the Third World Women's Alliance grew to about 200 third world women and many individuals expressed interest in establishing chapters in other states.[64] This tremendous response to the Alliance's call for third world solidarity and collective action to eliminate the triple oppression of third world women revealed the inadequacy of the TWWA administrative structure and the need for a well-defined ideology. In response, a small group of TWWA activists went into retreat in November 1970 to "formulate a workable structure" and to devise an ideological platform "based on scientific revolutionary analysis."[65]

The Third World Women's Alliance emerged from the winter 1970–71 retreat with a well-defined, independent organizational structure and a detailed ideological platform designed to facilitate the Alliance's growth into a national third world women's organization.[66] Guided by the principle of democratic centralism, the Third World Women's Alliance established a national and local organizational structure completely distinct from the Student Nonviolent Coordinating Committee. Democratic centralism ensured organizational and ideological unity through a centralized administrative structure and a decentralized implementation structure. In other words, individual members and chapters were directly responsible to the National Coordinating Committee for carrying out its directives, program and ideological platform, but how each chapter chose to do this depended upon local conditions and decisions. The organization supported collective leadership, collective decisions and input from all members, but abhorred individualism and disregard for the will of the majority. Unity and the revolution would be achieved only if the part submitted to the whole and chapters acted as one in principle, program, strategy and tactics.[67]

The Third World Women's Alliance identified its feminism as much different from that of other white and Black feminists. The women of the TWWA focused on eliminating economic exploitation, racism and sexism simultaneously.[68] Members embraced socialism to achieve this goal because they identified the system of capitalism as the basis of third world peoples' oppression.[69] In their eyes, capitalists used and encouraged racism and chauvinism "to divide, control and oppress the masses of people for economic gain and profit."[70] Since capitalism caused racism and sexism, and led to economic exploitation and inequality, the Third World Women's Alliance advocated armed revolution in order to establish "a truly socialist society where all oppression would be eliminated."[71]

The Third World Women's Alliance intended to take an active part in creating a socialist society, in building solidarity and sisterhood among third world women and in integrating women fully into society and the revolution.[72] To achieve these objectives, the TWWA recruited members, encouraged the development of local chapters throughout the United States, held weekly consciousness-raising meetings, participated in demonstrations and protest activities and published a newspaper, *Triple Jeopardy*.[73]

The members of the TWWA primarily centered their energies on *Triple Jeopardy*, and the paper represented the organization's main effort to attain a socialist society. Under the editorship of Frances Beal, the TWWA published *Triple Jeopardy* from September 1971 through the summer of 1975. Although occasionally irregular, the TWWA usually distributed five issues a year, its messages aimed at third world, working-class women and men. Each issue contained sixteen pages of articles, photographs, poetry and editorials, in both English and Spanish.[74]

Although the name *Triple Jeopardy* referred to the triple oppression experienced by third world women in the form of racism, imperialism and sexism, the paper focused on establishing capitalism as the basis of these oppressions and socialism as the only route to liberation for third world people. *Triple Jeopardy* presented information and facts about conditions in the United States under capitalism and promoted socialism as an alternative to the American system by illustrating life and conditions, particularly for women, in socialist nations around the world. By spreading this ideology and educating men and women about the nature of sexism, racism and the economic exploitation inherent in capitalism and imperialism, the TWWA used *Triple Jeopardy* to recruit members and to organize the masses.[75]

A majority of the articles and ideas found in the newspaper emphasized the evils of capitalism. Some features suggested the failure of capitalism by documenting the dismal state of the economy in the United States. Topics included high inflation, food costs, the energy crisis, monopolies and President Nixon's economic policies.[76] Other articles documented the economic exploitation of workers, the intolerable working conditions of the masses and the unequal distribution of resources in the United States. The TWWA primarily illustrated these points through the recurring column "On the Job." Members of the TWWA would interview third world women working in all kinds of jobs to show the similar oppressions experienced by each and to begin to identify ways to deal with the inequities.[77] *Triple Jeopardy* focused on not only the domestic effects of capitalism but also its international repercussions in the form of imperialism. Its writers demanded an end to the role of the United States and European nations in colonialism, the domination of the third world, economic exploitation and military occupation in areas such as Korea, Southeast Asia, Latin America and the Middle East. Although identifying imperialism worldwide, the TWWA devoted most of its effort and space in the publication to U.S. colonialism in Puerto Rico.[78]

Articles in *Triple Jeopardy* also documented the relationship between gender inequality and capitalism. Authors used examples from Puerto Rico, Africa, Mexico and the United States to show how sexism evolved out of capitalism.[79] The paper also revealed the group's belief that capitalists used sterilization to control third world people in the United States, arguing that the purpose was to curb population growth and solve the social problems caused by capitalism. Through *Triple Jeopardy* TWWA members tried to promote knowledge about the female reproductive system, birth control and sterilization to empower women to make their own choices about sexuality and procreation.[80]

Conversely, to show the relationship between women's equality and socialism, *Triple Jeopardy* carried numerous articles examining the conditions of women in socialist nations or in countries with the revolution ongoing and reported that socialism promoted women's equality. Every issue had one or more articles on women in Cuba, China, the Soviet Union, North Vietnam, North Korea, Sudan, Guinea-Bissau, Albania or Mozambique.[81]

The TWWA extended its critique of white society to include the women's liberation movement, rejecting it because white women demanded reform, not revolution. According to the TWWA, the majority of white feminists only wanted their piece of the pie, not to change the power balance of society.[82] In addition, white women pointed to men and male chauvinism as the enemy rather than identifying and fighting against deeper causes of sexism. The TWWA believed that middle-class white women, upon receiving equality in the white capitalist system, would use their privileged status to oppress third world women.[83]

Despite the ideological consistency of the Third World Women's Alliance, the organization disappeared shortly after the summer of 1975. After approximately five years of working to create a socialist society through its distinctive feminism, the Alliance ended its efforts to usher in a socialist revolution in the United States. However, the TWWA represents an important legacy of SNCC. As SNCC entered its last, chaotic years, a handful of African American female members merged SNCC's concept of Black nationalism with innovative ideas of feminism to create an independent organization aimed at alleviating the triple oppression of third world women based on class, sex and race. The feminism envisioned by these militants not only differed from that of the mainstream women's liberation movement but reflected its origins in SNCC. Black women adopted feminism in 1968, as did white women in 1964 and 1965, because a comprehensive ideology existed in SNCC. When a multifaceted belief system constituted the ideology of Student Nonviolent Coordinating Committee members, both Black and white women discovered their identity as women, developed a feminist consciousness and created distinctive forms of feminism.

NOTES

1. For example, see Clayborne Carson, *In Struggle: SNCC and the Black Awakening of the 1960s* (Cambridge: Harvard University Press, 1981), 147–8, 302; Mary King, *Freedom Song: A Personal Story of the 1960s Civil Rights Movement* (New York: William Morrow and Company, 1987), chap. 12; Sara Evans, *Personal Politics: The Roots of Women's Liberation in the Civil Rights Movement and the New Left* (New York: Alfred A. Knopf, 1979), chap. 4.

2. "What Is SNCC?" (*Student Voice* 1:1 [June 1960]: 2), in *The Student Voice, 1960–1965: Periodical of the Student Nonviolent Coordinating Committee*, ed. Clayborne Carson (Westport, Conn.: Meckler, 1991), 2; Howard Zinn, *SNCC: The New Abolitionists* (Boston: Beacon Press, 1964), 34; Ella Baker, interview by John Britton, Washington, D.C., 19 June 1968, tape 203, transcript, Civil Rights Documentation Project, Manuscript Division, Moorland Spingarn Research Center, Howard University, Washington, D.C., 41, 44. (Hereafter cited as CRDP.)

3. James Forman, *The Making of Black Revolutionaries* (Washington, D.C.: Open Hand Publishing, 1985), 237; Carson, 62, 75, 95; Emily Stoper, *The Student Nonviolent Coordinating Committee: The Growth of Radicalism in a Civil Rights Organization* (Brooklyn: Carlson Publishing, Inc., 1989), 35, 65, 108 (hereafter cited as *Student Nonviolent Coordinating Committee*); Baker, interview by Britton, 96; Jane Stembridge, "Interview with Jane Stembridge," interview by Emily Stoper, 1966, in *Student Nonviolent Coordinating Committee*, 258.

4. Stoper, 27, 122–3, 124, 132; Carson, 2; Zinn, 167; Forman, 307; Ella Baker, "Interview with Ella Baker," interview by Emily Stoper, 27 December 1966, in *Student Nonviolent Coordinating Committee*, 266; Dorothy Zellner, interview by James Mosby, New Orleans, 27 May 1970, tape 684, transcript, CRDP, 14, 15.

5. For a discussion of Freedom Summer and the problems arising from it, see

Carson, chaps. 9, 10; Forman, chaps. 48–50, 52; King, chaps. 10–12; Mary Aickin Rothschild, *A Case of Black and White: Northern Volunteers and the Southern Freedom Summers, 1964–1965*, Contributions in Afro-American and African Studies, number 69 (Westport, Conn.: Greenwood Press, 1982); Doug McAdam, *Freedom Summer* (New York: Oxford University Press, 1988).

6. King, 440, 447, 448, 485; Edward Brown, interview by Harold Lewis, Washington, D.C., 30 June 1967, tape 2, transcript, CRDP, 46; Cleveland Sellers, with Robert Terrell, *The River of No Return: The Autobiography of a Black Militant and the Life and Death of SNCC* (New York: William Morrow and Company, 1973), 130, 131; Baker, interview by Britton, 63–4; Baker, interview by Stoper, 270, 271; Zellner, 21–2; Julian Bond, "Interview with Julian Bond," interview by Emily Stoper [1966 or 1967], *Student Nonviolent Coordinating Committee*, 216; Betty Garmen, "Interview with Betty Garmen," interview by Emily Stoper [1966 or 1967], *Student Nonviolent Coordinating Committee*, 289; Stembridge, 250, 262; John Lewis, "Interview with John Lewis," interview by Emily Stoper [1966 or 1967], *Student Nonviolent Coordinating Committee*, 218.

7. Bond, 275; Baker, interview by Britton, 63; Brown, 46–7; Sellers, 132; Carson, 139; Stoper, 78; Garmen, 288, 294; King, 447.

8. Brown, 56.

9. Baker, interview by Britton, 65, 66; Carson, 192; Forman, 451.

10. Carson, 134, 135; Forman, 408, 411.

11. Carson, 137; Forman, 414, 420, 421.

12. King, 462; Carson, 144.

13. Carson, 151.

14. Garmen, 288; Baker, interview by Stoper, 270; "Position Paper," 6–12 November 1964, *Student Nonviolent Coordinating Committee Papers, 1959–1972*, microfilm ed. (Sanford, N.C.: Microfilming Corporation of America, 1982), A:6:25, 0785. (Hereafter cited as *Student Nonviolent Coordinating Committee Papers*, series: section: file, frame.)

15. "Position Paper," 0786.

16. King, 442–8; Casey Hayden, "Preface," in King, 9.

17. King, 445.

18. Ibid., 448.

19. Ibid., 442–8.

20. King, 458, 465; "A Kind of Memo," 18 November 1965, in King, 573.

21. Evans, 100; King, 460.

22. King, 460, 455–60; Hayden, 9.

23. Carson, 325 n. 32.

24. "A Kind of Memo," 571, 572, 573.

25. King, 450.

26. King, 450, 485. "Position Paper" supporters included Bob Moses, Charlie Cobb, Emmie Schrader, Theresa del Pozzo, Marie Varela and Dona Richards.

For their presence in the nonstructure faction, see Stembridge, 262; Bond, 276; Lewis, 218, 240; Brown, 47; Carson, 154; King, 337.

27. King, 467.

28. Cynthia Washington, "We Started from Different Ends of the Spectrum," *Southern Exposure* 4:4 (Winter 1977): 15.

29. Stembridge, 251.

30. Washington, 14; King, 465; Evans, 88.

31. Evans, 81; McAdam, 124; Jacqueline Jones, *Labor of Love, Labor of Sorrow: Black Women, Work, and the Family from Slavery to the Present* (New York: Basic Books, 1985), 312.

32. See, for example, Carson, chaps. 10–15; Forman, chaps. 51–55.

33. Stokely Carmichael, "Power and Racism" (September 1966), *The Black Power Revolt*, ed. Floyd B. Barbour (Boston: Extending Horizons Books, 1968), 61–4; Stokely Carmichael and Charles Hamilton, *Black Power: The Politics of Liberation in America* (New York: Random House, 1967), 46; Joyce Ladner, "What 'Black Power' Means to Negroes in Mississippi," *Trans-action* 5:1 (November 1967): 14.

34. Sellers, 156, 157; King, 500; Will Henry Rogers, Jr., interview by Robert Wright, Greenwood, Mississippi, 29 June 1969, tape 446, transcript, CRDP, 55; Carson, 201.

35. Betita Martinez, "Black, White, Tan" (summer 1967), *Student Nonviolent Coordinating Committee Papers*, A:3:1, 1266.

36. Forman, xiv, 475; Carson, 240; King, 508–9; Sellers, 193, 194.

37. Forman, 449, 476.

38. Ibid., 450.

39. Ibid., 509–18.

40. Ibid., 520; Carson, 271.

41. Carson, 265, 269, 276, 272; Angela Davis, *Angela Davis: An Autobiography* (New York: Random House, 1974), 149, 151.

42. Forman, 509–18; 520; 410; Carson, 269, 277; Davis, 158.

43. Martinez, 1266–68; Carson, 266; Forman, 480–1, 487, 518; Sellers, 188; Carmichael, *Black Power*, xi; Ladner, 9, 13.

44. Forman, 410, 460–71, 481, 504, 509–20, 522; Carson, chaps. 15–18; Sellers, 184, 207.

45. Carson, 296; BWLC Position Paper, n.d., Folders 1–21, BWA Correspondence, Frances Beal Papers, Records of the National Council of Negro Women, Bethune Museum-Archives, Washington, D.C. (Hereafter cited by document title or description, date, page number, box, folder, Beal Papers.)

46. Information sheet on *Triple Jeopardy,* n.d., 3, Folders 1–21, Typescript Reports and Transcripts, Beal Papers; Carson, 269.

47. "Transcript," 17 April 1969, 1, 15, Folders 1–21, Transcript Reports and

Typescripts, Beal Papers; Frances M. Beal, "Double Jeopardy: To Be Black and Female," *New Generation* 51 (Fall 1969): 28.

48. "Women in the Struggle," *Triple Jeopardy* 1:1 (September/October 1971): 8, *Herstory 1 Continuing Update*, microfilm ed., reel 4, Women's History Research Center, Berkeley, California. (Hereafter cited as *Herstory 1*, reel number.)

49. Kathleen Cleaver, "Black Scholar Interviews Kathleen Cleaver," interview by Julia Herve, *Black Scholar* 3:4 (December 1971): 55.

50. BWLC Position Paper; Frances M. Beal, "Slave of a Slave No More: Black Women in Struggle," *Black Scholar* 12:6 (November–December 1981; repr. 6:6 (March 1975)): 16; "Transcript," 17 April 1969, 2; "Women in the Struggle," 8.

51. Beal, "Double Jeopardy," 28; "Transcript," 17 April 1969, 2, 13; Davis, 161; Michele Wallace, *Black Macho and the Myth of the Superwoman* (New York: Dial Press, 1978), 47.

52. "Women in the Struggle," 8; Beal, "Double Jeopardy," 25; "Transcript," 17 April 1969, 8.

53. Beal, "Double Jeopardy," 25.

54. "Women in the Struggle," 8; Fran to Julia, 23 April 1969, box 8, unlabeled folder, Beal Papers; "Transcript," 17 April 1969, 3. Examples of Black nationalist men, such as Eldridge Cleaver, Malcolm X, Stokely Carmichael, H. Rap Brown and Huey Newton, who relegated women to a subordinate role are accumulated in Jones, 311–3; and Marable Manning, "Groundings with My Sisters: Patriarchy and the Exploitation of Black Women," *Journal of Ethnic Studies* 11:2 (Summer 1982): 25–31.

55. "Transcript," 17 April 1969, 3, 13; Beal, "Double Jeopardy," 28.

56. "Transcript," 17 April 1969, 1.

57. Ibid., 12, 7, 14, 15, 6.

58. "Women in the Struggle," 8.

59. Ibid.; Frances Beal to Sister, 30 April 1970, Folders 1–21, BWA Correspondence, Beal Papers.

60. BWA Statement and Objectives, n.d., Folders 1–21, BWA Pamphlet, Beal Papers.

61. "Transcript," 17 April 1969, 9–10.

62. "Women in the Struggle," 8.

63. "What Is the Third World?" *National SNCC Monthly* (March 1971): 10, box 8, Fran Beal, Beal Papers. The earliest reference to the Third World Women's Alliance is August 26, 1970 in "Women Strike But Equal to What?" *National SNCC Monthly* 1:3 (September–October 1970): 3, series 10, box 9, SNCC, Records of the National Council of Negro Women, Bethune Museum-Archives, Washington, D.C.; "Women in the Struggle," 8.

64. Charlayne Hunter, "Many Blacks Wary of 'Women's Liberation' Movement in U.S.," *New York Times*, 17 November 1970, 60.

65. Fran Beal to Betty McEady, 10 January 1971, 1, Folders 1–21, National Organization, Political Chapters, Beal Papers; Frances Beal to Mary Stone, 25 May 1971, Folders 1–21, National Organization, Political Chapters, Beal Papers; TWWA to Friends, 1 December 1970, box 8, loose, Beal Papers.

66. Beal to McEady, 10 January 1971, 1, 2; Beal to Stone, 25 May 1971; TWWA to Friends, 1 December 1970.

67. "Political Committee Meeting Minutes," 25 June 1971, Folders 1–21, TWWA Political Committee Meetings, Beal Papers; "Democratic Centralism," n.d., box 8, Political Education, TWWA, Beal Papers; Beal to McEady, 10 January 1971, 2.

68. "Women Strike But Equal to What?"; "Women in the Struggle," 8; Hunter, 60.

69. "Women Strike But Equal to What?"; "Women in the Struggle," 9; Beal, "Slave of a Slave," 22, 23; Beal, "Double Jeopardy," 24.

70. "Women in the Struggle," 9; Beal, "Slave of a Slave," 22, 23; Beal, "Double Jeopardy," 24.

71. "Women Strike But Equal to What?"; "Women in the Struggle," 8; Beal, "Slave of a Slave," 22, 23.

72. "Women in the Struggle," 8, 9; Beal, "Slave of a Slave," 23.

73. "Political Committee Meeting Minutes," 25 June 1971; "Third World Women's Alliance," n.d., box 8, unlabeled folder, Beal Papers; "Tuesday Meetings for September-October, 1971," *Triple Jeopardy* 1:1 (September-October 1971): 16, *Herstory 1*, reel 4; "Tuesday Meetings," *Triple Jeopardy* 2:1 (November–December 1972): 2, microfilm ed., State Historical Society of Wisconsin, Madison. (Hereafter cited as SHSW.)

74. This study is based on an examination of fourteen issues out of eighteen known issues, although it is unclear how many issues were published between January-February 1975 (4:2) and the Summer 1975 issue (no volume or number). All papers were microfilmed by either the Women's History Research Center, Berkeley, California, or the State Historical Society of Wisconsin, Madison; Information sheet on *Triple Jeopardy*, 4.

75. Information sheet on *Triple Jeopardy*, 1, 2.

76. Fourteen articles during the run of the newspaper analyzed the state of the U.S. economy and the failure of capitalism in the United States. See, for example, "Nixon's Nasty Economic Policy [NEP]," *Triple Jeopardy* 1:2 (November 1971): 7, *Herstory 1*, reel 16; "The Energy Crisis, A Matter of Profits," *Triple Jeopardy* 3:5 (Summer 1974): 11, SHSW.

77. Fifteen articles examined the plight of the laborer in the United States. See, for example, "On the Job: Telephone Operators," *Triple Jeopardy* 1:2 (November 1971): 3, *Herstory 1*, reel 16; Bernice Davis, "Farah Strike Gains Support," *Triple Jeopardy* 3:2 (November-December 1973): 2, *Herstory 1*, 7.

78. Seventeen articles analyzed U.S. and Western imperialism in third world

nations, and twenty-two documented U.S. imperialism in Puerto Rico and the Puerto Rican liberation movement. Examples include "Vietnam," *Triple Jeopardy* 1:5 (April-May 1972): 11, SHSW; Marilyn Aquirre, "Puerto Rico Is a Colony," *Triple Jeopardy* 3:1 (September-October 1973): 3, *Herstory 1*, reel 7.

79. See, for example, "Machismo," *Triple Jeopardy* 1:2 (November 1971): 5, *Herstory 1*, reel 16; Frances Beal, "Feminine Stink Mystique," *Triple Jeopardy* 3:4 (March-April 1974): 7, *Herstory 1*, reel 7.

80. Nineteen articles dealt with sterilization, birth control and other health issues. See, for example, Margo Jefferson, "North, South, East, West: Sterilization of Black Women Common in the U.S.," *Triple Jeopardy* 3:1 (September-October 1973): 1, *Herstory 1*, reel 7; "Vaginal Ecology," *Triple Jeopardy* (Summer 1975): 16, SHSW.

81. Twenty-seven articles examined the condition and experience of women in nations in which a socialist revolution had occurred or was in process. See, for example, "Korean Women in the Struggle," *Triple Jeopardy* 1:5 (April-May 1972): 4, SHSW; Margaret Randall, "Cuban Women Now," *Triple Jeopardy* (Summer 1975): 10–11, SHSW.

82. Frances Beal, "Let's Stop Chasing Shadows," *Triple Jeopardy* 3:3 (January-February 1974): 10, *Herstory 1*, reel 7; "Women Strike But Equal to What?", 3; Hunter, 60.

83. Beal, "Let's Stop Chasing Shadows," 10; Frances Beal quoted in Beth Day, *Sexual Life Between Blacks and Whites: The Roots of Racism* (New York: World Publishing, 1972), 285–6; "Women Strike But Equal to What?", 3; Beal, "Double Jeopardy," 23.

Chapter Five

The Making of the Vanguard Center
Black Feminist Emergence in
the 1960s and 1970s

Benita Roth

Introduction: Feminisms in the Second Wave

In the late 1990s, feminists in the United States have come to accept the idea that feminism means different things to different women located in different places in this society's race/class hierarchy. Scholarship on the feminist consciousness and activism of women of color and working-class women has shown us that the story of second-wave feminism—as the resurgence in feminist activism in the 1960s and 1970s is generally known—was and is really the story of feminisms.[1] However, to date, case studies of second-wave feminism have all but ignored the feminist social movement activism of women of color. African American feminist organizing has been given a nod in the form of mentions of the National Black Feminist Organization and lamentations as to why Black women did not join feminist groups in greater numbers.[2]

Generally, Black feminism is seen as emerging later than white feminism, and as varying a bit from white feminism's model by calling attention to the impact of racial oppression in Black women's lives. A couple of things are wrong with this picture, however. The reemergence of feminism in the 1960s and 1970s needs to be understood as the reemergence of "feminisms," plural form of the noun, because feminists from different racial and ethnic groups formed organizationally distinct feminist movements in the second wave. At the same time, these movements were linked in a crowded, competitive social movement sector, and there were mutual and complicated relationships between feminist activists from different racial/ethnic communities.

In the following discussion, drawn from a larger comparative research project on the emergence of feminisms in the 1960s and 1970s,[3] I challenge the idea that Black feminist organizing was a later variant of so-called mainstream white feminism by reexamining both the timing of Black feminist emergence and the content of the Black feminist critique of both the white women's liberation and the Black liberation movements. First, Black feminist organizing began roughly when white feminist organizing did; scholars have conflated the *timing* of Black feminist emergence with the separate analytical problem of the *numbers* of Black women involved in feminist groups. This has led to "model making," the implicit (and sometimes explicit) idea that white feminism—particularly the "younger," white women's liberation branch of second-wave feminism—was a template that African American feminists later used for their feminist politics.[4]

Second, Black feminist politics contained a strong class critique of both the white women's liberation movement and the Black liberation movement, a critique that transcended the additive approach of race being an overlay to gender oppression.[5] Black feminists' class critique of existing liberation movements was part and parcel of their feminist emergence, and not solely a reaction to their marginalization within those movements due to racism and sexism. The critique of class and race oppression by Black feminists led them to develop an idea of their movement as a "a vanguard center"; I use this term to describe the Black feminist assertion that the liberation of Black women—who were oppressed by the multiplicative systems of gender, race and class domination—would lead to the liberation of all.[6]

The Numbers Game, Model Making, and the Timing of Black Feminist Emergence

The issue of when Black feminism emerged is important because positing a later emergence for feminist activism by Black women bolsters the tendency in the literature on second-wave feminism to make white women's feminism a model from which other forms of feminist activism "deviate." Although never explicitly stated, it is assumed that early feminist organizing—presumably by white feminists—sets the stage for later movements, as earlier movements inevitably assume a "pride of place" as exemplars for later ones. Ironically, the impact of the Black civil rights movement on later movements—including women's liberation—has been duly noted by white feminist scholars and Black ones.[7]

But the issue of the *timing* of Black feminist emergence has been conflated in this literature with the issue of *numbers,* so that scholars search for large numbers of Black feminists in white women's organizations and find the Black women missing. The absence itself is then conscientiously explained; the conclusion drawn from this explained absence is the necessarily later emergence of Black feminism.

For example, Klein noted that although African American women supported women's liberation goals more strongly than white women in survey data, "(most) Black feminists are working outside of *mainstream* feminist organizations to create space for discussing the problems facing Black women."[8] Other scholars have argued that African American women were uniquely unattracted to [white] feminism, because of their being relatively better off vis-à-vis Black men; thus Black women have failed to join so-called mainstream organizations and presumably would not until they began to lose ground to Black men.[9]

By playing the "numbers game"—worrying why Black feminists did not join "mainstream" feminist groups—scholars have misunderstood the timing of Black feminist emergence, and thus missed the chance to fully map out second-wave feminist networks. The "numbers game" has obscured not just the feminist elements of Black women's activism on behalf of the race but early Black feminist activism itself. African American feminists have argued strongly against the model making of scholarship on second-wave feminisms; they have argued that a feminist consciousness was (and is) inherent both in the activities and the ideology of Black women active in behalf of the race.[10] These arguments of the inherently feminist nature of African American women's activism in the 1960s and 1970s are certainly persuasive, but so is the actual historical record of Black feminist organizing.

Black feminist organizing began at the same moment that white feminist organizing did, albeit on a smaller scale, and primarily in all-Black organizations. There were early challenges to male dominance in the civil rights movement. In 1964, Ruby Doris Smith Robinson, Casey Hayden, Mary King, Mary Varela and others began to discuss women's status in the Student Nonviolent Coordinating Committee (SNCC); Hayden and King (both white) wrote an "anonymous" memo to other SNCC members about the position of women in the movement.[11] Hayden and King were reluctant to sign their names to the document, and so speculation as to authorship fell on Smith Robinson, in part because of her position of authority within SNCC and her propensity for questioning gender inequities in it. Evans reports that in fact, Smith Robinson was important enough as a feminist presence so that later accounts by white feminists had her presenting "her" paper to SNCC herself.[12]

In 1965, Hayden and King wrote (and this time signed) a memo, "Sex and Caste," about women's status in the New Left at large, and accounts of white feminism move from that action to the formation, in November 1967, of a feminist group by white women, mostly "of the movement"— that is, of the New Left. These women published "Preliminary Statement of Principles" in *New Left Notes*, and then went on to publish the first white women's liberation newsletter, *Voice of the Women's Liberation Movement*, out of Chicago.

Only months later, in 1968, Frances Beal and other members of SNCC's Women's Caucus formed the Third World Women's Alliance (TWWA), a self-consciously Black *and* feminist social movement organization. TWWA had an explicitly anticapitalist critique of the middle-class style of the Black liberation movement and of white feminism.[13] In October 1968, MaryAnn Weathers, another TWWA member, argued for Black women's liberation in position papers published by TWWA. Entitled "An Argument for Black Women's Liberation as a Revolutionary Force" and "Black Women and Abortion," these papers were widely circulated in both Black and white leftist circles. Feminist ideas on the Left crossed racial boundaries as well when, in August of 1968, Gwen Patton sent a draft of her essay "Black People and the Victorian Ethos," to Robert and Pam Allen.[14] Patton's essay would shortly afterward appear in Toni Cade Bambara's 1970 collection, *The Black Woman*; Pam Allen was a white women's liberationist notably concerned with issues of racial difference and solidarity.

From the late 1960s on, Black feminist writing was being produced and read by both Black and white women. Frances Beal's oft-cited manifesto of Black feminism, "Double Jeopardy: To Be Black and Female," was written in 1969, and then published in both *Sisterhood Is Powerful*, Robin Morgan's edited collection, and Cade Bambara's *The Black Woman*. While Morgan's collection is considered a touchstone of second-wave feminism, Cade Bambara's collection is rarely treated by scholars as a product of feminist social movement activism, possibly because *The*

Black Woman also included the voices of Black women skeptical of the need for an autonomous Black feminist movement. But many of the pieces in *The Black Woman*—besides Beal's and Patton's, a list includes those by Jean Carey Bond and Patricia Perry, Joyce Green, Abbey Lincoln, Kay Lindsey, Pat Robinson and the Mount Vernon/New Rochelle Women's Group, and Toni Cade Bambara herself—clearly expose and oppose the specific forms of oppression that affected Black women.

As noted above, scholars have noted the impact that Black women civil rights activists had on emergent white feminists as role models; Sara Evans is especially convincing on this point. But Black women were not solely protofeminist role models for white feminists, who then set the feminist stage for Black women to reenter. Some early Black feminists were involved in political relationships with early white feminists, and influenced one another's thinking. For example, Pat Robinson, one of the founders of the Black feminist Mount Vernon/New Rochelle Women's Group, and author of several position papers reprinted in both Cade Bambara's and Morgan's collections, corresponded with Joan Jordan (aka Vilma Sanchez), a white West Coast feminist and labor activist, from October 1966 through at least 1971. From their correspondence, it is clear that the two influenced each other's thinking. Robinson quoted Jordan's writings on the position of Black women and their historical role in a letter to another "dear and hardworking sister":

> [O]nce the Black woman is unified her voice will be like thunder throughout the Americas and the world. . . . The opportunity to unify and develop is all there. This is the historical role . . . to push forward to progress and justice.[15]

And Sanchez/Jordan clearly drew from Robinson's experience as a practicing psychotherapist and Black activist; she wrote a piece in 1968 entitled "Black Women as Leaders in the Coming Crisis: A Psycho-Dynamic Approach," and writings by Robinson on Malcolm X were part of Sanchez/Jordan's extant papers (State Historical Society, Madison, Wisconsin). Robinson at one point even wrote Sanchez/Jordan that she thought more Black middle-class militant women would be supportive of feminism, if they were not "too scared to come out honestly for black women's liberation."[16] These kind of contacts between feminist activists mattered very much in the relatively small network of the Left in the 1960s, and become apparent only when we look for Black feminists outside mainstream feminist organizations.

In short, Black feminist activism began when second-wave white feminism began and was part and parcel of it. Playing the "numbers game" has obscured the simultaneity and *interrelatedness* of Black and white feminist emergence, the very mutual influence that some feminists had on one another across racial lines. If we dispense with "model making" and stop expecting large numbers of Black feminists to flock to white organizations, we can see that second-wave feminism was *at its roots* the creation of Black and white women.

Forming the "Vanguard Center": Black Feminism's Class Critique

Black feminist thought has been extremely influential in shaping feminist politics, and the phrase "the intersection of race, class and gender" is axiomatic now for doing feminist work. But accounts of how Black feminists arrived at the intersection do not always show that they were going down all three streets at once from the very start of their movement.

Black feminist ideology did not simply emerge from the empty space created by Black feminism's marginalization in the white women's and Black liberation movements; it is not simply a residual creation of adding a race component to the gender critique of society and a gender component to the critique of racism. To a remarkably consistent degree, African American feminists in the second wave developed what I call "a vanguard center" ideological approach to feminist activism: the idea that the liberation of Black women, oppressed by race, gender and class domination, would mean the liberation of all. Facing competing demands on their energies from the Black liberation and the white women's liberation movements, Black feminists did more than just reject Black liberation's sexism and white feminists' racism. Rather, Black feminists were critical of the middle-class assumptions and values that were built into *both* movements. In fact, the Black feminist critique of both Black and white women's liberation was in large part a class critique that posited that each movement's respective shortcomings—Black liberation's sexism and white women's liberation's racism—were in no small part *due* to activists' middle-class blinders.

It is hard to ignore Black feminist critiques of white women's liberation; criticism of "white middle-class" women's liberation was just that, with the word "white" seldom appearing without the words "middle class." From the beginning of their movement, Black feminists focused on the implicit racism of white feminism's neglect of poor and working-class women's issues of survival. This is not to say that Black women did not see white women as personally racist—many undoubtedly did because many white women undoubtedly were. But Black feminists argued that white women's liberation's neglect of economic survival issues were time and time again the main stumbling block to joint work with white women on feminist issues.

Given the relative economic power of the Black and white communities, the Black feminist critique of white feminism's middle-class blinders was both race *and* class conscious; white feminists were perceived as being indifferent to both race and class issues.[17] This made working with white feminists, who tended to focus exclusively on gender issues, difficult. Hunter, while interviewing several Black feminists, quoted Beal, who told of how white women marching in a liberation parade in August 1970 had objected to a sign reading "Hands Off Angela Davis"; these white feminists failed to see a link between Davis's incarceration and women's liberation.[18]

Many Black feminists felt that white women's class unconsciousness was the key obstacle to a linked feminist struggle; in a 1970 satirical piece, one Black feminist, Lorna Cherot, wrote that "I'll love you [white women] when my belly is full, there's clothes on my back and shelter over me."[19] Dorothy Pitman, a community organizer and Black feminist interviewed for *Mademoiselle* magazine, argued that "I can't really say I'm a sister to white women, unless they recognize how they also were oppressive in a capitalistic situation."[20] Pitman felt that white women needed a class analysis of oppression in order to understand how their class privilege contributed to the oppression of Black women. Without such an analysis, Pitman argued that white women working on their own oppression in a white-dominated society would not be able to do anything for the liberation of Black women.

Thus, the racism that many Black feminists saw in the white women's liberation movement was seen as rooted in white women's failure to look beyond their own racial and class experiences. Davenport wrote that because of this failure, Black feminists working with white feminists

are seen in only one of two limited or oppressive ways: as being white-washed and therefore sharing all their values, priorities, and goals, etc.;

or if we . . . mention something particular to the experience of Black wimmin, we are seen as threatening, hostile, and subversive to their interests.[21]

Barbara Smith and Beverly Smith characterized their experiences with the white middle-class women's movement in a similar fashion: white women were insensitive to the experiences of those without racial and class privilege. The Smith sisters especially challenged some white middle-class feminists' "arrogance" in seeing downward mobility as a measure of their politics. Material comfort, the Smith sisters argued, had a very different meaning for Black women, who had to struggle for it and thus did not take it for granted.[22]

Black feminism's class critiques help to explain differences between Black and white feminists on issues like reproductive rights and the family. In articles that appeared in the Philadelphia women's liberation newsletter "Women" in June of 1970, Black feminists assailed white women's failure to acknowledge class and racial aspects to the abortion issue. Abortion on demand—a key demand of white feminism—was seen by Black feminists as imperfect policy because it was not linked to other reproductive concerns that were tied to class power: involuntary sterilization; life circumstances that compel poor women to abort; and the possibility that women on welfare would be forced by the state to have abortions. The author(s) argued that if white women's liberationists really cared about having an impact in communities of color, they would expand reformist policies into a commitment to destroy the economic system.

Black feminists had different perceptions about the meaning of feminist struggles surrounding the family; class status, as well as racial status, played a role in creating these different perceptions. The white women's liberation movement was seen as trying to reshape a family structure that Black women were trying to stabilize.[23] While many white women experienced family obligations as exploitation, most Black women found that the family was the least oppressive institution in their lives and constituted a refuge from white domination.[24] bell hooks noted that white feminists who speculated about the feminist movement's leading to the abolition of the family were seen as a threat by many Black women, and she attributed the antifamily attitudes of some white feminists to their ability to rely on outside institutions to be cognizant of their needs; Black women, poorer as a group, could not rely on such support.[25] Both hooks and Toni Morrison pointed out that class privilege buys one out of many of the responsibilities of family; upper- and middle-class women can hire other (poor, nonwhite) women to do work for them.[26] And as Lewis argued, white feminist demands for work privileges did not resonate strongly with Black women, who had never been excluded from the privilege of working to support their families.[27]

Motherhood itself had different meanings for Black and white feminists, as a consequence of class and racial differences. Polatnik, looking at Black and white feminist groups in the second wave, argued that for many white feminists, becoming a mother meant being doomed to living a 1950s suburban housewife role, as their mothers had; therefore becoming a mother meant potentially participating in women's oppression.[28] Coming from less prosperous, more urban backgrounds, Black feminists knew that alternative mothering styles were possible; in the Black community, "othermothering," a more communal style of child rearing, existed. Thus, Black feminists did not reject motherhood but, instead, argued for choice and control over motherhood rather than a full retreat.

Black feminists were equally critical of the propagation of middle-class values by many Black liberationist groups, and saw Black liberation's sexism as emanating in great part from an embrace of middle-class values as a means of "fixing" what was wrong in the Black community. From the founding of the Third World Women's Alliance in 1968, Black feminists argued against the "middle-class style" of the Black liberation movement, along with the movement's sexism and masculinism.[29] Analogous to the critique of white women's liberation's racism, Black feminists saw Black liberation's sexism as rooted in an unexamined adoption of middle-class white values.

Segments of the Black Power/Black liberation movement ideologically favored entrepreneurial capitalism, inasmuch as the Black Power solution had African Americans turning back to the community and emulating other ethnic groups through self-help.[30] These tendencies were bolstered by the publication of the Moynihan report in 1965, in which the Black family was painted as deviant, and pathological in its being matriarchal.[31] Many Black liberationists advocated that the Black family remake itself along patriarchal lines; they urged Black women to take a step back from public activism into merely supportive roles, or to go all the way back into the home, away from public life altogether.

Black feminists countered that the idea of remaking the Black family along patriarchal lines was classist, foreign to the Black experience, and indicative of a lack of real revolutionary thinking when it came to the role of Black women in the community. Highly critical of the Moynihan report itself, Black feminists rejected the desire of Black liberationists to restructure the Black family along patriarchal lines. They saw "the myth of the matriarchy" as a "sledgehammer" being used to stop Black women from effective organizing, since the report had caused many Black women to feel that they had to step back from responsibilities and hand the reins over to men.[32]

Many of the contributors to *The Black Woman* anthology wrestled with the Moynihan report and what they saw as the Black liberationist "manhood" preoccupation that was restricting Black women's activism. They explicitly linked a fixation on "manhood" to the demands of capitalism. Essays by Pat Robinson and the Mount Vernon/New Rochelle group in *The Black Woman* were especially critical of those Black leaders who led poor Blacks down the garden path of capitalism. The Mount Vernon/New Rochelle group analysis of fighting for Black women linked class, gender and racial oppression; fighting these oppressions would require a united front of middle-class Black *and* white women who would join poor Black women in continuing to expose male oppression:

> Capitalism is a male supremacist society. . . . All domestic and international political and economic decisions are made by men and enforced by males. . . . Women have become the largest oppressed group in a dominant, male, aggressive, capitalistic culture. . . . Rebellion by poor black women, the bottom of a class hierarchy . . . places the question of what kind of society will the poor black woman demand and struggle for. Already she demands the right to have birth control, like middle class black and white women. . . . She allies herself with the have-nots in the wider world and their revolutionary struggles. . . . Through these steps . . . she has begun to question aggressive male domination and the class society which enforces it, capitalism.[33]

Robinson faulted her Black militant friends for their class biases, although she came from a middle-class background herself. She wrote Joan Jordan in 1970 that Black militants conflated class oppression with race oppression. Robinson's socialism impelled her to be friendly to the white women's movement from its beginning, and, as noted, she told Sanchez/Jordan that she thought more Black middle-class militant women would be too, if they were not afraid of the lack of support they would have in coming out in favor of a Black women's movement.

In "Double Jeopardy," Beal analyzed the cultural ideal of Black "manhood" and laid the responsibility for it at the feet of American capitalism. She argued that the construction of masculinity and femininity was necessitated by the need to sell products to men and women. The "typical" middle-class woman, staying home and buying these products, was not a Black woman, who had historically worked outside the home (and historically, mostly in white middle-class homes). Beal argued that male Black liberationists had failed to extend their class analysis to the position of women. She had sympathy for Black men's suffering in white society, but for Beal, consistent class analysis meant recognizing that the move to put Black women "back" in the home was futile in the face of technological advancement: "Black women sitting at home reading bedtime stories to their children are just not going to make it."[34] Thus, Beal argued that Black liberation needed to purge itself of middle-class ideas about gender relationships, and Black women's groups were needed to steer the course straight.

Gwen Patton also argued that the failure to apply class critiques to gender roles was at the root of Black liberation's sexism. She held that Black liberation had adopted a "Victorian Philosophy of Womanhood" and that Black men failed to realize that capitalism was responsible for their needing to feel like "men." Patton felt that Black militants should have been savvier about the intent and impact of the Moynihan report. She chastised Black male activists for not seeing through the report:

> Black men . . . respond[ed] positively toward Black Power and could assert their leadership, which included a strengthening of their masculinity and, unfortunately, an airing of their egos. Black women will now take the back position, and in so doing, Moynihan was justified in his observations. [A] victory for the capitalistic system! Black men are now involved with keeping their women in line by oppressing them more, which means that Black men do not have time to think about their own oppression. The camp of potential revolutionaries has been divided.[35]

Patton noted that white women had begun the challenge to a male capitalist order and recommended that Black women do the same.

Kay Lindsey agreed that Black militants were being seduced by capitalist promises. She argued that those in the "Black middle class" were "pseudo-escapees into the mainstream," where they assumed "many of the institutional postures of the oppressor, including the so-called intact family." Lindsey argued that white-establishment efforts to "encourage the acquisition of property among Blacks via Black Capitalism . . . would probably serve to further intensify the stranglehold on women as property," and therefore work against the liberation of Black women.[36]

The contributors to *The Black Woman* were not alone in their linking of Black liberation's sexism to a lack of awareness of class issues. Other Black feminists writing during this time period echoed the idea that Black liberationists were importing white middle-class values into the heart of the Black community. Margaret Wright, a member of the Los Angeles Black women's liberation group WAR, declared it impossible for Black families to be shaped like white ones:

> The black man is saying he wants a family structure like the white man's. He's got to be head of the family and women have to be submissive and all that nonsense. Hell the white woman is already oppressed in that setup. Black men have been brainwashed into believing they've been emasculated. . . . Black women aren't oppressing them. We're helping them get their liberation. It's the white man who's oppressing, not us. In black women's liberation we don't want to be equal with men, just like in black liberation we're not fighting to be equal with the white man. We're fighting for the right to be different and not be punished for it. . . . I want the right to be black and me.[37]

Nina Harding, a Black woman writing from a socialist perspective, lived in Seattle, 3000 miles away from most of the contributors to *The Black Woman*. In 1970, she wrote a position paper entitled "The Interconnections Between the Black Struggle and the Woman Question," which she presented at the Seattle Radical Women Annual Conference in February of that year. She echoed the idea that Black liberation, otherwise critical of capitalism, had accepted traditional ideas about women's roles:

> Where the Black man asserts to reject the values and mores of this capitalistic system . . . when it comes to the woman question, he imposes and demands that all Black women resume a sub-servient role and maintain the feminine qualities of what he considers to be lady-like. . . . Black men have even alleged that Black women have aligned with society to persecute and emasculate their manhood. As a consequence Black men DEMAND that Black women step back because the Black women hamper the leadership of the Black man within the struggle for liberation of all peoples.[38]

Harding was critical of Black "bourgeois sisters and silent sisters," who hold to "WASP standards, be those standards interpreted by the Muslim or Nationalist advocates." For Harding, the Black struggle would not succeed as long as it adhered to white middle-class family models.[39]

The Black feminist critique of Black liberation's middle-class biases was apparent in challenging that movement's take on the issue of birth control. Black feminists challenged Black liberationists' assertion that birth control was "genocide," arguing that charges of genocide took away poor Black women's right to control their lives. Black liberationists urged Black women to have children to thwart dominant white society; the racism present in some family-planning groups made this stance viable.[40] At times, Black militants took action to back up their assertions. In 1969, Black nationalists closed down a birth control clinic in Pittsburgh, which was subsequently reopened by community women.[41] Ross reported that other birth control clinics were "invaded by Black Muslims associated with the Nation of Islam, who published cartoons in *Muhammed Speaks* that depicted bottles of birth control pills marked with a skull and crossbones, or graves of unborn Black infants."[42]

Toni Cade Bambara, MaryAnn Weathers from the Third World Women's Alliance, and the Mount Vernon/New Rochelle group argued that abandoning birth control would deprive Black women of much needed control of their lives. Black feminists advocated the liberalization of abortion laws; they dismissed the idea that the use of birth control by Black women constituted "genocide."[43] The Mount Vernon/New Rochelle group's well-known statement "Poor Black Women" was published in Morgan's 1970 collection, and as a pamphlet; Patricia Robinson had formulated a version of the statement about two years earlier, in response to the "Black Unity Party's" stand against the use of birth control by Black women.[44] In "Poor Black Women," Robinson and her coauthors argued that the Pill gave "poor Black sisters" the ability to resist white domination; trading that ability in for a life of domesticity—a middle-class picture—would not work for poor Black women. More pointedly, the authors accused the anti–birth control Black militants of being "a bunch of little middle-class people" with no understanding of the Black poor:

> The middle-class never understands the poor because they always need to use them as you want to use poor black women's children to gain power for

yourself. You'll run the black community with your kind of Black Power—
You on top! The poor understand class struggle![45]

In summary, Black feminist responses to the traditional gender ideology that Black liberationists espoused saw sexism as generated by the Black liberation's adoption of white middle-class values that were alien to the Black community. Black feminists consistently blamed sexism on capitalism and linked struggles against sexism to struggles for economic justice; they linked their critique against white women's liberation's racism to white women's neglect of these same economic struggles. As the 1970s progressed, Black feminist organizations like the National Black Feminist Organization and the Combahee River Collective would add another street to the intersection, in the form of an analysis of the impact of heterosexism on Black women's lives. The understanding of how feminist activism had to take charge of fighting against intersecting, multiplicative oppressions was therefore a Black feminist legacy that could be expanded to reach out to more and more women. The vanguard center could thus grow.

Conclusion: A Different Picture of the Second Wave

From the standpoint of chronology and ideology, Black feminism is at the center of the story of second-wave feminism, not a variant but constitutive of the core of the feminist legacy of that era. It is a myth that Black women were hostile to feminism, as polls done during the era show.[46] Black feminists began their struggle at the same time white feminists did; they are absent from the story of feminism's emergence by virtue of the fact that they did not join white women's liberation groups in large numbers. And from the beginning of their feminist activism, they argued for opposition to gender, race and class oppression, and resistance to prioritizing any one of the three above the others.

By the mid–1970s, Black feminism had profoundly influenced the entire feminist movement—the so-called mainstream included. The "vanguard center" critique of interlocking oppressions strongly influenced feminist theory and continued to do so throughout the 1980s and 1990s.[47] Whatever problems remain in feminist practice, Black feminists succeeded in bringing their concerns to the center of feminist activism.

Scholars of social movements have to pay attention to the impact of numbers; social movements come from outside, and need numbers to gain the attention of the powers that be. But the impact of a social movement is never solely a matter of numbers, and social movement success and influence cannot be judged solely on this basis. The legacy of feminist activists consists of both solid achievements and of political ideas that last, that clarify the position of different groups of women in this society, and that motivate further activism. By these criteria, the Black feminist contribution has been central to the success of second-wave feminism, and telling the story of Black feminism needs to be a central part of telling the story of the second wave.

NOTES

The author would like to thank the following for their critical input: Duchess Harris (Macalester College), Cheryl Johnson-Odim (Loyola University, Chicago), Susan Markens (UCLA), and Kimberly Springer, as well as an anonymous reviewer at New York University Press. An earlier version of this chapter was published in *Womanist Theory & Research* 2:2. It is reprinted by kind permission of *Womanist Theory & Research*.

1. Gluck et al. 1998.

2. See Buechler 1990; Echols 1989; Freeman 1975; and Marx Ferree and Hess 1994.

3. The project, "On Their Own and For Their Own: African American, Chicana and White Feminist Emergence in the 1960s and 1970s," is a work of historical sociology that examines the structural, intramovement and intermovement factors that led to the emergence of feminist movements organized along racial/ethnic lines in the second wave.

4. See Freeman 1975 for analysis of the difference between "younger" and "older" branches of white feminism in the second wave.

5. See Spelman 1982.

6. See King 1988.

7. See Evans 1979; and Johnson Reagon 1978.

8. Klein 1987, 27 (emphasis added).

9. See Buechler 1990; Freeman 1975; and Lewis 1977.

10. See Giddings 1984; Hill Collins 1990; hooks 1981 and 1984; Omolade 1994; and Smith 1983.

11. Evans 1979.

12. Robnett (1997) noted that Hayden and King's paper was not so much an attack on SNCC's sexism as an attempt to bring up issues of patriarchy and hier-

archy as the group wrestled with its structure and direction. That the paper has been seen by subsequent scholars solely as evidence of SNCC's sexism is the result, Robnett argued, of a failure to take a womanist standpoint; such a standpoint would consider what Black women were doing in the organization and would not boil down gender relations to those between white women and Black men.

13. Third World Women's Alliance 1971.

14. Allen 1968.

15. Pat Robinson, 1967, letter in Robinson 1966–1971.

16. Pat Robinson, 1970, letter in Robinson 1966–1971.

17. White socialist feminist groups, like Boston's Bread and Roses, did have an anticapitalist critique of sexism from the late 1960s on. It is probably true that these socialist-feminist groups were initially distant from Black feminist networks. Later Black feminist groups like the Combahee River Collective had members with specific links to white socialist-feminist organizations. See Combahee River Collective 1981.

18. Hunter 1970. See also Giddings 1984, 305.

19. Cherot 1970.

20. Cantwell 1971, 183.

21. davenport 1981, 85–6.

22. Smith and Smith 1981, 113.

23. See Dubey 1994; and Ferguson 1970.

24. See White 1984.

25. See hooks 1981 and 1984.

26. See Morrison 1971.

27. Lewis 1977.

28. Polatnik 1996. To be fair, most white feminists were not hostile to motherhood; what they were hostile to was the suburban housewife role. But as Polatnik noted, some white feminists were deeply suspicious of motherhood and of works like Shulamith Firestone's (1970) *The Dialectic of Sex* (in which Firestone speculated about the future demise of biological motherhood in terms that left little doubt as to her opinion of it as an experience) that fed the idea that white feminists were widely hostile to being mothers.

29. See Giddings 1984, and before that, Third World Women's Alliance 1971.

30. See Cruse 1968; and Carmichael and Hamilton 1967. Black feminists had a more complicated relationship with the avowedly socialist Panthers. The Panthers were known for having strong women leaders; at the same time, the masculinism of much of the male leadership made women's lives within the party difficult. See Brown 1992; *The Militant* 1969; Newton 1970; Ross 1993; and Smith 1970 on the complicated and contradictory aspects of gender relations within the party.

31. United States Dept. of Labor Office of Planning and Research 1965.

32. See Weathers 1968a; and Murray 1975.

33. Robinson and Mount Vernon/New Rochelle Group 1970a.

34. Frances Beal, "Double Jeopardy: To Be Black and Female," in Cade Bambara (1970a, 345).

35. Patton 1970, 146–7.

36. Lindsey 1970, 86–7.

37. Wright 1972, 608.

38. Harding 1970, 2.

39. Space precludes consideration of the writings of other socialist-feminist Black women like Maxine Williams and Pamela Newman, who published essays critical of the middle-class biases of Black liberation in a widely circulated 1970 pamphlet, *Black Women's Liberation.*

40. See Ross 1993. As Rodrique (1990) noted, the racist, eugenic orientation of some in the birth control movement made advocacy of birth control practices difficult for Black women.

41. See Lindsey 1970.

42. See Ross 1993, 153.

43. Cade Bambara 1970b; and Weathers 1968b.

44. Robinson 1968. According to a 1967 letter from Robinson to Sanchez/Jordan, Robinson's father, a physician, had been on the national board of Planned Parenthood.

45. Robinson and Mount Vernon/New Rochelle Group 1970b, 361.

46. See Carden 1974; and Klein 1987.

47. See Gluck et al. 1998; Hill Collins 1990; hooks 1984; Johnson Reagon 1983; Joseph and Lewis 1981; King 1988; Moraga and Anzaldúa 1981; Smith 1979; Spelman 1982; and White 1984.

REFERENCES

Allen, Pam. 1968. Letter (August 29). Pam Allen Papers, State Historical Society, Madison, Wisconsin.

Beal, Frances. 1970. "Double Jeopardy: To Be Black and Female." In *The Black Woman: An Anthology*, edited by Toni Cade Bambara. New York: New American Library.

Brown, Elaine. 1992. *A Taste of Power: A Black Woman's Story*. New York: Pantheon Books.

Buechler, Steven M. 1990. *Women's Movements in the United States: Woman Suffrage, Equal Rights and Beyond*. New Brunswick and London: Rutgers University Press.

Cade Bambara, Toni, ed. 1970a. *The Black Woman: An Anthology*. York and Scarborough, Ontario: Mentor Books.

———. 1970b. "On the Issue of Roles." In *The Black Woman: An Anthology,* edited by Toni Cade Bambara. New York: Pantheon Books.

Cantwell, Mary. 1971. "'I Can't Call You My Sister Yet': A Black Woman Looks at Women's Lib." *Mademoiselle* (May).

Carden, Maren Lockwood. 1974. *The New Feminist Movement.* New York: Russell Sage Foundation.

Carey Bond, Jean, and Patricia Perry. 1970. "Is the Black Male Castrated?" In *The Black Woman: An Anthology,* edited by Toni Cade (Bambara). York and Scarborough, Ontario: Mentor Books.

Carmichael, Stokely, and Charles V. Hamilton. 1967. *Black Power: The Politics of Liberation in America.* New York: Vintage Books.

Cherot, Lorna. 1970. "I am What I am." *Liberation News Service* 294 (October 29): 16.

Combahee River Collective. 1981. "A Black Feminist Statement." In *This Bridge Called My Back: Writings by Radical Women of Color,* edited by Cherríe Moraga and Gloria Anzaldúa. Watertown, Mass.: Persephone Press.

Cruse, Harold. 1968. *Rebellion or Revolution?* New York: William Morrow & Company.

davenport, doris. 1981. "The Pathology of Racism: A Conversation with Third World Women." In *This Bridge Called My Back: Writings by Radical Women of Color,* edited by Cherríe Moraga and Gloria Anzaldúa. Watertown, Mass.: Persephone Press.

Dubey, Madhu. 1994. *Black Women Novelists and the Nationalist Aesthetic.* Bloomington and Indianapolis: Indiana University Press.

Echols, Alice. 1989. *Daring to Be Bad: Radical Feminism in America, 1967–1975.* Minneapolis: University of Minnesota Press.

Evans, Sara. 1979. *Personal Politics: The Roots of Women's Liberation in the Civil Rights Movement and the New Left.* New York: Vintage Books.

Ferguson, Renee. 1970. "Women's Liberation Has a Different Meaning for Blacks." *Washington Post* (October 3): D1–2.

Firestone, Shulamith. 1970. *The Dialectic of Sex: The Case for Feminist Revolution.* New York: William Morrow and Company.

Freeman, Jo. 1975. *The Politics of Women's Liberation.* New York & London: Longman.

Giddings, Paula. 1984. *When and Where I Enter: The Impact of Black Women on Race and Sex in America.* New York: Bantam Books.

Gluck, Sherna et al. 1998. "Whose Feminism, Whose History? Reflections on Excavating the History of (the) Women's Movement(s)." In *Community Activism and Feminist Politics: Organizing Across Race, Class and Gender,* edited by Nancy A. Naples. New York and London: Routledge.

Green, Joyce. "Black Romanticism." In *The Black Woman: An Anthology,* edited by Toni Cade (Bambara). York and Scarborough, Ontario: Mentor Books.

Harding, Nina. 1970. "The Interconnections Between the Black Struggle and the Woman Question." Reprint, published by Seattle Radical Women. Women's Liberation Ephemera Files, Special Collections, Northwestern University.

Hill Collins, Patricia. 1990. *Black Feminist Thought: Knowledge, Consciousness, and the Politics of Empowerment.* Boston: Unwin Hyman.

hooks, bell. 1981. *Ain't I a Woman: Black Women and Feminism.* Boston: South End Press.

———. 1984. *Feminist Theory: From Margin to Center.* Boston: South End Press.

Hunter, Charlayne. 1970. "Many Blacks Wary of 'Women's Liberation' Movement in the U.S." *New York Times* (November 17): B1.

Johnson Reagon, Bernice. 1978. "The Borning Struggle: The Civil Rights Movement." *Radical America* 12:6 (November/December): 9–25.

———. 1983. "Coalition Politics: Turning the Century." In *Home Girls: A Black Feminist Anthology*, edited by Barbara Smith. New York: Kitchen Table/ Women of Color Press.

Jordan, Joan (aka Vilma Sanchez). 1968. "Black Women as Leaders in the Coming Crisis; A Psycho-Dynamic Approach." Unpublished paper. Joan Jordan Papers, State Historical Society, Madison, Wisconsin.

Joseph, Gloria I. and Jill Lewis. 1981. *Common Differences: Conflicts in Black and White Feminist Perspectives.* Garden City, N.Y.: Anchor Books.

King, Deborah H. 1988. "Multiple Jeopardy, Multiple Consciousness: The Context of a Black Feminist Ideology." *Signs* 14:1 (Autumn).

Klein, Ethel. 1987. "The Diffusion of Consciousness in the United States and Europe." In *The Women's Movements of the United States and Western Europe: Consciousness, Political Opportunity, and Public Policy*, edited by Mary Fainsod Katzenstein and Carol McClurg Mueller. Philadelphia: Temple University Press.

Lewis, Diane K. 1977. "A Response to Inequality: Black Women, Racism, and Sexism." *Signs* 3:2 (Winter).

Lincoln, Abbey. 1970. "Who Will Revere the Black Woman?" In *The Black Woman: An Anthology*, edited by Toni Cade Bambara. York and Scarborough, Ontario: Mentor Books.

Lindsey, Kay. 1970. "The Black Woman as a Woman." In *The Black Woman: An Anthology*, edited by Toni Cade Bambara. York and Scarborough, Ontario: Mentor Books.

Marx Ferree, Myra, and Beth B. Hess. 1994. *Controversy and Coalition: The New Feminist Movement across Three Decades of Change.* New York: Twayne Publishers.

The Militant. 1969. "Panther Sisters on Women's Liberation." 1969. Unsigned article (September: 9–10).

Moraga, Cherríe, and Gloria Anzaldúa. 1981. "Introduction." In *This Bridge*

Called My Back: Writings by Radical Women of Color. Watertown, Mass.: Persephone Press.

Morgan, Robin, ed. 1970. *Sisterhood Is Powerful*. New York: Vintage Books.

Morrison, Toni. 1971. "What the Black Woman Thinks about Women's Lib." *New York Times Magazine* (August 22).

Murray, Pauli. 1975. "The Liberation of Black Women." In *Women: A Feminist Perspective*, edited by Jo Freeman. Palo Alto: Mayfield Publishing Company.

New Left Notes. 1967. "Chicago Women Form Liberation Group/"Preliminary Statement of Principles" (November 13).

Newton, Huey P. 1970. "A Letter from Huey to the Revolutionary Brothers and Sisters about the Women's Liberation and Gay Liberation Movement." Reprint from *Black Panther* 5:8 (August 21). Women's Liberation Ephemera Files, Special Collections, Northwestern University.

Omolade, Barbara. 1994. *The Rising Song of African American Women*. New York and London: Routledge.

Patton, Gwen. 1970. "Black People and the Victorian Ethos." In *The Black Woman: An Anthology*, edited by Toni Cade (Bambara). York and Scarborough, Ontario: Mentor Books.

Philadelphia Area Women's Liberation. 1970. "Abortion = Genocide? Letters from *Plain-Dealer* Women"; "Control of Our Bodies and Lives for White Women Only?"; "Abortion or Genocide?" *Women* 1:3 (June).

Polatnik, M. Rivka. 1996. "Diversity in Women's Liberation Ideology: How a Black and a White Group of the 1960s Viewed Motherhood." *Signs* 21:3: 679–706.

Robinson, Pat. 1966–1971. Letters to Joan Jordan (aka Vilma Sanchez), 1966–1971. Joan Jordan Papers, State Historical Society, Madison, Wisconsin.

———. 1968. "Poor Black Women," manuscript. Joan Jordan Papers, State Historical Society, Madison, Wisconsin.

Robinson, Patricia and the Mount Vernon/New Rochelle Group. 1970a. "Poor Black Women's Study Papers by Poor Black Women of Mount Vernon, New York." In *The Black Woman: An Anthology*, edited by Toni Cade (Bambara). York and Scarborough, Ontario: Mentor Books.

———. 1970b. "Statement on Birth Control. In *Sisterhood Is Powerful*, edited by Robin Morgan. New York: Vintage Books, 360–1.

———. 1970c. "Poor Black Women." Reprint. Somerville, Mass.: New England Free Press.

Robnett, Belinda. 1997. *How Long? How Long? African-American Women in the Struggle for Civil Rights*. New York and Oxford: Oxford University Press.

Rodrique, Jessie M. 1990. "The Black Community and the Birth Control Movement." In *Unequal Sisters: A Multicultural Reader in U.S. Women's History*, edited by Ellen Carol DuBois and Vicki L. Ruiz. New York and London: Routledge.

Ross, Loretta J. 1993. "African-American Women and Abortion: 1800–1970." In *Theorizing Black Feminisms: The Visionary Pragmatism of Black Women*, edited by Stanlie M. James and Abena P. A. Busia. London and New York: Routledge.

Smith, Barbara. 1979. "Notes for Yet Another Paper on Black Feminism, or Will the Real Enemy Please Stand Up?" *Conditions 5: The Black Woman's Issue*: 123–7.

———. 1983. "Introduction." In *Home Girls: A Black Feminist Anthology*, edited by Barbara Smith. New York: Kitchen Table/Women of Color Press.

Smith, Barbara, and Beverly Smith. 1981. "Across the Kitchen Table: A Sister to Sister Dialogue." In *This Bridge Called My Back: Writings by Radical Women of Color*, edited by Cherríe Moraga and Gloria Anzaldúa. Watertown Mass.: Persephone Press.

Smith, Fredi A. 1970. "Meet Women of the Black Panthers." *Daily Defender* (January 24).

Spelman, Elizabeth V. 1982. "Theories of Race and Gender/The Erasure of Black Women." *Quest: A Feminist Quarterly* 5:4: 36–62.

Third World Women's Alliance. 1971. "History of the Organization." *Third World Women's Alliance* 1:6 (March).

United States Department of Labor. 1965. *The Negro Family: The Case for National Action*. Washington, D.C.: U.S. Government Printing Office.

Weathers, MaryAnn. 1968a (October). "An Argument for Black Women's Liberation as a Revolutionary Force." Position paper issued by Third World Women's Alliance, Cambridge, Mass. Social Action Files, State Historical Society, Madison, Wisconsin.

———. 1968b. "Black Women and Abortion." Social Action Files, State Historical Society, Madison, Wisconsin.

White, E. Frances. 1984. "Listening to the Voices of Black Feminism." *Radical America* 18:2–3: 7–25.

Williams, Maxine, and Pamela Newman. 1970. *Black Women's Liberation*, reprinted in 1971, 1972. New York: Pathfinder Press.

Wright, Margaret. 1972. "I Want the Right to Be Black and Me." In *Black Women in White America: A Documentary History*, edited by Gerda Lerner. New York: Vintage Books.

Chapter Six

"Inside Our Dangerous Ranks"
The Autobiography of Elaine Brown and the Black Panther Party

Margo V. Perkins

Of the African American women who were active on the front lines of the Black Power movement in the United States during the late 1960s and early '70s, only three to date have published full-length autobiographies chronicling their experiences. In 1974, International Publishers issued Angela Davis's self-titled autobiography, a narrative composed largely while Davis awaited trial on FBI charges of murder, kidnapping, and conspiracy. Assata Shakur's autobiography, *Assata*, was published by Lawrence Hill & Co., thirteen years later, following her successful escape from New Jersey's Clinton Correctional Facility for Women and flight to Cuba. The most recent of the women's autobiographies to appear, Elaine Brown's *A Taste of Power: A Black Woman's Story*, was published by Pantheon in 1992. Because all three texts are ideologically situated at the intersection of the Black Power and feminist movements, their testimonies introduce important gender considerations into any retrospective assessment of the Black Power movement's achievements and shortcomings. Taken collectively, their stories offer broad insight into the range and quality of Black women's experiences in revolutionary nationalist struggle. While all three women shared a commitment to radical leftist politics in the struggle to end race and class oppression in the United States, the nature of their individual experiences in activist struggle, and the character of their respective narratives are notably different.

Compared to the earlier narratives by Davis and Shakur, which are closely tied to impending struggle both by virtue of the time they are written and each writer's personal circumstances, Brown's *A Taste of Power* is published some eighteen years after her association with the Black Panther Party. Consequently, her text emerges onto a completely different sociopolitical landscape. The implications of this difference are significant. Writing in the contemporary era and, consequently, from the vantage point of greater retrospective distance, Brown's reflections on the gender, sexual, and power dynamics at work within the movement are as unsettling as they are revealing.

Brown's autobiography, *A Taste of Power*, chronicles her political evolution and eventual ascension in 1974 to leadership of the Black Panther Party. The narrative begins with her "assumption" (literally the title of the first chapter) of power as head of the Party. The (deliberate?) play on words here is instructive since Brown both assumes power and assumes she has power. The fact that Huey Newton retains control over the organization in absentia, however, serves to undermine this assumption. Beginning with chapter 2, *A Taste of Power* travels back to Brown's childhood years in Philadelphia and works up through the narrative present—that is, the moment of Brown's departure from the Party. Unlike Shakur and Davis, whose respective associations with the Black Panther Party under Newton were fleeting (for reasons they each note in their narratives), Brown remained an active member until the organization's eventual demise in the mid–1970s. Although many individuals (including both fellow activists and movement scholars) date the Party's effective demise to even before Brown assumed leadership of the organization in 1974, a small and shrinking cadre of the Party did continue well into the late 1970s. Brown, who was pulled into the organization's innermost circle through her close association with Newton, became the first woman to lead the Party after Newton's flight to Cuba.

Even as Brown's narrative explores many of the same political issues and historical events treated by Davis and Shakur, she appears to enter into the autobiographical project with a markedly different sense of purpose. In many ways, Brown seems less concerned with writing a "political autobiography" (as Davis, for example, defined her own interest in such a project) than with reconciling the meaning of her own past involvement in political struggle. As a result, Brown's revelations tend to diverge in spirit and scope from Davis's and Shakur's. Because historically activists have used life-writing as another front on which to advance political struggle, many of the conventions of their narratives reflect an avowedly political agenda. Such conventions include emphasizing the story of the struggle over their personal ordeals; giving voice to the voiceless and names to the nameless; honoring strategic silences that both protect the integrity of the struggle and the welfare of other activists involved; and illuminating the oppressive conditions that call for organized resistance while also exposing the state's repressive tactics. With these conventions in mind, most activists use their texts as a form of political intervention to educate as broad an audience as possible to the nature and necessity of resistance struggle.

In *A Taste of Power* Brown, however, appears much less concerned with such conventions than with exploring the meaning of her own past involvement in the movement. Brown's narrative consistently transgresses the conventions noted above. Prime examples include the prominent status she affords her individual/autobiographical *I* in relation to the story of the movement, and her patent disregard for the kinds of strategic silences embraced by other writers. Because of the attention *A Taste of Power* affords to illustrating both the dynamics and abuses of power that transpired inside the highest echelons of the Party, Davis proposed in a June 1993 review of the book that its publication

> would have been inconceivable in the seventies—or even eighties. In radical circles, it would have been considered tantamount to treason, and among conservatives it would have been welcomed as the exposé of a fraudulent movement.[1]

It is precisely, however, Brown's disregard for strategic silences that makes her text an especially compelling study. Although many aspects of Brown's storytelling make her narrative worthy of careful deconstructing by autobiography critics and social historians alike, I wish to focus in this essay on the unique critique (i.e., vis-à-vis other Black Power activists' texts to date) her narrative presents of the nature of power itself, as experienced both within and without the Black Panther Party. It is, however, a critique much more implied than explicit.

Because of Brown's peculiar—and I would add, strategic—style of narrating, which avoids situating a present I in her text, her narrative is less an explicit critique of power dynamics in the Party than a presentation of episodes that *invite* such critique. That is, while Brown's repeated allusions throughout *A Taste* to the relationship between sex and power point to disturbing psychosexual dimensions of Party life and practices, we as readers are left largely to interpret the implications of these allusions on our own. Because Brown filters her story through the I of her past rather than present consciousness, there is rarely any authorial retrospective judgment passed on the episodes she recounts. Even so, the new insight to be gained into the Party, the era, and the power dynamics at work therein, marks *A Taste* as a unique and important instance of political witnessing.

Brown acknowledges that sexual openness was part of the spirit of the times. Having sex during the era, she writes, was "akin to drinking water" in terms of the casualness with which individuals experimented with different sexual partners (107). *A Taste* captures well the sense in which activists' acute awareness of their own mortality (the result of surviving under violent repression and of witnessing death repeatedly) led them to live fully in the present. Fellow Panther Masai Hewit, for instance, marvels with Brown over their having endured together six funerals in just six months time (195). Brown places the sexual openness and intimacy between men and women during the era in the context of war; sexual expression was one means of celebrating life against a backdrop of impending danger and devastating loss.

Although sexual openness was very much a part of the era, Brown's disclosure of intimate details about her own sexuality is paradigmatic of the kind of personal details that are largely absent in the autobiographies of other African American women activists. She recalls, for instance—in various degrees of detail—sexual affairs/encounters with at least twelve Party men, apart from her long-standing relationship with Huey Newton. The ethics of naming her lovers aside (many of whom were married or otherwise "committed" to others at the time), critics have noted that the sexual episodes described in *A Taste* certainly contribute to the narrative's rather racy, novelistic appeal. Is it merely sensationalism, though, that prompts Brown to include such highly personal details? Of course, that cannot be ruled out in a culture where sex is regularly marketed by print, television, and film media for profit. However, to read these episodes solely in terms of their sensational value is to miss other important issues raised by their inclusion.

Brown's frankness in *A Taste* about sexual matters challenges negative silences around Black female sexuality. Her identification of herself as a sexual being is a radical move in a society where Black women's sexuality is almost always overdetermined. Because racist ideology historically has marked Black women's bodies as hypersexed, many Black women choose to silence or minimize the sexual aspect of their identity so as not to fuel existing stereotypes. Against both the cultural dictates about the impropriety of women talking about or initiating or enjoying sex, and enduring racist assumptions about Black women as hypersexed, Brown is unapologetic about her own sexual desires and experiences. Her openness to sharing this part of herself is indicated by the details she supplies about intimate encounters with different men. Her description of making love with Larry is illustrative. Brown writes:

> His toughness was tender, I thought enveloped in his body, which was full and fit and dark and sweet. He made love with fire, a smoldering, satisfying heat. I caressed his muscular buttocks as we lay in the dark and dreamed out loud. (402)

The detailed passage significantly presents Brown as an unapologetically sexual being. Interestingly, it also inverts a conventional gender paradigm in which men describe and appraise the physical attributes of women. Rather than minimizing her sexual experiences, then, Brown insists upon their being seen as part of who she is. Even if Brown's self-revelations are partially motivated by a desire to undercut the potential for her detractors to use this information against her (a vulnerability peculiar to women), Brown's inclusion of such details works to affirm Black female sexuality as normal and healthy. Her articulation of the formerly unarticulated also widens a space in which Black women can share their experiences in a climate less laden with shame and censure. Because Brown is critical, at many points, of the nature of some of her sexual encounters, she portrays herself alternately in *A Taste* as sexual subject *and* object, noting the empowering aspects of the former and the dehumanizing tendency of the latter.

More than any other autobiography of the period, Brown's narrative also explores the extent to which women's sexual liberation was compromised within the movement. Specifically, she suggests ways in which the spirit of sexual freedom and openness during the era was often manipulated to reinscribe patriarchal privilege. While the Black Panther Party's rejection in principle of the commodification of intimate relationships under capitalism (specifically, the ownership of one's lover/partner) was liberating in many ways, Brown's narrative insists that the freedom to be intimate with multiple partners translated into substantially different consequences for women than for men. The combination of biology (the possibility of pregnancy) and ideology (the Party's rejection of birth control as genocide) created a situation in which women inevitably had more to lose. Brown's guilt feelings in the aftermath of an abortion she elects to have seem tied to Party ideology about contraception. She laments: "The immorality of it stung something deep in me. It was not in thinking that I had killed someone. I had done something worse. I had prevented someone from coming into being" (434). Narratives by women as well as some men from the period concede that Party women were sometimes coerced into sex by men who conveniently conflated women's capitulation to demands for sex with their commitment to the revolution. Brown remembers Panther Earl Anthony reminding her: "a true Sister would be happy to sleep with a revolutionary Brother" (115). Encouraged to regard birth control as genocide, many women who surrendered reproductive control of their bodies to the Party's line were left to rear on their own children born of tenuous relationships. Men, on the other hand, generally retained the freedom to accept or renege on parental responsibilities. Brown, who becomes pregnant by Masai Hewit, is left to rear their daughter, Ericka, without Hewit's support. She, in fact, learns during her fourth month of pregnancy that Hewit has married another woman (199). When Brown confides her feelings on the matter to fellow Panther David Hilliard, Hilliard chastises her for being petty, for allowing the "'subjective' to supersede the 'objective'" (199). The implication is not only that mind and body can be separated/severed (an assumption peculiar to Western rational thought) but also that interpersonal relationships are somehow outside the realm of politics.

As Brown's text repeatedly attests, men often managed to maintain male privilege even as radical shifts appeared to take place in the nature of interpersonal relations. While Newton, in accordance with Party ideology, rejected possessiveness in the context of intimate relationships, Brown notes that he often made it very clear to her potential suitors that she was, in fact, *his* woman (246). That is, his woman *along with* the many other women whose company he also continued to enjoy. Significantly, Brown—because of the power differential between herself and Newton, specifically, and between women and men, in general—could make no similar claim (i.e., one that was bound to be respected) on Newton. In his autobiography, *A Lonely Rage*, Bobby Seale maintains that

[t]he principle that backed up love relationships among Party members was simply that those who did not have an established one-to-one relationship with someone had the right, male or female, to make love with whomever they desired.[2]

However, who, in the relationship, enjoyed the privilege of defining whether or not the relationship was an "established one-to-one" was another matter. Black Power activists' narratives (including Seale's) repeatedly suggest that men were the ones who assumed this prerogative.

What is most compelling about Brown's treatment of sex and sexuality in *A Taste*, however, is the way in which power (often expressed as violence) is eroticized. For Brown, having and exercising power (i.e., the capacity to have one's communicated intentions met with acquiescence) is sensual. She confesses: "It was a sensuous thing to know that at one's will an enemy can be struck down, a friend saved. The corruption in that affirmation coexists comfortably with the sensuousness and seriousness of it" (319). Even the title she chooses for the autobiography renders power in sensual terms. Brown's illustrations of the internecine violence that eventually destroyed the Party repeatedly point toward not only sexual but, often, *sadomasochistic* underpinnings with fascinating implications.

Although neither the term nor the practice of sadomasochism is explicitly invoked in Brown's narrative, her rendering of a clearly sadomasochistic episode early in the autobiography (prior to her association with the Party) almost invites us to read other incidents recounted in her text through this lens. Shortly after her arrival in California at the age of 25, Brown's naive participation as a dominatrix in a sadomasochistic ritual becomes a symbolic trying on of power. Lured by the prospect of securing quick cash with seemingly little personal investment, Brown is, by her own admission, duped into meeting a man whom she is instructed to physically chastise. She writes:

> He hurriedly took off his clothes, while I remained, as instructed, in mine: tight Black pants, Black turtleneck sweater, and high-heeled Black shoes. . . . He threw his huge naked fleshiness onto my convertible bed and begged me to beat him. I grabbed the belt and simply whipped him, as though I had done it before. (74)

Before Brown is paid for her "services," however, the client makes a hasty departure, promising to come right back after removing his car from a no-parking zone. When he fails to return, Brown realizes that she is the one who has been the "trick." The client's seeming subjugation to her will is exposed as illusory. Reading Brown's text allegorically through this particular episode has fascinating implications because the episode parallels the manner in which she eventually is given leadership of the Party. Her status vis-à-vis the Party is similar to that of the dominatrix in that the extent of her power is rigorously circumscribed by the wishes of another. Since the authority Brown is permitted to exercise over the organization emanates from Huey Newton, Newton always retains the power to usurp control at any time. As with the dominatrix, then, Brown's power is merely "a taste."

In *Sadomasochism in Everyday Life*, author Lynn Chancer suggests that any hierarchical social structure potentially yields sadomasochistic dynamics. Thus, the Party's very structure meant that it was doomed from the outset to recapitulate many of the same regressive power dynamics at work in the dominant culture. Brown, in fact, acknowledges that it was the Party's rigidly authoritarian paramilitary structure that enabled her to realize power within the organization. She explains: "Within a chapter were branches, organized by city, and within the branches were sections. These were divided into subsections, which were divided into squads. Ideas and information flowed up and down the chain of command. Orders went from the top to the bottom" (135). Such a structure ensured respect for her authority, even as her gender was often resented by the predominately male membership consigned to follow her orders. Within this rigid chain of command, many activists, such as Assata Shakur and Angela Davis, found that there was little tolerance for constructive criticism, especially from rank-and-file members. Even Brown's narrative attests to the Party's practice of swiftly crushing signs of dissension or resistance within its ranks. Many activists who eventually broke with the Party found such pervasive "power-tripping" among the leadership antithetical to the interests of any serious liberation struggle.

Chancer's work would suggest that the apparent contradiction between the Party's authoritarian structure and liberatory ideals might best be explained by examining the larger context in which the Black Panther Party operated. That is, the exploitative nature of economic and social relations under capitalism and patriarchy, in general, provides an ideal context for the emergence of sadomasochistic dynamics. Chancer proposes:

> Rather than sadomasochism being merely the property of individuals, our culture itself is deeply oriented in a sadomasochistic direction. We are living in a society sadomasochistic in that it bombards us with experiences of domination and subordination far more regularly than it exposes us to sensations and inklings of freedom and reciprocity.[3]

In *A Taste*, Brown illustrates the fluidity between the positions of sadist and masochist, noting her own passage through both roles. In the role of sadist, Brown acknowledges ordering and supervising the vicious beating of Steve, a fellow Panther who allegedly challenged her authority. Once a victim of Steve's physical abuse herself, Brown admits that this motivated her desire to see him punished for his flagrant disrespect for her authority. In an analeptic narrative moment, she recounts her retaliation against Steve: "I had not intended committing an act of vengeance. Despite my memory of the fists that had brutalized my body a few years before, there were larger issues involved when I ordered Steve to Oakland" (368). Brown seems to make the latter assertion as an attempt to convince herself, simultaneously providing the reader insight into her own rationalizing of the incident at the time. Further, in asserting that she "had not intended committing an act of vengeance," she implicitly concedes that that is, in fact, what she did. Repeatedly, Brown's recollections of her own actions as titular head of the Party remind us that the capacity to abuse power is a non-gender-specific phenomenon.

In the role of masochist, Brown admits to a dependence on and need for validation from others to escape feelings of emptiness, learned self-hatred, and nonexistence. Her ascension to power in the Party allows her to shed the role of masochist. Addressing an assembly of Panthers she summons in order to announce her new position as head of the Party, Brown writes that "there was something in that moment that seemed a reparation for all the rage and pain of my life" (6).

In invoking a sadomasochistic paradigm to talk about power relations within the Party, I wish to stress that the plight of the masochist is less defined by pleasure in subordination (for that would be highly problematic in speaking about oppression) than by psychological or material dependence. Certainly, the nature of this dependence has been thoughtfully documented in the works of Frantz Fanon's *The Wretched of the Earth* and Albert Memmi's *The Colonizer and the Colonized*, among other studies. Dependence on the Party, once members became deeply involved and committed to its vision, almost guaranteed submission to the range of the Party's activities, including some of its more unsavory practices. After all, committing oneself to the Party generally involved profound sacrifice, both personal (alienation from one's family as well as the society at large), and financial (members turned over any individual income to the collective, and in turn, lived communally with other Party members). Furthermore, membership in the Party for some activists, including Brown by her own admission, provided for the first time, a sense of purpose and meaningful identity. David Hilliard, for instance, confesses in his 1993 autobiography, *This Side of Glory*, that he desired to leave the Party long before he actually did. Reasoning against his better judgment, he concluded, "but there's no place to go. The Party is home, where I am accepted; anyplace else is exile."[4] Hilliard's sentiment finds its echo in Brown's narrative more than once. Since the sadomasochistic dynamic is never static, the stakes are always being raised. Any increase in resistance from the dominated is always met with an increase in abuse/tyranny from the dominator. Only when the dominated succeed in leaving the situation, as both Brown and Hilliard among others, eventually do, can the sadomasochistic dynamic be broken.

Brown notes that prior to actually joining the organization, she, like many who witnessed the Panthers in action, was impressed by the spirit of resistance and self-determination that the Party exuded. As Angela Davis notes, the Panthers provided a "romantic revolutionary image" at the same time that they promoted active resistance. Style was an important part of their allure and thus a useful strategy in mobilizing communities of resistance.[5] Of course, style, in general was highly politicized during the era. The hippie movement, the cultural nationalists, and the Black Panthers all had their own unique dress styles vis-à-vis mainstream America, each connoting a particular set of politics. The Panthers habitual donning of Black leather (the official Party uniform) is just one example of an accouterment often associated with sadomasochistic sexual practice. As Brown and others have testified, much of the Party's immediate appeal to the uninitiated, in fact, had to do with their distinct appearance, notably the Black leather, the dark shades, the open display of weaponry, the use of military formations, and the aura of power associated with all four. The mixture of awe and fear the Panthers regularly inspired might be read as arising in part from the (unconscious) cultural fascination and titillation with the paraphernalia of sadomasochism, signifying as it does the forbidden or unknown, specifically, lawlessness and the deliberate transgressing of (sexual) taboos.

A much more disturbing manifestation of sadomasochism that Brown describes in *A Taste*, however, is the Black Panther Party's use of whips in administering corporal punishment, a practice ironically evocative of the historical experience of slavery. According to Brown, "disciplining" generally entailed being lashed across the back with a whip (275). Contrary to slaves, however, Party members willingly submitted to authoritarian rule and disciplining on account of their own commitment to and belief

in the ideals of the organization. The analogy to a sadomasochistic paradigm here is instructive. As Chancer indicates:

> both sadist and masochist remain rigidly within the parameters of their re-
> spective roles; they are symbiotically interdependent; and the masochist has
> been forcibly restricted in such a way that challenging sadomasochistic in-
> tercourse (literally or figuratively) is . . . only possible under certain rules of
> the game that do not ever really allow the power of the sadist to be chal-
> lenged.[6]

Brown's account of the violent expulsion of then Party chairman, Bobby
Seale, reveals that even members of the central committee (with the obvious exception of Newton) were not exempt from such disciplining.
Brown's account of Seale's expulsion, during one of Newton's drug-in-
duced rages (which became increasingly frequent in the later years of the
Party) is chilling. Brown writes that Newton became offended when Seale
repeated a third party's criticism of Newton's leadership. Though Seale
insisted that he avidly defended Newton to his detractor, Newton is not
appeased and continues to escalate the confrontation until the scene cul-
minates in Seale's violent lashing with a bullwhip. From her position as
voyeur, Brown recalls: "Though a relatively thin man, Bobby bent only
slightly with each lash, his head down, eyes tight, braced for the next
crack. I remained at the table, smoking" (351). Although Brown places
five other Party members at the scene, none of them makes an effort to
avert what all apparently recognized as an unprovoked and unjust attack
on Seale. All no doubt, rightly assumed, that such violence could be just
as easily turned on them.

As graphic as Brown's account of Seale's expulsion in the autobiography is, it merely hints, by other accounts, at the extent to which sadomasochism pervaded Party practices. Hugh Pearson's revealing though
not unproblematic 1994 study, *The Shadow of the Panther: The Price of
Black Power in America*, for instance, proposes an even more troubling
account of the circumstances surrounding Seale's expulsion. In his interviews with former Party member Mary Kennedy and with David
Horowitz, a onetime Party sympathizer later turned right-wing conservative, Kennedy and Horowitz maintained that Seale was not only violently beaten but also *sodomized* by Newton on the occasion of his expulsion. Pearson writes that "Newton dramatically beat Seale with a bullwhip and sodomized him so violently that his anus had to be surgically

repaired by a physician who was a party supporter."[7] Seale subsequently has denied not only that he was sodomized but also that he was beaten. Oddly, his 1978 autobiography, *A Lonely Rage*, omits any mention at all of the July 1974 expulsion. By his own account, Seale leaves the Party without incident and on his own volition. When confronted, in the aftermath of *A Lonely Rage*'s publication, by reporter Kate Coleman with contrary testimony/evidence from other Party members, Seale adamantly denied that he was beaten and further charged that the rumors were likely the result of a disinformation campaign initiated by the police. When Coleman indicated that her sources included someone who claimed to have actually treated his injuries, Seale allegedly screamed into the phone:

> "What injuries? . . . I had no injuries whatsoever! I don't give a damn who said it. Tell them I said they're a flat Black-ass, motherfucking liar, or a white-assed liar—whoever the hell they are."[8]

The tenor of Seale's extreme denial (i.e., extreme in the sense that nobody but Seale seems to deny the fact that he was at least expelled), as well as the bizarre nature of the charge itself, suggests that—at the very least—something traumatic transpired around Seale's abrupt departure from the Party. Given Newton's history of incarceration (and therefore, probable exposure to sodomy as an expression of violence and debasement among prisoners), and the Party's documented practice of corporal punishment as a disciplinary measure, Pearson's claim is not unfathomable. Furthermore, given the climate of homophobia in America, it is understandable that Party members, as well as Seale himself, might be reluctant to publicly corroborate/ acknowledge such an incident.

Assuming there *was* more to the episode than just the beating Brown's narrative recounts, Brown's decision to omit further detail could be out of a desire to protect the image of the Party, herself, or both. Several disparaging remarks about Seale in the autobiography make it appear unlikely that Brown would have been interested in protecting Seale's image by deliberately omitting such detail.[9] Furthermore, the suppression of sensitive information is hardly consistent with other moments in the narrative where Brown is quite candid in disclosing others' intimate secrets; for example her naming of former lovers and her treatment of Kathleen Cleaver as a victim of domestic violence being paradigmatic. It appears that Brown's omission is a calculated one. Disclosing the sodomizing of Seale—as if the beating alone were not damning enough—not only would have strained any lingering romantic images of the Party but would have even more deeply implicated Brown herself as a participant in the sado-masochistic dynamics that her narrative intimates were common, espe-cially since there is no indication in the autobiography that Brown subse-quently sought to distance herself from Newton's inner circle. The inci-dent points again to Brown's own move between the roles of sadist and masochist, or victimizer and victim, as the circumstances portend. While *A Taste* repeatedly gestures toward exposing the seedier side of the Party's activities, Brown generally avoids fully exploring the extent of her own complicity in such activities.

Brown's eventual break with the Party is also marked by what might be described as sadomasochistic violence. In *A Taste*, Brown indicates that Newton's increasing paranoia, which eventually alienated most of those closest to him, led her to believe that it would not be long before she, too, would become the victim of one of his irrational purges of Party activists (353). Weary over Newton's failure to seriously address sexist vi-olence against women and its negative impact on Party morale, and fear-ing that matters would only get worse, Brown claims that she determined to flee for her own safety. As in the case of her description of Seale's de-parture, however, other sources suggest a slightly different chain of events than what Brown recalls in the autobiography. Hugh Pearson maintains that just prior to her departure, Brown was brutally battered by Newton to the extent that she required hospitalization for her injuries.[10] Although Brown notes that she was once slapped by Newton, there is clearly no mention in *A Taste* of any assault this severe. In fact, in recounting the in-cident, which she describes as "commonplace inside our dangerous ranks," Brown writes:

> He struck me. It was a slap in my face after I had made an innocuous re-mark. Huey had not so much as raised his voice in anger to me prior to that, not even in that last month, when the snares of his madness had left so many others maimed. (9)

Brown's minimizing/omission of the beating is ironic, especially given her rather condescending portrait in *A Taste* of Kathleen Cleaver. It is also odd that Brown would choose to distance herself from Cleaver in the nar-rative rather than to use her own circumstance to express the kind of fem-inist solidarity her text argues for elsewhere.

While it is true, as some of her critics have charged, that Brown re-peatedly fails to explore the full implications of many of her own disclo-sures about abuses of power within the Black Panther Party, her narrative nevertheless opens new doors to public discussions about the organization and its operations, particularly during the Party's later years, that have not—and perhaps, as Angela Davis has argued, could not have—taken place prior to the 1990s. As late as his own study, Hugh Pearson admits that he had difficulty finding ex-Panthers willing to talk critically about Huey Newton and the Party. He writes:

> The horrific truth of the party's downfall was an open secret among Black Oaklanders and party veterans, but most of them insisted on silence (and still do to this day)—something akin to not discussing the state of a relative who has gone to pot, or, sensing that death might occur any day, preparing to recall only the best.[11]

The lack of respondents forthcoming meant that Pearson was left to rely largely, for his own study, on individuals openly disillusioned about both their own experiences within the Party and the direction the organization eventually took. Bob Blauner's review of *The Shadow of the Panther* in the *New York Review of Books* (July 19, 1994: 22) indicates that seven of Pearson's twenty-eight interviewees requested anonymity as a condition for their input.

One thing Pearson fails to note in his book is that activists' reluctance to talk about Newton and the Party arises at least in part from their awareness of how critical testimony can be and often is politically manipulated to reduce, undermine, and/or dismiss the movement in its entirety without appreciation for its complexity or achievements above and beyond whatever serious shortcomings also existed. It is in this context that Brown's own revelations must be considered. Even as Brown remains guarded in her confessions, the fact that she writes her autobiography in a different sociopolitical climate as well as from the psychological advantage of greater retrospective distance than either Angela Davis or Assata Shakur, for example, means that she enjoys greater freedom to probe potentially explosive internal issues. In grasping this freedom, Brown opens, through *A Taste*, new spaces for important discussions around gender and sexual politics, and around power dynamics in nationalist struggle that, to date, have been only cursorily explored in other activists' works from the period. In the end, contrary to what some of her critics have proposed, Brown's disclosure of explicit information about her own sexuality and illustrations of the psychosexual dynamics at work in the Party suggest a complex relationship between sex, violence, and power that is more instructive than gratuitous. The sensationalism such revelations lend to her narrative, notwithstanding, Brown engages, no less than the other prominent activists whose ranks she joins, in an important kind of political witnessing.

The issues Brown presents complement and expand the critiques offered by Davis and Shakur. Taken collectively, the women's autobiographies emphasize the extent to which the personal *is*, in fact, political, even as such recognition marks only the beginning of transformative struggle. Brown's text illustrates historian Michel Foucault's assertion that power passes everywhere. The kinds of episodes that *A Taste* highlights, as well as Brown's inability to escape acting out some of the very contradictions her narrative points to, give credence to Foucault's claim. Because we are at no time outside the power relations that structure social interaction, the prospect of making what is inside impermeable to the values, assumptions, and ways of knowing that are outside is exposed as a fiction; the reality, of course, is that the outside always already *is* inside. The women's texts most emphatically address the implications of this realization. Their testimonies, which broaden our understanding of the period, also impart valuable lessons for mapping resistance struggles today.

NOTES

1. Angela Davis, "The Making of a Revolutionary," review of *A Taste of Power*, by Elaine Brown, *Women's Review of Books* 10, 9, June 1993: 4.

2. Bobby Seale, *A Lonely Rage: The Autobiography of Bobby Seale* (New York: Times Books, 1978) 187.

3. Lynn Chancer, *Sadomasochism in Everyday Life: The Dynamics of Power and Powerlessness* (New Brunswick: Rutgers University Press, 1992) 2.

4. David Hilliard with Lewis Cole, *This Side of Glory: The Autobiography of David Hilliard and the Story of the Black Panther Party* (Boston: Little, Brown & Company, 1993) 309.

5. *A Place of Rage*, dir. Pratibha Parmar, with Angela Davis, June Jordan, and Alice Walker, Women Make Movies, 1991.

6. Chancer 11.

7. Hugh Pearson, *The Shadow of the Panther: Huey Newton and the Price of Black Power in America* (New York: Addison-Wesley Publishing Company, 1994) 264. In a footnote on p. 391, Pearson substantiates the claim, citing an August 29, 1982, interview with Kennedy in Oakland and an October 6, 1992, interview with Horowitz in Los Angeles. He further notes that "Horowitz also provides written confirmation for the sodomizing in [the] article 'Black Murder, Inc.,' by David Horowitz, Heterodoxy, March 1993." Mary Kennedy joined the Party

in 1968 and left in 1973, disillusioned by its apparent deterioration. David Horowitz, who became associated with the Party after 1971, left disgruntled in the aftermath of Betty Van Patter's mysterious disappearance and death. Van Patter was hired by Brown as an accountant to maintain the Party's finances.

8. Kate Coleman with Paul Avery, "The Party's Over," *New Times* 10 July 1978: 33.

9. Brown not only raises questions about Seale's intelligence but criticizes his general ineffectualness as a leader (273) and mocks several of his ideas—his cleanliness campaign, for example (347).

10. Pearson 281. Pearson's footnote of the incident cites the following: an "interview with Landon Williams [ex-Panther], Berkeley, October 1991; 'The Party's Over,' by Kate Coleman with Paul Avery, *New Times*, July 10, 1978; 'Ex-Comrades Return for Tomorrow's Rights,' by Bill Snyder, *Oakland Tribune*, August 27, 1989" (395).

11. Ibid., 292.

Chapter Seven

Racial Unity in the Grass Roots?
A Case Study of a Women's Social Service Organization

Kristin Myers

I was born into a white, middle-class family in the South in 1967, at the height of one of the most powerfully threatening challenges to the American institution of racism. In Mississippi, Alabama, Georgia, Tennessee, North and South Carolina, freedom riders and CORE and SNCC volunteers applied peaceful tactics in an attempt to end racial brutality and discrimination. The Black Muslims called for separatism. The Black Panthers called for revolution. Two years before I was born, Watts, Detroit and Newark burned in summer riots. In this period, whites, who had instilled fear in African Americans for centuries, were becoming afraid.

What strikes me about my experience as a child born into the middle of this conflict is my inability to recollect that any of it occurred. I was completely oblivious because my parents never problematized racism and violence for me. The social changes that affected me were such an *a priori* part of my life that I never knew they were innovations. I was among the first generation in the South to attend integrated schools. From the first grade on, I was bussed 20 miles from my suburban neighborhood to a historically Black elementary school. After integration, my school was reconfigured to be 60 percent white and 40 percent Black. As a first grader, my best friends were Lisa and Frederika, African American girls who lived across the street from the school.

I met Lisa on the first day of school; her mother was my bus driver, and Lisa rode the entire route with her, even though the school was only 100 yards away from her home. Our particular route picked up kids who lived on the fringes of suburbia, like me, and then wound through the prestigious neighborhoods of the financially endowed—past rolling lawns and sprawling, shaded homes, picking up children of prominent citizens. Lisa was the only Black child on the bus. I sat with her every day, and together we walked from the parking lot to our classroom. I thought Lisa was beautiful with her elaborate braids, caught at the ends by rubber bands adorned with marble-like plastic balls.

While Lisa was quiet and pensive, Freddie was raucous and adventuresome. She, too, was in my class, and became my gateway to fun. She and I smeared Elmer's glue on our hands during art, waited for the glue to dry, and then peeled it off to look at the patterns of our skin. Sitting in a circle on the carpet during show and tell, we would filch straight pins from the bulletin board and carefully slide them through the thin skin at our fingertips, allowing them to jut out. This created an ugly sight while producing no pain. Freddie and I waved our spiky fingers at the other kids, giggling when the other little girls winced.

These girls were my friends. We knew that we looked different: they with their brown skin and Black plaits; me with my pale, freckled skin and cowlicked orange hair. We knew we lived in different neighborhoods: Lisa lived beside a busy railroad crossing in a five-room house; I lived in a newly developed, cookie-cutter neighborhood of two-story houses. We saw these differences, but they had no meaning. In our world, we did not see them as cues for evaluating and ranking one another.

In the third grade we were all rearranged, and I was no longer in Lisa and Freddie's class. Instead, my new peers were privileged white girls who wore hand-knit Scottish cardigans and leather penny-loafers. In the fourth grade, racist indoctrination began to kick in, and I began to hang around only with other white girls. I never made a conscious decision to do this. It just seemed natural.

It was not until years in higher education as a sociologist that I began to critically examine my own experiences with racism, and only then through what I thought to be a side door: studying women. In studying the women's movement of the 1960's, I learned that many women's organizations attempted to end inequality for "all women," regardless of race, class, or creed. These groups were often led by middle-class white women who continually confounded "all women" with "white women," thereby ignoring the diverse needs of women of color and economically insecure women (Echols 1989; Ferree and Hess 1985; and hooks 1984).

Economically secure white women leaders called for the emancipation of all women, demanding that they be allowed to enter the paid work force. While being relegated to the home was a means of repressing and controlling upper- and middle-class women, this was not the case for all women: many women of color and/or working-class women did not have the luxury of economic security that would grant them reprieve from manual and servile labor in order to stay home to care for their own children. Consequently, they did not view paid employment as a means to freedom (Bulbeck 1988).

The same leaders of this time were fighting for the right to make choices concerning one's own body (Lewis 1983). Abortion was a key issue, one that many African American women experienced differently from white women. Rather than denying African American women the "right" to have an abortion, white male officials were often all too eager to force abortion upon them as a means of birth control. While the issue for Black women still centered around control over one's own body, the nuances of the debate took very different forms, and the Black woman's viewpoint was often ignored.

Consequently, it became clear to me that gender alone cannot explain social inequalities. Race and class are concomitantly important factors. Indeed, with regard to my own experiences, I began to realize that I had been buffered against the racial conflict of my youth because of my racial and class privilege. And, although being a woman placed me at a disadvantage by means of gender discrimination, I understood that the way I would experience this disadvantage would be different from what it would be for my old friends Lisa and Freddie.

The realization that women of different races experience life in markedly different ways led me to the writings of bell hooks (1984, 1993, 1995), Patricia Hill Collins (1990), Angela Davis (1983), Elaine Brown (1992), Patricia Williams (1991) and myriad other African American women. These are women who poignantly articulate their oppression, acknowledge experiencing life as the "other," and who are committed to abolishing inequality. But they find time and again that the intertwining forces of racism, classism and sexism create what Collins (1990) calls a "matrix of domination" that continually confounds their efforts. I began to wonder if this matrix makes it impossible for diversity to be used as a positive tool for overcoming the racial divide in the United States.

The Study

It was with this lens that I discovered an intriguing grassroots organization. When it began in 1968, this organization sought to use women's "unique powers" to end racial violence. I approached the organization with great expectations and wonder: here was a group of women— African American and white—who had actually been a part of the struggle of the civil rights and women's movements. These women had organized in my hometown one year after I was born, and they remained together. They appeared to have discovered the secrets of harmony, despite the divisive pressures of racism, classism and sexism. I believed that they held the key to equality. Here I tell their story. In many ways, these women were pioneers against prejudice and discrimination. However, this organization developed in the context of oppression that created inequalities in the first place. Over the years, this unequal social context affected policies, procedures, and members' interaction. In this paper, I demystify social relationships and organizational processes, and what remains is a more pragmatic and perhaps pessimistic portrait of organizational survival in a society where racism, classism and sexism persist and intertwine to create seemingly insurmountable obstacles.

Central to this study is Collins's (1990) matrix of domination. Recognizing West and Fenstermaker's (1995) critique of Collins's work, I want to further clarify my understanding of the matrix. Race, class and gender are each axes of domination that weave together to form a more oppressive structure as a matrix. Each axis represents *patterns of unequal social processes* whereby one subgroup is privileged over others. I do not treat race, class or gender as traits or static categories; however, in everyday life, everyday actors often approach them as absolutes (Williams 1991). Because race, class and gender are concurrently embedded in complex ways, we cannot understand the effects of one of these elements on a person's life without taking the others into consideration (for more on embeddedness, see Anderson 1996). For me, the effects of being white cannot be fully understood without simultaneously understanding the effects of being middle-class and female. I do not assume that key social categories affect all people similarly. Instead, race, class, gender and other dimensions are intertwined, and they cannot be separated for purposes of simplifying analyses.

Data and Methods

The data for this paper come from a larger case study of this interracial women's organization, founded by an elite African American woman in an attempt to unite women against violence in their community (Myers 1996). I call this organization Women Against Violence, or WAV. I discuss the history of WAV more fully below. Contemporary WAV functioned primarily as a small welfare agency (that I call "the Outlet") run by a small paid staff and volunteers. Funding came from a national nonprofit agency, public donations, and funds raised in an annual banquet. A large board of directors ran the organization, which had about 250 general members.

I collected data on this organization from 1992 to 1996, through archival data collection, participant observation—first as a volunteer in the Outlet and later as a board member—and through interviews with board and staff members. I spent about 150 hours in the field, and conducted 14 in-depth interviews with board and staff members. I have changed names of people, places and organizations in order to protect the anonymity of the people involved, but the central facts remain unchanged.

Women Against Violence: Responding to a Call for Action

As described in the introduction, the year 1968 began in the midst of menacing racial conflict. All over the country, confrontations raged. In Los Angeles and Oakland, Black Panthers demanded the release of Huey Newton from prison. Eldridge Cleaver declared war on "Babylon," or white America. Conflict over the Vietnam War tore families and communities apart ideologically and literally, as thousands of young men died each year. In April, Martin Luther King, Jr., was assassinated, "triggering the most massive uprising of Black people in the history of America, in over one hundred cities throughout the country, wherever Black people were concentrated. . . . Nonviolence was dead" (Brown 1992). As African Americans fought for legal protection, better education, job security and overall access to resources, white Americans clung to a system that had privileged them for centuries, often using violence to underscore their dominance.

In 1968, a prominent women's magazine held a national conference, "What Women Can Do to End Violence in America." The conference organizers gathered women together in hopes of uniting their "power" and using their strength to end the racial violence in their respective communities; to them, it was obvious that men could only *create* violence, not quell it. The organizers couched the conference announcement in terms that sent fear through the hearts of readers, offering pernicious examples, asserting that violence is everywhere:

> The sickness has been here a long time. It simmers and flares in the ghettos where people have felt its curse for years and would now pay it back in kind. It mows down our men—and theirs—in Vietnam. It erupts on the campuses of the nation, where some of our young men and women have turned against their own proclaimed abhorrence of violence and have disfigured not just their universities but their own lives. It stalks our cities, our parks, and subways, and destroys the green and gentle calm of the countryside. It rams its way into our homes on the television screen that brings instant brutality and savagery, instructing children in the ease and casualness with which life can be humiliated, tormented, twisted. . . . [I]t weakens those precious arts of gentleness, of compassion, of moderation, of love that women alone can give to their families and the world.[1]

An estimated 15 million women read about this insidious, ubiquitous violence that plagued their communities. The message was clear: it was *women's responsibility* to stop the madness. The magazine's editors elaborated,

> Women, with their capacity for compassion and their fear of a future darkened by violence, are no longer content to sit on the sidelines. . . . Political leaders and other decision-makers will recognize and respect woman power for what it is: the vital fraction that can be America's benevolent plurality, a new force to help build a more humane society, before time runs out. . . . The greatest power of all is theirs: woman power. No force on earth can stand against it.

The implication was that women were a different kind of being than men, with an ability and need to pacify. Attitudinal research echoes this notion, showing that since the 1960s, women in the United States have been more concerned than men about violence (Shapiro and Mahajan 1986). Even though they were largely outside the realm of politics, women were told that they had power. The editors did not define "woman power," but it seemed to be multifaceted. Women's power bubbled from an internal, natural font of gentility and nurturance. It derived, as well, from women's intimate relationships with men—the people who occupied the real positions of power. Women could use their influence over male leaders to achieve peace. And last, woman power was such a threat to violence because of the sheer number of women in the world. Were they to truly unite, they would be a force with which to be reckoned. Viewing men and women as fundamentally, naturally different is known as "essentialism" (Bem 1993; Lorber 1994). Essentialism exaggerates the differences between women and men and overlooks the myriad similarities. This perspective is often used to legitimate gender inequality. These women, however, saw it as *empowering*. With the weight of the world on their shoulders, 250 women went to the conference, hoping to learn what they needed to do to end violence.

WAV's founder was among them. She received the announcement in the mail anonymously. She told me, "To this day, I don't know why I was chosen to be invited." Although an African American woman, her personal history did not parallel that of most Black women of her time. She was raised with the resources and benefits of privilege: her father's peers included men of such stature as Booker T. Washington and W. E. B. DuBois, and he himself was a respected educator. As an adult, she married a successful businessman, who inherited his elite social and economic position from his father and uncles before him. Indeed, the political, social and economic history of the African American community in her city was largely a history of her husband's family, along with several other powerful African American leaders.[2] In the South, where even modest economic success was only a recent acquisition for most African Americans (Wilson 1980), the founder's family stood apart. However, her economic privilege only modestly shielded her from the palpable racism of the South.

In her community, WAV's founder witnessed the kinds of problems described by the magazine's message, and she recognized their interconnectedness with racism. WAV's founder explained that her children brought home filthy, secondhand textbooks from their school because the county did not provide new books for Black children. Some Black principals protested being denied materials:

> One day, one of the principals was down in the main school office and the door to the supply room was left open and no one was around, so he just

stepped in to look at all these wonderful supplies they had for children and schools; and that was at least an opening of getting more supplies than they had. They [Black principals] absolutely didn't even know the supplies existed.

In addition to the disparity in schools, trouble brewed between African Americans and whites with regard to business: white businesses were profiting from Black patronage without filtering the profits back into the Black community. The Black community threatened a boycott in 1968. As WAV's founder explained,

> [There was] no mixing of the races—no real caring or concern, except maybe some person-to-person kinds of contacts that men and women may have had. And the Blacks— they weren't heard. So they decided they would work on the pocketbook. And they closed down the stores, through boycotting. . . . And people were afraid to go downtown. It was really very upsetting.

The omnipresent threat of violence in the city compelled the founder to attend the conference. It was a three-day conference, with guest speakers including Coretta Scott King and Margaret Mead. Attendees were of different races and religions, and they came from all over the country. The major message of the conference was that they go back to their home communities and establish grassroots organizations geared toward ending racial violence.

Of all of the women at the conference, only two women subsequently founded antiviolence organizations. One of these was WAV's founder. She returned home and sent out a notice to all women in the city. A handful of women called to say that they were interested in helping. They scheduled the first meeting, and, to the founder's surprise and delight, 125 women attended. The membership soon grew to 200, and it included women from the most powerful, longtime families in the city, both white and African American.

The founder's husband delivered the kickoff speech at the first meeting. In her introduction, she praised him for his "long-standing interest in the maintenance of good will" in the city, and for his commitment to nonviolence. He said these things in his speech:

> If you are to persevere and to do an effective job, you must condition yourselves to face and deal with confrontations arising from all the weaknesses and frailties of man compounded by the nature of the arena of the life and

the environment of the community, and to deal with them calmly and intelligently, more rationally than emotionally.

Your challenge is to help man emerge from a tendency toward savage brutality to one of civilized human behavior. Violence can take on many forms: physical, mental, and moral; violence to one's person, property, personality, dignity, rights, etc. This is why an avoidance of inflammatory statements is so important.

His words echoed the messages from the conference: women should be the saviors of men, to actually transform them from "man" to "human." But they needed to do so in a particular manner, one that was rational and fit well with the needs of the community, that is, the status quo. He pointed to nonviolent techniques for making the necessary transformation without upsetting the existing power structure. It is important to reiterate that the early members of WAV were themselves part of the existing power structure, although it was a segregated power structure. By openly joining Black with white, they were already rocking the proverbial boat. Had they called for radical social change, they might have upset the boat completely. Thus, by calling for community change, they risked being shunned by their elite peers, floating without life preservers. It is common for voluntary organizations with elite memberships to emphasize working within the system rather than challenging it (Kaplan Daniels 1988; Ostrander 1984). What is uncommon is for elite organizations to have an intentionally interracial membership (Markham and Bonjean 1995). Thus, WAV was an unusual organization from the beginning.

The women of WAV took the speaker's words to heart. They adhered to a broad definition of violence from then on. As the founder explained at a board retreat 28 years later, violence comes in many forms: "Racism is violence; poverty is violence; even bad roads are violence. Anything which makes us feel unsafe and offends our sense of humanity is violence." Adopting such a broad conceptualization of violence had consequences for the organization. Likewise, WAVers' application of the tenets of nonviolence affected WAV as an organization.

They created WAV as a hierarchical organization run by a large board of directors.[3] They decided that half of the board would be African American women and the other half white women, and they gave the founder a permanent seat on the board. They stipulated that subcommittees' cochairs should be of different races so as to institutionalize racial equality in WAV.

O Pioneers!

As stated above, the very existence of an interracial women's organization in 1968 in a southern city was controversial. To understand the obstacles faced by these women, it is important to know more about the city itself. For shorthand, I refer to this city as "Nexus." Nexus, like many southern cities, historically relied on the tobacco industry for its economic stability. A handful of white families rose to political and economic power by capitalizing on the industry. Like most southern cities, Nexus had been largely segregated along racial lines since the abolition of slavery. However, unlike many cities, a large, powerful, Black upper and middle class developed and thrived in Nexus. One source linked the huge success of some African Americans in Nexus to the open-mindedness of the whites in power. In particular, those white tobacco magnates allowed, and perhaps even fostered, the growth of Black industry rather than quashing it as an economic threat. Powerful whites adopted a laissez-faire attitude toward Black business, thereby allowing it to grow to great heights. This situation was different from that of other southern cities, where Black and white elites often reached stalemates and de facto segregation persisted (Marable, 1977).

This is only one explanation for the success of Black Nexans. A class analysis is more critical of the motives of the whites in Nexus. If the white power structure "allowed" the success of certain Blacks, it had something to gain by doing so. No ruling group intentionally sows the seeds of its own destruction by training future competitors (Marx 1972). It is more likely that the whites saw the benefits of fracturing the African American community by elevating the position of some Black people. Divisions among a large, oppressed group protected the dominants from challenge because such division decreased the likelihood of Blacks creating a united front against whites. Allowing restricted mobility to African Americans also created a more complex division of labor among them as a group, so that there were manual laborers as well as professional/administrative managers. A complex division of labor also protected leaders by exacerbating material differences among a population (Giddens 1980). By dividing African Americans economically, white elites were better protected from collective challenges to their power.

The division helped to foster alliances between Black elites and white oppressors. Not all African Americans were given access to mobility. Restricting access to resources and mobility is known as "social closure"

(Parkin 1979). Only a cadre of African Americans became members of the Nexus elite. They had wealth and prestige, but they were not truly rulers; their fabricated success by means of social closure kept them at bay politically for many decades. Only in recent years did African Americans become a serious power force in Nexus. The white ruling class benefited from the existence of a small, yet controlled, Black elite.

This is not to say that African American progress went unchallenged by whites. As in most southern cities, there were numerous incidents of white aggression. The point, then, is not that whites in Nexus were consistently benevolent masters over their community. Instead, they refrained from exercising their superordinate power over some African Americans in Nexus. Through a combination of their own prowess and an atmosphere that did not punish their achievements, a cadre of African Americans achieved notable successes.

Despite the prosperity of some African Americans, many were still very poor. Segregation among the races was a de facto reality. Until the mid–1970s, hospitals and schools were segregated. A large section of the city was designated the Black section, and it consisted mostly of inferior, low-lying, poorly drained property. Whites moved to the suburbs, leaving older housing for African Americans. When African Americans moved in, rents went up, even though nothing was done to improve the condition of the homes. Streets were rarely repaired and were poorly lit. There was little fire-fighting equipment, and no housing codes. Despite some people's economic success, Jim Crow lived in Nexus. Consequently, WAVers faced obstacles in forming a boundary-spanning organization.

As the founder explained, even choosing places for these women to meet was a challenge. Often, they met in women's homes, and that was successful as long as the women were wives of academics or other "progressive" people.

> Now, as far as the traditional person, we were not invited to their homes. That would have been too much. To invite Blacks into your homes? We still suffered from the old mentality, the slave-plantation.

On at least one occasion, their husbands sat at the windows with guns to protect WAVers from outsiders. Usually, they held large public meetings in places like the YWCA, and an average of 200 people attended. WAVers held forums on controversial issues, and they played the role of moderators rather than taking a stand. The meetings often went late, to just before midnight, and the women worried for their safety: Black women caught after dark in white neighborhoods would have been at risk of violence in that period. According to the founder's recollection, these women risked physical harm and social ostracism by even participating in WAV, but they did so because they were committed to their goals. Between 1968 and 1971, or what the founder calls the "crisis years," WAV mediated in two major community conflicts: the Black boycott and school integration. While it never openly took an activist stance, its mediations and political influence over powerful members of the community helped maintain peace. In this sense, WAV fulfilled its goal by acting to avert violence.

WAV also mediated in problems as they arose. The founder described one case where an ex-Klansman-turned-activist called her for help. He was concerned about a situation at a school where a white girl had gotten involved with a Black boy, and the families and the school were in an uproar; violence was impending. WAV responded to the call:

> Usually when we went out, made trips out like that where there were sore spots, we usually made it a habit to send out a Black and a white female. In this particular instance, we decided not to, that it involved a white family situation and a Black boy, of course, and we would send two white women out. They went and visited with the parents, talked over the situation, and they assured them that things could be worked out. And it really toned things down, and we really never heard anything about it. So, that was one of the most crucial situations that we ran into head on.

Here, she explained the rationale for dividing tasks biracially: it was intended to further defuse racial tension. Interestingly, WAV appealed to the *white* family—the dominant party in the incident—rather than the Black family in its attempts to mitigate conflict. Because WAV existed in a context of institutionalized racism, placating the dominants was less threatening to organizational survival than the mollification of subordinates.

In sum, the women wanted changes, but they played by the rules; they did not challenge the rules themselves. It was a reformist rather than radical strategy for confronting social problems; they took the existing organization of society for granted instead of calling for a redistribution of wealth and equal access to material and ideological resources. Nevertheless, they took a stand in their community when it was largely taboo for Black and white women to interact, let alone collude. Their unity served as a role model for their community in general and other organizations in particular.

Flash Forward: The WAV of the 1990s

I was drawn to WAV as a study site because of its reputation. As I mentioned in the introduction, I thought WAV held the secrets of racial unity, and I greatly admired its grassroots activism in the community. Unlike most grassroots women's organizations of the 1960s, it had survived internal divisions and external pressures (Ferree and Hess 1985). I made contact with the founder and began volunteering in the office. In this hands-on contact with WAV, my grand illusions began to dissolve as I saw the daily reality of WAV in the 1990s. I volunteered in what I call the Outlet. WAV first established the Outlet in October of 1970. It operated out of various empty storefronts whose owners offered them low rent. The board members themselves staffed the office, providing information and referrals for people who had questions about unemployment, drug abuse, unwanted pregnancies, and medical care. The original program of the Outlet was this:

1. To provide call-in services to receive rumors, complaints, dissatisfactions, or problems that could cause tension.
2. To report rumors or complaints to the proper agency.
3. To receive citizen suggestions.
4. To work with other established agencies.

The Outlet functioned as a referral/information center for fifteen years. Very little changed in this time period.

In 1985, the purpose of the Outlet changed. As WAV achieved nonprofit status and acquired funding from outside sources, it was able to provide financial services for poor people. This transition from referral service to funding agency was consistent with its goal of preventing the causes of violence, with poverty deemed to be a major cause. After 1985, the Outlet operated as a resource providing emergency funds to people in financial crisis. The Outlet differed from other social service agencies in that it was privately operated and did not require extensive background information on clients. The board wanted to provide a personal, nonjudgmental place for poor people to receive relief. To run the Outlet, the board hired a full-time staff—an executive director, an assistant director, and a secretary—and relied on volunteers.

Because the board had become financially responsible to outside agencies, it began to implement more rigorous methods for recording spending, as well as criteria for deciding who qualified for funding. To be eligible, a client had to furnish proof of identification and an overdue bill or eviction notice. WAV helped with only power or gas bills, prescriptions, and past-due rent. It usually offered minimal assistance (during my study, aid ranged from $50 to $150 per person), and a client could receive assistance only once in a 12-month period. Assistance was not given directly to the client; instead, a voucher was given directly to the landlord, power or gas company, or pharmacist so as to help minimize client fraud.

The new rules established a formal, bureaucratic structure. Although there was a screening process, it was still less rigorous than that of the Department of Social Services or any other government-sponsored agency. During a typical screening session, the interviewer would ask a client her name, address, phone number (if she had one), her landlord's name, where she was employed (if at all), number of people in the household, marital status, and number and age of children. She also had to report income (from all sources, including AFDC) and monthly expenses. Other than examining the required paperwork, the interviewer rarely attempted to verify a client's word, unless she suspected fraud or if she had been warned about the client by another agency. The process was formal enough for the clients to see it as legitimate and fair, but it was not an interrogation. Consequently, the clients testified that they did not feel condemned or judged at WAV. Rather, they considered it a place they could go for emotional if not financial support.

With the inception of the staff, the board became completely separate from the day-to-day operations of the Outlet. The director reported monthly to the board and consulted with it on major decisions, such as whether to start a new project. Other than that, most board members had never even been to the Outlet offices and had only a glimmer of understanding about what occurred there. This was a major change from the early days when all board members were personally involved in WAV activities. In other words, the board had become "decoupled" from the daily activities of the organization (Meyer and Rowan, 1977), divorced from the procedures. For example, one longtime board member said this about the Outlet:

> They don't give out money knowing that next month the person will be in the same situation without making long term plans. They don't just give out money if this is something that the client ought to be able to think through on their own.

The above is inaccurate. When WAV set up the Outlet, the *intention* was to help people who needed a little boost—to help those who perhaps had had bad luck and needed short-term help to avoid losing everything. Very few of the people who came to WAV for services fell into this category. Included were people who had been employed for a long time but had been recently laid off, or people who were being overwhelmed by medical bills. There was no stipulation that WAV could help only people who would immediately recover from economic crisis, given a little boost.

Another board member described her vision of the Outlet:

> I think WAV functions in the same way that the extended family used to. What happens when your cousin wants to move out and get an apartment and doesn't have the money for the security deposit? It's not an ongoing sort of assistance as would be provided by Social Security. It is that one shot: let's help grandpa or cousin get over the hump.

In addition to romanticizing WAV's services, this member was incorrect about the type of aid offered by WAV. WAV never provided deposits for anything, even rent. Both of the above member descriptions focus on the few people who fell into the "one-shot" need category. Such clients, who received help from WAV and were subsequently able to overcome economic adversity, became its poster children, its success stories. WAV invited them to public functions and praised them for their accomplishments. Most board members perceived that these were the typical clients because those members believed their own propaganda. Because of the "decoupling" from the board to the Outlet, board members had little accurate information about it.

These more fortunate clients were the exceptions. The vast majority of WAV's clients were chronically unemployed, single mothers who received multiple services from state agencies on a regular basis. The following example, taken from my field notes, exemplifies the typical WAV client (about 90 percent of the clients were like her, although she had more children than most). One hot day, she came to the offices to get some Pampers, and I helped her:

> This woman was 25 years old, and she had an 8 month old baby with her as well as a 3 year old boy. The boy was cute and funny, saying "hello" and "goodbye" every time I passed him. He kept waiting for a mint that we had on the desk. The baby was in a stroller and was filthy. Her fuzzy pink sleeper—one obviously made for cooler weather—was covered with food crumbs and smeared dirt. The baby's face was dirty too, and she sucked a

bottle. When the bottle was empty, she dropped it on the floor and began to cry. This woman told me that there were 6 people in her household: one adult and five children. The children's ages were 11, 7, 5, 3, and 8 months. . . . We have to ask [as part of the documentation] if she's getting money from different sources: wages, AFDC, child support, etc. She got no child support—which I jokingly said she needed. The woman agreed. She just started a job at [a fast food restaurant] and doesn't know her wages yet. Other than that, she made about $526 in aid. . . . I gave her 10 Pampers and she left.

This typical client is in sharp juxtaposition to the common image of clients held by many board members. This perception reflected a lack of contact with the Outlet.

The Outlet received much of its budget from outside sources but nevertheless experienced financial crises. In 1990, WAV developed an annual fund-raiser—a banquet named after the founder—as an alternative source of funding. People pay a set price for a plate or a table. At the banquet, members recount WAV's beginnings, celebrate WAV's activism in a time of crisis, hallowing "women's powers" against violence. Black-and-white table cloths and napkins highlight WAV's success as an interracial organization. Above the head table a gigantic Black-and-white banner, emblazoned with WAV's name and seal sends the message to guests that WAVers are not hampered by racial divisions but surmount them. At each banquet, an invited speaker usually praises WAV's accomplishments, comments on the changing, violent times, and exhorts the members to keep up the good work. The evening ends with an award presentation to an outstanding member of the community who has helped in some way to eradicate violence or poverty. Following the racial structure of WAV, the speaker is alternately African American and white, and award recipients are racially balanced as well. The board spends most of its meetings planning the annual banquets. Indeed, the banquet is central.

Cataloguing the Changes

Within weeks of my entry into the field, I noticed three major departures of the 1990s WAV from the 1960s WAV. First, the 1990s role in the community is radically different from the 1960s role. WAV had all but abandoned its 1960s activism for a more traditional "good-works" program, the more typical role for elite women in the United States (Kaplan Daniels

1988). In addition, the banquet had become its major source of visibility in the community. In effect, it was no longer even marginally threatening to the existing power structure but, rather, was dependent on it for funding and legitimacy.

Second, I learned that the board had instructed the staff to avoid making any public statements that might be deemed political, including any statements relating to crime, violence, gun control, racism—all topics that were fundamental to WAV's original raison d'être. This was particularly ironic: in 1968, the founder and other early WAVers had thrown down the gauntlet in the fight against violence, declaring women to be the number-one enemy of violence and its causes. WAVers had attempted to attack violence by attacking the roots of violence—poverty in particular. They had also sought to alleviate emotionally charged tensions in their community, thereby averting future violent struggles. They had established the Outlet to educate people about one another and thereby had attempted to circumvent violence. They took an active role in their community. Over the years, WAV had tapered its goals and sheathed most of its weapons in the struggle against violence.

In order to understand this shift, I asked the founder about her views on activism. She told me that she did not want WAV to be seen as an activist organization; she disdained activists. In our interview, she said, "I don't care how good the ideas are, you can't carry an organization faster than it is able to travel." She believed activists to be people who press for change before the time is right. To illustrate, the founder described the early years, when some level of activism was acceptable because it was "a time of crisis." Even then, however, there were people who wanted too much too soon. Five white women came to the early meetings and "gave the president a hard time":

> They wanted things to happen right away, and they were activists. That's the nature of an activist: to want things now. Now and extreme. Not any in-between. Well, knowing the climate of this community and knowing that change is gradual yet constant, steady change can take place. But when you are putting more than what a person is willing or able to digest at a given point in time, then you run into problems of acceptance.

She saw activism as a white endeavor, and one that would threaten the legitimacy of WAV in the community. She feared that too much politicism would alienate the general community and jeopardize WAV's credibility. Again, it is not uncommon for elite members of community organizations to prefer the "volunteer" role to that of "activist" (Kaplan Daniels 1988); however, the founder went beyond a class-specific rationale and included a race-specific critique of activism.

In the 1990s, the only permissible political forum was the banquet. Banquets became the fundamental vehicles for political, antiviolence statements. For example, one invited speaker bemoaned the terrible conditions for children in society and challenged WAV and the people in the community to put their money where their mouths were by starting to attack violence at its roots. Another speaker said that women should be involved in antiviolence work because women are victims of a lot of violence. Her main point was that creating violence is a male endeavor. Yet another speaker provided demographics about who the violent criminals these days are: young Black males. She argued that schools, parents, and politicians needed to do something. She said that we need to get rid of guns because they are too accessible. All of these speakers made controversial statements, most of which WAVers would never be permitted to say in the name of the organization. For example, the Outlet director was forbidden to even attend meetings on gun control as a representative of WAV. The speakers, on the other hand, were reliable, credible sources who spoke publicly and passionately under the auspices of WAV. Despite their rules about members' maintaining silence on controversial issues, WAVers supported and agreed with the speakers' messages. Banquets were legitimate conduits for politics because the messages did not come directly from WAV but indirectly through the invited speakers.

WAV reached hundreds of influential community members with its messages annually. These people included CEOs and upper-level managers; physicians; city council members; school board members; lawyers; NAACP members; bank officials; and state, local and—occasionally— even national politicians. WAV used its community influence to gather together these people and then relayed its primary message: violence is everywhere, and we in our community complicity help to perpetuate it through collective inaction. Thus, WAV did not *abandon* its political ideology; it just relied upon more subtle ways to convey the message. Indeed, members relied upon their own embeddedness in the power structure in order to affect the power structure.

A third major departure of the 1990s WAV from the 1960s was that the class composition of the board shifted from predominantly elite, career volunteers (Kaplan Daniels 1988) to a growing contingent of professional women. This "new guard" included professors, lawyers, accountants, and even newscasters. They juggled families, paid careers, and volunteer work. This class shift probably contributed to the decoupling of the board from the Outlet in that most members had less free time to devote to hands-on community efforts. It also reflects a larger shift in the "public sphere" of the paid work force in general: opportunities for women and people of color to climb job ladders in more lucrative job markets has improved moderately since the 1960s. However, most women and people of color are still clustered in low-pay, low-mobility jobs (Reskin and Padavic 1994). The new guard at WAV had broken through the metaphorical "glass ceiling," at least compared to the majority of employed women of the 1990s. Thus, while a class shift has occurred compared to the early years, contemporary WAVers are still more economically well off than many women in the community. Their elevated status helped reinforce WAV's historical ties with the dominant power structure of the community. And, of course, the founder and a handful of her elite, African American peers remained active, influential members. The class shift did not necessarily correlate with a shift in organizational values. Research has shown that when new members join an established organization, their values tend to mirror those of the existing members (Betz and Judkins 1975). Thus, the entry of the new guard caused more pragmatic changes than ideological.

Summary

Overall, the three changes in WAV interacted to make it more passive in its community activities. I argue that this passivity resulted from the social context: a context of race, class and gender inequality. In other words, its social "environment" constrained WAV. The "institutional school" of social organizations argues that organizations change missions and goals to fit with their changing environments. Indeed, a central element of institutional theory states that "the process of institutionalization is the process of organic growth, wherein the organization adapts to the striving of internal groups and the values of the external society" (Perrow 1986, 167). For example, the Women's Christian Temperance Union had to change its mission after the repeal of Prohibition, so it focused instead on the morals of the middle class (see also Clark 1960; Gusfield 1955;

Messinger 1955; Meyer and Rowan 1977; Perrow 1961; Seeley et al. 1957; Selznick 1949; Zald and Denton 1963).

My study of WAV is consistent with studies in the institutional school in that it focuses on the effects of the environment as well as a disjuncture between goals and goal attainment. According to the literature, such a disjuncture is not surprising. My study *differs* significantly from these studies in that WAV did *not* change its mission in order to adapt to its environment.[4] In the almost 30 years since WAV's beginning, racial and gendered aspects of its community changed a great deal. The city changed from a place where white and African American people could not look one another in the eye or speak to one another in public to a place where African Americans and whites vie with one another in public elections for powerful positions. They compete in the marketplace; they go to school together. Black and white women work side by side, not just as domestic servants and mistresses of the house but as professional coworkers. This does not mean that racial and economic inequality are dead and gone. Far from it; there are still significant numbers of poor African Americans in the community. However, after decades of struggle, African American leadership is visible and viable, and not just within the African American segregated community—whites *had* to take notice.

Despite these changes in the environment, the women of WAV became more passive than they had been 30 years before. A passive approach was effective in the late 1960s because the environment was so hostile to women and to interracial contact of any kind. In the early days, WAVers all had economic privilege, which provided inroads to the power structure: they were married to elite men, both African American and white. However, as women and/or people of color, they were excluded from formal involvement in the dominant power structure in their community. The political position of the organization was tenuous because of the intersecting forces of racism, classism, and sexism. If the women began WAV by challenging male privilege or white privilege, they would have been immediately squashed. Being passive allowed them to conduct their business, affect the community, and gain local praise.

However, as time changed, the women did not adapt their strategies to the more accepting environment. They did not gradually become more outspoken on racism and violence. In fact, they became less active, holding fewer forums and speaking out less—and then only indirectly. One ex-

REFERENCES

Anderson, Cynthia D. "Understanding the Inequality Problematic: From Scholarly Rhetoric to Theoretical Reconstruction." *Gender and Society* 10 (1996) 729–46.

Bem, Sandra. *The Lenses of Gender.* New Haven: Yale University Press, 1993.

Betz, Paul, and Bennett Judkins. "Impact of Voluntary Association Characteristics on Selective Attraction and Socialization." *Sociological Quarterly* 16 (1975) 228–40.

Brown, Elaine. *A Taste of Power: A Black Woman's Story.* New York: Doubleday, 1992.

Bulbeck, Chilla. *One World Women's Movement.* London: Pluto Press, 1988.

Clark, Burton R. *The Open Door College: A Case Study.* New York: McGraw-Hill, 1960.

Collins, Patricia Hill. *Black Feminist Thought.* Boston: Unwin Hyman,1990.

Davis, Angela Y. *Women, Race and Class.* New York: Vintage, 1983.

Echols, Alice. *Daring to Be Bad: Radical Feminism in America, 1967–1975.* Minneapolis: University of Minnesota Press, 1989.

Ferree, Myra Marx and Beth Hess. *Controversy and Coalition: The New Feminist Movement.* Boston: Twayne Publishers,1985.

Giddens, Anthony. *The Class Structure of the Advanced Societies.* London: Hutchinson, 1980.

Gusfield, Joseph R. "Social Structure and Moral Reform: A Study of the Women's Christian Temperance Union." *American Journal of Sociology* 61 (1955) 221–32.

hooks, bell. *Feminist Theory: From Margin to Center.* Boston: South End Press, 1984.

———. *Sisters of the Yam.* Boston: South End Press, 1993.

———. *Killing Rage: Ending Racism.* New York: Henry Holt and Company, 1995.

Kaplan Daniels, Arlene. *Invisible Careers: Women Civic Leaders from the Volunteer World.* Chicago: University of Chicago Press,1988.

Lewis, Diane K. "A Response to Inequality: Black Women, Racism and Sexism." *Signs* 3 (1983) 339–61.

Lorber, Judith. *Paradoxes of Gender.* New Haven: Yale University Press, 1994.

Marable, Manning. "Tuskegee and the Politics of Illusion in the New South." *Black Scholar* 8 (1977) 13–24.

Markham, William T., and Charles M. Bonjean. "Community Orientations of Higher-Status Women Volunteers." *Social Forces* 73 (1995) 1553–71.

Marx, Karl. 1972. *Capital.* London: Lawrence and Wishart.

Messinger, Sheldon L. "Organizational Transformation: A Case Study of Declining Social Movement." *American Sociological Review* 20 (1955) 3–10.

Meyer, John W., and Brian Rowan. "Institutionalized Organizations: Formal Structure as Myth and Ceremony." *American Journal of Sociology* 83 (1977) 340–63.

Myers, Kristin A. "Sailing Under False Colors: Race, Class and Gender in a Women's Organization." Dissertation, directed by Barbara J. Risman, North Carolina State University, Raleigh, 1996.

Ostrander, Susan. *Women of the Upper Class.* Philadelphia: Temple University Press, 1984.

Parkin, Frank. *Marxism and Class Theory: A Bourgeois Critique.* New York: Columbia University Press, 1979.

Perrow, Charles. "Organizational Prestige: Some Functions and Dysfunctions." *American Journal of Sociology* 66 (1961) 335–41.

———. *Complex Organizations: A Critical Essay.* New York: Random House, 1986.

Reskin, Barbara, and Irene Padavic. *Women and Men at Work.* Thousand Oaks, Calif.: Pine Forge, 1994.

Seeley, John R., Bulford H. Junker, and R. Wallace Jones, Jr. *Community Chest.* Toronto: Toronto University Press, 1957.

Selznick, Philip. *TVA and the Grass Roots: A Study of Politics and Organization.* Berkeley: University of California Press, 1949.

Shapiro, Robert Y., and Harpreet Mahajan. "Gender Differences in Policy Preferences: A Summary of Trends from the 1960s to the 1980s." *Public Opinion Quarterly* 50 (1986) 42–61.

Stinchcombe, Arthur. *Handbook of Organizations* Chicago: Rand McNally, 1965.

West, Candace, and Sarah Fenstermaker. "Doing Difference." *Gender and Society* 9 (1995) 8–37

Williams, Patricia. *The Alchemy of Race and Rights: Diary of a Law Professor.* Cambridge: Harvard University Press, 1991.

Wilson, William Julius. *The Declining Significance of Race.* Chicago: University of Chicago Press, 1980.

Zald, Mayer N., and Roberta Ash. "Social Movement Organizations: Growth, Decay, and Change." *Social Forces* 44 (1966) 327–40.

Zald, Mayer N., and Patricia Denton. "From Evangelism to General Service: The Transformation of the YMCA." *Administrative Science Quarterly* 8 (1963) 214–34.

Chapter Eight

"Necessity Was the Midwife of Our Politics"

Black Women's Health Activism in the "Post"-Civil Rights Era (1980–1996)

Deborah R. Grayson

Introduction

During the 1980s, a time when the gains of most social movements of the 1950s and '60s were under attack, the contemporary Black women's health movement emerged. Arguing that women's health issues do not cut across race and class lines despite the perceived commonalties of women's health experiences and concerns, Black women health activists maintain that race and class are the source of their different experiences within health care. This belief led to a form of organizing among Black women on health issues that worked (1) to address the racial and sexual politics of, and government indifference to, Black women's health and health care needs and (2) to educate Black women not only to confront this indifference but also to help them address their own health needs.

This essay focuses on the health activism of Black women from 1980, usually marked as the beginning of the contemporary Black women's health movement, to the present.[1] Through an analysis of published reports I discuss the public health work of "lay" and professional women in order to demonstrate how they approach the litany of health problems that plague Black women at rates disproportionate to their percentage of the population. I argue that the work done by Black women health activists in behalf of themselves and their communities shows their deter-

131

mination to alter health policies that often serve as barriers to their physical and emotional well-being. For the purposes of my arguments here, Black women's activism is broadly defined. When talking about contemporary Black women's health activism in this essay, I am describing the critical community work Black women have engaged in.

First, I provide an overview of recent health activist work by Black women, discussing the strategies they have developed to combat the interlocking oppressions of race, gender, and class in their lives and in their communities. Next, I provide examples of Black women's community-based activism and how they work to inform individuals on health-related issues. The church, beauty salons, and grassroots organizations within the Black community have been transformed into "ground zero" for activism in connection with issues as AIDS and breast cancer. Last, I discuss how grassroots organizations can and should serve as models for outreach to scientific and medical communities charged with the task of addressing the future health needs of Black women.

"We've Got Your Back": The Birth of a Movement

Despite media claims to the contrary, neither technological innovation nor physician acumen alone can explain or solve the problems and the politics of health in American culture. In fact, the women's health movement evolved precisely because traditional strategies used to meet the population's health needs have failed to meet the specific health needs of women. Women are the majority users of health and medical services. They access the system nearly twice as often as men do.[2] In addition to seeking services for birth control, pregnancy, and childbirth, women, because they tend to live longer, are also frequently in need of treatment for chronic disease and impairment later in life. Finally, women, especially women of color, make up the majority of low-level health-care workers. Not only do they tend to assume responsibility for the health care needs of their families, which includes tasks such as making doctor's appointments or escorting family members to the doctor's office, women also provide regular care to others in their communities who are ill.

Compounding the familial and occupational responsibilities many women shoulder in their interactions with the medical system are the social, cultural, and political burdens of health care. Black women, for instance, have the additional burden of confronting the intersectional politics of race and class in their encounters with the health-care system. Too often, Black women meet with difficulty in obtaining sufficient facts to make informed decisions about their health. They frequently suffer from inappropriate medical intervention because of those barriers. The negative impact of this kind of treatment on the health and well-being of African American women, however, is often underestimated and overlooked.

In almost every category of disease African Americans have worse health outcomes than whites.[3] For African American women specifically, heart disease continues to be the leading cause of death. Sixty-five percent more Black women died from cardiovascular disease than did white women in 1992. This gap has not narrowed since the 1960s. Incidents of cancer, the second leading cause of death for Black women, also reveal a disproportionate difference. Whereas in the case of some cancers, like breast cancer, Black women have a lower rate of incidence; they are also much more likely to die than white women are because of late detection. Finally, AIDS is a leading cause of death among Black women, particularly between the ages of 25 and 35. From 1990 to 1992 new AIDS cases increased by 50 percent among Black women. Currently Black women make up close to 60 percent of cases of HIV/AIDS found among women.[4]

To combat these and other poor health statistics, Black women health activists have come up with an array of approaches in their community health work. Not simply privileging one oppression as their central target of political action, Black women health activists have devised strategies to address their specific historical and structural circumstances. As Black women have said many times now, the multiple statuses of race, gender, and class cannot be separated for them. Further, as long as these interlocking categories of oppression continue to exist, African American women will continue to have worse health outcomes than other groups of American women. This is true not because there is some biological deficiency among Black women due to race and gender, as is so often implied. Rather, it is because of the ways the cumulative effects of negative life stresses, such as racism, sexism, and classism, work together to produce "patterns of health and illness in groups that share certain characteristics."[5]

Believing that Black women needed a way to voice their concerns about their health, Billye Avery founded the National Black Women's

Health Project (NBWHP) to provide Black women with a forum from which to speak. Avery, often credited with being at the center of revitalizing the contemporary Black women's health movement, used strategies such as the concepts of self-evaluation, self-determination, and self-help to respond to the staggeringly poor health statistics of African American women. She lacked formal training as a health professional herself but nevertheless believed that she could take charge of her own health care and assist in the training of other Black women in self-care. With members of the Project, Avery worked to empower Black women to deal with the struggles they faced in their day-to-day lives that affected their health. Through a two-pronged approach, the NBWHP inspired the growth and development of self-help groups that would address the health needs and concerns of individual women. From these self-help groups, chapters often formed whose emphasis was to educate those working in federal and state agencies, and colleges, as well as health care providers, on the health concerns of Black women. Other components of NBWHP programs include the development of media and educational programs and an international branch of the project called SisteReach, which works in Black women's organizations in Africa and the Caribbean.[6]

What is still considered to be one of the most groundbreaking efforts of the NBWHP was the organization of the first-ever international conference on Black women's health. It was appropriately held in June 1983 at Spelman College in Atlanta, the nation's oldest and most well known college for Black women. The more than 2000 conferees discussed health issues related to Black women. The organizers sought to educate Black women, to define cultural and historical perspectives of health, and to instruct and guide in self-care skills and health promotion, which included becoming aware of public policies that impact their health access.[7] Organizers of this and subsequent conferences focused their efforts on establishing a network of Black women that would continue to carry out these tasks. Violence, dangerous work environments, and depression were among the issues Black women experienced that health statistics neither highlighted nor addressed.

It is clear that a central goal of all NBWHP programs is to organize Black women to take an active role in their health. Embedded in the community work of the National Black Women's Health Project and other organizations like it is a deep and abiding commitment to work for group survival. Recognizing that achieving good health is still a central component within the struggle for civil rights, Black women activists work to make the health needs of Black people a central political concern in the national arena. In conceptualizing the work of the NBWHP, one finds that there are at least two dimensions to its activism. First, Project workers emphasize the importance of group survival. Second, through lobbying and educational efforts, they work for institutional transformation—especially those forms of institutional transformation that will significantly alter if not completely eradicate existing structures of oppression.[8] More specifically, the activists make clear through their work that change can come about only through a willingness (1) to recognize that there is a problem; (2) to respond to the way the problem manifests itself in the community; and (3) to organize various strategies to challenge oppressive structures.

Community workers "argue, obstruct, organize, teach, lecture, demonstrate, sue, write letters," and form their own organizations in response to community needs.[9] In so doing, they create a "critical speech community around the problem—a group of people who share a point of view on a problem, acknowledging that it exists and that it is something in which public action is necessary."[10] The work of the National Black Women's Health Project and of Black women's health activists more generally, then, facilitates a "culture of resistance," to paraphrase Patricia Hill Collins, that is essential to Black female and Black feminist consciousness. It is Black women's culture of resistance, their refusal to internalize their own oppression by rejecting its ideological justifications, that enables, indeed demands that Black women work for political and social change. In the history of their health activism in particular, Black women have taken the narrow spaces of opportunity available to them and expanded them.

"Taking Charge and Taking Care"

Through self-help initiatives, initiatives that promote "taking charge and taking care," that is, taking responsibility for oneself, Black women health activists act as "primary health resources" for their families and communities.[11] Individual women and small groups of women organize to assess and to address specific issues related to particular diseases or health concerns of Black women. AIDS, currently a major life-threatening condition affecting a disproportionate number of Black women, is of great concern to many health activists. The problem of AIDS for Black women is exacerbated by concomitant problems of high rates of poverty in Black communities, poor nutrition, substance abuse, inadequate housing, under- or unemployment, and lack of access to preventative health care. Also, because early conceptualizations of AIDS described it first as a disease of gay white men and then as a disease of specific "risk groups," women were effectively preempted from consideration in AIDS research. The invisibility of women as a population affected by HIV/AIDS, especially the initial failure of the diagnostic criteria of the Centers for Disease Control and Prevention (CDC) to include gynecological conditions in the CDC definition has contributed to the underdiagnosis, misdiagnosis, and late diagnosis of HIV/AIDS in Black women. These failures also contribute to women's unnecessary suffering and dying more quickly from complications related to the disease. Taken together, all of these matters have a devastating effect on the health and well-being of Black women.

More than half of all women living with HIV/AIDS are Black, and yet on a national level, little is being done to address this overrepresentation. Much of the stigma and the silence related to AIDS has to do with how categories of sex, race, and gender are given meaning in U.S. culture. An elaborate network of sex, race, and gender dynamics shapes the history of sexual behavior in the United States, particularly as it pertains to sexually transmitted diseases. More specifically, for decades racial theories prevalent in American culture constructed Black women's bodies as the site and source of immorality and disease. Since at least the nineteenth century societal views of Black women's sexuality have constructed Black women as "promiscuous, irresponsible, and involved in illicit sexual activity such as prostitution."[12] This distorted perception contributes to defensiveness and hesitance among Blacks to openly discuss issues related to sex, sexuality, and their consequences in the age of AIDS. It also perpetuates the treatment of Black women as a risk to others (their children, their partners) rather than as individuals deserving of treatment and assistance themselves.[13] Oddly positioned as being both invisible and yet highly visible in AIDS discourse, Black women are being ignored in the AIDS prevention and education programs.[14] Rather than acknowledging how interlocking systems of race, gender, and class oppression cause Black women to be un(der)served in the health care system, Black women themselves are blamed.

Sister Care

In a recent publication on HIV/AIDS and women, *The Gender Politics of HIV/AIDS in Women*, Sheila Battle, a medical social worker with the San Francisco Department of Health, describes her work in counseling HIV+ African American women and their families. In her work Battle tries to make the specific health concerns of HIV+ African American women more visible. Citing indifference on the part of national, state, and local governments, as well as the minimal amount of funds allocated in her area for programs for women with HIV, Battle argues that change can occur only if communities work to educate themselves and one another through the development of their own programs. One such program is the one she works with, the Sister Care Project, which focuses on pregnant and postpartum Black women with HIV. This focus is extremely important because there are few prenatal care providers who are willing or able to care for pregnant women with AIDS, especially those who have contracted the disease through IV drug use.[15] Little education and under/unemployment plagues many of Battle's clients. Sometimes her clients also have problems with drugs and with the criminal justice system. Many of these women were physically and sexually abused. In some instances their families also abandoned them. According to Battle issues such as these faced by her clients in their day-to-day lives often take precedence over obtaining proper medical care.[16]

The Sister Care Project, which takes its name from its goal of "sisters taking care of sisters," provides comprehensive medical and social services. Realizing that many of the women they seek to reach were abandoned by their families or are homeless, workers in Sister Care try to reach women wherever they are emotionally, physically, or geographically. For poor women, this sometimes means counselors must provide information about nutrition and drug rehabilitation. For women who are middle class, this may mean counselors must provide them with information to overcome emotional paralysis because of feelings of shame related to their belief that they are "innocent" victims because they have not engaged in what have been described as "high-risk" behaviors. Battle argues that the way medical providers attempt to reach out to clients has a "very real impact on the success or failure of the relationship they have with one another."[17] This point becomes even more important when the history of mistreatment of Blacks by the medical establishment is taken into consideration. Annette Dula and others have written on the feelings of distrust and suspicion that many Blacks feel toward the medical community.[18] This lack of trust contributes to the underutilization of medical and social services by Blacks and makes it even more imperative that medical professionals as well as others concerned with the health of Blacks be willing to meet them halfway.

AIDS Ministries

In addition to the immediate physical problems of Black women with HIV or AIDS, larger issues related to their emotional and mental health must be addressed. Harvard AIDS Ministries has been focusing on community outreach to address the emotional and spiritual needs of Blacks, particularly Black women with AIDS. The Reverend Carol Johnson, founder of Harvard AIDS Ministries, uses curriculum development and training in AIDS prevention and education to form and lead affinity groups on AIDS in Black communities. In her essay "Healing from Within: Women, HIV/AIDS, and the African American Church,"[19] she describes the founding of Harvard AIDS Ministries and how she has worked to create a national forum on AIDS for African American religious leaders. This effort has led to a network of partnerships between diverse organizations, as well as to a national week of prayer to help combat the AIDS pandemic.

While still a student at Harvard Divinity School, Johnson established Harvard AIDS Ministries in 1992 to train herself and other seminary students about AIDS. She was motivated by a spiritual and intellectual desire to minister to people about AIDS, and by her prior community work relating to sex education. In its initial stages one of the goals of the program was to determine how to best utilize information about AIDS. Johnson's activism was inspired by gaps she had identified in the theological curriculum relative to AIDS. In particular, few facts were available pertaining to the growing numbers of women being impacted by it. Like Sheila Battle and other Black women organizing around the issue of AIDS, Johnson found that existing information and strategies were insufficient for an organized response from or about Black women. In particular, Johnson points to the limited effectiveness of safer-sex campaigns promoting condom use because they assume a certain equality of power distribution between sex partners.[20] According to Johnson, women's sexual experiences span a "continuum from consensual to coerced sexual encounters."[21] Issues related to gender, power, and sexuality, then, especially as they pertain to sexual abuse and other forms of bodily violence, need to be addressed before the high rates of AIDS in some Black communities can successfully be combated.

Religious institutions within Black communities historically played an important role in this kind of community outreach. More particularly, the Black church and other religious institutions were at the center of fostering spiritual, social, and political life for Black Americans, as well as of providing key health and human services to Black communities whose needs have gone unmet in the larger society.[22] Along with the community work facilitated by the church body, public health and medical professionals have called on the leadership of the church in attempting to reach segments of the Black population that are often missed by traditional mainstream strategies.[23]

Black women make up the vast majority of those who do church and community outreach. Operating as organizers and as advocates in their churches and in communities, they mobilize to "eliminate their own suffering as well as the suffering of their men, their children," and their fictive kin.[24] Even in the face of negative gender politics within the church and political institutions that have sometimes worked to stifle their ingenuity and activism, Black women continue to be an "effective force for social change and progressive thinking."[25] The work of Battle and Johnson are examples of how Black women build and maintain institutions in their communities. Their example and subsequent examples demonstrate how community work among Black women around issues of health continues an important tradition of organizing people to take public action.

Black Women Organizing against Breast Cancer

Breast cancer is the leading cause of cancer mortality among Black women. While overall, Black women have a lower rate of incidence of breast cancer than do white women, Black women nevertheless have higher mortality rates from breast cancer. The difference is said to be a result of Black women's often being diagnosed at more advanced stages of the disease. However, even when controlling for stage at diagnosis, Black women still have a higher mortality rate than white women. Currently, there is no single widely accepted explanation of the disparity. Reasons from socioeconomic status to lack of education and low perceptions of risk have been given. Black women's response to these statistics, generally speaking, has been twofold. First, they have worked externally to elicit government action in terms of research and funding to address issues specific to their experiences with breast cancer. Second, they have worked internally to create the support systems needed to help one another in battles against breast cancer.

SOS: Saving Our Sisters from Breast Cancer

In an attempt to answer the questions "Why are older Black women screened less for breast cancer?" and "What can be done to narrow the racial gap in mammography screening?" the Save Our Sisters (SOS) Project was founded.[26] Funded by the National Cancer Institute (NCI) the project is an attempt to respond to the dismal rates of participation of Black women ages 50 and older in mammography screening. A pilot program in North Carolina was undertaken to assist Black women 50–74 years old in obtaining mammograms. Under the premise that "women turn to other women they know for a helping hand, a shoulder to lean on, or advice," the program trained women described as "natural helpers" to become "lay health advisors."[27]

Natural helpers are individuals to whom others "naturally turn for advice, emotional support, and tangible aid."[28] Drawing on the work of Salber and others, Eugenia Eng and Jaqueline Smith assert that all communities have certain individuals with reputations "for good judgement, sound advice, a caring ear, and being discreet"[29] who are sought out by persons who have problems or concerns—before or, sometimes, instead of, resorting to professionals. Taking advantage of the fact that often the first contact persons in Black communities for those concerned about their health are natural helpers, individuals with substantial credibility in the communities, the SOS Project trained them as "lay" health advisors (LHAs). The role of the LHA was developed by the project to utilize resources within the community. The women chosen were willing and able to provide one-to-one assistance to women to get them to have mammograms; to facilitate community-based activities related to organizing around breast cancer issues; and to form a coalition of advisors and their networks to create a nonprofit organization[30] to bring into being community-based systems of care, as well as culturally sensitive and appropriate social support that complemented the role of health professionals.[31]

Eng found that lay health advisors are crucial to getting Black women to participate in education programs related to breast cancer. As members of the community, LHAs often have many things in common with the women they are working to educate, including a shared history of facing segregation and discrimination within the medical system. Because they largely have the trust of Black communities, LHAs are able to educate members of their communities as well as mediate and build coalitions between state and local health agencies and the communities. In addition, that trust enables the LHAs to break the silence about breast cancer and to demystify breast cancer screening. The community programs of the SOS Project, a nonprofit Black and female-controlled organization, educate Black women, especially those 50 and older about breast cancer and the importance of obtaining mammograms. The programs also provides information on navigating the health care system and its rules and regulations; train and recruit advisors from the community to assist in its education programs; and provide a support group for women diagnosed with breast cancer. In so doing, the programs of the project are uniquely able to meet the needs of Black women because the programs speak to the social, cultural, and structural barriers present in the professional system of services that help to maintain the disproportionately negative health outcomes of African American women affected by breast cancer.

"Beauty Shops . . . a Hell-of-a-Place to Ferment a . . . Revolution"[32]

Much of the current health literature on breast cancer points to the fact that traditional mechanisms for community outreach and education have failed to reach all populations. In addition to religious institutions, such as the church, delivering health and human services to the community, social and cultural institutions play a similar key role. Hair salons are culturally familiar settings in which African American women spend a significant amount of time. Serving as a site for the exchange of life stories and ideas, the hair salon by extension, hair stylists often function as principal sources of information. More recently, the beauty salon makes it possible to receive information about breast cancer.

Some beauticians in the Los Angeles area agreed to participate in a pilot study conducted by the Drew-Meharry-Morehouse Cancer Consortium. They were trained in the provision of detailed information on breast cancer, in this instance to their clients. Through oral and written narratives and through use of the 30-minute film "A Life Saving Choice" produced by the Revlon/UCLA Women's Cancer Research Program, African American women, particularly those older than 50, became the beauticians' target audience. Deirdra Forte notes that since African American women tend to "congregate, exchange information, and network in places that are different from those used by women in the mainstream,"[33] hair salons and other culturally familiar sites are effective settings for the dissemination of health information. By using beauty salons as a site of organizing and the passing along of information, study personnel hope that they can decrease the mortality rates of African American women from breast cancer.[34]

Rise, Sister, Rise: Sisters Supporting Sisters

Black women have also organized to help those sisters who must learn how to survive breast cancer. In 1989 Zora Kramer Brown, herself a breast cancer survivor, founded the Breast Cancer Resource Committee (BCRC). The committee, a group based in Washington, D.C., has as its aim helping Black women nationwide fight breast cancer. The BCRC's nationally recognized support group Rise, Sister, Rise is an important component in this process. It is one of a small but growing number of such groups in the United States focused on the needs and concerns of Black women. Members of its locals discuss the importance of having a group that they can go to where they can discuss "faith, food, family, and feelings"—issues they do not necessarily feel comfortable talking about in "mixed groups."[35] Rise, Sister, Rise deals with related matters such as diet and hair loss; provides a 16-month program that focuses on how to survive in the face of the disease and how to destigmatize the illness; and is a means to prevent isolation. Women who finish the program and eventually leave the group frequently continue to work as breast cancer activists.

Brown and her colleagues also work in Black communities, particularly poorer communities, that frequently have less access to health care and information about breast cancer. They lecture in churches, housing

projects, and neighborhood centers to combat the Black community's silence in regard to the disease. Brown and her colleagues are active, too,
in lobbying members of Congress as well as the health, business, and activist communities concerning research and treatment for breast cancer.
In dealing with Congress in particular, Brown presses for increased funding for research, especially research on manifestations of the disease specific to Black women. The women active in the BCRC, in other words,
make themselves visible in their communities, in churches, and in mainstream culture as resource persons and role models. Members of the
Women of Color Breast Cancer Survivor Support Project, interviewed by
Wanda Coleman for the *Los Angeles Times Magazine* make it clear why
the kind of support system afforded by the BCRC and their own organization is necessary: "Doctors are insensitive. They're the issue that started
this group. We face discrimination and neglect. . . . We tend to be given
the strongest medicines without necessarily needing them. Without any
concern as to what they might do to us. . . ."[36] Put another way, these
women feel that "[their] cultural background has put [them] in the background."[37]

Necessity Is the Midwife to Our Politics

Much of Black women's health activism is based on their ability to mediate between the "private lives of individuals and public institutions of the
wider society."[38] Through the representational politics of health advocacy, the activists continue their decades-old tradition of calling on health
professionals to pay attention to their health needs. Black women are
working to expand the repertoire of research questions to include the
kinds that health professionals raise and they demand that researchers include Black women in their studies. As activists, Black women challenge
the ways their bodies have been simultaneously used and ignored in
health research. Some of the ways they have issued their challenge is by
writing and lecturing about their own encounters with illness. Fueling
their activism is a deep sense of the history of African Americans' experiences with medical institutions. Their community work promotes and
provides advocacy and empowerment through education and role mod-
eling. They train and encourage women to actively participate in their
own health care. In so doing, they are able to translate the dismal health
statistics reported regularly about African American women into some-

thing meaningful: instead of focusing on what Black women are dying from, the activists are focusing on what Black women are living with. The work of Black women health activists puts them in the best position to facilitate and lead in setting the agenda for addressing health issues confronting African Americans in the coming decades. It is clear in the current work being done by Black women health activists that we are our resources.

NOTES

The author would like to thank Kimberly Springer and Charles Moore for their comments on earlier drafts of this chapter.

1. For an excellent analysis of the early history of the Black women's health movement, see Susan L. Smith, *Sick and Tired of Being Sick and Tired: Black Women's Health Activism in America, 1890–1950* (Philadelphia: University of Pennsylvania Press, 1995).

2. Norma Meras Swenson et al., "The Politics of Women's Health and Medical Care" in *Our Bodies, Ourselves for the New Millennium,* ed. Boston Women's Health Collective (New York: Simon & Schuster, 1998).

3. Health statistics have been compiled in the United States from at least colonial times, and statistics on such things as mortality rates, birth and fertility rates, and other health-related matters have been recorded since 1790 and in some cases 1770. See, for example, *Datapedia of the United States, 1790–2000: America Year by Year* (Lanham, Md.: Bernan Press, 1994), and *Historical Statistics of the United States, Colonial Times to 1970* (Washington, D.C.: Bureau of the Census, 1975).

4. For more information on the health statistics of Black women, see Centers for Disease Control, "Update: Mortality Attributable to HIV infection/AIDS among Persons Aged 25–44 Years—United States, 1990 and 1991," *Morbidity and Mortality Weekly Report* 42 (1993): 481–6; National Center for Health Statistics, *Health United States, 1989* (Hyattsville, Md.: U.S. Public Health Service, 1990); U.S. Department of Health and Human Services, *Health Status of the Disadvantaged—Chartbook.* DHHS Pub. No. [HRSA] HRS-P-DV90–1 (Washington, D.C.: U.S. Government Printing Office, 1990). See also Linda Villarosa, ed., *Body & Soul: The Black Women's Guide to Physical and Emotional Well-Being* (New York: HarperCollins, 1994); Evelyn White, ed., *The Black Women's Health Book: Speaking for Ourselves* (New York: Seal Press, 1994).

5. Sheryl Burt Ruzek, Virginia L. Olesen, and Adele Clark, "Intersections of Race, Class, and Culture" in *Women's Health: Complexities and Differences,* ed.

community. See Annette Dula, "African American Suspicion of the Healthcare System Is Justified: What Do We Do About It?" *Cambridge Quarterly of Healthcare Ethics* 3(1994): 347–57. See also Lynda Richardson, "Experiment Leaves Legacy of Distrust of New AIDS Drugs," *New York Times*, April 21, 1997, A1+; Jeff Stryker, "Tuskegee's Long Arm Still Touches Nerve," *New York Times*, April 13, 1997, sec. 4, p. 4.

19. Rev. Carol Johnson, "Healing from Within: Women, HIV/AIDS, and the African American Church," in *The Gender Politics of HIV/AIDS in Women*, 273–81.

20. See Z. Stein, "HIV Prevention: The Need for Methods Women Can Use," *American Journal of Public Health* 80 (1990): 460–2.

21. Rev. Carol Johnson, "Healing from Within," 274.

22. See Stephen B. Thomas et al., "The Characteristics of Northern Black Churches with Community Health Outreach Programs," *American Journal of Public Health* 84.4(1994): 575–79.

23. See ibid.

24. Jualyne E. Dodson and Cheryl Townsend Gilkes, "Something Within: Social Change and Collective Endurance in the Sacred World of Black Christian Women," in *Women and Religion in America*, vol. 3, *1900–1969*, ed. Rosemary Radford Ruether and Rosemary Skinner Keller (Cambridge: Harper & Row Publishers, 1981), 81.

25. Ibid., 86.

26. Eugenia Eng, "The Save Our Sisters Project: A Social Network Strategy for Reaching Rural Black Women," *Cancer* 107(1993): 1071–7.

27. Ibid.

28. Eugenia Eng and Jaqueline Smith, "Natural Helping Functions of Lay Health Advisors in Breast Cancer Education," *Breast Cancer Research and Treatment* 35(1995): 23–29.

29. Ibid., 24.

30. Eng, "The Save Our Sisters Project," 1074.

31. Eng and Smith, "Natural Helping Functions of Lay Health Advisors in Breast Cancer Education," 24.

32. From the Willi Coleman poem "Among the Things That Used to Be," in *Home Girls: A Black Feminist Anthology*, ed. Barbara Smith (New York: Kitchen Table, Women of Color Press, 1983), 221–22.

33. Deirdre A. Forte, "Community-Based Breast Cancer Intervention Program for Older African American Women in Beauty Salons," *Public Health Reports* 110 (March-April 1995): 179–83.

34. Forte, "Community-Based Breast Cancer Intervention," 181.

35. DeNEEN Brown, "Rise, Sister, Rise, Wipe Your Weeping Eyes: Black Women Find Strength in a Breast Cancer Support Group of Their Own," *Washington Post Health*, May 9, 1995, 10–13.

Sheryl Burt Ruzek, Virginia L. Olesen, and Adele Clark (Columbus: C
University Press, 1997).

6. For general information about the National Black Women's Healtl
see Martha Scherzer, "Byllye Avery and the National Black Women's He
ject" *Network News,* May/June 1995, 1–6; Gloria Naylor, "Power: Rx f
Health," *Ms.,* May 1986, 54–62.

7. For more on the conference and its goals, see Edith Butler, "The F
tional Conference on Black Women's Health Issues," in *Women's Healtl
ings on Social, Economic, and Political Issues,* ed. Nancy Worcester an
anne H. Whatley (Dubuque, Iowa: Kendall/Hunt Publishing Company, 1

8. See Patricia Hill Collins, *Black Feminist Thought: Knowledge, Con
ness, and the Politics of Empowerment* (Boston: Unwin Hyman, 1990), 1

9. Cheryl Townsend Gilkes, "'If It Wasn't for the Women . . .': African
ican Women, Community Work, and Social Change," in *Women of Color
Society,* ed. Maxine Baca Zinn and Bonnie Thornton Dill (Philadelphia: 1
University Press, 1994), 239.

10. Ibid.

11. Shay Youngblood, "Self-Help Groups: 'Taking Charge and Taking C
Network News May/June 1983, 8.

12. Beth Richie, "AIDS in Living Color," in *The Black Women's Health I*
184.

13. On this issue, see Sandra Crouse Quinn, "AIDS and the African Amei
Woman: The Triple Burden of Race, Class, and Gender." *Health Education Q
terly* 20.3 (Fall 1993): 305–20.

14. On the issue of Black women's invisibility in AIDS discourse, see e
cially Evelynn Hammonds, "Missing Persons: African American Women, A
and the History of Disease," *Radical America* 20 (1986): 7–23.

15. Richie, "AIDS in Living Color," 185.

16. On occasions when medical care is sought, it is usually only when
women find out that they are pregnant. It is also usually during the time wh
they go in for medical care that the women find out that they have HIV. She
Battle, "The Bond Is Called Blackness: Black Women and AIDS," in *The Gend
Politics of HIV/AIDS in Women: Perspectives on the Pandemic in the Unite
States,* eds. Nancy Goldstein and Jennifer Manlowe (New York: New York Un
versity Press, 1997).

17. Ibid., 287.

18. The Tuskegee experiment on 400 Black men immediately comes to the
minds of many Blacks when asked about why they do not trust the medical establishment. Other examples include discrimination against Blacks during the
sickle cell screening initiatives of the 1970s; forced sterilization of Black women
through the 1960s, '70s, and '80s; and, more recently, the view held by many
African Americans that AIDS is a genocidal plot aimed at the African American

36. Wanda Coleman, "Sisters in Arms: Breast Cancer Survivors Find, at Long Last, a Place to Tell It Like It Is," *Los Angeles Times Magazine*, February 6, 1994, 6.

37. Ibid.

38. Eng, "The Save Our Sisters Project," 1074.

RESOURCES

Below is a brief list of additional resources related to the issues raised in this chapter.

Organizations

Breast Cancer

African American Breast Cancer Alliance
P.O. Box 8987
Minneapolis, MN 55408
612–731–3792

Breast Cancer Resource Committee and Rise, Sister, Rise
1765 N. Street, NW
Washington, DC 20036
202–463–8040

Embracing Life
National Black Leadership Initiative on Cancer
University of Illinois Chicago
2121 W. Taylor Street, Suite 512
Chicago, IL 60612
312–996–8046 or 800–799–2542

God Cares Support Group
Church of the Great Commission
10137 Prince Place, #402
Largo, MD 20772
301–350–3113 or 301–735–7398

AIDS

National Red Cross
African American HIV/AIDS Programs
2025 E. Street, NE
Washington, DC 20006
202–728–6693

The Lesbian AIDS Project
129 West 20th Street, 2nd Floor
New York, NY 10011
212–337–3531

The Balm in Gilead Institute for Minority AIDS Prevention Studies
130 West 42nd Street, Suite 1300
New York, NY 10036

General

The National Black Women's Health Project (NBWHP)
1211 Connecticut Avenue NW, Suite 310
Washington, DC 20036
202–835–0117

Chapter Nine

Black Women in Congress during the Post–Civil Rights Movement Era

Sharon D. Wright

Introduction

The years 1954–1965 have often been described as the height of the civil rights movement. In *When and Where I Enter: The Impact of Black Woman on Race and Class in America,* Paula Giddings pointed out that "men led, but women organized" protests and other activities.[1] Beginning in the mid–1960s, Black men and women won elective offices mostly as a result of passage of the Voting Rights Act of 1965. Black voter turnout increased dramatically in states where Blacks had once been disfranchised and Black politicians won office for the first time since Reconstruction. Most of these politicians were male, but Black females experienced victories as well.

This chapter analyzes the experiences of Black women in Congress from the late 1960s to the late 1990s. Currently, 13 Black women serve in the House of Representatives and one in the Senate. Mainly, this chapter examines ways in which African American women have used their congressional offices to further the activism of the civil rights movement.

The chapter will focus on two main research questions. First, do Black political women face a double disadvantage because of their race and gender? Second, is there a Black woman's agenda? In the last two sections, I discuss the more recent issues for Black congresswomen, such as the implications of Supreme Court decisions on majority-minority districts and "the politics of charisma" for Senator Carol Moseley-Braun.

The Role of Black Women in the Women's Suffrage and Civil Rights Movements

Black women have had a long history of civil rights and political activism dating back to the Reconstruction years. During the women's suffrage movement, they joined interracial and predominantly Black women's organizations in support of women's suffrage. The Cooperative Women's League of Baltimore, Maryland, and the Commission on Inter-Racial Cooperation of the Women's Council of the Methodist Episcopal Church South were two groups in which Black and white women worked to ratify the 19th Amendment and to push for other rights for women. However, many of these interracial organizations had only token Black female members who were the wives of prominent men and/or had achieved stature in their own right.[2]

Agendas favoring white women usually dominated these groups. A number of white women felt uncomfortable addressing racial issues, and others had openly racist views toward African Americans. For example, white female suffragists suggested that the Susan B. Anthony amendment for women's suffrage be worded so that southern states could disfranchise Black women while still allowing white women to vote. In 1916, Carrie Catt, president of the National American Women's Suffrage Association (NAWSA) urged its white members not to attend its annual meeting in Chicago because a substantial number of the delegates would be African American.[3] Other white suffragists recommended that states include grandmother clauses in women's suffrage laws to disfranchise approximately three million Black women.[4]

As a result of these conflicts, Black women abandoned interracial civil rights organizations and formed their own. The Black women's club movement reached the height of its prominence during the 1920s. The National Association of Colored Women (NACW), the most well known of these social and civil rights clubs, consisted mostly of educated, middle-class women. It was the national headquarters that set the agenda for and disseminated information to local NACW chapters.[5] Since the majority of Black citizens belonged to the Republican Party before the 1930s, Black Republican women formed the National League of Republican Colored Women. Because the League of Women Voters usually excluded Black women from its membership, they organized separate local units of the league.[6]

After World War II, Black women continued their grassroots activism. Unlike the members of women's club organizations, these activists often had poor- and working-class backgrounds. For example, Mississippi's Fannie Lou Hamer and Unita Blackwell were sharecroppers and Rosa Parks was a seamstress. Black middle-class women were often indifferent to and passive about civil rights matters because of their belief that their problems differed from those of the poor. Eventually, communities abandoned class divisions and fully supported civil rights activities.

In an essay entitled "Men Led, But Women Organized: Movement Participation of Women in the Mississippi Delta," Charles Payne pointed out that Black women were more active in organizing civil rights protests in many areas, but men usually served as spokespersons. From the mid-1950s to the mid-1960s, women in Mississippi were active in trying to remove the obstacles to Black suffrage by filing lawsuits and organizing boycotts and marches.[7] Women such as Mary Fair Burks, Claudette Colvin, Rosa Parks and JoAnn Robinson were called "trailblazers" because of their role in the 1955 Montgomery bus boycott.[8] Other activists (e.g., Joyce Ladner, Anne Moody, Diane Nash and Ruby Doris Smith) were either high school or college students when they became involved in the movement or were members of the NAACP (e.g., Ella Baker, Daisy Bates, Septima Clark and Modjeska Simkins).

During the modern civil rights movement, which has also been called the second Reconstruction, Black women and men protested discrimination and legalized segregation. As a result of their efforts, federal, local and state civil rights laws were enacted and enforced for the first time since the late 1880s. The Voting Rights Act of 1965 resulted in substantial increases in Black voter registration and turnout rates and in the number of Black elected officials. By voting and electing representation, African Americans hoped that they would receive economic, educational, employment, housing and other opportunities.

Since the height of the civil rights movement from 1954 to 1965, a number of African Americans have won elective offices. Most have been male, but Black women have made strides as well. Jewel L. Prestage in "In Quest of the African American Political Woman" found that Black female voters had higher levels of turnout than both Black men and white women; held a larger number of elective offices than white women; were more likely to join women's organizations; and generally promoted issues of concern to women and to Blacks while in office.[9] In the 1970s and

1980s, Black women made greater gains than white women in winning congressional, mayoral and state legislative offices.[10]

The Double Disadvantage Hypothesis: Issues of Racism and Sexism

In 1968, Shirley Chisholm (D.-New York) became the first Black congresswoman. She was joined by Yvonne Braithwaite-Burke (D.-California), Cardiss Collins (D.-Illinois) and Barbara Jordan (D.-Texas) in 1972. During the 1980s, Katie B. Green-Hall (D.-Indiana) served for one term (1983–1985). During the 1990s, several Black women were elected: Corrinne Brown (D.-Florida), Julia Carson (D.-Indiana), Carolyn Cheeks Kilpatrick (D.-Michigan), Donna Christian-Green (D.-Virgin Islands), Eva Clayton (D.-North Carolina), Eleanor Holmes Norton (D.-District of Columbia), Eddie Bernice Johnson (D.-Texas), Cynthia McKinney (D.-Georgia), Carrie Meek (D.-Florida), Juanita Millender-McDonald (D.-California), Barbara Rose-Collins (D.-Michigan) and Maxine Waters (D.-California).

A statement by Maxine Waters pointed out the unique experience of African American women in Congress: "The Founding Fathers never envisioned Black women being in this place. So every time another one of us comes, we jolt the system just a little bit more, simply by being here. . . ."[11] According to the double disadvantage hypothesis, Black female candidates and officeholders have been disadvantaged by both racism and sexism.[12] Darcy and Schramm found in "When Women Run Against Men" that female candidates were disadvantaged by stereotypical, sexist beliefs that they were less capable of governing than men.[13] These views were stronger for younger women with small children.[14] In addition, women in Congress and in state legislatures have been assigned to "feminine" committees, which handle issues of child care, education and health care.[15]

Often subtle forms of sexism are worse than the overt. Many congresswomen have been mistaken for spouses and staff. When Carol Moseley-Braun sought a congressional identification card and received one that identified her as a "spouse," she responded "try again."[16] When U.S. Representative Maria Cantwell (D.-WA) locked herself out of her office and asked a security guard to open it for her, she overheard him say,

"You know, they don't make these guys like they used to."[17] Shortly after her 1992 victory, Cynthia McKinney filed a complaint against a security officer who grabbed her arm to prevent her from entering the building where her office was located. McKinney was wearing the gold pin that indicated that she was a member of Congress.[18]

For Black women in Congress, racism rather than sexism has always been a more oppressive problem. African American candidates usually raised fewer campaign funds than white males and females.[19] A number of Black congressmen and women have been the subject of federal investigations that they viewed as harassment.[20] Also, Cynthia McKinney once referred to a North Carolina poll in which 30 percent of whites admitted that they would not vote for a Black candidate "under any circumstances."[21]

Although African American women have been victimized by both racism and sexism, many scholars have found that they have not experienced a double disadvantage because of their race and gender. Darcy and Hadley in "Black Women in Politics: The Puzzle of Success" found that a greater proportion of Black women were elected officials than white women because of their higher levels of political ambition and because of the experience they gained as activists during the civil rights movement.[22] Black women also benefited from the ratification of the Voting Rights Act of 1965, reapportionment and redistricting.[23] The Voting Rights Act resulted in tremendous increases in Black voter registration and turnout that benefited Black candidates. In addition, reapportionment laws required that states redraw district lines each decade according to population shifts. As a result of the "reapportionment revolution," new, predominantly Black districts were created. Thus, Black candidates ran for office without having to challenge an incumbent.[24]

Despite these findings, Shirley Chisholm's 1972 presidential campaign provided evidence that Black women faced prejudices because of their race and gender that have inhibited their abilities to seek offices. In *The Good Fight,* Chisholm pointed out that her gender was as much as or more of an obstacle to her political career as her race:

> Black women . . . have to realize what they are in for when they venture into politics. They must be sure they have the stamina to endure the endless obstructions that are put in their way. They must have enough self confidence so they will not be worn-down by the sexist attacks that they will encounter on top of racial slurs.[25]

After she announced her plans to seek the Democratic nomination, Chisholm did not receive endorsements from three groups that she had cofounded: the Congressional Black Caucus, the National Organization for Women (NOW) and the National Women's Political Caucus (NWPC). She was an outspoken advocate of equal rights for minorities and women, but the most prominent Black and female leaders refused to support her candidacy. At the 1972 National Black Political Convention in Gary, Indiana, the delegates chose not to endorse a presidential candidate.[26] NOW would have lost its tax-exempt status if it had publicly endorsed a political contender, and the NWPC announced that it would remain neutral by not campaigning for or against her.[27] Representative Bella Abzug (D.-New York) said she supported the "idea" of Chisholm's candidacy but never campaigned for her. Many other NWPC members were Republicans who were solidly behind Richard Nixon. Those who backed Chisholm's campaign included author Betty Friedan, civil rights activist Fannie Lou Hamer and *Ms. Magazine* editor Gloria Steinem.[28]

Chisholm's issues with the Congressional Black Caucus were even more complex. Representatives Ronald Dellums (D.-California) and Parren Mitchell (D.-Maryland) and Manhattan Borough President Percy Sutton supported Chisholm throughout her 1972 campaign.[29] However, other Black elected officials questioned whether she would be a candidate for Blacks or for women. Many believed that Chisholm planned her campaign without consulting with them and that she lacked credibility as both a presidential and congressional candidate. In his book *Just Permanent Interests: Black Americans in Congress, 1870–1991*, Representative William L. Clay (D.-Missouri) called Chisholm's 1972 presidential campaign a "failure":

> Shirley Chisholm was never a potential or real "vote-getter." She served in the U.S. Congress not by any particular mandate of the vote but rather due to the apathy and indifference of her Brooklyn constituency. . . . More serious candidates who are defeated for Congress receive more votes in being denied a seat in the House than Chisholm ever received in winning office.[30]

Chisholm was also said to be on an ego trip because of her refusal to support other Black political women, such as the 1972 nomination of Yvonne Braithwaite-Burke for vice-chairman of the Democratic National Convention. She instead favored Asian-American congresswoman Patsy Mink (D.-Hawaii). Chisholm also objected to the nomination of former U.S. ambassador to Luxembourg and secretary of housing and urban development Patricia Roberts Harris as chairman of the credentials committee at the DNC.[31]

Despite the fact that Black women compose less than 3 percent of U.S. representatives and less than 1 percent of U.S. senators, scholarly research has found little evidence that they face a double disadvantage when running for congressional and other political offices.[32] However, Chisholm's 1972 presidential campaign proved that they have faced "prejudices" because of their race and gender. Chisholm may not have won the Democratic nomination and subsequent presidential election even if she had been endorsed by the majority of Black and women leaders. Yet, white women and Black men probably would have been more supportive of her if she had been a white female or Black male candidate.

Is There a Black Woman's Agenda?

Kelly and colleagues, in "Female Public Officials: A Different Voice?" found that female elected officials "represent other women, speak for women's interests and change the context and direction of public policy."[33] White political women were expected to serve the interests of women, but what about Black women? In this section, I analyze the ways in which Black women in Congress served their constituents. In other words, was there a Black woman's agenda?

Edith Barrett defined the terms "woman's agenda" and "Black agenda" in her analysis of whether Black women had a distinctive agenda in state legislatures. Women legislators primarily promoted legislation on parental leave, affirmative action or comparable worth, child care and housing discrimination against families with children. African American legislators were more concerned with affirmative action, urban education, hiring opportunities, protesting investment in South Africa during apartheid and the awarding of contracts to minority-owned businesses. Black women focused on a combination of these issues by promoting educational opportunities, accessible and affordable health care, economic development, employment opportunities, child care, and the poor.[34] Yet, they were more preoccupied with racial rather than gender issues.

The same can be said for Black women in Congress. Most Black representatives have served districts with large minority populations and disproportionate numbers of poor residents. In 1990, the average household income in districts represented by Black congressmen and women was $31,921; the national average was $38,453. Per capita incomes averaged $11,715 in Black congressional districts and $14,420 in others.[35] Approximately 23.1 percent of these districts' residents lived at or below the poverty level; the national figure was only 3.1 percent. Last, unemployment averaged 10.3 percent, whereas the national average was 6.3 percent.[36]

Because of the needs of their urban, disproportionately poor and mostly Black constituents, Black congresswomen focused more heavily on a Black rather than a woman's agenda and all were liberal Democrats. The earliest Black congresswomen—Yvonne Braithwaite-Burke, Shirley Chisholm, Cardiss Collins, Katie B. Green-Hall and Barbara Jordan— were more likely to sponsor legislation concerning affirmative action, busing, civil rights for minorities and women, and unemployment opportunities.[37] B. Green-Hall sponsored the Dr. Martin Luther King, Jr., federal holiday bill during her term in office. The Black congresswomen who were elected during the 1990s focused on affirmative action, Black youth, child care, crime (law and order), immigration and job training. All opposed President Clinton's Omnibus Anti-Crime ("three strikes, you're out") Bill, which required life in prison for anyone convicted of a third violent crime, and the Hyde Amendment, which prevented poor women from using Medicare to fund abortions, and the welfare reform bill, but they supported the James Brady bill for handgun control.

Are Majority-Minority Congressional Districts Unconstitutional?

The year 1992 was called the "year of the woman" because a record number of women sought and won elective offices. In Congress, four women, including Carol Moseley-Braun, were elected to the Senate. Twenty-four women including nine African Americans, three Latinas, one Puerto-Rican and one Asian American won seats in the House of Representatives. As a result of these victories, the numbers of women rose from one to five in the Senate and from twenty-nine to forty-seven in the House.[38] Possible reasons for the successes of women candidates in 1992 included the increased number of women who ran for political office, the 1991 Thomas-Hill hearings, the House bank scandal and redistricting.[39]

Like their predecessors, the Black congresswomen who were elected in 1992 owed their victories to redistricting. A record number of women won congressional races in 1992, but a record number of Blacks won as well. The Congressional Black Caucus increased from 26 to 40 members and became an even more powerful voting bloc. In 1992 states such as California (Walter Tucker), Florida (Corinne Brown, Alcee Hastings and Carrie Meek), Georgia (Sanford D. Bishop and Cynthia McKinney), Illinois (Carol Moseley-Braun, Mel Reynolds and Bobby Rush), Louisiana (Cleo Fields), Mississippi (Bennie Thompson), North Carolina (Eva M. Clayton and Mel Watt), South Carolina (James E. Clyburn), Texas (Eddie Bernice Johnson) and Virginia (Bobby Scott) elected Black congressional representatives.

After these new representatives took office, plaintiffs filed lawsuits that challenged the constitutionality of their districts. In the 1993 *Shaw v. Reno* case, the U.S. Supreme Court ruled that the North Carolina legislature had engaged in racial gerrymandering—creating districts in a way that discriminated against a certain group of voters. Accordingly, Eva Clayton's and Mel Watt's districts were redrawn. The Supreme Court also invalidated districts in Florida, Georgia, Louisiana, South Carolina, Texas and Virginia; all now have white population majorities. In Georgia, George DeLoach, the white Democrat whom Cynthia McKinney defeated in 1992, filed a federal lawsuit against the state after he switched to the Republican Party.[40]

These decisions did not result in a decrease in Black congressional representation. Cleo Fields (D.-Louisiana) declined a reelection bid, but all of the Black congresswomen and men whose districts had been challenged were reelected in 1994 and in 1996. However, long-term implications of the Supreme Court decision remained unclear. With the exception of Representatives Julia Carson (D.-Indiana), Carolyn Cheeks-Kilpatrick (D.-Michigan), Cardiss Collins (D.-Illinois), Katie B. Green-Hall (D.-Indiana) and Carol Moseley-Braun (D.-Illinois), Black women have represented new, majority Black districts in Congress.[41] By receiving most of the minority vote and percentages of the white vote, they were able to win these elections. Carol M. Swain in *Black Faces, Black Interests: The Representation of African Americans in Congress* suggested that Black congressional candidates should develop coalitions among Black and white voters and run for office in predominantly white districts because of the inability of courts and state legislatures to create Black districts in the future.[42] Swain's argument was logical; however, most Black candidates were far less successful when seeking office in predominantly white districts because of the unwillingness of white voters to support them.[43] If federal courts and legislators had not created majority-minority districts, most of the Black members of Congress would not have been elected. During the civil rights movement, Black women and men fought for the right to vote and elect representation, but they must develop new strategies to hold on to these gains in the postmovement era.

Senator Carol Moseley-Braun and the Politics of Charisma

Before Carol Moseley-Braun's 1992 victory, three African Americans had served in the Senate: Blanche K. Bruce of Mississippi (1875–1881), Edward K. Brooke of Massachusetts (1966–1978) and Hiram R. Revels of Mississippi (1870–1871). When Moseley-Braun entered the Senate race in Illinois, she was not expected to win. Her opponents in the primary election, incumbent Democratic Senator Alan Dixon and Albert Hofeld mainly attacked each other and ignored Moseley-Braun's candidacy. She had served as a state representative from 1978 to 1988. During that period, she became the first African American and first woman to serve as assistant majority leader in the Illinois House.[44] In 1988, she became the first African American to serve in a countywide elective position: Cook County Recorder of Deeds.

Moseley-Braun realized that she could not win election to the Senate with the Black vote alone. Therefore, she used a "deracialized" strategy in order to attract support from white, female, middle-class, rural and Republican voters. A deracialized campaign is one in which Black and other minority candidates place less emphasis on racial issues.[45] Moseley-Braun emphasized gender and economic issues more than race.

Alan Dixon, a conservative Democrat who had been involved in Illinois politics for more than 40 years, had voted in favor of Clarence Thomas's nomination to the Supreme Court. Moseley-Braun capitalized on the Hill-Thomas sexual harassment hearings by mobilizing suburban white women—many of whom switched from the Republican to the Democratic Party to vote for her. The charismatic Moseley-Braun had widespread appeal. Her celebrity supporters included Goldie Hawn and Barbra Streisand. Women's groups that seldom supported Black female candidates such as Illinois Women for Government, or "Babes in Government," raised funds for her.[46] During the last days of the primary campaign, Emily's List, a national group that donates money to women candidates, contributed to her campaign, which by that time was thousands of dollars in debt. Approximately 62 percent of Moseley-Braun's support came from white female voters and she received more than 99 percent of the Black vote. Moseley-Braun won the primary election with 38 percent of the vote; Alan Dixon, 35 percent; and Hofeld, 27 percent.[47]

In the November general election, Moseley-Braun defeated Republican lawyer Richard Williamson despite a campaign that was described as "disorganized" and "chaotic." Two female members of Moseley-Braun's staff anonymously accused her campaign manager and boyfriend Kgosie Matthews of sexual harassment. An investigation later found that these charges were without merit. On election day, Moseley-Braun received 53 percent of the votes cast, and Williamson received 43 percent.[48]

Moseley-Braun's election to the Senate showed that it was possible for a Black female candidate to build coalitions among voters beyond class, gender, partisan and racial lines. However after taking office, she found it difficult to please her vast array of supporters—all of whom had different interests. Voters had the same high expectations for the first Black female senator that they would have had for any "first" minority or female political figure. However, they were soon disappointed by Moseley-Braun's excessive campaign debts and other problems; her debts totaled $563,000. Eventually, the Federal Election Commission conducted a two-year audit of how she and Matthews had spent $6.7 million in the campaign.[49] Moseley-Braun's supporters and staff were angered even more because shortly after winning the election, she, Kgosie Matthews and her son Matthew took a 27-day South African vacation and bought a lavish co-op apartment near Lake Michigan rather than meeting with constituents in her district and paying her campaign staff.[50] She also offended many African Americans when she endorsed Chicago Mayor Richard M. Daley's 1995 reelection bid over two Black candidates who had backed her run for the Senate. At one appearance, Moseley-Braun said that she would "bake cookies for Mayor Daley."[51]

In 1998, Carol Moseley-Braun will seek reelection to the Senate. She faces an uphill battle against her white Republican opponent, Peter Fitzgerald, a wealthy banker with a prolife platform. She will again attempt to develop a multiracial coalition that heavily targets minority and women voters. However in a recent poll conducted by her campaign, voters in her district gave her a 41 percent disapproval rating.[52] Because of the difficulties she faced during and after her 1992 campaign, she must again use her charismatic personality as well as her incumbency advantages to win reelection.[53]

Conclusion

This chapter analyzed the experiences of Black women in Congress and the ways they furthered the activism of the civil rights movement. During the women's suffrage and modern civil rights movement, Black women were involved in efforts to increase the numbers of Black registered voters, Black districts and Black elected officials. The Black women who served in Congress from the late 1960s to the late 1990s have not experienced a double disadvantage because of their race and gender when seeking and holding office, but have experienced prejudices. Shirley Chisholm's 1972 presidential campaign showed that white women and Black men were not as willing to support a Black female candidate for a major office.

Concerning their agenda, Black women in Congress focused mostly on issues of concern to Blacks rather than to women. Whereas the earliest Black congresswomen were concerned with civil rights legislation, redistricting has been the main issue for those elected in the 1990s. If the federal courts refuse to create majority-minority districts in the future, a sharp decrease in Black congressional representation will result. Last, the Carol Moseley-Braun campaign in 1992 showed that the politics of charisma can lead to victories, but Black women must learn to avoid controversies and to satisfy the needs of their diverse array of supporters after taking office. The activists of the women's suffrage and civil rights movements paved the way for a new generation of Black women who are carrying on their legacy.

NOTES

1. Paula Giddings, *When and Where I Enter: The Impact of Black Women on Race and Class in America* (New York: Bantam Books, 1984).

2. Rosalyn Terborg-Penn, "Discontented Black Feminists: Prelude and Postscript to the Passage of the Nineteenth Amendment," in *Decades of Discontent: The Women's Movement, 1920–1940*, edited by Lois Scharf and Joan M. Jensen (Westport, Conn.: Greenwood Press, 1983), 271.

3. Ibid., 263.

4. Ibid.

5. Charles H. Wesley, *The History of the National Association of Colored Women's Clubs, Inc.: A Legacy of Service* (Washington, D.C.: National Association of Colored Women's Clubs, 1984), 55–100.

6. Evelyn Brooks Higginbotham, "Clubwomen and Electoral Politics in the 1920s," in *Women and the Vote, 1837–1965*, edited by Ann D. Gordon with Bettye Collier-Thomas, John H. Bracey, Arlane Voski Avakian, Joyce Avrech Berkman (Amherst: University of Massachusetts Press, 1997), 140.

7. Charles Payne, "Men Led, But Women Organized: Movement Participation of Women in the Mississippi Delta," in *Women in the Civil Rights Movement: Trailblazers and Torchbearers, 1941–1965*, edited by Vicki L. Crawford, Jacqueline Anne Rouse and Barbara Woods (Bloomington: Indiana University Press, 1993), 1–11.

8. Mary Fair Burks, "Trailblazers: Women in the Montgomery Bus Boycott," in *Women in the Civil Rights Movement: Trailblazers and Torchbearers, 1941–1965*, edited by Vicki L. Crawford, Jacqueline Anne Rouse and Barbara Woods (Bloomington: Indiana University Press, 1993),71–83.

9. Jewel L. Prestage, "In Quest of the African American Political Woman," *Annals of the American Academy of Political and Social Science* 515 (May 1991): 88.

10. Robert Darcy and Charles D. Hadley, "Black Women in Politics: The Puzzle of Success," *Social Science Quarterly* 69 (1988): 642.

11. Ibid., 43.

12. Gary Moncrief, Joel Thompson, and Robert Schuhmann, "Gender, Race, and the State Legislature: A Research Note on the Double Disadvantage Hypothesis," *Social Science Quarterly* (October 1991): 481.

13. Robert Darcy and S. Schramm, "When Women Run Against Men," *Public Opinion Quarterly* 4 (1977): 1–12.

14. Ronald D. Hedlund, Patricia K. Freeman, Keith E. Hamm and Robert M. Stein, "The Electability of Women Candidates: The Effects of Sex Role Stereotypes," *Journal of Politics* 41: 1–2 (1979): 513–24.

15. Alice S. Rossi, "Beyond the Gender Gap: Women's Bid for Political Power," *Social Science Quarterly* 64 (1983): 718–33.

16. Clyde Wilcox, "Why Was 1992 the 'Year of the Woman'? Explaining Women's Gains in 1992," in *The Year of the Woman: Myths and Realities*, edited by Elizabeth Adell Cook, Sue Thomas and Clyde Wilcox (Boulder: Westview Press, 1994), 2. Also in 1993, Senator Jesse Helms sang "Dixie" in an elevator to Orrin Hatch (D.-Utah) and to Moseley-Braun: "I'm going to make her cry. I'm going to sing Dixie until she cries." Moseley-Braun's response was "Senator Helms, your singing would make me cry if you sang Rock of Ages."

17. Marjorie Margolies-Mezvinsky. *A Woman's Place: The Freshman Women Who Changed the Face of Congress* (New York: Crown Publishers), 1994.

18. Francis Wilkinson, "Guess Who's Coming to Legislate?" *Rolling Stone*, May 19, 1994, 43.

19. Darcy and Hadley, "Black Women in Politics," 630.

20. See William L. Clay, "A Conspiracy to Silence Dissent" in *Just Permanent*

Interests: Black Americans in Congress, 1870–1991 (New York: Amistad Press, 1992), 312–38.

21. Cynthia A. McKinney, "The Politics of Geography: The Voting Rights Act Strengthened the Black Vote, Remapping Could Weaken It," *Emerge,* December/January 1996, 64.

22. Darcy and Hadley, "Black Women in Politics," 642.

23. Ibid., 629.

24. Charles S. Bullock III, "Minorities in State Legislatures," in *Changing Career Patterns in State Legislatures*, edited by Gary Moncrief and Joel Thompson (Ann Arbor: University of Michigan Press, 1992).

25. Shirley Chisholm, *The Good Fight* (New York: Harper and Row Publishers, 1973), 32.

26. Ibid., 31.

27. Laverne M. Gill, *African American Women in Congress: Forming and Transforming History* (New Brunswick: Rutgers University Press, 1997), 30.

28. Chisholm, *The Good Fight,* 75–77.

29. Ibid., 73.

30. William L. Clay, *Just Permanent Interests: Black Americans in Congress, 1870–1991* (New York: Amistad Press, 1992), 224–26.

31. Gill, *African American Women in Congress,* 32.

32. Both Black women and men remain underrepresented in Congress. African Americans constitute 12 percent of the U.S. population, yet Black women are approximately 2.9 percent of the House membership and less than 1 percent of the Senate membership, and Black men 3.9 percent and zero percent respectively. White men and women are 90 and 99 percent of the House and Senate memberships. Despite the underrepresentation of African Americans in Congress and in other elective offices, the literature has found that so few are elected because of their inability and/or unwillingness to run for office.

33. Rita Mae Kelly, Michelle A. Saint-Germain and Judy D. Horn, "Female Public Officials: A Different Voice?" *Annals of the American Academy of Political and Social Science* 515 (May 1991): 77–87.

34. Edith J. Barrett, "The Policy Priorities of African American Women in State Legislatures: Is There a Black Woman's Agenda?" (paper presented at the Annual Meeting of the American Political Science Association, Washington, D.C., August 1993).

35. David A. Bositis, *The Congressional Black Caucus in the 103rd Congress* (Washington, D.C.: Joint Center for Political and Economic Studies, 1994), 25.

36. Ibid., 26.

37. Gill, *African American Women in Congress.*

38. Wilcox, "Why Was 1992 the 'Year of the Woman'?" 1.

39. Carol Chaney and Barbara Sinclair, "Women and the 1992 House Elections," in *The Year of the Woman: Myths and Realities*, edited by Elizabeth Adell

Cook, Sue Thomas and Clyde Wilcox (Boulder: Westview Press, 1994), 123–139.

40. McKinney, "The Politics of Geography," 62.

41. In 1996, Julia Carson was elected in a predominantly white congressional district in Indiana. Cardiss Collins was elected in a 1972 special election to succeed her husband U.S. Representative George Collins, who had died in a plane crash. From 1982 to 1984, Katie B. Green-Hall completed the term of Congressman Adam Benjamin Jr., who died in office. Carolyn Cheeks-Kilpatrick defeated incumbent Representative Barbara Rose-Collins in 1996. Carol Moseley-Braun defeated incumbent Senator Alan Dixon and Republican Richard Williamson in 1992.

42. Carol M. Swain, *Black Faces, Black Interests: The Representation of African Americans in Congress* (Cambridge: Harvard University Press, 1993).

43. The 1996 reelection of Representative Cynthia McKinney proved the validity of Carol Swain's argument but also provided evidence that Blacks and whites continue to vote along racial lines. After the Georgia legislature redrew McKinney's district, its Black population fell from 60 to 33 percent. During her reelection campaign, McKinney focused on developing coalitions with white voters, particularly with white women. In the November 1996 general election, she received approximately 30 percent of the white vote and was reelected with 58 percent of the total vote. Despite her victory and impressive white crossover vote, voting remained racially polarized with 90 percent of Black voters supporting McKinney and almost 70 percent of whites voting for her white male Republican opponent.

44. Gill, *African American Women in Congress,* 150.

45. Charles V. Hamilton, "Deracialization," *First World* 1 (1977): 3–5.

46. John R. Coyne Jr., "Woman of the Year?" *National Review,* September 14, 1992, 24.

47. Ibid., 51.

48. Ted G. Jelen, "Carol Moseley-Braun: The Insider as Insurgent," in The *Year of the Woman: Myths and Realities,* edited by Elizabeth Adell Cook, Sue Thomas and Clyde Wilcox (Boulder: Westview Press, 1994), 83.

49. John McCormick and Daniel Klaidman, "The Trials and Tribulations of a Symbolic Senator: How an Icon Got Mired in Debt and Disappointment," *Newsweek,* April 8, 1996, 34.

50. Eloise Salholz, "A Senator's Uneasy Debut: Carol Moseley-Braun Arrives in Washington," *Newsweek,* January 18, 1993, 26.

51. McCormick and Klaidman, "The Trials and Tribulations of a Symbolic Senator," 35.

52. Richard Dunham, "Why Moseley-Braun Has Top Dems Scared," *Business Week,* June 1, 1998.

53. Editor's note: Moseley-Braun narrowly lost the November 1998 election by roughly three percentage points (source: http://www.state.il.us/election/).

Part III

Contemporary African American Women's Activism

Chapter Ten

Engendering the Pan-African Movement
Field Notes from the All-African
Women's Revolutionary Union

M. Bahati Kuumba

Women of African descent are situated at the apex of national oppression, class domination, and gender inequality. Response to and resistance against these intersecting and multiplicative oppressions have been constant and varied. Resistance has included involvement in social movements primarily seeking racial equality and/or national liberation.[1] "Nation/race-identified" movements in which African women have participated have included national liberation struggles in Africa, Latin America, and the Caribbean; the civil rights and Black Power/consciousness movements in the Americas and South Africa; and the twentieth-century Pan-African movement. The nation/race-identified movements, for example, have historically placed the issue of gender inequality and patriarchy in secondary or tertiary positioning in lieu of seemingly more pressing emphasis on nation/race political, economic/class, and cultural liberation. Until very recently, the Pan-African movement continued this tradition.

While African women experience nation/race/class/gender oppressions simultaneously and interactively, most social movements have dealt with these sites of struggles in piecemeal fashion. Contemporary Pan-Africanism has been forced to more effectively negotiate the continuities and discontinuities implicated by this nation(race)/gender/class dialectic. The Pan-African movement incorporated women from its emergence, yet the ideologies and practices of its organizations and conferences were male-dominated and did not deal directly with issues of gender. The labor of

African women was crucial to the movement, yet they routinely experienced marginalization within the structures and were often sidelined from official leadership roles.[2]

The following discussion explores the struggle to create and practice gendered Pan-Africanism and apply a nation(race)/gender/class analysis in the context of a contemporary Pan-African organization. Women's wings and organizations such as the All-African Women's Revolutionary Union (AAWRU or the "Union"), the U.S.-based women's wing of the All-African People's Revolutionary Party (AAPRP), established in 1980, emerged specifically to address this question of women's oppression and liberation in the Pan-African movement. Its emergence was reflective of the tension within the movement between African nationalism, women's liberation, and class struggle.

While the formation of the AAWRU represented a qualitative leap in gendering Pan-Africanism, it also heightened old struggles around African women's roles in the movement, thus creating new gender/race/class contradictions. Many movements have illustrated the explosive role that gender inequalities, hierarchies, and divisions of labor play in creating splinter and breakaway organizations devoted to women's liberation.[3] The AAWRU represents an imploding of these contradictions.

This study explores overlapping and conflicting nation/class/gender processes as they relate to African women in a Pan-Africanist organization using the AAWRU as a contemporary example. It rests on an examination and analysis of AAWRU organizational documents and speeches, the results of a 1990 survey of 44 AAWRU members, and the author's "conscious partiality" based on personal experience of political education and activism within the organization from 1982 to 1992. In order to offset the insider privilege of access to internal AAWRU records and discussions, the analysis rests mostly on public AAWRU documents and minimizes direct reference to and specific information about internal organizational documents and specific individuals. In a general sense, this study seeks to situate the AAWRU, as a case study, within the broader context of women's liberation in nationalist and Pan-Africanist social movements.

African Women and Nation/Gender/Class Struggles

Women numerically dominated in many nation/race-identified movements and played crucial leadership and "bridging" roles on the grassroots level but have scarcely been represented in the more official leadership roles.[4] Gender asymmetry in perceptions and assignments of leadership obscured the central roles that women played. For example, the work that the Women's Political Council and "The Club from Nowhere" performed in initiating and sustaining the Montgomery bus boycott of 1955–56 has been overshadowed in our collective memory by the sole focus on its male leadership.

Civil rights scholars and activists have argued that Ella Baker, for example, would have received more recognition for her role had she been a man, particularly a male minister. The same is true for other central female organizers in the movement such as Fannie Lou Hamer, Diane Nash, Septima Clark, and Gloria Richardson. The limitations imposed by gender have served as both impediments and opportunities. Blocking women from official leadership positions often enhanced their more broad-based, substantial community levels of involvement.[5] The gender dynamics within the context of nation/race-identified movements like the civil rights, Black Power, and Pan-African movements essentially reproduces the same tensions existent between national and women's liberation in many social movements. The complexities of the relationship between national liberation and women's emancipation have been observed on a global level.[6] According to Orayb Aref Najjar (1992):

> The tension between women's needs and rights and perceived national needs has led some to wonder whether the national struggle is retarding the efforts for women's equality. . . . On the other hand, the strain has led others to dismiss women's emancipation as a "secondary contradiction" . . . one that is not important enough to distract from the all-consuming struggle for national self-determination.[7]

A national liberation struggle, by definition, places the objective of nation/race independence, equality, and self-determination in prioritized position. From the nationalist perspective, national independence is posed as a necessary precondition for women's liberation. At the same time, women's contributions are sought after and needed in the struggle for nation/race independence and equality. Substantive participation on the part of women presupposes a certain degree of equality and, sometimes for these purposes alone, national liberation struggles alter the status of women in different and complex ways.[8]

At the same time, the primacy of nation-class liberation over women's emancipation, as opposed to the simultaneity of struggle, glosses over women's differential experience within and as a result of the national liberation struggle. In many historical and cultural contexts, "nationalist" tendencies are linked to traditions and belief structures that disadvantage women. National liberation, in fact, often leads to the regression of women's status and a backlash of rekindled "traditional" patriarchal practices and structures.[9]

The relegation of women's oppression and inequality to the background, despite its interactive linkage to nation/race inequality, has repercussions. In many instances, the submersion of gender, class, and/or cultural factors creates a virtual "pressure cooker" effect. By heightening contradictions, these "secondary" struggles are propelled into the forefront. Nationalist and race-based movements are notorious for stimulating gendered consciousness and offshoot movements of autonomous or semiautonomous women's movements and organizations.[10] The groundswell of postcolonial women's liberation movements in Africa and the African diaspora, Asia, and Latin America were incubated in the context of national liberation struggles.[11] Once the gender dialectics in a national liberation or racial equality movement reach a zenith, they either explode into autonomous women's organs or implode resulting in internal women's wings, secretariats, and ministries. The twentieth-century Pan-African movement is no exception.

The Pan-African Woman Question: Married or Just "Shacking Up"?

African women's involvement in movements that seek racial equality and/or national liberation has included the Pan-African movement. The Pan-African movement was formally initiated by twentieth-century organizations, congresses and conferences, and political-cultural activities that share a view of the fundamental commonalities in the history, conditions, and destiny of African people worldwide.[12] Its many expressions are linked by a common focus on the liberation of Africa from the vestiges of European colonialism and imperialist relations; continental unity among the independent African nation-states; and racial equality for and unity among people of African descent globally. Ideologically, these aims are viewed as prerequisites for the liberation of any specific sector of the African population, for example, women, youth, and workers. From a social movement perspective, Pan-Africanism can be viewed as a collective-action frame that explains, rationalizes, and directs political action.[13] It is through the collective-action frame that movement participants connect with the larger objectives and structures of the struggle.

The Pan-African movement is the totality of the strategic and organizational expressions that have embodied the Pan-African ideology/collective-action frame. It has included seven Pan-African Congresses, a host of organizations, and both localized and transnational actions and insurgencies. While the Pan-African movement has always incorporated women, the ideologies and practices of its organizations and conferences, as well as women's experiences within its structures, have not reflected explicit attention to or analysis of "women's interests."

While most of the leaders and delegates to the early Pan-African meetings and organizations were educated and relatively privileged men (such as W. E. B. DuBois, Kwame Nkrumah, and George Padmore), numerous women of African descent have documented participation. Anna Julia Cooper, radical educator and scholar, attended the first Pan-African Congress in 1919. In attendance at the Second Pan-African Congress of 1921 were Jesse Fauset, literary editor of *The Crisis* (journal of the NAACP); Helen Curtis, an African American teacher, social worker, and activist; and Mrs. I. G. Hunt. Later, Addie W. Hunton, leader in the Black women's club movements, assisted organizational efforts for the Fourth Pan-African Congress in New York (1927), and Amy Ashwood Garvey, former wife of Marcus Garvey, chaired a session at the Fifth Pan-African Congress (1945).[14]

The involvement of African women in the early Pan-African movement did not, in an of itself, constitute the merging of Pan-African and women's interests, however. Concern for African women's inequality and issues have virtually no mention in the early records of "official" Pan-Africanism. Only the "Resolutions Adopted by the All-African People's Conferences" of 1958 and 1961 and the "Charter for Union of African States" reference women at all. All three documents merely encourage regional and continental conferences of "women's organizations" to promote Pan-African unity and coordination. Thus, women and the "woman question" were treated as more of a "special interest" category than an integral part of the struggle.

African diasporan women in the United States and the Caribbean were prominent in Pan-African organizations like Marcus Garvey's Universal Negro Improvement Association (UNIA), as well. In fact, the Black Cross Nurses, the women's auxiliary of the organization, was a substantial segment of the UNIA's membership.[15] There were also a "Lady President" for each chapter and women in key leadership positions, such as Henrietta Vinton Davis, the director of the UNIA's Black Star Shipping Line.

Despite women's numerical prominence and the provision for women's rights in the UNIA constitution, women "faced resistance (and often outright hostility) from the male dominated officers and membership."[16] A gendered division of labor existed within the UNIA that relegated women to "expressive" and supportive roles and maintained the dominance of men in "instrumental" roles and leadership positions.

> In this scheme, the wife/woman's sphere (and her roles as mother, teacher, nurse, or office worker) was deemed important but secondary to and supportive of that of the husband/man (and his roles as policy maker, executive, or diplomat). Many women accepted these gender definitions and their attending roles, but others rebelled against them, creating modified positions of authority for themselves and reconstructing the prevailing views of womanhood and manhood in the process.[17]

In an effort to address the gender differentials and bring alternative notions of women's liberation into the UNIA, women delegates to the 1922 convention took the stage and put forth several demands in favor of gender equality.[18] These resolutions included the request that women be given greater recognition, power, and input into "setting international policy" so that, in their words, "women all over the world can function without restriction from the men."[19]

Other African women asserted gendered demands and resisted patriarchy with their feet. Many prominent women in the Pan-African movement left organizations like the UNIA to organize alternative and sometimes rival movements.[20] Laura Kofey and Mittie Maud Lena Gordon left the UNIA to create their own "Back to Africa" movements. Some women left Pan-African organizations to create alternative "spaces" and structures that thrust women's issues and gendered realities into the forefront. Examples include Adeline Casely Hayford's school for girls established in the 1920s and Addie W. Hunton's involvement in the Black women's club movement.

It is clear that the early Pan-Africanist movement, conferences, and ideology entailed masculinist conceptions of liberation. It is also clear that ideological and structural efforts to address the confluence of the nation, class, gender oppressions has historical precedence in the Pan-African movement.

The All-African People's Revolutionary Party emerged as a U.S.-based Pan-African organization in response to a call made by Kwame Nkrumah his 1968 manuscript *Handbook of Revolutionary Warfare*. In this political treatise, Nkrumah called for a political party that would strive to unify independent African nation-states into a United States of Africa and link African people globally. Beginning in the early 1970s, a core of activists with experience in organizations from the previous movement era (e.g., the Student Nonviolent Coordinating Committee and the Black Panthers) began forming All-African People's Revolutionary Party study circles on college campuses initially in the United States, but also in the United Kingdom, the Caribbean, and (to a limited extent) in Africa. The growing membership divided time between attending study circles mainly devoted to discussions of assigned readings; committee meetings and seminars that focused on party business; passing out literature and "propagandizing"; public speaking; and organizing political education events on African historical and contemporary politics. Themes for external events mainly dealt with the nature of capitalist colonialism and imperialism, the role of youth and women in revolutionary struggles, and the imperative for Pan-Africanism and socialism. The largest of the events was African Liberation Day held in May of each year.

The AAPRP forged and adopted an Nkrumah-Toureists ideology, named after two male icons in the struggle to create and theorize the Pan-African ideal. Kwame Nkrumah was the first president of the independent Ghana in 1957, leader of the Convention People's Party (CPP), and convener of the first All-African People's Congress (1958). Sekou Toure held the same honor as first president in newly independent 1958 Guinea. Both men were staunch Pan-Africanists who theorized and made policy with African continental unity as the objective.

The ideologies and organizations of the civil rights, Black nationalist, and left-wing student movements of the 1960s also had an impact on the political line and strategy of the AAPRP. Kwame Ture (Stokely Carmichael), along with his cofounders of the AAPRP, brought histories of struggle from the voter registrations in Mississippi, the Student Nonviolent Coordinating Committee (SNCC), and the Black Panther Party (BPP).

This mass approach to organizing, coupled with the emphasis on participatory democracy and anti-imperialist/socialist ideals that were legacies of the 1960s movement era and these particular movement organizations, had an impact on AAPRP philosophy and practice. While the civil rights/Black Power movement had been officially male-led, the pre-dominance of women as "grassroots" leaders and participants gave the AAPRP founders an appreciation of the importance of the imperative for active female participation.[21]

While the AAPRP shared the Pan-African objectives of its predeces-sors, it was also influenced by movements of the 1970s and 1980s, in-cluding the international women's liberation movement. In this contem-porary mode of the Pan-Africanist movement, the All-African People's Revolutionary Party (AAPRP) was driven to more effectively articulate the problems facing African people by infusing gender into its political line and organizational structure. The seeds of a more sophisticated ap-proach to the "African women's question" planted in the earlier phase of the Pan-African movement would reemerge fifty years later in the form of the All-African Women's Revolutionary Union.

Labor Pains: The Emergence of the All-African Women's Revolutionary Union (AAWRU)

The emergence of the All-African Women's Revolutionary Union (AAWRU) in 1980 and the complexities surrounding the activist experience of its members illustrate the uneven and dynamic process involved in formu-lating and implementing a race/class/gender praxis (i.e., combined ideol-ogy and action). Its formation signaled greater ideological and structural appreciation of African women's oppression and liberation within the Pan-African movement. It stimulated the development of a nation (race)/class/gender analysis, provided a space for women's ideological and or-ganizational skill development, and stimulated the recruitment of women into the All-African People's Revolutionary Party. At the same time, its structure and mandate conflicted with African women's liberation in the short run and exemplified recurrent issues related to women's experiences in nation/race-identified movements.

The Women's Union of the AAPRP was an ideological and strategic re-sponse to the international women's movement, in general, and the heightening gender consciousness in the All-African People's Revolution-ary Party, specifically. This women's wing of the party, established in 1980, emerged specifically to more effectively address the simultaneity of gender oppression with racism and classism. These theoretical problems were coupled with the need to more practically address problems women faced within the AAPRP.

Birthing the AAWRU was not an easy process. It was the culmination of seven years of hard labor, intense internal struggle, discussion, and debate. Many of the contradictions evident at formation of the AAWRU would continue to manifest themselves in years to come. Here again, the gender constraints dialectically provided both impetus and impediment to the interests of African women's liberation.

The need to examine the "woman question" from a Pan-African perspective was initially introduced in the AAPRP at the African Liberation Day of 1973 held in Washington, D.C. The AAPRP sat on the panel with members of the Congress of Afrikan People (CAP) and the Youth Organization for Black Unity. Exploration of women's role in the struggle continued the next year when the AAPRP presented the position paper "The Role of African Women" at the Congress of Afrikan People–sponsored African Women's Conference at Rutgers University. At this 1974 meeting, the formation of an African Women's United Front was proposed, with a kickoff scheduled for the next year.[22]

Although many "sisters" in the AAPRP were involved in the organizing efforts for the conference, the official position of the AAPRP was against the formation of an autonomous African women's organ or women's wing at that time. This resistance was informed, in part, by the long-standing argument within nationalist discourse that efforts directed solely toward "women's liberation" could be divisive to the overall goal of African liberation. There was additional concern that a more reformist than revolutionary solution would be proposed by an autonomous African women's movement. The AAPRP counterproposed the formation of an African United Front that could incorporate a Women's United Front under its umbrella. This position was overruled in favor of forming a Black Women's United Front (BWUF), which emerged from the 1975 meeting in Detroit, Michigan, under the leadership of CAP.

Despite the official AAPRP position against the women's organization, "sisters" in the AAPRP participated in the Black Women's United Front in limited ways and on local-chapter levels. This involvement with women's organizing outside the AAPRP structures, coupled with the growing discussion of the oppression and liberation of African women internal to the AAPRP, fueled a growing women's consciousness. There had already been complaints regarding the underrepresentation of "sisters" in leadership positions within the AAPRP and their exposure to insensitive practices and harsh treatment in some AAPRP chapters. Problems of recruitment of women into the AAPRP chapters and of their retention were cited in organizational documents (AAPRP n.d.(c)). These initial efforts served to catalyze scrutinization and critique of the AAPRP's ideology (Nkrumah-Toureism), its political positions, and day-to-day practices regarding women members, specifically, and the issue of gender, more generally. The first structural response to these "rumblings" came two years later. The AAPRP set up a task force in 1977 to investigate the relationship of women's oppression to that of nation/class oppression and marginalization of women in various AAPRP chapters. The Political Education Committee of the AAPRP was subsequently charged with researching African women's oppression in search of the best strategy for addressing the "woman question" within AAPRP ideology and structure. Its recommendations included the formation of a women's wing to be called the All-African Women's Revolutionary Union and its birth date was scheduled for October 11 and 12, 1980. The site for the birth would be Columbus, Ohio.

The formation of the AAWRU, a qualitative leap in the gendering of the AAPRP and the Pan-Africanist movement, was modeled after a number of other national liberation organizations and revolutionary parties on an international level that had created internal structures to mobilize women and address internal gender contradictions. Parties such as the Democratic Party of Guinea (PDG), Zimbabwe African National Union (ZANU), the Front for the Liberation of Mozambique (FRELIMO), the African National Congress (ANC), and the Palestinian Liberation Organization (PLO) all had women's wings.

The AAWRU's role had ideological, structural, and strategic components. Ideologically, its charge was to spearhead political education on the historical development of African women's oppression. Structurally, AAWRU meetings and programs were to provide a "space" for women's leadership to blossom and for the "sisters" to freely participate without the intimidating influences from their "brothers." This structure would also be responsible for internal and external programming on women and youth. Strategically, the AAWRU was viewed as a vehicle to recruit and retain African women for the All-African People's Revolutionary Party and, ultimately, the Pan-African movement.

Thus, the role/tasks of the AAWRU could be broadly categorized as follows:

1. political education: conscientization around the "woman question" in a Pan-African context;
2. recruitment and retention: efforts to mobilize a greater number of women and expand their roles in the AAPRP;
3. diplomatic liaisons: to develop and strengthen relationships with the women's wings of other revolutionary parties/organizations; and
4. child/youth coordination: to organize child care and a political education program for the Young Pioneer's Institute (YPI).

Support for the creation of the women's wing was not universal within the Party. There was resistance to the idea of a women-focused entity within the AAPRP. But by the AAWRU's Tenth Anniversary Conference in 1990, the AAWRU could boast of more than 100 hardworking, militant women within its ranks. The conference, held in London, England, had well over 75 AAWRU/AAPRP members in attendance. A survey of 44 AAWRU attendees profiled them as well-educated, predominantly U.S.-born women of African descent with an average age of 33 years. Reflective of the AAPRP's ideological emphasis on youth and students as the "spark of the revolution" and its strategy of organizing on college campuses, the AAWRU members were highly educated. Most surveyed AAWRU members had been recruited to the AAPRP as college students (66 percent), almost all had at least a bachelor degree (91 percent), and a significant number had attended or were in graduate school (48 percent).[23] It is highly likely the exposure to material by and about women during their college careers heightened the gender consciousness of these women.

The span of membership ranged between 4 months and 18 years, with the average being 7 years. More than half of the women in the AAPRP at that time had been recruited since the formation of the All-African Women's Revolutionary Union. This increased quantity would have qualitative effects.

Ideological Struggle: Forging a Nation/Class/Gender Analysis

The creation of the AAWRU and emphasis by the All-African People's Revolutionary Party catalyzed the formation of an official position on the oppression of women of African descent and their role in the Pan-African movement. Within the AAPRP, the nation/class emphasis of Nkrumah-Toureist ideology was expanded to include the "woman question," resulting in a "nation/class/gender" political line. This perspective emphasized the triple oppression of racism, classism, and sexism in the historical and contemporary oppression of African women; the commonality of the problems facing women of African descent globally; the necessity for unified struggle by African men and women to address the conditions faced by African people; the need for women of the African diaspora born all over the world to unite around the commonalities of their conditions; and European colonialism and capitalism/imperialism as the underlying cause of racism, classism, and sexism.

Treatises like Sekou Toure's (1983) "The Role of Women in the Revolution" and Thomas Sankara's (1988) "The Revolution Cannot Triumph Without the Emancipation of Women" provided the theoretical core and basis for AAWRU ideas and practice. They linked the gender and nation problematics from an African perspective. These writings commonly prefaced their analysis with the centrality of African women's role and their relatively high status in precolonial African societies. They go on to locate the roots of African women's oppression in the onslaught of European colonialism and capitalist penetration. Most important, these writings stressed the imperative for African women to be mobilized equally into the liberation struggle to ensure its success.

Concomitantly, the ideological positions of Engels (1972) and Lenin (1938) were used to establish the connection between gender oppression and class relations. Their examination of gender oppression as related to the rise of private property and capitalism was also incorporated into the AAPRP/AAWRU's political line. Simultaneously, the need to equally include women to ensure success in the liberation struggle and for Pan-Africanist socialist revolution to secure the emancipation of women were embodied in the AAWRU's ideological "line."

While the AAWRU pushed for a nation/class/gender analysis, it defined itself as decidedly and consciously antifeminist. The Pan-African, anti-capitalist ideological perspective toward liberation emphasized the interdependence of African men and women in the struggle for race/class/gender equality and justice. "Feminism" was viewed as a Western perspective based solely on the experiences of middle-class, European-American women. Feminism was charged with being ultimately a reformist strategy that inherently supports the national oppression and class exploitation that set men against women. According to the AAWRU Manifesto (n.d.):

> Feminism, epitomized in the European "Women's Lib Movement," is a bourgeois distraction from the real struggle we as Africans need to be involved in. . . . It pushes separate organizations and activities excluding men as a desperate attempt to achieve the progressive development of women individually and collectively while leaving intact the pervasive, devastating capitalist system.[24]

The nation/class/gender line as articulated placed capitalism and racism as the main sources of the oppression of women of African descent. An AAWRU recruitment pamphlet states it succinctly: "The emancipation of African women must be associated with the liberation of the African nation and the African working class because if the nation and class are not liberated, then women will not be liberated."[25]

To some extent, this notion of Pan-African socialist revolution as the panacea for African women's liberation was informed by a selective reading of African history and of the fate of postcolonial revolutions in the underdeveloped world. Early AAWRU memos provide an uncritical and almost romanticized reading of the precolonial status of African women. In addition, the "antifeminism" line restricted AAWRU members from the study of Africana feminists and womanist theoretical work that was also attempting to reconcile their analysis of interlocking and multiplicative oppressions.[26] This restricted scope of study limited the degree to which the emergent nation/class/gender ideology was truly gendered and representative and inclusive of African women's perspective and input.

An additional ideological concern was the way in which the antifeminist line was often used to derail charges of patriarchy and male chauvinism raised by AAWRU members. A memo from the Bay Area Chapter illustrates the problem by asking: "Sistas, have you ever been called that dirty "F" work, FEMINIST, just because you raise your voice too loud in criticizing a Brotha inside the Party?"[27] From an AAPRP perspective, being labeled "feminist" was tantamount to being called an "Uncle Tom" or "sellout." This charge was often used strategically as a subterfuge to undermine charges of patriarchy or sexism in the Party, thus undermining one of the purposes for establishing the AAWRU. The unevenness of the race/class/gender approach contradicted the simultaneity of oppressions experienced by the AAWRU.

The Revolutionary "Double Day": The Realities of the Militant African Women

Contradictions and debates evident at the formation of the All-African Women's Revolutionary Union were to emerge again later during the implementation of AAWRU work. These conflicts were both ideological and structural. Ideologically, there were struggles around fusing gender into the nation/class line while maintaining a staunch antifeminist position. Structurally, the very structure of the AAWRU heightened party contradictions surrounding the gendered division and distribution of labor.

Most "sisters" in the AAWRU conformed to the condition of the larger African-woman reality of juggling a variety of social responsibilities. At the time of the 1990 survey, most AAWRU respondents were still attending college (53 percent), rearing children (73 percent), working full-time (66 percent), and serving as primary household head bearing primary (or sole) child-rearing responsibility (63 percent). These race/class/gendered life realities for AAWRU members as students, mothers, and workers often clashed with their political obligations.

A major structural contradiction lay in the fact that AAWRU members were overburdened by the work associated with the very entity intended to seek their liberation and relieve their burden within the struggle. Even at the birth of the AAWRU, women were given disproportionate amounts of work without being relieved of regular AAPRP responsibilities. A 1980 AAWRU task force memo, for example, charged the total membership of the AAPRP (i.e., "sisters and brothers") with the responsibility of "organizing the Union." Indeed, the rationale behind forming the AAWRU was to educate the entire AAPRP membership on the sources and manifestations of African women's oppression. The sisters in the AAWRU were given sole responsibility for organizing the seminars on women that led up to the founding conference and most subsequent "women's programs." Later, AAWRU work would consist of organizing and attending AAWRU meetings, coordination of women's programs, organizing and supervising youth activities, and writing on the role of African women in the Pan-Africanism movement. The men of the Party were allowed, and encouraged, to attend most AAWRU meetings, although they were restricted from voting. Needless to say, despite the fact that the stated role of the AAWRU was to organize and mobilize the entire organization (men included) to participate in politicizing around the issues of sexism, most of this work fell upon the shoulders of AAWRU women.

The birth of the AAWRU also initiated the struggle over the coordination of child care and the politicization of African youth. From the outset, the Young Pioneer's Institute (YPI), the youth wing of the AAPRP, was intended to relieve the "sisters" from primary child-care responsibilities. Some factions in the AAPRP argued that care for the children and political education of the youth of AAPRP members were collective responsibilities to be shared by all. Others evoked the essentialist view that women, by virtue of their particular relationship to children, should be responsible for coordinating the YPI. The decision made at the founding conference was to place the coordination of YPI under the purview of the AAWRU.

Despite the AAWRU's existence, underrepresentation of women in leadership positions continued to be a problem faced by the AAPRP. The lower levels of official leadership positions held by women was often explained away as an "ideological" problem. That is, it was posed as a reflection of the lack of clarity or consciousness of the sisters and brothers of the party. I contend that this contradiction also had a structural basis and was a function of the contradictory and unifying forces of race/class/gender operating both internally and externally to the AAPRP.

The All-African Women's Revolutionary Union was formed to address the oppression of women from a gendered Pan-Africanist perspective. The race/class/gender analysis emphasized the "triple burden" carried by women of African descent. The irony is, however, that AAWRU work often became a fourth burden and a form of oppression as a result of breakdowns in the implementation of the race/class/gender informed praxis. The very structure of the All African Women's Revolutionary Union created tasks for women in the AAPRP over and above their regular AAPRP duties, which included AAWRU meetings, organizing and attending programs on women, and coordinating the Young Pioneers Institute.

In 1990, members reported an average of 10 additional hours per week spent specifically on Union work, that is, meetings, seminars/programs, reading, and propagandizing. Overburdening, burnout, and dropping out were common responses. In the 1990 survey, many members cited these conflicting responsibilities and role conflicts as major obstacles to full participation. Their multiple pressures of being mothers, students, workers, AAPRP members, *and* AAWRU members were not offset by any institutional or organized support. Ironically, then, while the increased recruitment of women into the AAPRP and AAWRU were major objectives in the creation of the AAWRU, its very structure and processes militated against the sustained participation of women.

The additional work placed on women in the AAWRU was not offset by assistance with the "triple oppression" experienced by African American women, as the nation/class/gender political "line" promised. In fact, one of the major ironies in my experience and the experience of other "sisters" in the All-African Women's Revolutionary Union was coordination of child care. Not only did this add to their multiple responsibilities, it also contradicted the more progressive position promoted in AAPRP discourse of collective responsibility for the children. It essentially mirrored the conservative position on the roles of women and men in society and reinforced the public/private split that oppresses women in Western patriarchal capitalist society.

The real-life, day-to-day realities of most AAWRU sisters already entailed primary responsibility for household production (that is, child care, domestic responsibilities, and so on), full- or part-time school, *and* employment. Despite the fact that the AAWRU Manifesto states as an objective, "liberating African women from the domestic slavery that subjugates them to the eternal drudgery of kitchen and nursery work 7 days a week while working other jobs," the Party often failed to actualize this goal.

These contradictions between ideology and practice came to a head at the 1990 anniversary meeting of the AAWRU held in London. Where the AAWRU spearheaded a call for a "social revolution" within the All-African People's Revolutionary Party. The underlying charge was that principles of egalitarianism and humanism, central ideas in AAPRP ideology, were not practiced in the social relations and interpersonal interactions within the party. In many AAWRU chapters, sisters' charges of mistreatment by men were being dismissed as "personal problems." Thus, despite the AAWRU's decidedly antifeminist stance, it was, in effect, posing a very "feminist" challenge to the larger body of the AAPRP. It was arguing that these seemingly "personal" issues should be seen within their larger "political" context, reiterating a long-standing "feminist" idea—"the personal is political."

"Women on the Front Lines": Revolutionary Cadre or Cannon Fodder

> Far from creating divisions, the struggle of our women is a sector of the front in the great movement for African emancipation; it is one of our instruments to speed up the liberation and social advancement of our peoples.[28]

The All-African People's Revolutionary Party's (AAPRP) sought to "place African women in the forefront of the struggle for African liberation" because of their positioning at the bottom of the race/class/gender hierarchy. The formation of the AAWRU did succeed in recruiting women into the AAPRP and promoting them into leadership positions. In 1990, close to one-half of the AAWRU members had held some leadership role in the Party. A major irony of this "front-line" position was the increased work and responsibility that came with being on the forefront. There was a degree of overburdening that resulted from activity within an organizational structure developed to address issues of oppression against women both inside the party and outside.

The "triple oppressions" of racism, classism, and sexism that challenged African women in the wider society were, to some extent, recreated in the structure and processes of the AAWRU.

The added labor associated with organizing "women's" programs, attending AAWRU meetings, and writing propaganda around the "woman question," often made the union a burden in and of itself.

Care for the AAPRP's youth, theoretically organized to relieve AAWRU members of the "burden" of child care, became an additional responsibility. The AAWRU was supposedly responsible for coordinating, not being the main caretakers of, the Young Pioneer's Institute (YPI). In reality, though, members disproportionately took on the task of pressing for, organizing, and working with the Party's youth wing. The structural relegation of the Young Pioneers Institute to the purview of the union and the conservative nuclear family-oriented approach to child rearing were also an added burden.

The AAPRP also benefited from the domestic and child-rearing labor of many ex-AAWRU members who maintained primary responsibility for children of AAPRP unions. Women external to the AAPRP continued to subsidize the work of the AAPRP male members to the extent that they often continued to be responsible for domestic labor associated with the children and households of AAPRP unions. The fact that AAPRP "brothers" were often able to do their party work unhampered by the constraints of family labor in some ways mirrors the exploitative processes characteristic of patriarchal capitalist accumulation.[29] This unpaid and unrecognized women's labor against which the Party fought was capitalized upon, on some levels, for the party's growth and development. Many of the mothers of the youths of the YPI had themselves been AAWRU/AAPRP members at one time but had dropped out due to heavy workloads associated with juggling AAWRU/AAPRP work, school, and workforce and family responsibilities.

The gendered Pan-Africanism of the AAWRU exemplified the best of merged movements. In many ways, the Union is a clear example of the growing internationalism and clearer ideological connection to women of other postcolonial/neocolonial nations. It was also a logical continuation of processes incubated earlier in the struggle of women of African descent within U.S.-based struggles, such as the Third World Women's Alliance that emerged from SNCC in the 1970s.[30] That is, to better address the contradictions and continuities surrounding the struggle for Pan-Africanism, socialism, and women's liberation.

In spite of the contradictions, participation in nation/race-identified movements has historically heightened the gender/women's consciousness of African women. The need for women's participation forces a level of gendered struggle over traditional gendered norms and structured inequalities that sets the stage for gendered consciousness. The All-African Women's Revolutionary Union was both a cause and effect of the nation(race)/class/gender dialectic. The officially stated race/class/gender political line of the AAPRP was expressed through, and at the same time conflicted with, the All-African Women's Revolutionary Union. This reflects the continuum of dialectical struggle between African nationalism, women's liberation, and class struggle within which women of African descent in movements must negotiate.

NOTES

1. See Barnett 1993, 1995; Gilliam 1991; Johnson-Odim 1991; King 1988; Robinson 1987; Robnett 1996, 1997.

2. See Lemelle 1992.

3. Evans 1979; Freeman 1975.

4. See Barnett 1993; Payne 1990, 1995; Robinson 1987; and Robnett 1996, 1997 for fuller treatment of grassroots and bridge leadership.

5. For example, see Barnett 1993, 1995; Gilkes 1988; Robnett 1996, 1997.

6. The relationship between nationalism and women's liberation/feminism is explored in Alexander and Mohanty 1997; Gaidzanwa 1988; Jayawardena 1986; McFadden 1992; and Mies 1986.

7. Najjar 1992:144.

8. See Kuumba and Dosunmu 1995.

9. Rowbotham 1992; Gilliam 1991.

10. See Evans 1979.

11. See Gilliam 1991; Jacquette 1994; and Jayawardena 1986.

12. See Legum 1962; Lemelle 1992.

13. A fuller discussion of the collective action frame concept can be found in Snow et al. 1986.

14. For more information on the Pan-Africanist Congresses see Delamotte, Meeker, and O'Barr 1997; Legum 1962; and Lemelle 1992.

15. The UNIA and the Black Cross Nurses are explored further in Bair 1992; Garvey 1986; Giddings 1984; and Lemelle 1992.

16. Lemelle 1992:92.

17. Bair 1992:155.

18. See Lemelle 1992.

19. Bair 1992:160.

20. Lemelle 1992.

21. Barnett 1993, 1995; Robnett 1997.

22. AAWRU Organizing Task Force. "Recent Developments and Decisions," A-APRP Memo, 1980.

23. AAWRU, "Tenth Anniversary Conference Report." Memorandum, 1992.

24. AAWRU n.d.(a):6.

25. AAWRU n.d.(b).

26. For discussions of the multiple and interlocking race/class/gender oppressions, see Barnett 1993; Brewer 1993; Collins 1986; hooks 1984; King 1988; and Lorde 1984.

27. AAWRU 1994:1.

28. Toure 1983:267.

29. For expansive discussion of the global accumulation and the capitalist patriarchy, see Mies 1986.

30. Giddings 1984.

REFERENCES

Alexander, M. Jacqui, and Chandra Talpade Mohanty. *Feminist Genealogies, Colonial Legacies, Democratic Futures.* New York: Routledge, 1997.

All-African People's Revolutionary Party. n.d.(a). Assorted AAPRP memos and notes.

All-African Women's Revolutionary Union. n.d.(a). "Manifesto."

———. n.d.(b). "Organizing African Women for Revolution." Pamphlet.

———. "Ready for the Revolution." Working document, Greater Bay Area California Cadre Circle, 1994.

———. "Tenth Anniversary Conference Meeting Report." Memorandum, 1992.

AAWRU Organizing Task Force. "Recent Developments and Decisions." Memorandum, 1980.

Bair, Barbara. "True Women, Real Men: Gender, Ideology, and Social Roles in the Garvey Movement." Pp. 154–66 in *Gendered Domains: Rethinking Public and Private in Women's History*, edited by Dorothy O. Helly and Susan M. Reverby. Ithaca: Cornell University Press, 1992.

Barnett, Bernice McNair. "Black Women's Collectivist Movement Organizations: Their Struggles during the "Doldrums." Pp. 199–219 in *Feminist Organizations: Harvest of the New Women's Movement*, edited by Myra Marx Ferree and Patricia Yancey Martin. Philadelphia: Temple University Press, 1995.

Barnett, Bernice McNair. "Invisible Southern Black Women Leaders in the Civil Rights Movement: The Triple Constraints of Gender, Race, and Class." *Gender and Society* 7(2) (1993): 162–82.

Brewer, Rose. "Theorizing Race, Class and Gender: The New Scholarship of Black Feminist Intellectuals and Black Women's Labor." Pp. 13–30 in *Theorizing Black Feminisms: The Visionary Pragmatism of Black Women*, edited by Stanlie M. James and Abena P. A. Busia. London: Routledge, 1993.

Collins, Patricia Hill. "Learning from the Outsider Within: The Sociological Significance of Black Feminist Thought." *Social Problems* 33(6) (1986): 514–32.

Davis, Angela. "Reflections on the Black Woman's Role in the Community of Slaves." *Black Scholar* (December 1971): 3–15.

Delamotte, Eugenia, Natania Meeker, and Jean O'Barr. *Women Imagine Change: A Global Anthology of Women's Resistance*. New York: Routledge, 1997.

Engels, Friedrich. *The Origins of the Family, Private Property and the State*. New York: Pathfinder Press, 1972.

Evans, Sara. *Personal Politics: The Roots of Women's Liberation in the Civil Rights Movement and the New Left*. New York: Vintage Books, 1979.

Freeman, Jo. *The Politics of Women's Liberation*. New York: David McKay Company, 1975.

Gaidzanwa, Rudo. "Feminism: The Struggle Within the Struggle." *Network: A Pan-African Women's Forum* 1(1) (1988): 4–13.

Garvey, Amy Jacques. 1986[1923]. *The Philosophy and Opinions of Marcus Garvey*. Dover, Mass.: Majority Press.

Giddings, Paula. *When and Where I Enter: The Impact of Race and Sex in America*. New York: William Morrow, 1984.

Gilkes, Cheryl Townsend. "Building in Many Places: Multiple Commitments and Ideologies in Black Women's Community Work." Pp. 53–76 in *Women and the Politics of Empowerment*, edited by Ann Bookman and Sandra Morgen. Philadelphia: Temple University Press, 1988.

Gilliam, Angela. "Women's Equality and National Liberation." Pp. 215–36 in *Third World Women and the Politics of Feminism*, edited by Chandra Mohanty, Ann Russo, and Lourdes Torres. Bloomington: Indiana University Press, 1991.

hooks, bell. *Feminist Theory: From Margin to Center*. Boston: South End Press, 1984.

Jaquette, Jane S. *The Women's Movement in Latin America: Participation Democracy*. 2d ed. Boulder: Westview Press, 1994.

Jayawardena, Kumari. *Feminism and Nationalism in the Third World*. London: Zed Books, 1986.

Johnson-Odim, Cheryl. "Common Themes, Different Contexts: Third World Women and Feminism." Pp. 314–27 in *Third World Women and the Politics of Feminism*, edited by Chandra Mohanty, Ann Russo, and Lourdes Torres. Bloomington: Indiana University Press, 1991.

King, Deborah. "Multiple Jeopardy, Multiple Consciousness: The Context of a Black Feminist Ideology." *Journal of Black Studies* 18(4) (1988): 395–414.

Kuumba, M. Bahati, and Ona Alston Dosunmu. "Women in National Liberation Struggles in the Third World." Pp. 95–130 in *The National Question: Nationalism, Ethnic Conflict, and Self-Determination in the 20th Century*, edited by Berch Berberoglu. Philadelphia: Temple University Press, 1995.

Legum, Colin. *Pan-Africanism: A Short Political Guide*. New York: Frederick A. Praeger, 1962.

Lemelle, Sid. *Pan-Africanism for Beginners*. New York: Writers and Readers Publishing, 1992.

Lenin, V. I. *Women and Society*. New York: International Publishers, 1938.

Lorde, Audre. *Sister Outsider*. Freedom, Calif.: The Crossing Press, 1984.

McFadden, Patricia. "Nationalism and Gender Issues in South Africa." *Journal of Gender Studies* 1(4) (1992): 510–20.

Mies, Maria. *Patriarchy and Accumulation on a World Scale*. London: Zed Books, 1986.

Najjar, Orayb Araf. "Between Nationalism and Feminism: The Palestinian Answer." Pp. 143–61 in *Women Transforming Politics: Worldwide Strategies for Empowerment*, edited by Jill M. Bystydzienski. Bloomington: Indiana University Press, 1992.

Nkrumah, Kwame. *Handbook of Revolutionary Warfare*. New York: International Publishers, 1968.

Payne, Charles. *I've Got the Light of Freedom: The Organizing Tradition and the Mississippi Freedom Struggle*. Berkeley: University of California Press, 1995.

Payne, Charles. "Men Led, but Women Organized: Movement Participation of Women in the Mississippi Delta," Pp. 1–11 in *Women in the Civil Rights Movement: Trailblazers and Torchbearers, 1941–65*, edited by Vicki L. Crawford, Jacqueline Anne Rouse, and Barbara Woods. Bloomington: Indiana University Press, 1990.

Robinson, Jo Ann Gibson. *The Montgomery Bus Boycott and the Women Who Started It*. Knoxville: University of Tennessee Press, 1987.

Robnett, Belinda. *How Long? How Long? African-American Women in the Struggle for Civil Rights*. New York: Oxford University Press, 1997.

Robnett, Belinda. "African-American Women in the Civil Rights Movement, 1954–1965: Gender, Leadership, and Micromobilization." *American Journal of Sociology* 101(6)(1996): 1661–93.

Rowbotham, Sheila. *Women in Movement: Feminism and Social Action*. New York: Routledge, 1992.

Sankara, Thomas. "The Revolution Cannot Triumph Without the Emancipation of Women." Pp. 201–27 in *Thomas Sankara Speaks*. New York: Pathfinder Press, 1988.

Snow, David A., E. Burke Rochford, Jr., Steven K. Worden, and Robert D. Benford. "Frame Alignment Processes, Micromobilization, and Movement Participation." *American Sociological Review* 51 (August 1986): 464–81.

Toure, Sekou. "The Role of Women in the Revolution." *Black Scholar* (September-October 1983): 8–12.

Toure, Sekou. *Africa on the Move*. London: Panaf Books, 1979.

Wilkins, Fanon. "Which Way for Africans in the United States? The Seventh Pan African Congress and Beyond." *African Journal of Political Science* 1(1) (1996): 34–44.

Chapter Eleven

Talking Black, Talking Feminist
Gendered Micromobilization Processes in a Collective Protest against Rape

Aaronette M. White

The contemporary Black feminist movement took most of its shape during the late sixties and early seventies. Black feminist groups like the Combahee River Collective and the National Black Feminist Organization rose to the surface expressing their dissatisfaction with the sexism of Black civil rights organizations and the racism of white feminist organizations.[1] Contemporary Black[2] feminism has been described as the nexus between Black liberation and women's liberation movements.[3] Although Black feminism has ties to both the Black civil rights and women's liberation movements, it has its own distinct ideologies and notions of collective action, given its emphasis on Black nationalist, feminist, and socialist oriented struggles.[4]

The Black feminist movement does not mobilize through an institutionalized formal social movement organization. In fact, historically, most Black feminists fought (and many still fight) for gender equality through African American organizations.[5] Most recently, however, Black feminist collectives have operated through local communities in decentralized, often segmented ways referred to in the literature as "submerged networks."[6] Some informal networks include self-help groups, book clubs, "girlfriend" (women only) parties and gatherings, and explicit political education (or consciousness-raising) groups.[7] This chapter examines race, gender, and class factors regarding the mobilization strategies used by a local Black feminist collective in organizing a protest against rape within the African American community. The protest occurred

189

during the highly publicized appeals case of convicted rapist and professional boxer Mike Tyson and served as a springboard for antirape education. Organizers challenged rape-supportive discourse using a distinct Black feminist master frame that was influenced by structural as well as culturally engendered factors. Frame alignment processes are described here, with particular attention given to the dialectical relationship between organizers and supporters when frames are being negotiated. A coalition-focused view of the framing process is presented, and its usefulness in Black feminist collective action is underscored.

Theoretical Perspectives

Feminist standpoint epistemologies challenge how truth is known and identifies subjective experience as a critical source of social knowledge.[8] The notion that subjective experience and knowledge are central to our understanding of women and other oppressed groups rests on the assumption that oppressed groups have subjugated knowledges and perspectives, which are not reflected in the conceptual schemes of dominant groups.[9] Rather than seeking a single truth about a phenomenon, research guided by recent feminist standpoint epistemologies seeks to uncover the multifaceted nature of women's reality or "multiple truths" that are shaped by different sociopolitical contexts.

Black feminist standpoint epistemology "encompasses theoretical interpretations of Black women's reality by those who live it."[10] Black feminists are highly critical of dichotomous, hierarchical, and oversimplified additive models of oppression.[11] These models suggest that as Black women, they must identify as Black or women, women first and Black second, Black first and women second, or that their reality is simply "the Black experience" plus "the woman experience." Black feminist perspectives stress how various forms of gender, race, and class oppression interlock, forming a matrix of social domination.[12] Gender, race, and class are interrelated systems of oppression that profoundly affect Black women. I use Black feminist thought as a framework for the analysis and link it with literature on contemporary social movement theory to understand Black feminist collective action.

Until recently, many analysts of social movements focused on the role of formal social movement organizations and the external political processes and internal organizational dynamics that influenced institutional reform.[13] This approach inadvertently privileged white, middle-class, male-dominated organizations and emphasized structural factors as explanations for periodic shifts in social movement activity.[14] "New" social movement theorists have highlighted micromobilization factors and informal social movement communities in order to bring balance to the field.[15] Specifically, some contemporary theorists have analyzed the process by which consensus is formed and collective action mobilized.[16] In addition, others have analyzed how culture and gender-related factors affect micromobilization and the ultimate success of a movement.[17] I address these questions through a close analysis of the process of consensus formation and mobilization in grassroots movement.

This chapter highlights how Black feminist organizers incorporated racialized, gendered, and class-based mobilizing strategies in a collective protest against rape. I borrow extensively from Snow and colleagues' 1986 seminal work on frame alignment processes because it explicitly describes the processes I experienced as a participant observer. In addition to delineating how frame alignment theory applies to this case, I demonstrate how structural and culturally engendered factors shaped the framing processes generally and how racialized and gendered coalitions at the community level affected frame negotiations specifically. In what follows, I present an overview of the collective action. Then, I describe the structural and culturally engendered contexts that have both generated and inhibited Black feminist social movement activity. Finally, I describe particular frame alignment processes, related mobilizing strategies, and the aftermath of the collective action. A Black feminist frame transcends the frames of feminist and Black nationalist-civil rights social movements, when a coalition-focused approach to micromobilization was adopted.

The Protest

The rape trial and the appeals process regarding convicted rapist and heavyweight boxer Mike Tyson generated much public interest and debate. A disproportionate amount of public sentiment about the case reflected racist and sexist attitudes about rape, rape survivors, and rapists. Tyson's accuser, Desiree Washington, was a Black woman. Thus, within the African American community, denigrating comments about Black women and their credibility were often made on local Black radio talk shows and by prominent African American men in nationally televised interviews. One month after the announcement that Tyson's appeal had been filed and in response to public insensitivity toward the sexual abuse of Black girls and women, 92 African American women of St. Louis, Missouri, placed a full-page ad in a local weekly Black newspaper protesting against sexism and related ignorance surrounding rape (see Appendix). The first ad was printed on April 15, 1993.[18] A second ad was printed in the same Black weekly newspaper on October 21, 1993, one month after Mike Tyson's second appeal to the Indiana Supreme Court was denied.[19] This ad included the original list of 92 Black women's names and the additional names of 148 Black men supporters.

Letters that accompanied the protest statement explained that the purpose of the ad was to (1) educate the African American community about rape, (2) create dialogue about rape beyond the "mythical gutter wisdom" level, (3) educate the community about the multiple forms of oppression that Black women endure, (4) teach Black women to "speak out" about their realities without fear of repercussion, and, (5) provide support for the countless number of silent and outspoken rape survivors. Hence, an antirape campaign was launched that included obtaining signatures in support of the ad while simultaneously speaking to various Black community networks about racist and sexist rape myths. These initial efforts resulted in a rape-prevention speaker's bureau and a coalition of Black women and men concerned about sexual violence against women and other Black feminist issues. In order to fully grasp the significance of the campaign, activists' efforts must be placed within the proper historical and sociopolitical contexts.

Rape and Related Systems of Oppression

The Legacy

Analysts of grassroots movements have demonstrated that so-called single-issue protests are about more than just the single issue and are often linked to broader historical issues of power inequities.[20] Such is the case for the seemingly "single issue" of rape, which in the United States occurs in a context of male supremacy *and* white supremacy.[21] As a result of racist ideology developed to justify slavery, the history of rape in the United States has narrowly focused on the rape of white women by Black men.[22]

The emphasis on white victims and Black perpetrators reflects the prevailing racist stereotype that Black men's sexuality is bestial, criminal, wild, and uncontrollable.[23] Although many terrorist lynchings of Black men were driven by white men's fear of Black economic progress, lynchings of Black men were frequently justified by "the myth of the Black rapist" who preys on white women.[24] A related mythical belief is that Black women are chronically promiscuous and, as a result, cannot be raped.[25] This myth about Black women's sexuality was used to justify white men's sexual abuse of Black women during slavery.

Today, the public and the criminal justice system continue to treat the rape of Black women less seriously than the rape of white women.[26] Judges and white jurors generally impose harsher sentences for the rapes of white women.[27] The harshest sentences (capital punishment and maximum prison time) are reserved for Black men who have raped white women.[28] No man has ever been executed for the rape of a Black woman.[29]

Popular Sentiment and the Privileging of Black Men's Oppression

The differential impact that rape has on Black women and Black men creates considerable tension and ambivalence surrounding the topic in African American communities. On the one hand, African American women are highly vulnerable to rape victimization, less likely to report rapes, and less likely to take advantage of support services.[30] On the other hand, existing disparities in punishment, particularly between Black men and white men, is also a social justice issue and further alienates African Americans from the system.

Given these biases within the criminal justice system, rape is frequently seen as a form of racist oppression rather than sexist oppression among African Americans.[31] However, the history of false accusations of rape and thus the racist oppression of Black men is often highlighted, as opposed to the history of rape victimization among Black women. Although the question of whether Black women are victimized by rape more than Black men are victimized by false accusations of rape is an empirical question, the disproportionate rates of rape victimization among Black women and the fact that most rapes go unreported suggest that the former is more likely than the latter. Furthermore, the privileging of Black men's suffering ignores the fact that most Black women are raped by

Black men. Therefore, within these popular seemingly "race-based" analyses of rape (and within antiracist public discourse in general), Black men become the "default gender."[32] The rape trial of Mike Tyson painfully highlighted this reality.

Tyson's trial occurred on the heels of the highly publicized rape trial and acquittal of William Kennedy Smith. The different verdicts for the cases had a profound effect on African Americans. Many African Americans believed that Black men were being "set up by others" and targeted as failures in a racist conspiracy designed to keep them powerless.[33] The popular press suggested that a significant number of African American men and women believed that racist stereotypes about Black men's sexuality and a conspiracy against successful Black men had more to do with the guilty verdict handed down in the Mike Tyson rape trial than the evidence presented in court.[34] For some African Americans, Smith's acquittal and Tyson's conviction highlighted their race and class differences (Smith was white and from a wealthy background, while Tyson was Black and from a working-class-poor background). Many who supported leniency for Tyson contrasted his conviction with the acquittals of Smith and three white St. John's University students accused, but cleared, of raping a Black woman in New York City.[35]

Various prominent men in the African American community, such as filmmaker Spike Lee and former president of the National Baptist Convention the Reverend T. J. Jimerson, supported a "Free Mike Tyson" campaign in order to raise funds to support Tyson's appeal.[36] Most of these supporters were previously involved in letter-writing efforts and in circulating national petitions seeking leniency for Tyson before he was sentenced.[37] Tyson supporters saw him as a victim joining the ranks of Clarence Thomas and even District of Columbia Mayor Marion Barry as high-profile Black martyrs persecuted for behavior that white men get away with on a daily basis.[38] Supporters relied on sexist rape myths to justify their argument for the release of Tyson ("She was in his room so she must have wanted sex"). Disparaging remarks were made about Black women on various radio talk shows ("First Anita Hill, now Desiree Washington, why are Black women compromising Black men's upward mobility and embarrassing the Black community?").

Therefore, one year later on February 15, 1993, when the appeals hearing occurred and was announced by media sources, old wounds were opened and inflammatory issues were reignited. Members of a local Black feminist self-help group network began discussing their alternative perceptions of the case. Many Black women were concerned about the tendency within the African American community to emphasize "the powerless and endangered Black male," thereby reinforcing a male-centered definition of African American oppression. Most Black feminists believe the alarming statistics concerning Black men's suffering (e.g., homicide, unemployment, imprisonment, and illiteracy rates) should be seriously addressed. However, the allegation that Black men are being targeted for special oppression carries with it the implicit notion that African American women are exempt from special abuses and inadvertently renders the suffering of Black women invisible.[39] In addition, the misogynist charge that Black women are puppets of the power structure and play a role in a conspiracy against Black men blatantly ignores the sexism that Black women endure in support of "Black unity."[40] As a result, some Black women found it necessary to organize separately in order to address the sexism within Black communities.[41]

A local group of Black feminists in St. Louis, Missouri, decided to publicize their concerns about Tyson's appeals process by launching an anti-rape campaign designed to educate the Black community about harmful rape myths. Popular Black radio talk shows in St. Louis suggested that the local context mirrored the popular biases and "pro–Mike Tyson" sentiment characteristic of the national context. In addition, boxing is a popular sport in St. Louis, and its popularity is symbolized by the success of two Olympic medalists and professional Black boxers known as "the Spinks Brothers" (Leon and Michael Spinks). Organizers knew they were going against popular sentiment and were clearly outnumbered. However, they felt that dissident voices should be heard and in a public format. Organizers used the *New York Times* ad where over 1600 Black women supported Anita Hill as a model for how concerns should be framed and conveyed to the public.

The Contemporary Black Feminist Social Movement and Its Master Frame

Participants involved in collective action "frame or assign meaning to and interpret, relevant events and conditions in ways that are intended to mobilize potential adherents and constituents, to garner bystander support, and to demobilize antagonists."[42] Frames are cognitive understandings of certain issues, events, or problems that guide action.[43] Certain grievances are frequently expressed in Black feminist collective action frames. A number of such grievances were revealed in a historic statement in support of Anita Hill that appeared November 17, 1991, in the *New York Times* and six Black newspapers.[44]

The full-page statement was a national educational and fund-raising campaign launched by three Black feminists and a loose network of Black women.[45] It emphasized the importance of (1) highlighting the race, gender, and class implications of the hearings, (2) speaking out against any form of sexual abuse, and (3) countering myths about Black women's sexuality. Overall, the statement stressed the need to view Hill's mistreatment and Thomas's nomination as part of a larger framework of social injustice, linked to the dismantling of policies that protect "the rights of all women, poor and working class people, and the elderly."[46]

A Black feminist frame consistently acknowledges grievances or discontents regarding racism and its debilitating effects on African Americans.[47] Grievances or discontents regarding sexism and its debilitating effects on women are also acknowledged.[48] Speaking out against sexism, particularly men's violence against women, is characteristic of a feminist frame. A Black feminist frame, however, uniquely emphasizes how racism, sexism, and often class dynamics intersect and profoundly affect the lives of Black women.[49] Using the *New York Times* ad as a model, local Black feminist organizers decided to sponsor an ad that addressed popular misconceptions about issues related to the Tyson trial. Their first task was to frame the most critical issues.

Framing the Issues: Development of the Protest Statement

Snow and colleagues in 1986 identified four common frame alignment processes. *Frame transformation* is a process that occurs when organizers put forth ideas that radically challenge existing beliefs of potential recruits on an issue. *Frame amplification* is used by organizers to highlight how their interpretation of an issue is compatible with the underlying values and beliefs of potential supporters. *Frame extension* is used by organizers to expand the boundaries of their primary interests to additional interests of potential recruits as a strategy for increasing support. *Frame bridging* involves providing individuals who share similar grievances with information that persuades them to participate in the collective action. Core framing tasks include diagnosing a problem, proposing a solution, and engaging in a call to arms or stating a rationale for corrective action.[50] A frame's resonance is the degree to which it facilitates or constrains the mobilization of participants; thus, the greater the frame's resonance, the greater its mobilizing potential.[51] In the following sections I illustrate aspects of these processes and provide an insider's view of framing negotiations.

Core Framing Tasks

I worked on the core framing tasks with four other Black feminist primary organizers and a loose network of African American women in an organization called The Sisterhood; these women worked at a local Jesuit university during the period 1991–1994. Members organized a brown-bag-lunch series on topics of interests to Black women (i.e., breast cancer awareness, spirituality and emotional healing, Black women and psychotherapy, stress management, etc.). Members were mainly staff workers; however, there were a few active faculty and administrators. I was an active faculty member. Most of the women in The Sisterhood had prior experiences in antiracist and antisexist collective efforts, and many either knew about or had supported the *New York Times* ad. Even though our perceptions of the critical issues regarding the Tyson case were similar at the first meeting, we decided to gather additional information about the case before drafting our statement.

Some organizers were responsible for listening to various local radio talk shows and noting the most frequent comments about the appeals case. Others were responsible for gathering current and previous information from print media sources and noting the most common remarks about the 1993 appeals case and the 1992 trial. One person was responsible for gathering information about the *New York Times* ad and obtaining the *Court TV* video of the 1992 rape trial. I was asked to gather scientific information on rape statistics, rape myths, and historical information on rape and Black women. Everyone was encouraged to discuss the case with family and coworkers in order to gauge local popular sentiment about the case.

Data gathered from the various sources suggested that popular opinions and judgments covered three major themes: (1) the belief that there was a white conspiracy against prominent Black men that used Black women as pawns in "entrapment schemes"; (2) the idea that Black people should not "air their dirty (racial) laundry" in public regardless of whether a rape occurred; and (3) numerous misunderstandings about rape, rape survivors, and rapists.

We diagnosed the problem as a misunderstanding of the seriousness of rape in the African American community. This problem is due to an oversimplified analysis of oppression (racism as primary), the acceptance of rape myths, and other forms of sexism that silence rape survivors. Our prognosis included sociopolitical antirape education that emphasized (1) a race, gender, class analysis of rape and related issues, (2) replacing rape myths with facts about rape, and (3) encouraging Black women to stand up and speak out about sexual abuse and other forms of sexism. The rationale we provided for "standing up and speaking out" emphasized our moral obligation, given that misinformation about the sexual abuse of Black women "is an attack on our collective character" that allows "the physical and emotional scars that rape leaves on Black girls and women" to be ignored, and is an "insult not only to African American women but to African American men and all people concerned with social justice" (see Appendix).[52] Given the numerous misconceptions about rape, rape survivors, and rapists, a major portion of the statement had to challenge these false beliefs. Thus, frame transformation strategies were necessary.

Rape myths are "attitudes and beliefs that are generally false but are widely and persistently held, and that serve to deny and justify male sexual aggression against women."[53] We were determined to cease the view of rape as an unfortunate circumstance "to which only some unlucky women fall victim, to a conception that the sexual coercion of women is pervasive, multivariate, and wholly unacceptable in every form."[54] We countered rape myths with FBI statistics and social science research in an attempt to lend "empirical credibility" to our frame transformation efforts.[55] We relied on other frame alignment strategies to increase our statement's resonance.

In order to amplify our frame, we highlighted "social justice" as a value in the statement's introduction, mentioning how "comments we have heard regarding this case as an attack on our collective character and an insult not only to African American women but to African American men and all people who are concerned with social justice" (see Appendix). Social justice strikes a familiar chord with African Americans, given our ongoing civil rights struggles. We also highlighted in the introduction and conclusion what Snow and colleagues (1986) refer to as "beliefs about the necessity and propriety of standing up," reminding potential supporters that when we are silent "the various forms of oppression we experience are casually dismissed."[56]

We extended our Black feminist frame to address concerns that Black people have about the criminalization versus the rehabilitation of Black men in the prison system. We wanted to highlight how it is the Black working-class poor and illiterate who disproportionately populate prisons with a long-term presence. Given the debilitating conditions of racism, poverty, and alienation that many Black men grapple with prior to prison, the prison system needs some form of intervention that can counter such experiences. However, supporters of the statement agreed unequivocally that one cannot simply use racism, poverty, or anything else as a justification for rape. After organizers discussed an article about Tyson by Black feminist writer June Jordan (1992), we decided to capture some of the article's sentiment in our statement's conclusion.[57]

We pointed to the nonrehabilitative environment of U.S. prison systems and how our sufferings as Black women and men are interconnected. For example, many Black feminists realize that simply throwing Black men in these prison warehouses tends to further develop the criminal mind and one's sense of alienation. The lack of balance between punishment and rehabilitation only increases the chances of Black women's being the victims of these same men when they are eventually released! Rapists should be punished, but punishment alone will not deter rape given that it does not address the conditions of women's subordination that create a climate for rape. Hence, the statement emphasized how the lack of effective rehabilitation programs in the prison system means "men who rape will not get the help they need." It also demonstrated our understanding of the limitations of merely increasing rape convictions (especially given the racially biased way these convictions are meted out). Equally important, however, is the fact that addressing this issue demonstrated our understanding and continued acceptance of the well-known Afrocentric ethos "when one of us suffers, we all suffer."[58] Our concluding statement acknowledged how it is difficult for us to "rejoice" under these circumstances. The statement also declared "we will not, however, be silent about rape or excuse its perpetrators" (see Appendix).

Frame Bridging: Negotiations and Modifications

Frame bridging activities pointed out some of the shortcomings in our original statement and highlighted the dialectical relationship between organizers and supporters at various phases of a collective action. We "bridged our frame" by soliciting initial support of the statement and feedback from individual members of The Sisterhood and other known Black feminists in the St. Louis area. Many Black women were willing to support the statement and assist with further recruitment. Our initial recruitment efforts were successful probably due to the shared collective identity of members of these informal networks.[59] However, feedback from these supporters suggested that the statement was "too academic, too long, and addressed too many issues." Furthermore, there was disagreement on whether we should use the word *feminist*, include explicit socialist language when addressing class issues, defend a rape victim's right to financial compensation, and include Black men's names.

Terminology issues. Organizers can frame an issue in terms that render the frame inaccessible to all but a select few. This pitfall constrains mobilization efforts. Snow and Benford (1988) use the phrase "narrative fidelity" to describe the degree to which frames resonate with the "cultural narrations" or "stories, myths, and folk ideas" of potential supporters.[60]

Some early supporters suggested that we remove the word *feminist* and eliminate socialist jargon in order to make the statement more accessible to potential supporters, especially members of the Black working classes. Although contemporary Black feminist frames tend to be Black nationalist, feminist, and socialist, Black feminists are not a monolithic group.[61] Some Black women prefer the term *feminist* while others prefer the term *womanist* popularized by Alice Walker.[62] A number of Black women associate the term *feminist* with white-middle-class and/or lesbian women. Although socialist *principles* are familiar among many African Americans, socialist *jargon* may be less familiar and potentially alienating. The importance of the Black family, constant concern about "Black-on-Black crime," and ongoing discussions about the economic plight of Black communities are issues that resonate with existing cultural narratives and experiences of many African Americans. Thus, we used phrases like "mythical gutter wisdom about rape" and "rape as a Black-on-Black crime" to convey feminist ideology about rape, and phrases like "the importance of related economic issues" and "class dynamics" to subtly convey socialist ideas.

A major revision included changing the last sentence of the statement to "we speak out as your mothers, sisters, and daughters" versus the previous wording, "we speak out as Black feminists and as the allies of feminists." Using familial expressions (i.e., *sister, brother*) is very common in the Black community and emphasizes an Afrocentric ethos of interconnectedness.[63] By presenting feminist and socialist ideology in ways consistent with Black nationalist concerns about the Black family and crime in Black communities, we increased the statement's "narrative fidelity." By increasing the statement's narrative fidelity, we also increased its mobilizing potential to attract immediate supporters (signatories) and its potential to attract future support from readers once the ad was published.

Statement length and extraneous issues. Criticism about the statement's being "too long" and "addressing too many issues" led organizers to delete the section that addressed a rape survivor's right to pursue compensatory damages for pain and suffering through the civil courts system. Apologists for Tyson emphasized how Desiree Washington "set Tyson up to rape her just for the money, then she and her mother dumped the father and filed the civil suit."[64] We decided that addressing the multiple misogynist underpinnings of this argument was not in our interest and beyond the scope of our protest. Furthermore, we believed that persons espousing this argument were unlikely supporters. Finally, we thought that this issue directed attention away from the most popular misconceptions about rape. Snow and Benford (1988) mention how organizers often find themselves confronted with the problem of "frame over-extension" (206). Organizers must be careful not to include too many issues that are only incidental to their primary framework, thereby "muddying the waters" unnecessarily.

The "man question." The majority of Black feminists in our network supported the view that women gain a liberating sense of power by temporarily and strategically organizing separately from men. Most Black nationalist organizations also express this sentiment and organize separately from white people. However, a meeting was convened to discuss the issue because of the popular sentiment among Black feminists that we "need to struggle together with Black men against racism, while also struggling with Black men about their sexism."[65] Most of us agreed with Alice Walker's (1983) definition that a Black feminist is "not a separatist, except periodically, for health," and is "committed to survival and wholeness of entire people, male and female."[66] Many of us also believed that feminist revolution should not be solely "women's work" and that "men should assume some responsibility for actively struggling to end sexist oppression."[67]

We reached consensus (after an intense debate), deciding that men's names would not be included in the initial ad because we needed to benefit from the experience of standing alone and defining our reality without Black men's approval. We discussed our willingness to run a second ad including the names of supportive men if a group of men were willing to assist in face-to-face recruitment. Regarding the inclusion of white supporters, no debate was necessary. All organizers and initial supporters agreed that signatories should be African Americans since the statement was directed to the African American community. White signatories might arouse suspicion among African Americans about the intentions of organizers, given the historical association of rape with racism and related "cultural distrust" regarding the motives of white people.

The final, ninth draft. After heated debates, late-night conversations, seemingly endless caucusing, and numerous drafts, consensus was reached by the primary organizing committee's and initial supporters' accepting the ninth draft as final. Other modifications included an emphasis on "issues" as opposed to the "personalities" of Mike Tyson or Desiree Washington. We made the statement "less academic" and cumbersome by graphically creating a question-and-answer cutout section for the "rape myths–rape facts" part of the ad and by using the informal language of radio talk show callers when presenting each rape myth. These revisions potentially made the ad more accessible to a Black working-class audience than earlier versions. Furthermore, incorporating suggestions from initial supporters created a mobilizing atmosphere of democratic accountability and mutual respect—heated debates notwithstanding. The interaction between organizers and initial supporters was one of exchange, as opposed to one where organizers solely controlled the imparting of knowledge. "Framing is less like a completed symphony than like improvisational jazz: composers provide the initial 'head' for a jam session, but the improvisations depend on a group of players over whom they have little control."[68] My experiences as an organizer confirmed that this is an accurate and marvelous metaphor.

Recruitment Networks and Culturally Engendered Strategies

Some gender-segregated groups are fertile grounds for the growth of feminism and represent potential mobilizing networks for collective action.[69] Given the differential impact that rape has on Black women and Black men, the organizing committee decided that recruitment strategies should rely heavily on preexisting social networks of African American gender-segregated organizations. Other mobilizing strategies included engendering cultural rituals with potential women supporters and distributing culturally engendered literature to potential men supporters.

Women Supporters

Social networks. The goal was to gather at least 100 Black women's names in support of the ad in one month while the issue of Tyson's appeals case was salient in the minds of the public. Media sources had also suggested that a decision on the appeals case could be handed down in 4 to 6 weeks. Recruitment activities included mailings to known allies of Black feminists; an information packet (copy of the statement, a stamped envelope, and response sheet) was mailed to these potential supporters.

Face-to-face recruitment included presentations at the meetings of professional and sociopolitical Black women's organizations. We also targeted "girlfriend parties" (a local expression used for women-only social gatherings). These parties allowed Black women to pamper themselves and "hang out with the girls." Potluck dinners were common, and items such as jewelry, cosmetics, African American paintings, and lingerie were frequently advertised and sold. Some of the most elaborate girlfriend socials included an artistic presentation (usually poetry reading) by a Black woman, card games, business networking, and informal discussions. One member of The Sisterhood was also a member of this network and arranged for organizers to present at parties. I attended most of these activities and evaluated their effectiveness.

Successful strategies and the significance of rituals. Our face-to-face recruitment strategies at girlfriend parties and the meetings of sociopolitical organizations were evaluated as most successful in recruiting women supporters, based upon the number of supporters gathered from these

encounters. Recruitment drives at girlfriend gatherings were transformed into rap sessions and testimonials about how Black women have
been sexually abused across a variety of contexts (i.e., work, home,
church). Women shared their deepest, most painful stories about rape at
some of these events while others listened, cried, and offered rape survivors support. At another girlfriend party we informally adopted Sweet
Honey in the Rock's song "Women Should Be a Priority" as our protest
anthem and sang other songs that expressed Black feminist sentiment. A
Black woman poet at another gathering read poems that facilitated discussions about sexual harassment, rape, and how to heal emotional
wounds.

At recruitment sessions involving women members of sociopolitical
organizations, we delighted in the opportunity to pay homage to Black
women ancestors through "libation ceremonies" before reading the statement and answering questions. A libation ceremony is an African ritual
in which water is used to represent the spirits of the ancestors. As each
drop of water is poured from a vessel, members of the gathering are invited to call out the names of Black people (in this case Black women)
"who are no longer with us in the flesh but whose wisdom, courage, vision, and other qualities have had an impact on us." Women called out
the names of their mothers, grandmothers, "other mothers," teachers as
well as high-profile Black women like Harriet Tubman, Sojourner Truth,
and Audre Lorde.

Social movement theorists have noted how rituals can serve as important mechanisms for challenging dominant norms and mobilizing participants.[70] The Black liberation movement thrived on songs, poetry, rallies,
chants, and a host of other rituals to evoke certain emotions that drive
protest.[71] The feminist movement also uses a variety of rituals to produce
solidarity among women such as speakouts on rape, healing circles, and
"Take Back the Night" marches.[72] Rituals dramatize inequality and injustice; at the same time they allow feelings of "fear, shame, and depression to be transformed into feelings conducive to protest and activism
rather than resignation and withdrawal."[73] The rituals performed at
these meetings (libation ceremonies, testimonials, and singing) may have
increased the salience of a Black feminist perspective and identity in a
supportive environment. In addition, most of these women belonged to
organizations and networks that emphasized the empowerment of
women—economically, spiritually, emotionally, and physically (health-
wise). Combined, these embedded networks, direct contact with organiz-

ers, and the rituals created some of the important conditions for participation as described by recruitment analysts.[74]

Although allowing one's name to be printed in an ad against rape may seem like a simple, low-risk act, we were countering public sentiment and using a public forum to do so. Recall, there was strong opposition in the Black community against Desiree Washington for airing dirty (racial) laundry in public. McAdam and Paulsen (1993) mention how the ultimate decision to participate in a collective action also depends on "the absence of strong opposition from others on whom other salient identities depend." Our mobilization efforts were competing with this reality. For example, a woman at one of the girlfriend parties pulled me aside and said, "I agree with everything you said and I think I may even be a feminist, but there are too many men in my household who think Mike Tyson is a hero and if I signed that ad and they saw it, I would never hear the end of it."

We stopped gathering names exactly one month later, as planned. A total of 112 women supported the ad; however, only 92 women wanted their names printed. Thus, ten women supported the ad but requested that their names not be printed. Two of the most common reasons women gave for not wanting their names printed were fear of reprisals by Black men and "not wanting people to think that they weren't loyal to the [race] Black community."

The First Ad Is Printed and Black Men Offer Support

The ad was printed in the April 15–21, 1993, edition of the *St. Louis American*, a Black weekly newspaper. This paper was chosen over the major St. Louis daily newspaper and two other local Black weekly newspapers for several reasons. This particular Black weekly was the only free newspaper at the time, it had the widest readership, it was the most accessible, and organizers knew the publisher. Moreover, the intent of organizers and supporters was to increase dialogue about rape among women and men in the African American community. Thus, printing the ad in the most popular Black newspaper was congruent with these interests. This newspaper was freely distributed on college campuses, in grocery stores, restaurants, movie theaters, and a variety of other public locations in Black middle-class and working-class neighborhoods.

Organizers received a few letters from men and women commending us on the ad and requesting that we add their names. One local radio talk show discussed the ad with listeners when a caller asked the commentator what he thought about "those misguided women who placed that ad in the paper about Mike Tyson." Another local radio talk show invited organizers on their show to discuss relevant issues. Given the verbal support of men via letters and phone calls, we felt we could mobilize enough men to run a second ad. We knew we still represented a minority perspective; however, we believed it was important to expose people to an alternative viewpoint and rape prevention education. We made plans to publish a second ad.

Recruitment of Supportive Men

The organizing committee decided that they would assist in recruitment mailings, however, face-to-face recruitment would be the primary responsibility of Black men. The rationale was that Black men should assume their share of responsibility for the "emotional work" involved in debating the issue of rape, particularly among their peers. A Black man who was a community organizer and university student expressed the desire to organize the campaign for men's support of the ad. He belonged to several grassroots organizations, had taken women's and Black studies courses, was known among organizers, and was a native of St. Louis.

The primary organizing committee for the first ad decided to assist in two major mailings. A package of cultural and gender-sensitive propaganda was created that included a copy of the newspaper ad with the women's names, a copy of an editorial by Edward Lewis (CEO and publisher of *Essence* magazine) denouncing the Free Mike Tyson campaign, and a letter from the organizing committee.[75] The letter attempted to dissuade internecine fighting among Black women and Black men about who is the most oppressed and borrowed extensively from Black feminist writer Pearl Cleage's booklet on sexism in the Black community:

> Although Black women can benefit from the experience of standing up and speaking for ourselves, any war against racism, sexism, and economic oppression must be fought *together* by Black women and Black men. The ad does not support petty politics about who is "the most oppressed" within the group. The ad simply addresses the *differential* impact of oppression on Black women. Being Black and male isn't any worse than being Black and female, it's just different. Black men get shot disproportionately, Black women get raped disproportionately. We all suffer due to multilayered forms of oppression. Debates about who is most victimized

by the system is nonproductive, divisive and only takes us deeper into re-actionary victimhood.[76]

The letter maintained aspects of the African ethos that suggests "what affects one of us, affects all of us; I am, because we are."[77] It amplified values of a Black nationalist–civil rights frame by emphasizing the inter-connectedness of our suffering as Black people and the interconnected-ness of our struggles. The letter's feminist aspect highlighted the preva-lence of rape. However, the letter maintained the distinctive core of a Black feminist frame by highlighting "how the multilayered forms of op-pression" must be fought, and those include (but are not limited to) racism, sexism, and economic oppression. Information packets were sent to every woman supportive of the first ad with a request to share the in-formation with any Black man or men they thought might support the ad. A second mailing of packets targeted chairpersons of local Black men's service organizations.

Black men organized face-to-face recruitment. They approached gen-der-segregated grassroots organizations that worked with African Amer-ican boys and young men such as Black male role-model programs and rites of passage "manhood" training programs. Men-only sessions were scheduled, and materials included in the information packet were hotly debated. Our organizer was affiliated with most of these organizations. He also had a team of university students recruiting Black men on college campuses. Black feminist organizers had little face-to-face contact with men during this recruitment phase. Interviews with the organizer sug-gested that he recruited members of preexisting social networks where he had considerable influence.[78]

The Second Ad Is Printed and the Next Phase of the Antirape Campaign Is Launched

Given the meager contact that we had with most of the men, a primary organizer and I called every man whose name we received in support of the ad to verify his support, the spelling of his name, and his address. After two months of organizing, a total of 148 men's names were gath-ered and printed with the names of the initial Black women supporters. The ad was delayed for three weeks due to unforeseen complications with the publisher about space limitations. It was finally published on October 21, 1993, one month after Mike Tyson's second appeal was denied.[79]

After the second ad was printed, a Black man who was a columnist for the major (white) newspaper in St. Louis requested an interview with organizers to discuss the ad, rape myths, and the response of the African American community to Tyson's case. For the next year, organizers spoke to community organizations about rape prevention and organized ongoing men's and women's groups to discuss the race, gender, and class complexities of rape. This later phase of the antirape campaign was a welcomed but unanticipated outcome of our initial efforts and allowed us to delve further into the issues presented in the ad. The initial campaign also provided us with a network of women and men who advocated feminism and supported community activities (e.g., panel discussions, lectures, speakouts) that we sponsored.

Conclusion

Oppressed groups have subjugated knowledges and perspectives which are not reflected in the conceptual schemes of dominant groups.[80] Thus, in order to uncover such perspectives, each group must be allowed to speak from its own partial, situated reality.[81] Black feminist organizers publicized their reality by launching an antirape campaign that included obtaining signatures in support of a full-page ad while simultaneously educating the Black community about racist and sexist rape myths. What began as a protest and educational campaign about misconceptions concerning Mike Tyson's appeals trial became a broader story about how rape and its relationship to overlapping systems of oppression profoundly affect Black women and Black men. However, Black women and Black men experience the effects of these structural factors differently. A coalition-focused approach to the framing process led to a distinct Black feminist frame.

The protest statement was informed by Black nationalist–civil rights and feminist social movement frames. For example, aspects of the statement that emphasized social justice, concerns about Black-on-Black crime, the criminalization versus the rehabilitation of convicted felons, and Afrocentric humanism ("I am, because we are") are characteristic of a contemporary Black nationalist–civil rights frame with Black-working-class sensitivities. The emphasis on the prevalence of rape, the rights of women to speak out about sexual abuse, and feminist perspectives on rape myths is characteristic of a feminist frame. Thus, a distinct Black feminist master frame emerged with its blend of race, gender, and class dynamics in the analysis of rape.

All four frame alignment processes outlined by Snow and colleagues (1986) were utilized, and frame resonance was maximized by using informal language that was congruent with the cultural narratives and experiences of potential supporters across various socioeconomic strata. However, Black feminist organizers also used explicit racialized and gendered recruitment strategies in significant ways. For example, only African Americans were recruited since the campaign targeted the African American community. Furthermore, women engaged in face-to-face recruitment with potential women supporters and men engaged in face-to-face recruitment with men supporters at meetings of gender-segregated organizations. Women organizers used gendered cultural rituals to increase the salience of a Black feminist collective identity during recruitment drives. Men recruiters distributed culturally engendered literature that directly challenged the privileging of Black men's suffering. However, these same materials reconstructed the different gendered experiences of African Americans into a broader experience of shared suffering. Finally, the ad was published in a popular Black weekly newspaper widely distributed in Black middle- and working-class settings. These strategies, combined with the direct contact potential supporters had with organizers, may have enhanced participation. However the mobilizing potential of organizers' approach to framing negotiations merits special attention.

Frame bridging processes highlighted the dialectical relationship organizers had with supporters during certain phases of social movement activity. For example, feedback from initial supporters suggested shortcomings in at least eight earlier drafts of the protest statement. Initial drafts were perceived as overly academic, too lengthy, and potentially alienating due to explicit feminist and socialist jargon. A coalition-focused approach to the framing process was adopted that emphasized the interaction between organizers and initial supporters as one of exchange and democratic accountability. Organizers brought knowledge and information to the framing process; however, they also respected and incorporated the knowledge and information that supporters brought to the situation. Although the relationship had its tensions, organizers felt that modifications did not compromise the major purposes of the ad. In fact, initial feedback and resultant modifications increased the narrative fidelity, and thus the mobilizing potential of the ad. These Black feminist mobilizing strategies vividly demonstrate how frame alignment processes are shaped by race, gender, and class macrolevel factors that are further negotiated by racialized and gendered microlevel factors in complex ways.

On a practical note, the antirape campaign and the support of the full-page ad demonstrate that when the experience of gender is linked with equally elaborate systems of race and class, Black women as well as Black men are willing to participate in antirape collective action. Furthermore, when a coalition-focused approach to the framing process is adopted, a Black feminist frame can transcend the master frames of the Black nationalist–civil rights and feminist social movements and serve as the nexus between both movements.

Appendix

Rape in the African American Community

As Black women, we are deeply troubled by the oversimplification of the Mike Tyson–Desiree Washington rape case offered by certain producers of the media, supporters of the "Free Mike Tyson" campaign, and members of society at large. This is not a statement about who was right, who was wrong, who won and who lost. When Black men and Black women are forced to fight this way with one another we all lose. It is clear to us that both Mike Tyson and Desiree Washington are going to have to do a few things differently in the future. We are most bothered by the one-sided sexist assumptions being made about rape in the African American community specifically and Black women generally. This case and its related underlying issues involve race, gender, and class dynamics. We interpret some of the comments we have heard regarding this case as an attack on our collective character and an insult not only to African American women, but to African American men and all people concerned with social justice.

We resent the fact that many people in our community consistently feel that when an African American woman tells her story of sexual abuse, harassment, or rape in connection with a prominent African American man, that she *obviously* has to be a part of a "set up," deserving of the maltreatment, or she is lying. The possibility of her actually being raped, harassed, or abused isn't even considered by many! It has become apparent that Black women who speak of these matters are not likely to be believed or are indirectly asked by other African Americans to place race issues first and gender issues second. We are concerned about the dangerous message this kind of attitude sends to any woman who might contemplate reporting a rape. We find race and gender issues inseparable and will address them simultaneously along with related economic issues.

When Black-on-Black crime is mentioned, rarely do we discuss the sexual brutalization of Black women. Missing from the Black liberation movement is an understanding of rape and the physical and emotional scars that it leaves on Black girls and women. If a woman uses poor judgment, that does not mean that she deserves to be raped. Men are constantly telling us we should trust them, and when we trust them and they rape us, they act like it is our fault. We too are tired of the mixed messages. We are also tired of the "mythical gutter wisdom" about rape and want it replaced by the facts:

Mythical Gutter Wisdom: "Mike Tyson is rich and popular. He doesn't have to rape to get sex. There are too many women who he can get sex from without a fight!"

Facts About Rape: Most rapists have active sex lives. Thus, their need is not for sexual fulfillment but for power and control over their victims. Rape is not just sex, but violence committed though sexual activity. Rape is a *crime* motivated by anger, the need to feel powerful, and the need to control and dominate others.

Mythical Gutter Wisdom: "Desiree was allegedly kissing and embracing him earlier that day. She must have wanted sex."

Facts About Rape: One should not assume that the desire for affection is the same as the desire for sex. A person may be interested in some sexual contact other than intercourse. Do not assume that the other person wants the same degree of sexual intimacy as you. Everyone has the right to say "NO" to sexual activity, regardless of what has preceded it and to have that "NO" respected. Sexual excitement does not justify forced sex. Forced sex is rape.

Mythical Gutter Wisdom: "What was Desiree doing in his room at that time in the morning? She must have wanted to have sex. No one is that naïve! She was asking for it."

Facts About Rape: Psychologists have found that people hate to admit they are vulnerable. As a result, they tend to "blame the victim" for negative or criminal events instead of the perpetrator. This helps people falsely believe that certain horrible things couldn't possibly happen to them and that bad things simply happen to bad people. Myths like these suggest that rape is the justifiable punishment for poor judgement! Obviously, when you trust someone, you feel there is no need to believe they might rape you, regardless of the time. In at least 50% of all rapes, women know their attackers. Even in situations where a woman is flirtatious or dressed "provocatively" she is not asking for *rape*. No person asks for or deserves such an assault. Being in a man's hotel room, car, or apartment does not mean a woman has agreed to have sex with him. Women are not responsible for men's aggressive sexual impulses and actions. Men are responsible for their impulses and actions and need to accept such responsibility.

Mythical Gutter Wisdom: "If Desiree was raped, how could she have been dancing like that the next day?"

Facts About Rape: There is no single "normal" reaction to rape. Reactions vary according to the victim's "pre-assault" mental state and values, the nature of the assault, and the support system she has available after the assault. A woman may show emotions or *appear* calm after the attack.

Mythical Gutter Wisdom: "Women are always lying about rape."

Facts About Rape: Studies show that only 2% of rape calls are false reports, which is no more than the false reports of other felonies. One out of four women will be raped in her lifetime, but only one out of ten will report it. Rape is the most underrepresented and least successfully prosecuted crime.

Mythical Gutter Wisdom: "Most rapes involve Black men and White women anyway."

Facts About Rape: FBI statistics show that 3% of rapes involve Black men and White women and 4% involve White men and Black women. Most rapes involve a rapist and victim of the same race. Black women are twice as likely to be raped than White women and are less likely to report.

Mythical Gutter Wisdom: "If women were more careful, they wouldn't get raped."

Facts About Rape: Women can take precautions and learn how to protect themselves, but this is no guarantee that they won't be raped. This myth implies that women cause rape. For the most part, men rape and they can stop rape by accepting their responsibility not to harm another person, by accepting a woman's "no" as meaning "no," and by being sensitive to women who are unsure whether or not they want to have sex. A man can also prevent rape by speaking up and asking a woman to clarify what she wants if he feels he is getting a double message, by remembering that a woman who turns him down for sex is not necessarily rejecting him as a person, and by ultimately accepting responsibility for his actions. When men don't do these things, they run the risk of a charge of rape.

We are concerned about the historical vulnerability of Black women that includes the idea that the sexual abuse of a Black woman is not really a crime. We understand how this male supremacist society creates rapists. Therefore, we do not necessarily rejoice when a Black man is imprisoned for this crime. We know that prisons are not really institutions of rehabilitation, and we are concerned that men who rape will not get the help they need. We will not, however, be silent about rape or excuse its perpetrators. We speak out as your mothers, sisters, and daughters and we will continue to speak out when the various forms of oppression we experience are casually dismissed.

NOTES

I gratefully acknowledge the support of the following organizations: The Sisterhood of St. Louis University, the Organization for Black Struggle, St. Louis members of the National Black Women's Health Project, The African American Role Models, Better Family Life Inc., and the All-African People's Revolutionary Party. This essay is reprinted by kind permission of Sage Publications from *Gender Society* 13 (1999).

1. Paula Giddings, *When and where I enter: The impact of Black women on race and sex in America* (New York: Bantam, 1984), 299–324; E. Frances White, "Listening to the voices of Black feminism," *Radical America* 18 (1984): 7–25.

2. The word *Black* is used interchangeably with *African American* throughout this article. However, the usage of racial terminology in this article in no way supports biological, deterministic definitions of race. Social constructionist perspectives are accepted regarding the historic use of racial terminology, the shifting meaning of race, and the role that politics and ideology play in shaping such meanings. The first part of this chapter's title is a paraphrase of bell hook's (1989) book entitled *Talking back: Thinking feminist, thinking Black*.

3. White, "Voice of Black Feminism."

4. Combahee River Collective, "A Black feminist statement"; bell hooks, *Feminist theory: From margin to center* (Boston: South End, 1984); Barbara Omolade, *The rising song of African American women* (New York: Routledge, 1994).

5. Patricia Hill Collins, *Black feminist thought: Knowledge, consciousness, and empowerment* (New York: Routledge, 1991); Giddings, *When and where I enter*.

6. Alberto Melucci, *Nomads of the present: Social movements and individual needs in contemporary society* (Philadelphia: Temple University Press, 1989); V. Taylor and N. Whittier, "Analytical approaches to social movement culture: The culture of the women's movement." In *Social movements and culture*, edited by H. Johnston and B. Klandermans (Minneapolis: University of Minnesota Press, 1995).

7. Byllye Y. Avery, "Breathing life into ourselves: The evolution of the National Black Women's Health Project." In *The Black women's health book: Speaking for ourselves*, edited by E. C. White (Seattle: Seal, 1990); bell hooks, *Sisters of the yam: Black women and self-recovery* (Boston: South End, 1993); Omolade, *Rising song of African American women*.

8. For example, Collins, *Black feminist thought*, and Sandra Harding, *The science question in feminism* (Ithaca: Cornell University Press, 1986).

9. Collins, *Black feminist thought*.

10. Ibid., 22.

11. S. M. James, and A. P. A. Busia, eds., *Theorizing Black feminisms: The visionary pragmatism of Black women* (New York: Routledge, 1993).

12. Collins, *Black feminist thought*; bell hooks, *Talking back: Thinking feminist, thinking Black* (Boston: South End, 1989); James and Busia, *Theorizing Black feminisms*; Omolade, *Rising song of African American women*.

13. H. Johnston and B. Klandermans, eds., *Social movements and culture* (Minneapolis: University of Minnesota Press, 1995); Carol McClurg Mueller, "Building social movement theory." In *Frontiers in social movement theory*, edited by A. D. Morris and C. Mueller (New Haven: Yale University Press, 1992).

14. A. Bookman and S. Morgen, eds., *Women and the politics of empowerment* (Philadelphia: Temple University Press, 1988); Mueller, "Building social movement theory"; Nancy Whittier, *Feminist generations: The persistence of the radical women's movement* (Philadelphia: Temple University Press, 1995).

15. Johnston and Klandermans, *Social movements and culture*; Mueller, "Building social movement theory"; Whittier, *Feminist generations.*

16. William Gamson, "The social psychology of collective action." In *Frontiers in social movement theory*, edited by A. D. Morris and C. M. Mueller (New Haven: Yale University Press, 1992); Bert Klandermans, "The social construction of protest and multi-organizational fields." In *Frontiers in social movement theory*, edited by A. D. Morris and C. Mueller (New Haven: Yale University Press, 1992); Sidney Tarrow, "Mentalities, political cultures, and collective action frames."

17. Bernice McNair Barnett, "Invisible Southern Black women leaders in the civil rights movement: The triple constraints of gender, race, and class," *Gender & Society* 7 (1993): 162–82; Belinda Robnett, "African-American women in the civil rights movement, 1954–1965: Gender, leadership, and micromobilization," *American Journal of Sociology* 101 (1996): 1661–93; V. Taylor and N. Whittier, "Collective identity in social movement communities: Lesbian feminist mobilization." In *Frontiers in social movement theory*, edited by A. D. Morris and C. M. Mueller. New Haven: Yale University Press, 1992.

18. "Rape in the African American community," *St. Louis American*, 15 April, 1993.

19. "Rape in the African American community," *St. Louis American*, 21 October, 1993.

20. Celene Krauss, "Women and toxic water protests: Race, class and gender as resources of resistance," *Qualitative Sociology* 16 (1993): 247–62; Karen Brodkin Sacks, "Gender and grassroots leadership." In *Women and the politics of empowerment*, edited by A. Bookman and S. Morgen (Philadelphia: Temple University Press, 1988).

21. Kimberle Crenshaw, "The marginalization of sexual violence against Black women," *National Coalition Against Sexual Assault Journal* 2 (1994): 1–3, 5–6, 15; Angela Y. Davis, *Violence against women and the ongoing challenge to racism* (Latham, N.Y.: Kitchen Table, 1985); Nancy A. Matthews, *Confronting rape: The feminist anti-rape movement and the state* (New York: Routledge, 1994).

22. Davis, *Violence against women*; Jennifer Wriggins, "Rape, racism and the law," *Harvard Women's Law Review* 6 (1983): 103–141; Gail E. Wyatt, "The socio-cultural context of African American and white American women's rape," *Journal of Social Issues* 48 (1992): 77–91.

23. Giddings, *When and where I enter*; Davis, *Violence against women.*

24. Giddings, *When and where I enter*; Davis, *Violence against women.*

25. Davis, *Violence against women;* Wriggins, "Rape, racism and the law."

26. Crenshaw, "The marginalization of sexual violence"; Matthews, *Confronting rape;* Wriggins, "Rape, racism and the law."

27. Susan Estrich, *Real rape* (Cambridge: Harvard University Press, 1987); Wriggins, "Rape, racism and the law."

28. C. R. Mann and L. H. Selva, "The sexualization of racism: The Black as rapist and White justice," *Western Journal of Black Studies* 3 (1979): 168–77; Wriggins, "Rape, racism and the law."

29. Mann and Selva, "The sexualization of racism"; V. Schneider and J. O. Smykla. "A summary analysis of 'Executions in the United States, 1608–1987: The Espy file.'" In *The death penalty in America: Current research*, edited by R. M. Bohm. (Cincinnati: Anderson, 1991).

30. Collins, *Black feminist thought;* Matthews, *Confronting rape;* Wyatt, "The socio-cultural context of African American and White women's rape."

31. Crenshaw, "The Marginalization of sexual violence against Black women."

32. Ibid. Of course, in mainstream feminist discourse, white is the (unarticulated) default race. Thus, the experiences of white women are often privileged.

33. Earl Ofari Hutchinson, *The assassination of the Black male image* (New York: Simon & Schuster, 1996); Pamela Newkirk, "Tears for Tyson's fall," *Sports Illustrated*, 24 February 1992.

34. "National petitions seek leniency for Mike Tyson," *Jet,* 30 March 1992; Newkirk, "Tears for Tyson's fall"; Sonja Steptoe, "A damnable defense," *Sports Illustrated*, 24 February 1992.

35. "National petitions seek leniency for Mike Tyson"; Newkirk, "Tears for Tyson's fall."

36. *Christian Century*, "Tyson support defended," 15 April 1992.

37. "National petitions seek leniency for Mike Tyson."

38. Steptoe, "A damnable defense."

39. Barbara Ransby, "The gang rape of Anita Hill and the assault upon all women of African descent." In *Court of Appeal: The Black community speaks out on the racial and sexual politics of Thomas vs. Hill,* edited by R. Chrisman and R. L. Allen (New York: Ballantine, 1992).

40. Omolade, *Rising song of African American women;* Ransby, "The gang rape of Anita Hill."

41. Omolade, *Rising song of African American women;* Joy James, "Anita Hill: Martyr heroism and gender abstractions." In *Court of Appeal: The Black community speaks out on the racial and sexual politics of Thomas vs. Hill*, edited by R. Chrisman and R. L. Allen (New York: Ballantine, 1992).

42. D. A. Snow and R. D. Benford, "Ideology, frame resonance, and participant mobilization," *International Social Movement Research* 1 (1988): 198.

43. Gamson, "The social psychology of collective action" ; D. A. Snow, E. B. Rochford, S. K. Worden, and R. D. Benford, "Frame alignment processes, micro-

mobilization, and movement participation," *American Sociological Review* 51 (1986): 464–81; Snow and Benford, "Ideology, frame resonance, and participant mobilization"; Tarrow, "Mentalities, political cultures, and collective action frames."

44. "African American women in defense of ourselves," *New York Times*, 17 November 1991.

45. James, "Anita Hill"; Ransby, "The gang rape of Anita Hill."

46. "African American women in defense of ourselves."

47. Giddings, *When and where I enter*; hooks, *Talking back*; Omolade, *Rising song of African American women.*

48. Davis, *Violence against women*; Omolade, *Rising song of African American women*; Ransby, "The gang rape of Anita Hill."

49. Collins, *Black feminist thought*; hooks, *Talking back*; James and Busia, *Theorizing Black feminisms.*

50. Snow and Benford, "Ideology, frame resonance, and participant mobilization," 199.

51. Snow and Benford, "Ideology, frame resonance, and participant mobilization."

52. Our statement mirrored the Black feminist frame of the *New York Times* ad by (1) emphasizing the need for a race, gender, and class analysis of issues, (2) describing public responses to the case as "an attack on our collective character," and (3) by championing Black women's efforts to speak out about sexual abuse from our standpoint.

53. K. A. Lonsway and L. F. Fitzgerald, "Rape myths: In review," *Psychology of Women Quarterly* 18 (1994): 134.

54. Wriggins, "Rape, racism and the law," 140.

55. Snow and Benford, "Ideology, frame resonance, and participant mobilization."

56. Ibid., 469.

57. June Jordan, "Requiem for the champ," *Progressive,* 15 April 1992.

58. Molefi Kete Asante, *The Afrocentric idea* (Philadelphia: Temple University Press, 1987); F. L. Hord and J. S. Lee, *I am, because we are: Readings in Black philosophy* (Amherst: University of Massachusetts Press, 1995).

59. D. Friedman and D. McAdam, "Collective identity and activism: Networks, choices, and the life of a social movement," in *Frontiers in social movement theory,* edited by A. D. Morris and C. M. Mueller (New Haven: Yale University Press, 1992).

60. Snow and Benford, "Ideology, frame reference, and participant mobilization," 210.

61. Combahee River Collective, "A Black feminist statement"; James and Busia, *Theorizing Black feminisms*; Omolade, *Rising song of African American women.*

62. Alice Walker, *In search of our mother's gardens* (New York: Hartcourt Brace Jovanovich, 1983).

63. Asante, *The Afrocentric idea;* Hord and Lee, *I am because we are.*

64. Jennet Conant, "Desiree vs. Mike (round two)," *Mademoiselle* 99 (1993): 188–91.

65. Combahee River Collective, "A Black feminist statement," 16.

66. Walker, *In search of our mothers' gardens,* xi.

67. hooks, *Feminist theory,* 67.

68. Charles Tilly, "Speaking your mind without elections, surveys, or social movements," *Public Opinion Quarterly* 47 (1983): 463.

69. For example, hooks, *Sisters of the yam;* Verta Taylor, "The revolution from within: Gendering social movement theory." In V. Taylor, *Rock-a-by-baby: Feminism, self-help, and postpartum depression* (New York: Routledge, 1996).

70. Taylor and Whittier, "Analytical approaches to social movement culture."

71. Giddings, *When and where I enter.*

72. Taylor and Whittier, "Analytical approaches to social movement culture."

73. Ibid., 178.

74. D. Friedman and D. McAdam, "Collective identity and activism"; D. McAdam and R. Paulsen, "Specifying the relationship between social ties and activism," *American Journal of Sociology* 99 (1993): 640–67.

75. See Edward Lewis, "What it means to be a Black man," *Essence,* June 1992.

76. Pearl Cleage, *Mad at Miles: A Blackwoman's guide to truth* (Southfield, Mich.: Cleage Group, 1990), 38.

77. Asante, *The Afrocentric idea;* Hord and Lee, *I am because we are.*

78. Survey responses of women and men supporters regarding why they supported the ad are analyzed in A. M. White, *I am because we are: Collective identity among African American women and men antirape activists,* book manuscript currently under review. See A. M. White, C. A. Potgieter, M. J. Strube, S. Fisher, and E. Umana, "An African-centered, Black feminist approach to understanding attitudes that counter social dominance," *Journal of Black Psychology* 23 (1997): 398–420, for additional information on the attitudes of men supporters. See A. M. White, M. J. Strube, and S. Fisher, "A Black feminist model of rape myth acceptance: Implications for anti-rape research and anti-rape advocacy in Black communities," *Psychology of Women Quarterly* in press, for additional information on the attitudes of women supporters.

79. On August 6, 1993, seven days after recruitment for men's names had begun, the Indiana Court of Appeals denied Tyson's first appeal. Tyson's second appeal, to the Indiana Supreme Court, was denied on September 23, 1993. Tyson was released from prison March 25, 1995, after serving 3 years of his 6-year term.

80. Collins, *Black feminist thought.*

81. Ibid.

Chapter Twelve

ONAMOVE
African American Women Confronting the Prison Crisis

Jennifer E. Smith

We say the words "onamove"
because that's what we are
and that's what we want to encourage
all of you to be—onamove.
Not to stagnate,
not to sit back in apathy and accept illusions.
> —Ramona Africa, survivor of the MOVE
> bombing and ex-prisoner

One by One, Two by Two: The Emergence of the Prison Crisis

The mass incarceration of African Americans exploded in 1972 with the rise of the Black Power movement and the decline of civil rights activism. There were five times more people imprisoned in 1995 than in 1972 (Committee to End the Marion Lockdown 1995; Bureau of Justice Statistics 1960–1995). The prison crisis has erupted not only because of the startling numbers of individuals under the control of the criminal justice system but because of the disproportionate ratio of imprisoned African Americans. The injustice of the criminal justice system—in recent years, largely facilitated by the U.S. war on crime and escalated by the passing of parts of the Omnibus Crime Bill—has resulted in disparity along both racial and class lines.[1] This inequality is most pronounced and most evident in terms of sentencing. For example, crack cocaine dealers and users—mostly poor and Black offenders—are much more likely to receive harsher sentences than those who use powder cocaine. The latter, largely white and middle class, experience far lesser legal consequences, particularly in terms of punitive punishment resulting in time behind bars, than do the former (Tucker 1997). The targeting of African Americans by the criminal justice system, in fact, is traceable through examination of the epidemic-like rise in incarceration figures. The number of Blacks in prison has gone from 146,900 in 1980 to 541,900 in 1995, and the number of Blacks on probation and parole from 410,000 to 1,395,000 (Lotke 1997).

In the Tradition: Linking Arms in Dangerous Times

While far fewer Black females, at least for now, are incarcerated than Black males, African American women, like Ida Wells-Barnett, who led a crusade against lynching (Duster 1970; Thompson 1990), have a tradition of organizing against repressive social and political conditions. Riding a wave of momentum generated for prisoners' rights by the '60s civil rights movement, the challenges of the U.S. prison crisis are being met head-on by the activism of African American women (Walker 1987). At the grassroots level, African American women have been involved in frontline struggle that includes relentless resistance to mass incarceration, political imprisonment and police repression through organizing protests, lobbying for changes in sentencing guidelines, working with legislatures, educating the public, forming self-help groups and initiating crime-prevention programs.

Yet African American women's activism should not be defined only within traditionally rigid realms. This means that it extends beyond the scope of the *Merriam Webster's Collegiate Dictionary* definition of activism: "a doctrine or practice that emphasizes direct vigorous action [as in mass demonstration] esp. in support of or in opposition to one side of a controversial issue." Every day rebellions are a crucial part of resisting. As feminist scholar Patricia Hill Collins (1990) asserts in referring to previous movements, "without this key part of Black women's activism, the struggle to transform American education, economic, and political institutions could not have been sustained" (140). Her suggestion that

"African Americans' resistance to racial oppression could not have occurred without an accompanying struggle for group survival" is absolutely true when applied in describing the role Black women have
played in minimizing the intended affects of punitive punishment—deha-
bilitative institutionalization through a process of disassociation.

While broadening the definition of Black women's activism to include
behind-the-scenes women, this certainly does not consider the aiding of
misogynist behavior as such. For example, codependency on a prisoner
who verbally abuses or manipulates through inconsiderate and unrea-
sonable demands would not be included. Specifically, the activism referred to comes in the form of, for instance, spontaneous verbal protest
to a correctional officer or counselor over an incident perceived as unfair.

One of the most common ways African American women involve
themselves at the grassroots level is through prison ministries often affiliated with their church. At this stage of involvement, activism often includes visiting, counseling or writing inmates. Participation by African
American women is also higher in the religious arena because, first, it is
an essential part of meeting moral and spiritual commitments; second,
prison officials find these groups less threatening to the safety of the institution; and finally, the protection of the constitutional rights of inmates related to religious freedom gives religious clergy members and
other representatives more access than the general public to these institutions. Some outreach services even have special training sessions for
volunteers. For a few African American women, active interest through
organized religious activities—after ascertaining more knowledge on the
atrocities of the prison system—can lead to involvement with some of
the local organizations. For example, coming in contact with an astute
and literate prisoner such as Annette Sanders (1996), an African American female, who writes of the plight of HIV-infected prisoners and the
inadequate health care in prison, can politicize one to higher levels of
organized activism.

However, because so much of religious indoctrination focuses on good
and evil, rather than cause and effect, politicization is likely to be limited
in the range and scope of the process. This reality is unfortunate because
African American women are involved at the grassroots level in larger
numbers than African American men. In fact, African American women
often provide the majority of the assistance with laborious administrative
and fund-raising tasks as well as material donations to organizations
involved with prisoner-support projects and/or confronting the prison

crisis. It is not unlikely, however, that a male figurehead attempts to dominate the organization's decision-making process. A male prisoner may even seek to "rule" an outside-based organization through threatened violence by way of an outside contact. The sexism that permeates the antiprison movement is a hindrance to the movement's development because it discourages crucial analysis from women. Not to dismiss input from prisoners, but such individuals may not be in as advantageous a position as those living as freeworlders to access and formulate strategy.[2] Furthermore, underlying the need for men to seek control of an organization is "[t]he underlying assumption that we need strong Black patriarchs to give moral direction to the floundering female-headed households that have destabilized the Black community" (Ransby and Matthews 1995, 527). Because so much of the Black community's focus has been on the racist aspect of mass incarceration—specifically on "Freeing the Brothers"—little attention has been focused on the masculinist connections between control and violence. African American women's involvement in organizations concerned with dissolving the prison crisis is imperative because aside from the current adverse effects of white radicals' domination of what little media attention the prison crisis receives, the women's voices are often silenced. Take for example, the issue of restorative justice, which can involve restitution to victims through community service. This is an agenda item that an African American male–dominated movement is far less likely to advocate simply because the process inherently involves a confrontation with behavior patterns that may be both sexist and misogynist in nature. Black women's continued and increased participation in organizing against mass incarceration involves resisting and challenging masculinist constructs. This is essential to further development and implementation of a feminist agenda in the largely gender-biased antiprison movement.

In examining recent successful challenges to the U.S. prison crisis, one finds that inside and outside solidarity to implement action campaigns, such as boycotts and letter-writing campaigns, offers crucial forms of resistance aimed at offsetting and turning back repressive institutional policies. So as some African American women contribute by way of more radical politics and social activism, such as organizing demonstrations and protests, others engage in more moderate activities, such as coordinating van rides to prisons for family members and friends. In terms of cooperation and survival, the networking among women involving seemingly simple acts, such as the passing of messages and ridesharing, is important because the devastating impact on the social and economic, and even political conditions facilitated by the mass incarceration binge is mounting and far-reaching.

The U.S. Incarceration Binge and Its Impact
on African Americans

"The crisis of imprisonment produces a double crisis for the family—demoralization and dismemberment . . ." (Swan 1989, 151). Largely African American, the families, friends and supporters of offenders absorb enormous expenditures that are hidden from the public eye. While the most well known prisoner from the Black Power movement, George Jackson (1970), sentenced astonishingly to one year to life, denounced a Western culture of materialism, his prison letters published in *Soledad Brothers* indicated the constant emotional and financial demands. Jackson, for an example, writes to his father:

> Anything that you send me in the way of finances is a good investment.
> . . . I want you to send me a portable typewriter and, of course, the carrying case. . . . I want three cartons [of cigarettes] in each box; four pounds of nuts in each box, walnuts and Brazil nuts only; the full quota of cigars (150 in each box); and finally the salami (two pounds, one in each box).
> (1970, 148)

While the request for material resources is burdensome, it is linked to one of the most important aspects of an offender's rehabilitation and recidivism: maintenance or establishment of strong family ties (Bennett 1988). These connections are discouraged by prison officials who undermine inside-outside bonds by, for example, severely limiting inmate telephone privileges through tough rules and regulations. Collect-call surcharges from prison are much higher than those originating outside correctional facilities. Inmates are allowed to talk in only 20-minute intervals before being disconnected, which, of course, benefits both the telephone carrier and the department of corrections. This institutional policy often results in the need for several calls to complete a conversation or to relay a message or concern. Each call carries the operator-assistance charge. It is no wonder that the correctional telephone business is a staggering billion-dollar-a-year industry. In other words, families not only bear emotional burdens and economic weight from loss of income but are often overtaxed in terms of expenditures as well. Profit margins have been as high as 57.5 percent for some states (Fischer 1997).

With the rise of the "prisons for-profit" trend, inmates are "farmed out" by the state as human chattel in an era of advanced capitalism that involves the privatization of prisons. IBM, Honeywell, Motorola, and Microsoft are all alleged to have been involved with prison labor markets where inmate earnings (as low as ten cents per hour) fell far below the minimum wage (Appea 1998). Privatization of prisons began in the mid-1980s, facilitated by free enterprise, the rise in the number of prisoners and the increase in expenditures for incarcerations. Activists are calling attention to the phenomenon of the prison industrial complex and its relation to the exploitation of labor, but relatively little focus has been on the loss of income (both legal and illegal) suffered by African American households as a result of the incarceration explosion. While the incarcerated are not counted among the unemployed by the U.S. Bureau of the Census, the following are the theoretical earnings of African American prisoners. Males are estimated to have a 14.2 percent unemployment rate and a median annual income of $16,006; females, 9.2 percent and $10,961, respectively (U.S. Bureau of Census 1996a, 1996b). Hypothetically, this loss of potential income to African American households is more than $7 billion a year. The harsh economic reality for families of incarcerated adults is that it is likely that their expenditures for telephone usage and transportation are on average much higher than for families with no incarcerated adults. For example, 1,500 of the male prisoners of Washington, D.C., were transferred to a privately owned facility in Youngstown, Ohio. Almost immediately, the negative aspects of cost and time associated with visiting overwhelmed many of their families. Of foremost concern was the feeling of powerlessness upon receiving reports of abuse involving unnecessary and arbitrary use of mace, pepper spray and shackles on inmates (Park 1998). This also means, in terms of demands on family and friends of prisoners, that attention has to be shifted to the advocacy aspect of dealing with the criminal justice system because Black inmates often do harder time than their white counterparts (Cole 1995).[3]

The complexities and frustrations of dealing with a prison system, [fraught] with bureaucrats and demagogues, are difficult for newcomers to tackle. To effectively advocate requires those who cannot afford the enormous legal fees charged by lawyers—who are the majority as the poor are disproportionate casualties of the U.S. war on crime—to become experts in Department of Corrections policy. One must learn to think and speak in terms of set-off time, classification processing, parole hearing lingo and so on. (J. Smith 1997, 192)

Other areas of concern are mandatory minimum sentences and sentencing guidelines, reduction and/or discontinuance of prison educational programs, limited legal and health care access, racial disparity in capital punishment, and decitizening. Decitizening is a process that is primarily achieved through criminalization. The implementation of mass incarceration eliminates access to participation in the democratic process.Because Blacks are overrepresented in the criminal justice system, the destruction of the Black community through the loss of Black political power, potential and actual, is inevitable. Those labeled "felon offenders" suffer from both loss of voting privileges and lack of access to employment and educational opportunities even after release from prison. "One in seven (14%) African American males is either currently or permanently disenfranchised from voting as a result of a felony conviction" (The Sentencing Project 1998).

A particularly troublesome trend in the U.S. corrections industry involves the proliferation of control units. Control units are also known as supermaximum prisons. Supermax prisons are high-tech facilities appropriately stamped as "torture chambers" by prisoners'-rights activists (Committee to End the Marion Lockdown 1992). Behavior modification mechanisms such as sensory deprivation involve only half an hour a day out of isolation in combination with very limited or nonexistent visitation. With Nazi Germany war-camp origins, this barbaric practice is extremely detrimental to both physical and mental health. Prisoner psychosis with tendencies toward delusional episodes and violent behavior is a probable outcome (Grassian 1983). An investigation into Maryland's Control Unit prison led Deval L. Patrick, a former Department of Justice assistant attorney general of the Civil Rights Division, to express his utter disbelief of what was found. In a May 1996 letter to Maryland's governor, he wrote the following: "Conditions of extreme social isolation and reduced environmental stimulation, like the conditions of Supermax violate evolving standards of humanity and decency" (Patrick 1995). Supermaximum prisons' devastating impact on Black communities are cyclical in nature because such conditions will, first, "drive men mad"; second, "predispose them to violence"; and thus in sequence, "legitimize their solitary confinement" (Cummins and Weinstein 1993, 44). Violence recycled through revolving prison doors could very well be, in part and parcel, responsible for the continual victimization of African American women by African American men.

Consequently, complicated by the continual economic and physical limitations placed on offenders (primarily Black and male), the mass incarceration binge has also further served to reinforce patriarchal notions of the Black woman caretaker (Smith 1997). In turn, and largely because of the victimization African American women have experienced, dealing with the double-barreled issue of criminal justice is overwhelming. Menacing gender-specific issues involving race and gender for women are the crimes of battering, rape, stalking and sexual harassment. Whereas incarceration rates indicate marked increases in drug-related offenses, abusive behavior associated with addictions can be troublesome for those closely associated with such individuals. Dealing with these difficult issues, along with feelings of helplessness and apathy, more than likely account for some of the silence and frustration surrounding the Black community and the prison industry. Former-prisoner Jerome Washington (1994) summarizes the relationship between the level of frustration prevailing in prisons and the human condition: "In prison memories become hope, and hope is an absolute trap, yet to do nothing is treacherous" (122).

As confused as one can feel about the issues of crime and punishment, solutions must be considered in terms of the eradication of criminality by examination of the social process by which one is criminalized. The slogan of Citizens United for the Rehabilitation of Errants (CURE) (1997), a national criminal justice reform advocacy group, is "Today's prisoners are tomorrow's neighbors." African Americans personalize the relationship between criminality and social causes even further with wisdom from the adage "There, but for the grace of God, go I."

Black females are entering prison in record numbers and are as over-represented as their male counterparts. They are seven times more likely than white women to serve a prison sentence. Just as for men, prisons are mechanisms of control for women. There are some notable differences, however. Female offenders are subjected to the same but more intensified restrictions. "Where society is sexist, racist, and classist—the criminal justice system will be likewise" (Price and Sokoloff 1995, xix). Kurshan (1992) warns, "[W]hile imprisonment rates for women are low, they are rising rapidly, after having remained more or less constant for the previous fifty years. . . . [I]mprisonment of women, as well as all the other aspects of our lives, takes place against a backdrop of patriarchal relationships." Kurshan further suggests that imprisonment in the United States has always been different for women in that once women go to prison, they are more likely to "endure different conditions of incarceration." Although the poor bear the weight of incarceration, the same safety net of economic and family support in existence for white women offenders does not exist for women of color. While almost 90 percent of male prisoners indicate that their children's mothers were caring for their children during their incarceration, only 25 percent of jailed mothers indicated that their children were being care for by their fathers (Chicago Legal Aid to Incarcerated Mothers n.d.). Many of the advocacy groups having to do with the imprisonment of men have centered on racial disparity and poor prison conditions. For women, the thrust of the organizing has been on enabling them to maintain some connection to their families during imprisonment, primarily their children. The mitigating factor for African American women, however, is that many of the prison programs aimed at aiding mother-child bonding have been primarily established in systems and/or institutions where the African American female populations do not reflect national averages. For African American women, this disadvantage is further complicated by a policy of exclusion. As with all institutional programming, prison officials approve the participants.

In *The Black Woman's Health Book*, health-care worker Sean Reynolds (1990) observed:

> There are some physical, mental and social problems that are more pronounced among Black women in custody. I have observed more drug and alcohol dependency, unemployment, illiteracy, homelessness and isolation among incarcerated Black women than in the general population. (194)

Although Black men are incarcerated in greater numbers, Black women do even harder time than their male counterparts. Women prisoners, for example, have, for one thing, less access to educational programs than do their male counterparts, and, on average, spend 2 hours more a day in their cells than do men (Prison Activist Resource Center n.d.). Second, factors such as the rural location of women's prisons means confrontation with majority white correctional personnel is virtually unavoidable. Additionally, there is the expectation by parole boards that women meet higher standards of conduct than men. The above two elements when juxtaposed with the "Jezebel" stereotype of Black women are problematic to receiving positive parole hearing outcomes (Mann 1996).

Because imprisonment for both males and females means prolonged periods of extreme isolation, the establishment of support mechanisms is essential to reducing the negative conditioning caused by imprisonment. This fact is supported by research findings that current U.S. incarceration practices are not conducive to societal transformation (CURE-N.Y. 1997). Research highlights the importance of preserving family connections during an individual's incarceration (Hostetter and Jinnah 1993). Studies indicate a positive correlation between inmate visiting and successful inmate transition to the free world (Bennett 1988). Fathers Behind Bars was founded in 1993 by inmates Arthur L. Hamilton, Jr., Darryl K. Brown and Jerome Morton X to enable prisoners to make some positive connections with their children in spite of their circumstances (Hamilton and Banks 1993; Roberts 1995). Yet and still, even when children maintain some communication with an incarcerated parent, disappointment and confusion are tremendous. It is estimated that 1.5 million children have at least one parent behind bars (Hostetter and Jinnah 1993), and another 3.5 million have a parent on probation or parole (Prison Law Project 1996). It can, therefore, be suggested that the first line of struggle and resistance against the targeting of Blacks by the criminal justice system comes from the thousands upon thousands of Black women who are the sole caretakers of Black children.

From Osage to Jericho: Sounding the Alarm

In terms of African American women's involvement in organized struggle, it is important to note that many who played critical roles in the development of the social and political movements of the '60s and '70s found themselves in either prison or jail or exile. Some of the most-noted and serious criminal justice cases involved Angela Davis, Safiya Bukhari-Alston, Assata Shakur and Ramona Africa. Davis, the most well known of the four, spent 18 months in jail on charges of planning an alleged kidnapping of three San Quentin prisoners, as well as with having supplied the gun that killed four people in a thwarted escape attempt. She was tried and acquitted of the charges. Bukhari-Alston was first arrested in Virginia in 1975 for "attempted robbery, attempted murder, and possession of a machine gun" (Landas 1997). In 1979, Shakur, then leader of the Black Liberation Army, was tried and convicted of killing a state trooper. After escaping from a New Jersey prison, she fled to Cuba, where she now resides. MOVE survivor Ramona Africa spent seven years in prison for rioting relative to the events surrounding the MOVE bombing. Connecting three decades of political imprisonment, each of their experiences is a reminder of the extreme challenges faced by organizers. Threatened and actual violence against both organizers and inmates is of primary concern. The possibility of an organizer's becoming a political prisoner is always imminent. For instance, an unfortunate incident involved Mona Lisa Gaffney, who was active with the movement to free political prisoners, as well as in organizing to garner support for freeing her imprisoned brother in 1997. The possibility that she was set up by the criminal justice system itself as a result of her activism is a very strong one.

> Friends and supporters believe that Mona Lisa is one of the approximately 6,000 innocent people arrested and imprisoned each year in the United States. She was convicted of drug trafficking by an all-white jury without a shred of hard evidence of even possession—only the contradictory testimonies of a drug dealer who had been granted immunity and convicted drug dealers who were vulnerable to pressure from prosecution. (D.C. Coalition 1997)

Prison officials retaliate against inmates for filing grievances, acting as jailhouse lawyers, and participating in protests by imposing arbitrary disciplinary actions. Retaliation often includes transfer to segregation or a supermax, cancellation of parole hearings and reduction of good-time credits.

Nevertheless, as retaliatory as the criminal justice system can be to those who challenge its persecutory policies, the determination of those committed to social change is equally evident. For Davis, Bukhari-Alston, Shakur and Africa, their activism around criminal justice issues intensified *after* their imprisonment. Two of these women were seriously injured in confrontation with police. Africa suffered serious burns, and Shakur was injured by gunfire. In her essay "Incarcerated Women: Transformative Strategies," Davis (1996) suggested that her "interest in the penal system comes out of [a] personal history as a political prisoner during the early 1970s, and as an activist from the late 1960s on, engaged in projects that have contested the political imprisonment of activist around the world" (21). As a popular public lecturer, she is adamant in raising the issue of the prison industry's devastating impact on society. Challenging one to see beyond the political hype of crime and violence, she sounds a call to focus on the roots of the problem—

unemployment, drug addiction, illiteracy—whereby social transformation could then be possible. The eradication of the isms—racism, sexism and so on—is central to her theme of prison abolition. Davis (1997) writes:

> An expanding prison industry is the contemporary stage for large-scale violations of human rights, ideologically sustained by the criminalization of young people of color. At a time when activists, elected officials, and concerned individuals should be countering these trends with demands for jobs, education, and serious alternatives to imprisonment, there is relative silence. (378)

As a trailblazer in the tradition of African American women's activism, Davis has set out to break the silence surrounding imprisonment, encouraging progressive organizations to increase their intensity in dealing with prison issues.

A vocal activist even while exiled, Shakur speaks out from abroad. In an interview in *Essence*, she spoke of relentless concern for Blacks in the United States (White 1997). Her autobiography, *Assata*, is an eye-opening memoir about the process of self-discovery that led to her activism (Shakur 1987). It also gives prolific testimony about the role and depth of the FBI's infiltration by way of counterintelligence programs, namely, COINTELPRO, in social and political movements, forecasting early the allegations of a CIA–crack cocaine connection to the destruction of Black communities. In exposing political imprisonment in the United States through her writings, and while championing the causes of other political prisoners such as Mumia Abu-Jamal, she has been loyal to her comrade and codefendant, Sundiata Acoli. Shakur often collaborates in efforts with other writer-activists. In a special issue of *(Think Black) Journal of Black Thought* (1995), she urges "[one] not to forget, and not to betray our living heroes. If we ignore their struggle, we are ignoring our own."

Always quick to remind one not to forget those locked-down, Ramona Africa is the epitome of East Coast steamroller in terms of activism around the criminal justice system. "You know these people are not separate from us; they are us and we are them. What we allow to happen to them, leaves the door open for it to happen to us" (Africa 1995). As a champion of political prisoner Mumia Abu-Jamal, Africa takes on a huge number of public appearances as an opportunity to expose the injustices of the system. Her speaking style is a charismatic, powerful, folksy blend of down-home gentleness and big-city red-hot. Often visible, burn scars on her arms are a gruesome reminder of still another harassing aspect of the criminal justice system: police brutality. In 1996, Africa sued the city of Philadelphia over the MOVE bombing that resulted in the deaths of 11 MOVE members. She was awarded $500,000. However, Africa is quick to respond with her own commentary on the system. "This ain't about money, this is about taking a stand for all people, so that this government knows that the people ain't gonna have them bombing people and burning people alive" (Reuter News Service 1996). In fact, this is not the first compensation related to the MOVE tragedy. Thus far, the city has been forced to pay $30 million to the victims, including those who lost their homes in the blaze (Overbeck 1996).

Of the African American organizations involved with organizing against the mass incarceration binge and political imprisonment in the United States, the New African movement has spearheaded grassroots involvement. Safiya Bukhari-Alston is vice president of the Provisional Government of the Republic of New Afrika (RNA), a Black nationalist organization. While membership in the RNA is relatively small, its influence in the Black community is substantial. One of the goals of the RNA is to "bring before the United Nations Decolonization Committee the right of Black people in the United States to self-determination and independence (like Canada and Mexico) for those who want this, and the right of Black people to reparations paid by the United States [for slavery] and to the freedom of Black Liberation army personnel and other freedom fighters now in U.S. prisons" (The Peoples Center Council Information 1996). After being arrested, Bukhari-Alston escaped but was later reapprehended. She has been a consistent organizer of forums and film festivals since her release. Following a tradition of community activism, she served as national coordinator of Jericho '98 (1996), a march and demonstration held in Washington, D.C., on March 27, 1998, which called for "recognition and amnesty for U.S. political prisoners." Of the four activists, Bukhari-Alston is the most underacknowledged, but like Afrika, whose political views are religion-based, she fails to *adequately* address the dynamics of gender-based oppression on the African American community but, rather, panders to "excuse making." For instance, Bukhari-Alston (1995) believes that the "sexism of the Black community has its basis in racism and self-hate." Black male misogyny is a racist trap as far as the criminal justice system is concerned in that white males are not punished as often as Black males for their victimization of women.

While Black males *do not* share the same level of male privilege as their white counterparts, they still share in a brotherhood of sorts. The behavior patterns associated with this intricate, yet delicate connection, as hooks (1995) argues, must be examined outside the parameters of race as well.

As evidenced by Africa's suit, the call to resist the prison machine requires the activism of speakers and writers, as well as a succession of demands on the legal system. African American women in the legal profession have added firepower to the arsenal of activity surrounding the injustices in the criminal justice system. Many of these women wear the three hats of lawyer-writer-activist. In the early 1970s one such individual, Evelyn Williams, defended her niece, Assata Shakur. While unsuccessful in the highly political case, Williams in the years since has had various careers, including "that of a social worker, a professor, and the continuing practice of one of the most successful criminal trial lawyer activists in the country" (Chinsole 1995). Williams's (1993) autobiography, *Inadmissible Evidence*, is a hard-hitting indictment of the criminal justice system. Warning of the implications of society's failure to eradicate injustice, Williams writes:

> If history has a lesson to demonstrate, it is that repression of an entire segment of society will backfire. White society cannot continue to fasten the consequences of its own selfish, destructive design on its victims in order to escape its own responsibility. If there is ever to be change, white society must first recognize and accept the fact that the Black condition was intentionally fashioned by whites and that if there is no change in that circumstance, whites too will suffer. (228)

Some of the legal challenges presented by the criminal justice system are met in the form of acceptance by African American women in the legal profession of no-pay, pro-bono or low-paying public defender positions. Flowing in the tradition of activism by way of unleashing an arsenal of legal challenges to the system are two of Williams's protégées, Nkechi Taifa and Adjoa Aiyetoro.

Both Taifa and Aiyetoro previously worked for the American Civil Liberties Union's National Prison Project. Now professor of law at Howard University, Taifa has instituted an award winning public service program and is involved in the legal cases of political prisoners. The Howard University program links volunteer law students with organizations. She collaborated with Chokwe Lumumba on the book *Repara-*

tions, Yes!, and published a visionary article on the negative implications of criminal justice policy, in "Three Strikes and You're Out: Mandatory Life Imprisonment for Third Time Felons" in the *University of Dayton Law Review*. As legislative counsel for the ACLU, Taifa (1995) provided expert analysis of the crime bill through organizational press releases, statements and briefings.

ONAMOVE: Assessing Needs, Meeting Challenges

In terms of providing vehicles for sounding the alarm about the prison crisis, advocacy organizations, such as The National Center for Women in Prison, are headed by African American women like Margaret J. B. Owens. The center focuses primarily on policy issues relating to women prisoners and their family members. Pat Clark, a veteran organizer as former director of KlanWatch and the Alabama Prison Project, heads the Criminal Justice Program of the American Friends Service Committee, instrumental since the 1960s in leading the fight for prison reform. Lois Williamson, whose husband was killed in a robbery, is former chairwoman of National CURE (Citizens United for the Rehabilitation of Errants) and currently director of Pennsylvania CURE. She brings with her leadership tools by means of which reconciliation between offenders and victims can be possible. Primarily a lobbying group—one of the largest focused on political reform issues—Williamson's affiliated organization, National CURE, pushes for rehabilitation and alternatives to incarceration through policy reform. Meeting the challenges resulting from California's 200,000 prison population, Mothers Reclaiming Our Children (Mothers ROC) was formed by African American mothers whose children were facing life imprisonment as a result of California's "three strikes" law. Another California-based organization, Families with a Future, dedicated to the needs of women prisoners serving long sentences, was founded by Adia McCray Robinson. Other influential African American women organizers include Olinda Boyd (Baltimore ACLU); Beverly Nur (Maryland Prison Renewal Committee); Azora Irby-Muntasir (Maryland CURE); Joyce Miller (Come into the Sun; Coalition for California Women Prisoners; National Network for Women in Prison), Brenda Smith (Women's Legal Defense Fund); Marpessa Kupendua (nattyreb.com); and Jackie Walker (ACLU National Prison Project AIDS Awareness Program).

Second only to slavery in its devastating impact on African Americans, the mass incarceration of hundreds of thousands of individuals calls on collaborative activism and collective genius. Working to meet the challenges caused by draconian criminal justice policies passed since the early 1970s, an African American women's vanguard, determined to dissolve the prison crisis, is onamove.

NOTES

1. The Omnibus Crime Bill was heralded as "sweeping" criminal justice reform legislation in 1994 by President Bill Clinton. It contained repressive measures such as the "three strikes" rule for convicted felons and failed to include a Racial Justice Act provision to eliminate the racial disparity resulting from its passage.

2. *Freeworlder* is an activist term for individuals who are not incarcerated.

3. *Hard time* refers to the Black experience with a criminal justice system that is not only inhumane but characteristically harsher than the white experience. For instance, a breakdown by race indicates that Blacks are 8.5 times more likely to go to prison than whites. Other areas of concern include comparatively higher bails (or no-bail situations), lack of adequate and affordable legal representation, higher conviction rates, longer sentences, fewer positive parole and probation hearing outcomes, and more complicated prerelease and release issues for Blacks than whites. For instance, in Maryland, white prisoners tend to cluster at lower security levels, where violence is less of a threat. Prison authorities often assign white offenders to single cells at an institution, if available, while Black offenders are forced into double cells or dormitory housing. Also, because many prisons are rurally located and African Americans represent a small percentage of the free-worlder population, employment discrimination at the work-release level is rampant. For African American women, "hard time" is further intensified by the triple jeopardy of being Black, poor and female. (See Reiman 1979; Bell 1980; Committee to End the Marion Lockdown 1995; and Rosenblatt 1997.)

RESOURCES

Crossroad Support Network
3420 W. 63rd St.
Chicago, IL 60629
Tel/Fax: 773-737-8679
Email: crsn@aol.com
Web address: <http://afrikan.net/crossroad/index2.html>

Crossroad publishes a newsletter by and for New Afrikan prisoners. Its primary focus is to increases community awareness and garner support for prisoners.

Prison Activist Resource Center
P.O. Box 339
Berkeley, CA 94701
Tel: 510-845-8813
Fax: 510-845-8816
Email: parc@prisonactivist.org
Web address:

PARC is a grassroots collective project that has an activist community center and a political library. Its web site is a vital instrument in linking the various organizations concerned with the prison crisis.

The National Center on Institutions and Alternatives
3125 Mt. Vernon Avenue
Alexandria, VA 22305
Tel: 703-684-0373
Fax: 703-684-6037
Email: ncia@igc.apc.org
Web address: <www.ncianet.org/ncia/>

The National Center on Institutions and Alternatives (NCIA) is primarily a nonprofit, research-based institution. Its many publications address issues such as overcrowding, alternative sentencing and racial disparity in sentencing. They are excellent research materials and are available to the public.

Stop Prisoner Rape, Inc.
333 North Avenue 61, Suite #4
Highland Park, CA 90042
Tel.: 213-257-6164
Email: webmaster@spr

SPR is a national nonprofit organization dedicated to combating the rape of prisoners through challenges to the legal system, and prisoner and public education. It also provides assistance to survivors of jailhouse rape. Much of SPR's work focuses on eradicating the silence that surrounds rape and prison.

Families Against Mandatory Minimums Foundation
1612 K Street NW, Suite 1400
Washington, DC 20006
Tel: 202-822-6700
Fax: 202-822-6704

Email: famm@famm.org
Web address: <www.famm.org>

FAMM, a nonprofit organization, was founded by family members of inmates, as well as judges and criminal justice experts, as a result of the penalties associated with mandatory minimum sentencing policies. It seeks to bring an end to harsh sentencing. One of the more powerful prisoner rights organizations, it has chapters in 25 states and 33,000 members.

Center for the Children of Incarcerated Parents
65 South Grand Ave.
Pasadena, CA 91105
Tel: 626-397-1396
Fax: 626-397-1304
Web address: <www.amandla.org/osepp/resources/child_family.html>

CCIP is an advocacy group for children whose parents are incarcerated. The organization was founded and is staffed by former inmates. It is an excellent resource because it is a clearinghouse of information resources at both the national and local levels.

Critical Resistance
P.O. Box 339
Berkeley, CA 94701
Tel: 510-643-2094
Fax: 510-845-8816
Email: critresist@aol.com

Critical Resistance is a campaign to resist the expansion of the punishment industry by strategizing with activists, scholars and policy makers, former prisoners and others. The organization held its first national conference at the University of California, Berkeley in 1998.

National Campaign to Stop Control Unit Prisons—East
972 Broad St., 6th Floor
Newark, NJ 07102
Tel: 201-643-3192
Email: 103137.3272@compuserve.com

National Campaign to Stop Control Unit Prisons—Midwest
P.O. Box 144
Boulder, CO 80306
Tel: 303-823-5207
Email: ecorrine@scicom.alphacdc.com

National Campaign to Stop Control Unit Prisons — West
P.O. Box 2218
Berkeley, CA 94702
Tel: 415-452-3359

NCSCUP is dedicated to abolishing control unit prisons throughout the United States. The organization exposes the human rights violations that occur with conditions of extreme isolation and sensory deprivation through monitoring and education projects, as well as protests and lobbying activities.

REFERENCES

Acoli, Sundiata. *A Brief History of the New Afrikan Prison Struggle*. Leavenworth, Kans.: 1992 Pamphlet.

Africa, Ramona. "On a Move!" *Wazo Weusi (Think Black) Journal of Black Thought: Schooling the Generations on the Politics of Prisons* 2, no. 2 (1995). Online, http://www.efn.org/~chinosol/ramonmu2.

Appea, Pamela Jane. "Angela Davis Draws Capacity Crowd." *Maroon News*, January 20, 1998.

Bell, Derrick A. *Race, Racism and American Law*. Boston: Little, Brown, 1980.

Bennett, Lawrence, A. "Current Views of Inmates Visiting." *Voices and Visions: The Family and Corrections, Proceedings of the First National Conference on the Family and Corrections*. Sacramento, Calif., April 24–27, 1988.

Bukhari-Alston, Safiya. "On the Question of Sexism and the Black Panther Party," March 9, 1995. Online, hartford-hwp.com/archives/.

Bureau of Justice Statistics. Washington, D.C.: Department of Justice, 1960–1995.

Chicago Legal Aid to Incarcerated Mothers. "Fact Sheet." Chicago: n.d.

Chinsole, ed. *Wazo Weusi (Think Black) Journal of Black Thought: Schooling the Generations on the Politics of Prisons* 2, no. 2 (1995). Online, http://www.efn.org/~chinosol/ramonmu2.

Citizens United for the Rehabilitation of Errants (New York Chapter). "Seven Recommendations on Investment and Incentives for Addiction Treatment and Education." New York: February 10, 1997 Report.

Cole, Yoji. "At Calipatria: Black Inmates Get Stiffer Punishments." *Los Angeles Sentinel,* November 29, 1995.

Collins, Patricia Hill. *Black Feminist Thought*. Boston: Unwin Hyman, 1990.

Committee to End the Marion Lockdown (CEML). "Alcatraz to Marion to Florence—Control Unit Prisons in the United States." Chicago: 1992 Report.

———. "The Continuing Crime of Black Imprisonment." Chicago: 1995 Report.

Cummins, Eric, and Cory Weinstein. "The Crime of Punishment at Pelican Bay Maximum Security Prison." *Covert Action Quarterly,* no. 45 (Summer 1993).

Davis, Angela Y. "Incarcerated Women: Transformative Strategies." *Black Renaissance/Renaissance Noire (*Fall 1996): 20–34.

———. "Untitled Review." *Criminal Injustice.* Boston: South End Press, 1997.

D.C. Coalition to Free Mumia. "Support Mona Lisa Gaffney." Washington, D.C.: 1997 Leaflet.

Duster, Alfreda M. *Crusader for Justice: The Autobiography of Ida B. Wells.* Chicago: University of Chicago Press, 1970.

Fischer, David. "Reach Out and Gouge Someone: The Boom in Prison Phone Systems." *U.S. News and World Report,* May 5, 1997.

Grassian, Stuart. "Psychological Effects of Solitary Confinement." *American Journal of Psychiatry* 140, no. 11 (November 1983).

Hamilton, Arthur, Jr., and William Banks. *Father Behind Bars.* Waco, Texas: WRS Publishing, 1993.

hooks, bell. "Feminism: It's a Black Thing." *Killing Rage: Ending Racism.* New York: Henry Holt, 1995.

Hostetter, Edward C., and Dorothea T. Jinnah. "Families of Adult Prisoners." Reston, Va.: Prison Fellowship Ministries, 1993.

Jackson, George. *Soledad Brothers: The Prison Letters of George Jackson.* New York: Bantam Books, 1970.

Jericho '98. "Amnesty & Freedom for Political Prisoners & Prisoners of War!" New York: 1996 Leaflet.

Kurshan, Nancy. "Women and Imprisonment in the U.S.—History and Current Reality." Online, http://www.prisonactivist.org, 1992.

Landas, Marc. "Interview with Safiya Bukhari-Alston." *Urban Dialogue.* Online, http://www.unsociables.com, 1997.

Lotke, Eric. "Hobbling a Generation: Young African American Men in D.C.'s Criminal Justice System Five Years Later." Alexandria, Va.: National Center on Institutions and Alternatives, August 1997.

Mann, Coramae Richey. "Women of Color and the Criminal Justice System." *The Criminal Justice System and Women: Offenders, Victims and Workers.* New York: McGraw-Hill, 1996.

Overbeck, Ashley. "MOVE survivor Ramona Africa Sues City of Philadelphia." *Parascope*: parascope.com/mx/move5.htm, 1996.

Park, Paula. "Two Dead in Ohio." *Washington City Paper,* April 17, 1998. Online, http://www.washingtoncitypaper.com.

Patrick, Deval L. U.S. Department of Justice, Civil Rights Division, Letter of Findings (Maryland Correctional Adjustment Center). Washington, D.C.: 1995.

People's Center Council Information, The. "Republic of New Afrika Prepared for Increased Effectiveness as Blacks Turn to Nationalism." Washington, D.C.: 1996 Press release.

Price, Barbara Raffel, and Natalie J. Sokoloff. *The Criminal Justice System and Women: Offenders, Victims, and Workers.* New York: McGraw-Hill, 1995.

Prison Activist Resource Center. "Eleven Things You Should Know about Women in Prison." San Francisco: n.d. Leaflet.

Prison Law Project of the National Lawyers Guild. "Fact Sheet." San Francisco: 1996.

Ransby, Barbara, and Tracye Matthews. "Black Popular Culture and the Transcendence of Patriarchal Illusions." In *Words of Fire*. Beverly Guy-Sheftall, ed. New York: New Press, 1995.

Reiman, Jeffrey H. *The Rich Get Richer and the Poor Get Prison*. New York: John Wiley, 1979.

Reuter News Service. "MOVE Militant Wins Suit Against Philadelphia," June 25, 1996.

Reynolds, Sean. "Bar None: The Health of Incarcerated Women." *The Black Women's Health Book: Speaking for Ourselves*. Seattle: Seal Press, 1990.

Roberts, Penni. "Outside the Prison Walls: The Families Left Behind." *Philadelphia Tribune*, September 9, 1995.

Rosenblatt, Elihu. *Criminal Injustice*. Boston: South End Press, 1997.

Sanders, Annette. "Letter to the Pelican Bay Prison Express." *Pelican Bay Express* (1996): 23.

Sentencing Project, The. "Intended and Unintended Consequences: State Disparities in Imprisonment." Washington, D.C.: 1998 Report.

Shakur, Assata. *Assata: An Autobiography*. Chicago: Lawrence Hill Books, 1987.

———. "Message to Mumia." *Wazo Weusi (Think Black) Journal of Black Thought: Schooling the Generations in the Politics of Prisons* 2, 2 (1995). Online http://www.efn.org/~chinosol/mumass.

Smith, Jennifer E. "Function Fuckin', Phone Sex and Prison Marriages: The Effect of Incarceration on Black Male-Female Relationships." *Black Renaissance/Renaissance Noire* (Fall 1997).

Smith, Phil. "Private Prisons: Profits of Crime." *Covert Action Quarterly* (Fall 1993).

Swan, Alex. "Families of Imprisoned Black Men." *Crisis in Black Sexual Politics*. San Francisco: Black Think Tank, 1989.

Taifa, Nkechi. "ACLU Background Briefing: Crime Bills Tread Heavily on Fundamental Liberties." Washington, D.C.: ACLU, 1995.

Thompson, Mildred I. "Ida B. Wells-Barnett: An Exploratory Study of an American Black Woman, 1893–1930." *Black Women in the United States* (vol. 15). New York: Carlson Publishing, 1990.

Tucker, Cynthia. "Unequal Drug Law Fuels Sense of Injustice." *Atlanta Journal and Constitution*, April 20, 1997, R05.

U.S. Bureau of the Census (1996a). "Selected Economic Characteristics of Persons and Families, by Sex and Race: March 1996." Washington, D.C.: June 1997.

U.S. Bureau of the Census (1996b). "Total Money Income in 1996 of Persons 15 Years Old and Over, by Sex, Region, and Race." Washington, D.C.: June 1997.

Walker, Samuel. "Sixties Civil Rights Gave Momentum to Prisoners' Rights." Journal of the National Prison Project no. 13 (Fall 1987).

Washington, Jerome. *Iron House: Stories from the Yard*. Fort Bragg, Calif.: 1994.

White, Evelyn C. "Prisoner in Paradise." *Essence*, June 1997.

Williams, Evelyn. *Inadmissible Evidence*. New York: Lawrence Hill Books, 1993.

Williams, Susan Darst. "A CURE for America's Prisons." *Corrections Compendium* (March 1991).

Chapter Thirteen

Behind But Not Forgotten

Women and the Behind-the-Scenes
Organizing of the Million Man March

Wendy G. Smooth and Tamelyn Tucker

In the fall of 1995, organizers headed by the Nation of Islam sought to assemble one million Black men in the nation's capital for the purpose of atonement and revitalization of the Black community. This historic gathering, the Million Man March, was an unprecedented event in that its aim was the healing, improvement and revitalization of the Black community, yet the call to march was directed only to Black men.[1] Though Black women were not initially asked to participate in the march, a number of Black women responded with overwhelming support.

This article analyzes the roles women played as behind-the-scenes organizers of the Million Man March. As we analyze the roles women played, we ask whether Black women's roles have changed in Black liberation political activity since the civil rights movement. Black women's responses in terms of both endorsements and condemnations of the march serve as the foundation of our analysis. Using Black feminist theory as a theoretical framework, we discuss how Black women confront the "woman question" and the "race problem" in their activism.

The Million Man March marks the first massive organizing of the Black community since the civil rights movement. The march occurred after the first and second waves of the women's movement, which resulted in women asserting a much more substantial role in society. In our analysis, we explore the roles Black women assumed and their varied responses to the march. While one would expect that the role of women in the Million Man March would reflect the expanded roles of women in the society, women's roles in the 1995 march differed little from their roles some 30 years before. In light of our findings, we raise questions concerning the connectedness of Black feminist theory to the lives of Black women.

The Million Man March/Day of Absence

In calling one million men to assemble in the nation's capital on October 16, 1995, Minister Louis Farrakhan of the Nation of Islam (NOI) marked a new page in U.S. history. The Million Man March, despite low estimates by the National Park Police, was one of the largest assemblies ever held on the Washington Mall.[2] The march organizers included many faces from Black liberation struggles across history. Benjamin Chavis, former executive director of the NAACP, cochaired the march with Farrakhan. In addition, the executive organizing committee included notables such as Mayor Marion Barry, Haki Madhabuti, Maulana Karenga, and Rev. Jesse Jackson. The march was the result of months and months of planning across the country by churches, mosques and community activists.

Minister Farrakhan made the call for march attendance exclusively to Black men. Black women (as well as Black men unable to make it to Washington) were asked to participate in a Day of Absence. This required that they stay home from work, school, businesses and places of entertainment to reflect on the sacredness of the day. Women were encouraged to stay home, pray and teach children the importance of family values. This call by Minister Farrakhan was answered by an overwhelming number of men from all walks of life and all areas of the country. In making a call to only men of the Black community, he launched a controversial debate over the exclusion of women. The march sparked a plethora of reactions and controversial public debates. In this article we focus on "women and the Million Man March" on various levels. These include the gender-exclusive call to march, the roles women assumed as behind-the-scenes organizers and leaders, and women's condemnation of the march and its goals.

Black Women in Racial Liberation Politics

The history of Black women in racial liberation politics is an ever-growing area of inquiry. While many accounts of racial liberation politics fail to analyze the roles of women, some scholars have begun to use gender as a major factor in their analysis. Evidence from this expanded look at racial liberation politics suggests that generally women perform background duties, or supportive roles and that few women act in traditional leadership capacities.[3] Perhaps, no stronger example exists than the civil rights movement. Accounts of the civil rights movement suggest that women assumed organizational and supportive roles in racial liberation politics. Their activism typically took the form of behind-the-scenes organizing and did not include traditional leadership roles. Many progressive researchers are now directing their efforts toward clarifying the roles of Black women in social change movements; however, Black women's activism still struggles to gain the historical reverence it deserves.[4] Prior to the increased interest in Black women's social activism, research related to social movements was confined to the recording of a series of great deeds by great men.[5]

The lack of the recognition of women can partially be explained by the fact that the acknowledged leaders of the movement, who were chosen to receive the media attention, were Black ministers.[6] During this period few women served in ministerial capacities.[7] By virtue of the role they played, women were ignored in media coverage as the media sought to follow high-profile male leaders. Despite recent discoveries of a number of women working and leading in all phases of the movement, there is still much work to be done.[8] The dominant historical recording of the movement minimized, if not erased, the organizational and leadership roles of Black women.

Few women have been highlighted in historical accounts of the civil rights movement. This holds true with the exception of select cases such as the highly publicized role of Rosa Parks. A deeper look reveals a more interesting picture illustrating that much of the organizing was done by women.[9] Women such as Ella Baker (the SNCC coordinator who assisted the organization and implemented its participatory leadership style), Mary Fair Burkes and JoAnn Gibson Robinson(leaders of the Women's Political Council in Montgomery, the group that initiated the Montgomery bus boycotts) and countless others are representative of the critical roles women played.[10] In his research on grassroots organizing in the Mississippi Delta during the movement, Charles Payne found that Black women were the sustaining force supporting the Student Nonviolent Coordinating Committee's voter registration drives and economic liberation programs. Payne concludes that during the most turbulent period of civil rights activities in the Mississippi Delta, "men may have led but the women organized."[11]

On the one hand, Black women were kept out of key leadership roles, but on the other hand, they were the sustaining force carrying the movement along. As Payne and others recognize, many Black women served in incredibly valuable positions but were not placed before the cameras or given historical credit as great minds in the movement.[12] In Belinda Robnett's recent and thorough analysis of women in the civil rights movement, she finds that while women were neither in high-profile nor traditional leadership roles, they performed the duties of "bridge leadership"—connecting vastly different people to the movement, an activity that the movement heavily depended upon.[13] Despite the absence of women in publicized key leadership positions, women worked diligently as organizers for social change.

As Black women carried out their behind-the-scenes roles in the civil rights movement, there is evidence that they expressed concern that sexism limited their leadership opportunities.[14] While this critique was not a central issue during the movement, this tension was one of the most prevalent issues surrounding the 1995 Million Man March. Cheryl Towsend Gilkes finds women's limited leadership roles to be quite common in the Black community. In her work on women and community work, Gilkes concludes that if Black women had not engaged in organizing activities, many institutions associated with the Black community such as the Black church, would not exist as we know them today.[15]

Though sexism still exists, women obtained a higher status in society following the civil rights movement and the women's movement. Having learned valuable lessons from both of these movements, women have become more vocal in society. Black women, like all women, have taken on a much more public role in society and have assumed a more politicized voice. Since the 1960s there has been an increase in the number of women in occupations outside the home, and there has been a strong increase in the number of women elected to political office.[16] The Million Man March marks the first massive organizing of the Black community since women have assumed these more prominent roles in the larger society. It would be expected that the role of women in the Million Man March would reflect the change in the role of women in society.

While significant changes in women's roles were expected, from our study we found little difference in the roles women played during the Black liberation movement of the 1960s and the 1995 Million Man

March. Our data show that the roles of women were strikingly similar to those of the 1960s despite the change in social conditions. Though women held positions key to the success of the Million Man March, they did not occupy high-profile positions nor were they publicly regarded as leaders. Women did much of the behind-the-scenes organizing in the Million Man March, as they had in the civil rights movement. Like the women who were involved in the civil rights movement, the women who were involved in the Million Man March received little acknowledgment of their behind-the-scenes activism, nor were they recognized for the key leadership roles they played. The most salient difference between the 1960s civil rights movement and the 1995 Million Man March from our findings is the aggressive manner in which women confronted the roles prescribed for them in 1995.

To test our hypothesis, we employed a number of data-collection methods. First we conducted document analysis, reviewing both print and electronic media sources. Utilizing "women" and "Million Man March" as key terms, we collected data both before and after the march. Drawing upon the data gathered from newspapers, several women were identified for interviews. Personal and telephone interviews were conducted with several women who were involved in the organizing of the march. In addition, we collected a substantial amount of data as participant observers volunteering with the Health Task Force, a component of the march's organizational structure.

Women's Responses to the Million Man March

Women's responses to the Million Man March varied. Many women, inspired by promises that the march would bring peace to their communities, fathers to their single-parent families, and a higher-level sense of responsibility, were elated that Black men would gather together and profess intentions to improve their individual lives and their communities. These women supported the march in its entirety. On the other hand, many women believed that the march symbolized a regression in gender relations in the Black community. These women openly spoke out against the march. Of the women supporting the march, some had to reconcile their support in their own minds. Reasons for this need for reconciliation varied. For example, there was the issue of separating the message from the messenger. The fact that Minister Louis Farrakhan was the one who called the march was troubling for many who considered him and the Nation of Islam insensitive to the problematic nature of gender hierarchies. For some, the importance of racial solidarity and the critical situation of the Black community far outweighed any problems they had with Farrakhan. Others found this conflict irreconcilable and chose not to support the march.

Those Who Answered the Call

An in-depth look at the roles and viewpoints of two women contributes to our understanding of the leadership roles women held in relation to the march.[17] E. Faye Williams held a key organizational position as a cochair of the local organizing committee in Washington, D.C. In this position, she chaired organizational meetings and coordinated various logistical committees such as the hospitality and voter registration committees. Williams also served as a national spokesperson for the march. She was one of the few women slated to speak on the program the day of the march.[18] Williams said her expectation, hopes and dreams for the march were, first, to get one million men to attend, a goal that was far exceeded; second, she wanted the march to be a catalyst for the establishment of a trust fund to build African American businesses in communities across the country. A third goal was to improve the moral standing and enhance the spiritual development of Black men. She cited as a long-term goal, the uniting of brothers and sisters in the African diaspora and the adoption of 25,000 Black children.[19]

According to Williams, the role that women were asked to play in the march was not a problem. The march was to enhance male-female relationships and to honor women.[20] Williams, a self-proclaimed feminist, said that she was pleased with the request to stay home, reasoning that Black women should welcome Black men's taking on more family and community responsibilities. In addition, she claimed that Black women were never told that they could not participate. In fact, women participated in very profound ways; they coordinated the hospitality committees as well as the public relations committee. Williams named Sister Angela 6X Bone and Linda Greene as two of the most active organizers. She also mentioned that the "elders," such as the late Betty Shabazz, Coretta Scott King and Rosa Parks, were all honored guests at the march and these women were also invited to speak. In Williams's opinion, the Million Man March was a time to focus on the men, and she was glad of the opportunity. To women who complained that the march was for men only, Williams responded that next year we could have a *two* Million Woman March. According to Williams, very few of the women who participated in the march felt any misgivings about their roles as participants.[21]

Another influential woman in the organizing and execution of the march was Linda Greene, who served as the director of fund-raising. Greene traveled extensively with Minister Farrakhan and Benjamin Chavis, raising money from corporations, entertainers and professional athletes. In addition, she was in charge of some 300 fund-raising groups positioned all across the country. These groups—many headed by women—held dinners, car washes, bake sales and other fund-raising activities, and proceeds were reported to Greene. In her travels, Greene met many women who were extremely pleased to see a woman as a key figure in the organizational structure.

Like Williams, Greene also expressed a sentiment that the march should be focused on Black men. Her sympathies for the long suffering of Black men served as a catalyst for her activism. Greene stated, "For so long the Black man has been kicked and kept down, it's time he had some support." Greene strongly believed that Black men needed to see that Black women supported them. Greene also maintained that Black men needed to bond with one another, something that she said women do all the time. Black men needed this to help them heal and to make a new start. Greene had no problem with not being invited to gather at the march itself. She went on to compare this event to annual men's and women's days, traditionally celebrated in Black churches. "No one gets mad when women want to celebrate women's day or [men want to celebrate] men's day. In the Black church, men help women with women's day and vice versa." Despite the fact that Greene was "very prepared to stay at home," in actuality she attended the march. She hosted the VIPs and celebrities attending the march, as well as supervised additional volunteers.[22]

The roles played by E. Faye Williams and Linda Greene are representative of the key roles women played in the organizational structure of the march. While these women were key players in its execution, neither was regarded as a public figure associated with the event. Though both women held positions key in making the march a reality, neither was acknowledged as serving in a leadership capacity. Though not publicly recognized as march leaders, the activities of these women warrant such recognition. Just as these women are representative of those serving in executive capacities, many women contributed in other ways to the success of the march.

As volunteers with the Health Task Force, we observed firsthand the intricate planning and activity done mainly by women to make the march run smoothly. Led by the Nation of Islam's minister of health and human services, Dr. Abdul Alim Mohammed, the task force was responsible for minor first aid and medical attention to the march's attendants. Though the task force largely comprised women, Dr. Mohammed was its spokesperson. Much of the organizing was done by women in and around the Washington, D.C., area, but there were other branches of the task force as far away as California. Like the Washington, D.C., group, their volunteers were trained to perform various medical tasks on the day of the march. The women of the Health Task Force not only volunteered their time months before the march, they also provided medical supplies and contributed money and room and board for out-of-town marchers. Their involvement was extremely energetic. Each week the group met, there were always many new volunteers wanting to be trained to participate.

On the eve of the march, the Abundant Life Clinic, which was the meeting place of the task force, overflowed with volunteers. Women from all over the country waited there for hours as volunteers were processed and supplies were labeled and packaged for use the next day. Despite the fact that many had made tiring trips across the country, they remained eager and willing. Many worked until late in the evening preparing medical supplies and processing additional volunteers. Another force of women worked around the clock at the Imani Temple, a Washington church that served as temporary housing for out-of-town marchers and as the main command post for medics the day of the march. Women there organized medical supplies, communication devices, identification badges, and other supplies collected by the Health Task Force for the 18 first aid stations to be set up on the Mall. Women were also instrumental in facilitating a twenty-four-hour hotline that provided specific information concerning the next day's events.

The day of the march, the Health Task Force volunteers arrived on the Mall long before dawn, and a steady stream flooded the first aid stations, eagerly awaiting their opportunity to render assistance. Because of the large number of volunteers the day of the march, some local volunteers had to be turned away because preference was given to trained volunteers who had come from great distances.

While the results of our participant observation illustrate the role of women with the Health Task Force, women made significant contributions in other facets of the march as well. In keeping with the call of the march, women were responsible for the teach-ins that constituted the major activity of the Day of Absence. Cora Masters Barry, wife of Washington, D.C., mayor Marion Barry, led a massive voter registration drive that was facilitated by women. While her participation in particular has not been highlighted, the voter registration drive has been cited as the most tangible success of the march for having registered thousands of men.[23] Many women simply participated in the Day of Absence by reflecting on the spiritual significance of the day, as one group of women did at the Imani Temple.[24] The *Washington Post* reported that a group of four women demonstrated their support for the men attending the march by greeting them at Metro Transit stations.[25]

Exploring women's contributions to the Million Man March from leadership roles in fund-raising and strategizing to the grunt work associated with the Health Task Force and compliance with the Day of Absence allows us to critique the roles of women in executing the march. These accounts reflect women who chose to participate in activities supporting the march. However, these were not the only responses from Black women in relation to the march. There were many Black women displaying and articulating strong opposition to the march.

Those Who Spoke Out against the Million Man March

Women's reasons varied for speaking out against the march, but their primary concern was the same: they vehemently opposed the message they felt the Million Man March propagated. To these women, by its simply excluding women, calling on men to "take back their rightful place in the home," or some combination of both, the march signified a reinforcement of a detrimental patriarchal system. Black feminists and Black progressives, such as Angela Davis, Michelle Wallace, Rebecca Walker, Paula Giddings, Jewell Jackson McCabe and Derrick Bell assembled the day of the march and held a press conference/teach-in. The gathering resulted in the establishment of African American Agenda 2000 and a written statement protesting the march. For this group, the march represented a nonprogressive politics that attempted to reinforce patriarchy and capitalism.[26]

Economist Julianne Malveaux was one of the most outspoken Black women against the march. In an interview with Jesse Jackson, Malveaux expressed fear that the call for Black men to "stand up and take their rightful place" was a call for them to take control from Black women, as if they were to blame for the conditions of the Black family today. She asked, "Why do I think that one of the first steps some man might take is on a woman's back?" Though Malveaux felt that most men who attended the march were not there under the pretense of learning how to oppress women, she was upset because of the ways in which the march reinforced a patriarchal system.[27] Dr. Linda Williams, a political scientist at the University of Maryland was also critical: "This is a regressive move for the Black community. Though previous social movements may have had elements of sexism and gender classification, never before have women been asked not to attend at all."[28]

bell hooks deeply and profoundly opposed the march. Interestingly enough, she did not believe that it should be shunned or criticized simply because it invited only men. hooks classified herself as one of the women who "could not separate the message from the messenger." In an interview with Charlie Rose, she said, "I feel like men could march for days by themselves and I'd sit at home and cook and clean if they were marching for principles, values and politics that would actually aid Black self-determination. I happen to think patriarchy has been deadly." hooks reasoned that the main goals of the march were not about promoting self determination but instead were about reinforcing certain "notions about family," notions based on false assumptions, for example, the notion that Black men have not been productive leaders in Black resistance. According to hooks, the notion is inconsistent with history; in fact, Black men have contributed to race struggles in profound ways. In her words, "[W]hen someone tells me in their mission statement that no nation sends its women to war while the men sit in the kitchen . . . [t]hat to me is a real gender dialogue about conventional masculinity, which denies a history of race relations where the engagement of Black men in resistance struggles has been so meaningful and so crucial."[29] Beverly Hall Lawrence echoed a similar concern in asking the question "Where do Black women go now that Black men have Marched ahead? The issue isn't an easy one, and it comes down to this: Am I part of the problem? Has the rise in Black female independence made Black men feel superfluous?"[30]

The dissension surrounding the Million Man March among Black women illustrates a split over several issues concerning the march. First of all, the women held varied interpretations of the goals of the march. For example, Doris Lewis, a local Chicago organizer, said, "I have absolutely no problem with this March. It's time for Black men to stand up and say to Black women 'We are sorry.'" Lewis did not hold the opinion that Black men were trying to reinforce patriarchy or keep women in a subordinate position.[31] Her thought was echoed in march propaganda: "Black Woman this March is for You."[32] On the other hand, there were those like bell hooks and Kimberle Crenshaw who saw the march as an extremely sexist venture.

Not only were Black women split as to who supported and did not support the march, many also experienced inner conflict. This conflict is parallel to what W. E. B. Dubois termed *dual consciousness* and what various Black feminists attribute to concepts such as Deborah King's *multiple jeopardy*, Evelyn Higginbotham's *metalanguage of race* and Kimberle Crenshaw's *ordering of differences*.[33] Dubois describes the phenomenon as the attempt of African Americans to reconcile their African ancestry and their American ancestry when these two identities clash. However, these Black feminist theorists discuss a similar phenomenon in their attempt to reconcile gender and race.

The conflict has manifested itself in most struggles for social and political equality for Blacks. In the struggle to obtain voting rights at the turn of the century, Black women questioned whether they should align with women suffragists and fight for their own rights to the ballot, or forsake their own rights to support at least Black men's receiving rights to the ballot. In the latter scenario, Black women would not obtain suffrage but their interests would be somewhat articulated through their intimate relationships with Black men.

In conversations with many women participating in the march, we heard the strain of this duality. Making the decision to participate in the march echoed the dilemmas faced by Black women at the turn of the century and throughout history as the race question and the woman question intersect. Dr. Linda Williams expressed this conflict in a different way, saying that though she felt that the march might possibly have some positive outgrowth such as strengthening Black institutions, helping to mobilize voters and increasing community service, it was one of the most regressive incidents for gender relations in recent history. Critical of the March, she nevertheless wanted it to succeed. She reasoned that an unsuccessful march would be even more detrimental to the plight of African Americans.[34]

Deborah King's description of the "multiple jeopardy" faced by Black women is especially apt in regard to the feelings of duality expressed by women concerning the Million Man March. This duality was an issue for participants and supporters as well as many who spoke in opposition to the march. King describes Black women as dealing with the multiplicative effects of oppression occasioned by their being both Black and female. What is more, she describes the race treason Black women are accused of when they are confronted with an ordering of racial and gender issues and choose gender over race. As a result of their position in society, Black women must practice monist politics, wherein gender, class and other differences are superseded by race and thus neglected. This is problematic when the politics of race does not encompass differences such as gender and class, particularly when male issues are seen as the norm.[35]

For example, because Black men are seen as the norm of blackness, their issues are seen as the issues of the Black community; issues of Black women are seen as Black women's issues. Thus, one would not have Black men participating in a million woman march in the same way Black women participated in the Million Man March. This raises the question as to whether "all the Blacks are men, all the women are White" is still the case today.[36]

Higginbotham makes a similar argument on the "totalizing effect" race has on gender and class. Focusing on one of these categories(for example, race), serves to obscure the others of these socially constructed politicized categories.[37] Manning Marable echoes this sentiment in his critique of the Million Man March. According to Marable, by focusing on Black nationalism, the march falsely homogenized the Black community. The march platform did not recognize or address class hierarchy or gender hierarchy and instead reinforced a class hierarchy by legitimizing a reliance on capitalism to solve problems in the Black community. It reinforced gender hierarchy by reinscribing patriarchal tendency to "relegate women to a secondary status."[38]

Both the Million Man March and the civil rights movement prompted women to subscribe to the monist politics of racial liberation. Both events had as their goal the advancement of African Americans. It is of particular interest to note the activism of women in both events despite the fact that in the name of dealing with the ailments of the Black community, both of these historical events failed to directly encompass the issues and concerns that face Black women as women. Although the agendas of both would contend that their intentions were to benefit Black men and women alike, their immediate agendas held men as the focal point. This is clearly displayed through the neglect to incorporate women in a visual leadership capacity in either act of Black liberation politics, for the public crafting of the agendas was done by men and in the case of the Million Man March, directed toward men.

In the 1960s, gender was not the controversial category of analysis it is today. According to Cynthia Washington in her account of Black and white women in the civil rights movement, Black women were so focused on the issues of racial discrimination that they were blinded to other issues.[39] Paula Giddings argues that Black women were not aware of the sexism in SNCC. She recounts the words of one activist who stated that she had heard the sexist comments in the organization and was angered by them. However the comments did not prompt her to conclude sexism existed, namely, because she could see women in some decision-making positions though they were not in the "top hot spots."[40] In the 1990s, following the women's movement, women have pushed sexism and gender exclusion forward as a topic of public discussion. The question of whether or not there has been any progression in society's ideas about women and leadership roles remains an important issue.

Conclusion

The participatory roles of women were strikingly similar in both the Million Man March and the civil rights movement despite the societal conditions. Though women such as E. Faye Williams and Linda Greene held key positions as facilitators of the march, managing the finances and monitoring the organizational structure, they did not occupy high-profile positions, nor were they publicly regarded as leaders. Women did the behind-the-scenes work in the march just as they had in the civil rights movement. In neither case did the leadership roles women played receive adequate recognition in the media. The march's Health Task Force, a major behind-the-scenes support group, was heavily populated with women. E. Faye Williams also noted that "women almost always outnumbered men in the organizational meetings."[41] The actual duties performed by women in the Million Man March distinctly parallel the roles played by women in the civil rights movement.

In light of the fact that we found Black women participating in the Million Man March in largely the same ways they had during the civil rights movement, we surmise the role of Black women in racial liberation politics has not changed in the past thirty years. The role of women in the march demonstrates the sentiment Black feminist theory has generally articulated. The thoughts of Black women appear parallel to what King describes as "monist politics," in which the issues of the Black community were put ahead of their equal inclusion in the march. E. Faye Williams clearly articulated this sentiment in her discussion of the march when she suggested that it is the Black man's time to solve some of the problems of the Black community, and that women can deal with their issues another day.[42]

Some questions arise from these conclusions. First, why have women's roles in racial liberation politics not changed significantly? Second, is there a need for a movement that is conducted by Black women, as Black women, promoting the issues of Black women?

Kristal Zook took up these questions in writing a Black woman's manifesto in which she discusses the isolation of Black feminist in the academy. Zook concludes that in the ivory tower Black feminists are not successfully applying their theories to the lives of the Black community. She complains:

> Still, for all our "double jeopardy" consciousness about being both Black and female, progressive Black women have yet to galvanize a mass following or to spark a concrete movement for social change.[43]

Is it the case that Black women do not relate to a double-jeopardy consciousness, dual consciousness or any other conflict with their race and gender? Furthermore, is the end of patriarchy one of the goals of the Black community?

Zook's comments are of particular interest in light of the fact that two years after the Million Man March, the Million Woman March was held on October 25, 1997, in Philadelphia. While the Million Woman March was organized by Black women for Black women to attend, a brief look at the march's official platform finds no mention of ending patriarchy or the problems that Black women may face "existing on the matrix between race and gender." It is necessary to conduct an analysis of the march's propaganda and platform to discern whether the marching took place on behalf of Black women in particular or the needs of the overall Black community. Research comparing the platforms and agendas of the two marches is also needed.

Whatever the role of Black women in the Million Man March—organizational leaders, behind the scenes organizers or avid supporters—it is extremely important that their roles be accurately documented. Maulana Karenga, member of the executive board of the Million Man March/Day of Absence and author of the Million Man March mission statement, states that the day of absence—as was all of the organizing that made the march and the Day of Absence successful was overshadowed by the March itself. "Its name, its leaders and organizers, its focus in the capital, its concentration of forces in a single spot, the media generated from this all contributed to its overshadowing of the day of absence."[44] If this is true, it means that the aspects in which women were most instrumental—the organizing, the fund-raising, the grunt work—will not be remembered but conveniently forgotten. This chapter scratches only the surface of the magnitude and importance of women's participation in the organization and execution of the Million Man March. It took nearly 20 years to make substantial headway uncovering the dynamic work of women in the civil rights movement. Without a commitment from scholars to accurately record women's contributions to the success of the Million Man March, another 20 years may go by without acknowledging the hard work and dedication that the Black woman exhibited in relation to the march. If this were to happen, once again history would render a depiction of a monumental event that is incomplete.

NOTES

1. Officially, this event was referred to as the Million Man March/Day of Absence. Women were asked to participate in the day of absence. For the purpose of this analysis, we focus primarily on the march itself rather than the day of absence.

2. Michael A. Fletcher and Hamil R. Harris, "Black Men Jam Mall for a 'Day of Atonement'; Fiery Rhetoric, Alliance, Skepticism Mark March," *Washington Post,* 17 October 1995.

3. While some authors mention women, they do not discuss women's leadership nor do they discuss women's roles as central to the execution and sustainment of the movement. Such authors include Aldon Morris, *The Origins of the Civil Rights Movement* (New York: Free Press, 1984). David Garrow, *Bearing the Cross: Martin Luther King, Jr. and the Southern Christian Leadership Conference*

(New York: William Morrow, 1986). John White, *Black Leadership in America, 1895–1968* (New York: Longman, 1987).

4. For an in-depth review of women in various movements, see scholars such as Paula Giddings, *When and Where I Enter* (New York: Bantam, 1984); Cheryl Towsend Gilkes, "If It Wasn't for the Women . . . African American Women and Community Work and Social Change," in *Women of Color in U.S. Society*, ed. Bonnie Thornton Dill and Maxine Baca Zinn (Philadelphia: Temple University Press, 1994).

5. Bernice McNair Barnett, "Invisible Southern Black Women Leaders in the Civil Rights Movement: The Triple Constraints of Gender, Race, and Class," *Gender and Society* 7, no. 2 (1993): 162.

6. See Morris, *The Origins of the Civil Rights Movement*.

7. Evelyn Brooks Higginbotham, *Righteous Discontent* (Cambridge: Harvard University Press, 1993).

8. Melanie B. Cook, "Gloria Richardson: Her Life and Work in SNCC," *Sage* 5, no. 2 (1988): 51; Vicki Crawford, "Beyond the Human Self: Grassroots Activist in the Mississippi Civil Rights Movement," in *Women in the Civil Rights Movement: Trailblazers and Torchbearers, 1941–1965*, ed. V. Crawford, J. A. Rouse and B. Woods (Brooklyn: Carlson Publishing, 1990); Charles Payne, "Men Led but Women Organized: Movement Participation of Women in the Mississippi Delta" in *Women in the Civil Rights Movement: Trailblazers and Torchbearers, 1941–1965*, ed. V. Crawford, J. A. Rouse and B. Woods (Brooklyn: Carlson Publishing, 1990).

9. As discussed in our analysis, substantive discussions of the pivotal role women played in the civil rights movement are scarce. However, two volumes are exceptions to this rule and make great contributions to understandings of the dynamics of the movement by focusing on women: the edited volume by Crawford, Rouse and Woods, *Women in the Civil Rights Movement: Trailblazers and Torchbearers, 1941–1965* (Brooklyn: Carlson Publishing, 1990), and the recently published volume by Belinda Robnett, *How Long? How Long? African American Women in the Struggle for Civil Rights* (New York: Oxford University Press, 1997).

10. For example, the women behind the Montgomery bus boycott are seldom discussed in dominant narratives, but see Mary Fair Burks, " Trailblazers: Women in the Montgomery Bus Boycott," in *Women in the Civil Rights Movement: Trailblazers and Torchbearers, 1945–1961,* ed. V. Crawford, J. A. Rouse, and B. Woods (Brooklyn: Carlson Publishing, 1990). For a thorough discussion of the life and leadership of Ella Baker, see Joanne Grant, *Ella Baker Freedom Bound* (New York: John Wiley and Sons, 1998).

11. Payne, "Men Led but Women Organized."

12. Ibid.

13. Robnett, *How Long? How Long?*

14. Sara Evans, *Personal Politics* (New York: Random House, 1979). Cynthia Washington, "We Started from Different Ends of the Spectrum," *Southern Exposure* 21, no. 1–2,(1993): 14.

15. Gilkes, "If It Wasn't for the Women."

16. For a discussion of women's changed roles, see Marianne Githens and Jewel Prestige, *A Portrait of Marginality: The Political Behavior of the American Woman* (New York: Longman, 1997). In this early volume, the writers capture the change/increase in women's public activity—a sentiment often articulated in discussions of women's roles in society.

Editor's note: See also Sharon D. Wright, "Black Women in Congress during the Post–Civil Rights Movement Era," this volume.

17. Hamil R. Harris, "Despite Paradox, Black women Support March; Though Excluded, Many Endorse Event's Theme of Male Atonement," *Washington Post* 1 October 1995.

18. Haki R. Madhubuti and Maulana Karenga, *Million Man March/Day of Absence: A Commemorative Anthology* (Chicago: Third World Press, 1996).

19. E. Faye Williams, telephone interview by authors, October 1995.

20. Ibid.

21. Ibid.

22. Linda Greene, telephone interview by authors, October 1995.

23. David A. Bositis, "The Farrakhan Factor, Behind the Big Increase in Black Men Voting," *Washington Post*, 8 December 1996.

24. Marcia Slacum Greene and Tracey Thompson, "A Welcome on the Mall; Most Heed Call to Stay Away from March, Meet Elsewhere," *Washington Post*, 17 October 1995.

25. Ibid.

26. "Shun the March Activist Group Urges," Ft. Lauderdale: *Sun-Sentinel*, 14 October 1995.

27. Julianne Malveaux, "A Million Men Can Be Wrong," Ft. Lauderdale: *Sun-Sentinel*, 22 September 1995.

28. Linda Faye Williams, personal interview by authors, November 1995.

29. *Charlie Rose Show*, Sunday edition (MPR), 24 October, 1995. Transcript Number 1493.

30. Beverly Hall Lawrence, "What Now Sister? One Woman's Experience at the Million Man March" *Newsday*, 18 October 1995.

31. Byron P. White, "Women on the Outside Looking in at D.C. March," *Chicago Tribune*, 15 October 1995.

32. The Nation of Islam's publication *The Final Call* was full of propaganda on the purported benefits of the march for Black women. Many such writings appeared in the column "Eleven Fifty Five," such as "Black Woman This March Is for You," *The Final Call* 14, no. 22 (1995).

33. Kimberle Williams Crenshaw, "Beyond Racism and Misogyny: Black

Feminism and 2 Live Crew," in *Words That Wound: Critical Race Theory, Assaultive Speech, and the First Amendment*, ed. Mari J. Matsuda (Boulder: Westview Press, 1993). Evelyn Higginbotham, "The Metalanguage of Race," *Signs: Journal of Women in Culture and Society* 17, no. 2 (1992): 251. Deborah K. King, "Multiple Jeopardy, Multiple Consciousness: The Context of a Black Feminist Ideology," *Signs: Journal of Women's Culture in Society* 14, no.1 (1988): 42.

34. Linda Faye Williams, personal interview by authors, November 1995.

35. King, "Multiple Jeopardy, Multiple Consciousness."

36. This phrase is taken from the title of the book Gloria T. Hull et al, *All the Women Are White, All the Blacks Are Men, But Some of Us Are Brave* (New York: Feminist Press, 1982).

37. Higginbotham, "The Metalanguage of Race."

38. Manning Marable, "A Black Tie Occasion," *Guardian* 16 (October 1995).

39. Washington, "We Started from Different Ends of the Spectrum."

40. Giddings, *When and Where I Enter.*

41. Marc Fisher, "Million Man March; Behind the Scenes, the Women Count," *Washington Post* 14 October 1995.

42. E. Faye Williams, telephone interview.

43. Kristal Brent Zook, "A Manifesto of Sorts for a Black Feminist Movement," *New York Times,* 12 November 1995.

44. Maulana Karenga, "The March, The Day of Absence and the Movement" in *Million Man March/Day of Absence: A Commemorative Anthology,* ed. Haki R. Madhabuti and M. Karenga (Chicago: Third World Press, 1996).

Chapter Fourteen

Crossing Lines
Mandy Carter, Grassroots Activism, and Mobilization '96

Lynn M. Eckert and Dionne Bensonsmith

Introduction

Mandy Carter, an African American grassroots feminist activist from North Carolina whose career spans more than twenty-five years, is a significant leader both historically and politically. Continuing a long tradition of African American feminism that builds from the principles espoused by Sojourner Truth, Ida Wells-Barnett, and Ella Baker, Carter contributes to that tradition in a variety of ways. As a Black lesbian feminist, she gives voice to a group historically silenced within the women's, civil rights, and gay rights movements. Equally important, Carter's political activism and organizing are occurring at a unique moment in political history, a moment when organizations in those movements are willing to confront issues of diversity and difference within their memberships. This fact is strategically significant because it provides greater opportunities for cross-movement alliances, and for groups to challenge cultural assumptions our political culture makes regarding race, class, gender, and sexuality. Finally, Carter's experiences raise important questions about the viability of identity-based movements.

This chapter analyzes Carter's political history of activism. The experiences described and assessed are highlighted because they are relevant to Carter's maturation as an activist and point to a change in identity-based social movements dealing with difference across race, gender, class, and sexual orientation. The chapter traces her activism from the Vietnam

War to her most recent organizing with North Carolina Mobilization '96, a political action committee (PAC) created to defeat Senator Jesse Helms in his reelection bid. The latter part of the chapter explains the significance of Carter's activism and its connection to broader historical and political issues. The purpose here is not to valorize Mandy Carter's work but to suggest that the connections she develops across movements are politically important and tap into larger social changes.

The Ongoing Tradition of African American Feminist Activism

To fully appreciate the significance of Carter's organizing, her particular brand of activism needs to be placed in a tradition of African American feminism. African American women have always been a part of the feminist movement, but often organizations were segregated according to race and class. To many African American women, the behavior of white women in the movement was contradictory. Most Black women, Carter included, found that although many white women employed a rhetoric of inclusiveness, they had no problem with excluding or marginalizing Black women and working women from full participation within their organizations. A hallmark of Black feminist activism has been an understanding that oppressions overlap, and many like bell hooks, Audre Lorde, and Angela Davis have pushed the women's movement to conceptualize discrimination in more expansive and complex terms.

In terms of grassroots activism, parallels can be drawn between Mandy Carter and three African American feminists, Sojourner Truth, Ida Wells-Barnett, and Ella Baker, to demonstrate the continuity of a tradition of Black feminist thought of which Carter is a part. The first two activists, Sojourner Truth and Ida Wells-Barnett, were part of the first wave of the women's movement. The third activist, Ella Baker, was part of the second wave of the women's movement during the 1960s. A common theme that each addresses is the need for the women's movement to address issues of the intersection of race, class, and gender; to develop unity among women that allows for difference; and to develop a commitment to grassroots activism that empowers African American women.

While these women fought for the women's movement to develop a more complete understanding of how oppressions can overlap, it is important to recognize that in the earlier two waves of the women's movement, diversity was perceived as a group weakness rather than an advantage. The first wave's organizational focus was the right of universal suffrage. Prior to gaining suffrage many African American and white women divided. The debate became warped around the question of which group—Black men or white women—should vote.[1] After women gained the right to vote, the movement factionalized. Some believed voting rights entitled women to full citizenship and equal participation in political parties and government. Others wanted to maintain the gender division in the political sphere. According to the second perspective, women were properly concerned with health, education, and child welfare. Moreover, race and class often segregated women's organizations. White suffragists, due to wealth, status, and privilege, maintained greater political influence than other groups.

This era saw the emergence of Black feminists such as Sojourner Truth. A suffragette, Truth also saw the need for a more complex understanding of race, class, and gender. In a speech entitled "Ain't I a Woman," Truth implored white women to consider their own privileges as whites and to develop a truly inclusive movement representative of the experiences of all women. Implicitly, her speech conveys that gender oppression is affected by race, class, and social conditions. In another famous speech, "When Woman Gets Her Rights Man Will Be Right," Truth argues that women should be included in passage of the Fifteenth Amendment, which disallows the abridgment of suffrage on account of race but not sex. Truth did not support the amendment, and opposed Frederick Douglass and other feminists who believed including women weakened the likelihood of the amendment's ratification. Truth argues in her speech that Black men cannot claim that their race is emancipated when half of it remains unable to exercise a basic right of citizenship.

Similarly, Ida Wells-Barnett argues that suffragettes needed to address lynchings in the South in a context that took account of racism. Many Black men were lynched under the pretense of protecting white women's reputations. The women's movement during the first wave, however, failed to connect lynching with feminism. Wells-Barnett's article "Lynch Law in America" implicitly argues two points. First, feminists should be concerned about the erroneous way in which white women's sexual purity disguises brutal violence. Second, under political conditions permeated by racism, white and Black women could not forge a permanent alliance because African American women, in contrast to white women, interpreted lynching as a crime against race, and more specifically Black men, not gender. Wells-Barnett tacitly expresses a sense that gender oppression is connected to broader issues, and social location matters in experiencing oppression. Her point was that for African American women, race and gender were intrinsically linked, and until African American women's white counterparts addressed issues dealing with race equally with issues dealing with gender, a unified women's movement was unlikely to happen.

Feminism's second wave burgeoned from the turbulence of the 1960s. Here women of different backgrounds experienced unequal treatment within movements differently. For example, African American women played substantive roles within organizations, like the Student Nonviolent Coordinating Committee and the Southern Christian Leadership Conference, even though kudos for leadership responsibilities were given to men. The exclusion or relegation to "behind-the-scenes" positions in the civil rights and student protest movements led many women, especially women of color, to seek a movement of their own.

Some feminists like Deborah King questioned the actions of groups within the feminist movement during this wave. King writes:

> The history of racism in the early women's movement has been sustained by contemporary white feminists. Within organizations, most twentieth-century black women encounter a myriad experiences that deny their reality.[2]

King believes "monistic" approaches, frameworks that isolate one form of oppression as generative of all others, are reductive. A more "interactive model" placing women in a material context is needed. Thus, organizational practices become scrutinized and assumptions grounding the practices are challenged and reformulated.

Carter's activism is imbued with some of the same principles as the activism of Wells-Barnett and Truth. According to Wells-Barnett, the only way to achieve a lasting alliance is to understand how an individual from a different social location experiences sexism and racism. Carter extends the logic of Wells-Barnett's writings by including homophobia as another social location worthy of inclusion. No single referent exists for the way in which all women are discriminated against as women; rather, race, sex, and class influence how we experience sexism. Carter's objective is to get organizations within different movements (women's, gay and lesbian, civil rights) to understand this reality and broaden their appeal to become one movement that truly represents a diverse number of people.

At a time when we see an increase in organizations and movements based on single identities, like the Million Man March and the Promise Keepers, an ideal like Carter's has come under more and more scrutiny. Carter mirrors Truth's argument in that she refuses to rank oppression and understands that as long as some women are oppressed by racism and/or homophobia then feminists have failed in their goal of liberating all women.

Adding to the activism of Wells and Truth, Carter's activism builds upon some of the same principles as Ella Baker's. Carter, like Baker, believes that the process of change begins on the local level, slowly accumulating enough force and numbers to influence the national level. Baker, advisor and founder of the Student Nonviolent Coordinating Committee (SNCC), was critical of the patriarchal and hierarchical tendencies of organizations such as the Southern Leadership Council, which depended upon charismatic male leadership. Baker argued that the success of any movement depends upon the empowerment and self-reliance of the membership, not leaders. She also rejected the premise that organizations must be nationally rather than locally oriented. Both she and Carter realized that participants are more engaged, organized, and mobilized in the local community. According to Carter, local politics is a place where individual participation can directly shape a community. Because local government is the most accessible level of government, Carter believes that it is the foremost arena for political change.

Mandy Carter's Early Activism

Growing up in the politically charged sixties, Mandy Carter cites many factors that led her to a career as an activist. Although too young to participate during the early sixties, she was heavily influenced by the civil rights movement. Her first experience came in her senior year of high school when a representation of the American Friends Service Committee (AFSC) addressed her class. The AFSC had created an outreach program designed to teach students during the turbulent '60s about nonviolent grassroots activism. It was here that Carter realized the power of one person to inspire political change in a politically charged environment where individuals were compelled to address the failings of politics.

Her galvanizing moment as an activist arrived during the time of the Vietnam War when she became an organizer for the War Resisters League and acquired some of the organizing skills so vital later in her career. According to Carter, the war in Vietnam posed such an immediate threat to so many young people's lives that it united individuals with very different identities and backgrounds. What mattered most to those opposing the war was a commitment to peace; concerns about race, gender, or sexual orientation were secondary. Furthermore, organizing against the war proved to many people that they could induce political change. The opposition to the war imparted a sense of agency: a faith in the ability to recast the politics that affected their lives directly. Carter blames feelings of cynicism and alienation today on the absence of such a direct threat as war.

For Carter, antiwar organizing, the successful bringing together of a variety of individuals from diverse backgrounds, was evidence of the potential for alliances across race, gender, and even sexual orientation. It also sustained her faith in the political system and belief in the efficacy of grassroots activism. As an organizer against the Vietnam War, she understood that persistent and strategic actions such as protesting and mobilizing support through rallies and editorials affected government policy. The more vocal the resistance to the war, the more informed and aware the public was about the war, the greater the support to withdraw troops.

After the war in Vietnam ended, Carter moved to San Francisco, where she matured as an activist in a politically charged environment of a unique nature. During the late 1970s, the gay rights movement was building strength, and the gay and lesbian community became aware of its burgeoning political power. The political influence of gays and lesbians in San Francisco is more powerful than in any other city in the world, and it was here that the focus of Carter's activism shifted from the war to the rights of gays and lesbians.

Carter's perspective on politics evolved while working at Maude's, a landmark lesbian bar in San Francisco. Maude's figured so prominently in Carter's development as an activist for two reasons. First, it was there that Harvey Milk's murder took on particular significance. Second, Ricki Striker, then owner of Maude's, inspired Carter because she was an intelligent, successful, politically active, lesbian businesswoman. Harvey Milk was one of the first openly homosexual individuals elected to the San Francisco Board of Supervisors. Milk, along with Mayor George Moscone, was murdered by a disgruntled former supervisor named Dan White, made famous in his trial by the "Twinkie" defense. After the homicides in November 1978, many in the gay and lesbian community realized the importance of having "out" gays and lesbians in politics, a circumstance that raised the community's consciousness not only in San Francisco but around the country. It was in this politically charged environment that Carter began to reevaluate her career and deeply consider the significance of minority groups' pooling their numbers and resources.

The Cincinnati antigay ballot measure passed in November 1993 but was rendered unconstitutional when the Supreme Court struck down all such ordinances in the *Romers v. Evans* case.[3] The measure had passed in part because the Christian Coalition was able to exploit divisions within and between the Black community and gays and lesbians.

The Christian Coalition funneled large sums of money to local Black ministers to defeat the ordinance. A *New York Times* editorial described the Christian Coalition's actions, stating:

> For ambitious Black ministers in Cincinnati like K. Z. Smith and Charles Winburn, the media exposure they got for their anti-gay activism was priceless. And the passing of the measure won't end their mutually beneficial alliance with the religious right, which has sent a stream of cash into their coffers. One group, Coloradans for Family Values, sent $400,000 into Cincinnati before the vote.[4]

The Christian Coalition also sought to sever any analogies between the civil rights movement and the gay and lesbian movement. Gay rights were portrayed as "special, not equal rights." The same editorial continues:

> They [the Christian Coalition] produced and distributed a manipulative video called "Gay rights, Special Rights," which cleverly and misleadingly juxtaposes images from recent gay rights rallies and Black civil rights marches of the 60's. Using footage out of context, the video implies that the two movements are at odds and that gay and lesbian gains will detract from those made by Blacks.

The ordinance passed without much opposition from the Black community. Carter noted that several Black preachers rejected the position of ministers like Smith or Winburn but did so too late in the campaign to change opinions. She states, "Cincinnati is a classic example of what happens when you're silent and invisible."[5]

In Carter's own analysis, the responsibility for the success of the antigay measure must also be shared by the gay rights movement itself, which is overwhelmingly represented by gay white males. The cost of failing to reflect the diversity of the movement is that the Christian Coalition easily misrepresented reality. It were able to fragment the gay community along racial and gendered lines. Few Black gays or lesbians felt comfortable proclaiming their sexual orientation to the community because their families resided there, thus they failed to become part of the group of gays and lesbians fighting the ordinance. Others may have been willing but remained unmobilized or outside the grassroots network. Denials of white-male hegemony within the movement appear unpersuasive without significant numbers of Blacks in leadership positions in national gay and lesbian organizations.

Carter warns that until many in the gay community recognize the need to expand issues of concern beyond purely gay rights, similar vulnerabilities will persist. Issues of racism and sexism need attention to optimize the movement's numbers and strength. When blindly ignoring crosscutting issues, people of color and women remain marginalized and uninvolved in the gay rights movement. The gay and lesbian community needs "bridge builders," like Carter, to forge important political connections with other minority communities. These coalitions are necessary to overcome both the Black, and gay and lesbian communities' discrete and insular status.

North Carolina Mobilization '96

In 1996, Carter formed North Carolina Mobilization '96 (Mobe '96), a political action committee (PAC) to defeat Senator Jesse Helms in his re-election bid. Mobe '96 had three main objectives in the Senate race between incumbent Helms and challenger Harvey Gantt. The goals were to educate, register voters to "get out the vote" on election day, and train volunteers to organize and utilize the media. Mobe '96 recruited volunteers from the gay, lesbian, bisexual, and transgendered communities.

The central underlying purpose of the organization was to establish lasting links and encourage participation with other progressive communities within North Carolina. Carter hoped this progressive infrastructure would be sustained after the election. Thus, her objective was twofold: mobilize voters and organize a grassroots network. Of course, Mobe '96's objective also included ousting Helms from office. Carter's Mobe '96 takes on particular significance when placed in the changing context of North Carolina politics and when juxtaposed to the ideological positions of Helms.

Carter's kind of political organizing could take place only in the "New South." So what does this "New South" look like, especially in North Carolina? North Carolina is the tenth-largest state in the country, and at this writing has the country's lowest unemployment rate (approximately 6 percent). It is home of the Research Triangle area, which encompasses Raleigh, Durham, and Chapel Hill, and is a hotbed of high-tech industry growth. The Research Triangle contains the highest concentration of Ph.D.'s in the country. Moreover, North Carolina has become the banking center of the region, serving as headquarters for Nation's Bank, the country's fourth-largest bank.[6]

However, ideological and economic vestiges of the "Old South" endure. African Americans remain on the periphery of politics in the South. Earl and Merle Black note in *Politics and Society in the South* that the circumstances of African Americans are different and improved, but their political influence remains tangential.[7] This fact raises two important strategic issues. One, Mobe '96 will have to attract white, working-class supporters. Two, suppressing wedge issues like race, which typically divides working-class or populist alliances in the South, is necessary over the long term. Even with economic conditions that rival many third-world countries, most of North Carolina's political conflicts center on cultural rather than economic differences, mirroring the partisan divisions in the country as a whole.[8] Approximately 76 percent of the population is white, 22 percent Black, 1 percent American Indian, and 1 percent Hispanic, making cross-cultural coalition building essential if minorities in North Carolina expect any type of political power.[9]

The second aspect that makes Carter's Mobe '96 significant is the fact that it attempted to oust Helms, one of the most vociferous conservative critics in the country. Even as the state continues to change, maturing into a more progressive South, North Carolina continues to elect Helms, someone who represents old southern values. If his opponent Harvey Gantt, former mayor of Charlotte, had been elected, he would have been the first African American senator from the state since the Reconstruction era. Helms is more than a senator from North Carolina. He chairs the Foreign Relations Committee, one of the most powerful committees in the Senate, and is in a position to stall bills not in accord with his own political agenda. Also, he is a vocal national spokesperson for the conservative right in this country.

One needs only to examine the campaign strategy of Helms to understand precisely how divisive he can be. Helms and Gantt had faced each other once before, in 1990. During that race Helms gained crucial support in the last weeks of the campaign by televising several ads with racist overtones. The first accused Gantt of financially benefiting from a racial set-aside program. The others attempted to portray Gantt as a radical liberal supporting abortion for sex selection and racial quotas. Helms also suppressed Black voter turnout by mailing voter-fraud warnings to heavily populated Black districts.

Gay baiting has been another persistent theme in several of Helms's campaigns. Ironically, while Helms elevated issues like condemnation of homosexuality to the top of his campaign ads, he also enlisted help from the same corner. Arthur Finkelstein, Helms's lead pollster and consultant, recently revealed his sexual orientation, and adopted two children with his partner in Massachusetts.[10]

For these reasons, challenging Helms was important in its own right. The race took on added significance with Carter's social-movement-building activities. Given that the South is historically a conservative region with power concentrated in the hands of white heterosexual males, even the appearance of an organization such as Carter's is an indicator of a changing South. The failure of Gantt to win is not the central issue in assessing Mobe '96's success or, more generally, the success of Carter as an activist. Instead, through Carter's leadership, Mobe '96 was able to establish a progressive political infrastructure poised to build upon important links and to pool resources across organizations. "The Gantt campaign was not just about defeating Jesse Helms but about building coalitions and movement-making in North Carolina."[11] Mobe '96 worked alongside the National Organization for Women, Mothers Against Jesse in Congress (MAJIC), and the North Carolina Committee Against Extremism (NC Cares). Carter proved that such an organization was politically viable and influential by raising close to $250,000. Mobe '96 also coordinated with the North Carolina Democratic Party to defeat Helms.

Bridge building across communities takes time to establish. No gay and lesbian political network existed before 1990, and only skeletal organizations continued afterward. Following the 1996 election, gay and lesbian political networks were more firmly rooted, and developed important relationships with feminist organizations and the Black community. The ultimate force of this strategy is to educate and raise awareness, elucidating the fundamental similarities between identity-based oppressions. To repudiate one manifestation of oppression and not another only redirects rather than resolves the core problem. According to Carter, we are in an important moment in the gay and lesbian movement because a change in attitudes about homosexuality is rapidly occurring. African American lesbians are in a particularly important position because they are situated in other communities and can encourage understanding and alliances between groups across communities.

In sum, the most important issue for Mobe '96 was recognizing the complexity of identity as an opportunity to forge new political relationships through its participants' connection to and membership in other identity-based movements.

Carter's Political Significance: The Challenge of Cross-Movement Alliances

To Carter, factionalizing within various social movements is debilitating. Feminists, African Americans, and gays and lesbians are potential allies as marginalized and outnumbered groups in the political system, and their memberships overlap. Carter has worked toward making these groups acknowledge the possibility of forming coalitions, and to reflexively examine the prejudice within their own respective groups.

Like bell hooks in *Killing Rage*, Carter fears a rigid conceptualization of unity, or a unity thought of only in terms of sameness. hooks critiques demands to create an "onerous kind of unity" in the Black community, where gays, lesbians, and feminists—or any variation from a "normative ideal"—are suspect. Carter's activism extends the logic of hooks's argument to other groups within the gay rights or women's movement. According to hooks, Black identity is complex, multiple, and fluid; gender, class, and sexual orientation matter when constructing self and identity. Therefore, theorizing about Black identity from multiple locations is necessary.[12] She would add that organizing from multiple locations is also necessary, something that Carter attempts to recognize in all her organizations. Carter's organizing transfers this message to the gay and lesbian movement and to the women's movement, posing the challenge that true equality will remain unattained as long as any community preserves a simplistic image of unitary subjectivity. Imposing such a monistic image fragments the movement. This conclusion is counterintuitive to many in the African American, and gay and lesbian communities (and also in other identity-based communities) who believe losing a "unitary representation" will destroy the basis of organizational resistance.[13]

Carter's objective, one that is essential for the success of any identity-based movement, depends upon a recognition and acceptance of diversity. Yet persuading organizations within movements to understand the crosscutting connection of race, class, and gender and to willingly consolidate forces is difficult. It requires heightened consciousness from members to recognize the reciprocal value in not only understanding and respecting each other's differences but being willing to find some common ground on which to unite. Movements are also legitimately concerned about factionalizing and dilution. Factionalizing becomes more probable in social movements that include greater diversity. Organizing around an abstract goal will inevitably foment disagreement about concrete policies to end social injustice. Broad objectives can create friction between the dual functions of leadership, which include mobilization and articulation.[14] Both functions are correlated because successful mobilization requires heightened articulation: the two are integral to each other for success. Mobilization allows organization leaders to cultivate greater participation and is achieved when the organizational message is distinctive enough to target and prompt particular groups to act. However, when the message is pointed and sharpened it may also divide.

One of the reasons Mobe '96 was so successful in gaining membership has to do with its clearly defined objective of defeating Jesse Helms. Most agree that the goal of ending all oppression is worthy. Yet when called to act, some may disagree about what constitutes oppression. For example, when organizing for the Human Rights Campaign Fund, Carter confronted many gays and lesbians who declared that affirmative action is not a "gay issue."[15] Moreover, creating distinctive messages for the purpose of mobilization becomes difficult when the message is complex pointing toward multiple root causes. The content of Carter's message is nuanced; explaining the interconnection of oppression is no easy task. Moreover, communicating complexity in the American political system is not often rewarded.

The fear of dilution both of resources and attention from women, for example, to other groups is also a prevalent concern. "The larger question . . . at a time when women are under attack on all sides, is how to fight against racism and organize on a multitude of fronts, yet still keep the focus on women."[16] For feminists, this is a genuine worry, considering that groups in other movements had previously requested that women postpone demands for equality until after the more significant demands of other groups were realized. The closely related concern is that sometimes systems of oppression not only overlap but collide. The question remains whether groups have the prudence to seek justice by deconstructing streams of oppression through examining the relevance and propriety of claims in context specific situations, rather than unreflexively calling for what Cornel West describes as a "closed ranks mentality." Otherwise, minority group demands are easily dismissed as cross-movement alliances deteriorate.

A New Political Reality

One may ask what really makes Mandy Carter's activism all that unique. She deals with overlapping identity issues and the idea that organizations appealing to principles of nondiscrimination often practice a similar form of discrimination within their own group. These are principles for which antecedents such as Sojourner Truth, Ida Wells-Barnett, and Frances Beal, Pauli Murray, and Angela Davis have argued. Carter is clearly a part of that African American feminist tradition. However, she also contributes to that tradition in a number of ways. First, it must be noted that Carter's activism takes place at a unique moment in political history, a moment when organizations within the gay rights, racial equality, and women's movements are more willing than ever before to confront issues of difference and to reconceptualize "unity." This term has a more fluid meaning, one that embraces differences and challenges dominance.[17] The concern is not to question what it means to be Black, gay, or a woman but, rather to critique whiteness, heterosexuality, and maleness. This strategy dislodges the dominant group whether it be whites, heterosexuals, or men as referents, and questions the validity of the very distinctions that maintain their epistemic primacy. In this sense, Carter's activism, the very premises of the organizations she has helped to found, has more far-reaching objectives than did the activism of her predecessors.

Second, Carter's activism is unique because she gives a voice to an exceptionally marginalized group, African American lesbians. All of the movements of which she is a part have historically ignored her lesbianism, her blackness, or her gender. Her representation of these groups is important to the women's and gay/lesbian movements not simply to promote diversity but as a central epistemological issue.[18] A representation of women's experiences from a full-life spectrum is necessary to avoid the pitfalls of using one dominant group within any movement as a referent. In fact, internal debates within the women's movement question whether women are able to organize a movement around the basis of gender alone. What do low-paid, unskilled, third-world, female laborers have in common with educated, upper-class, white, Western women?

Thus, to fully understand the mechanisms through which patriarchy works, women with a variety of experiences need to convey the way that sexism has affected their lives.[19] In the case of the antigay statute in Cincinnati, the gay rights movement was portrayed largely as white and male. As a result, it appeared hegemonic and unable to connect with other minority communities. More important, when one group dominates a movement and serves as a referent for the entire group, division weakens the movement and policy outcomes are skewed toward the privileged group.

Carter's activism also raises some significant questions about the potential for cross-movement alliances. Fears of factionalizing and dilution are issues that threaten alliances. To succeed, organizations such as Mobe '96 have to labor at educating their memberships about how different streams of oppression interact, which is a complicated process.

The purpose of writing about Mandy Carter is not to issue a glowing assessment of her organizing. In her career, she has had both successes and failures. Rather, the focus is on telling a historically untold story that should provide a better picture of the ongoing tradition and ideas of African American grassroots feminist activism. This chapter also provides a fuller sense of our political times, a sense of the totality of political debates and ideas not simply recorded by the powerful or the winners, and also the important conversations taking place within social movement organizations.

In the past, the dominant group's assumptions about race, class, gender, and sexuality were rarely critiqued, leaving the epistemic validity of their claims unchallenged. This era is different because minority groups are able to question claims about whiteness or heterosexuality. As a result, no one group's experiences are considered authoritative or serve as a referent. Instead, a more legitimate dialogue about the foundational assumptions or epistemic claims are opened so that we develop a fuller understanding of the requirements or policies necessary to ensure fairness and equality.[20] Mandy Carter's activism and organizational philosophy push us to realize that in order to remain vital and effectively meet the challenges of our changing political landscape, organizations within

movements must interact, interorganize, and engage in a multifaceted and multicultural relationships.

NOTES

1. Deborah K. King, "Multiple Jeopardy, Multiple Consciousness: The Context of Black Feminist Ideology," in *Words of Fire: An Anthology of African American Feminist Thought*, with an epilogue by Johnetta B. Cole, ed. Beverly Guy-Sheftall (New York: New Press, 1995), p. 295.

2. Ibid., p. 305.

3. The Supreme Court decision declared unconstitutional a statewide referendum that prohibited at any level (legislative, executive, or judicial) discrimination of gays and lesbians. Justice Kennedy, writing for the Court, argues that Colorado's amendment imposed a liability rather than prohibited special rights for gays and lesbians. The Court concluded that the amendment was so broad and sweeping that its only possible purpose was to direct animus toward one group of citizens.

4. Editorial Desk, "Cincinnati's Odd Couple," *New York Times*, 13 December 1993, sec. A, p. 17.

5. Mandy Carter, interview by authors, Durham, N.C., 13 March 1997.

6. Peter Applebome, "In North Carolina, the New South Rubs Uneasily with the Old Ways," *New York Times*, 2 July 1990, sec. A, p. 1.

7. Earl and Merle Black, *Politics and Society in the South* (Cambridge: Harvard University Press, 1987), p. 293.

8. Infant mortality rates in North Carolina are high; SAT scores are low; 40 percent of wages fall below the poverty line; unions and industry regulations are few; and a sewage problem in the eastern part of the state produces conditions comparable to third world countries. Applebome p. 1.

9. *The Almanac of American Politics* (Washington DC: National Journal, 1996).

10. Rob Christiansen, "Tried-and-True GOP Strategy: Using Homosexuality as a Wedge Issue," *Raleigh News and Observer*, 7 October 1996, sec. A, p. 3.

11. Mandy Carter interview.

12. bell hooks, *Killing Rage: Ending Racism* (New York: Henry Holt and Company, 1995), p. 248.

13. Ibid., p. 249.

14. Mayer D. Zald and Roberta Ash, "Social Movement Organizations: Growth, Decay, and Change," in *Frontiers in Social Movement Theory*, ed. Aldon D. Morris and Carol McClurg Mueller, (New Haven: Yale University Press, 1992), p. 337.

15. Mandy Carter interview.

16. Helen Zia, "How NOW?" *Ms.*, July/August 1996, pp. 52–53.

17. hooks, *Killing Rage*; Judith Butler, Drucilla Cornell, Nancy Frasier, *Feminist Contentions* (New York and London: Routlege, 1995).

18. Satya Mohanty, *Literary Theory and the Claims of History: Postmodernism, Objectivity, Multicultural Politics* (Ithaca: Cornell University Press, 1997).

19. Ibid.

20. Butler, *Feminist Contentions.*

Chapter Fifteen

Documenting the Struggle
African American Women as Media Artists, Media Activists

Frances Gateward

Books, newspapers, magazines, radio, motion pictures, and television. Whether we like it or not, mass media are an integral part of our lives. As an industry, they provide billions of dollars in profit for a multinational oligarchy; as an information source, they are consumed by audiences to obtain knowledge, to seek advice and opinion, and to satisfy curiosity; and as an entertainment, they fill time, furnish companionship, and allow an escape from "reality." But the media's all-pervasive, powerful presence also works as a significant part of our cultural consciousness. Through media we can determine our personal identities, find models of behavior, and gain a sense of belonging. They not only influence how we think of others but also of ourselves—what we take ourselves to be, and what we want to become. And like all cultural products, mass media encode relations of power. Like other institutions, they reflect, reinforce, and help sustain the racist hegemonic order of the United States. This chapter examines the work of three African American women documentary film and video makers whose productions, unlike that of conventional media producers, seek to create a truly egalitarian society by challenging the racist, sexist, classist, and homophobic status quo. Madeline Anderson, Portia Cobb, and Cyrille Phipps, women who, like their predecessors in print (e.g., Maria W. Stewart, Mary Shadd Cady, and Ida B. Wells-Barnett)[1] "despite racial and sexual discrimination, [fight] back against their oppression and [are] at the forefront of major events in American history" (Streitmatter 1994: 2). As media artists, whose productions are diverse in style and content, they present new and unique aesthetic visions. As media activists, they give voice to the disenfranchised and marginalized, addressing the concerns and struggles of African American women and the African American community at large. But these artist/activists do more than just document the struggle. They use their talents and their respective mediums to, as Waugh states, "intervene wherever they have been challenging the inherited structures of social domination" (1984: xii).

One of the earliest African American women filmmakers who sought to use the medium of film for change was Eloyce Patrick Gist, born in Hitchcock, Texas, in 1892. She and her husband, James, directors of film dramas in the 1930s, knew that film could serve as more than entertainment. Gist, "based on her religious faith, believed cinema could unite Black people, promote Christian values and racial pride, and communicate a social message" (Gibson 1994: 21). Today there are hundreds of African American women writing, producing, and directing film and video. Though most of them can be considered activists because they challenge the exclusionary practices of Hollywood and free African Americans from the confines of conventional one-dimensional stereotypes, I focus on Anderson, Cobb, and Phipps because each is what Thomas Waugh (1984) terms "a committed filmmaker, one who not only observes, but also participates in socio-political transformation. He/she is not only content to interpret the world, but is also engaged in changing it" (14).

Before I address the work of the artist/activists noted above, I would like to briefly review areas of relevance to the discussion of African American women media producers: the control of media representation; conventional constructions of African American images; film and video as signifying practices; and the politics of film form, for as Fiske (1987) states, "[F]orm is just as much a bearer of meaning and content . . . as a bearer of ideology, form is considerably more effective than content" (23).

By virtue of race, class, gender, and heterosexual privilege, peoples of color, as well as women, gays and lesbians, and others, have had virtually no control over the creation of their images. In the United States, the television and film industries are heavily unionized, making it difficult for those "outside the system" to gain entry. Despite a pact made between the NAACP and the major studios in 1942, and more recent actions such as hearings in 1982 by the Los Angeles Human Relations Commission, a class action discrimination suit against the television networks and film studios in 1983, and investigations by the U.S. Commission on Civil Rights in 1997, employment discrimination continues to plague the industry.[2] One week before the 68th annual Academy Awards presentation, the popular publication *People Magazine*, created a flurry of controversy with its March 1996 issue. The cover featured actors Angela Bassett, Denzel Washington, Laurence Fishburne, and Whitney Houston, all celebrities with box-office clout. The uproar that followed was not caused by the photographs of African American celebrities but by the cover headline: "HOLLYWOOD BLACKOUT: The film industry says all the right things, but its continued exclusion of African Americans is a national disgrace." The article "What's Wrong with This Picture" examined discrimination in Hollywood from the perspectives of African American actors, media executives, and a production crew. As noted previously, union membership is crucial in mainstream Hollywood, and the statistics quoted are dismal: only 2.3 percent of Director's Guild of America members are African American, and just 2.6 percent of the Writer's Guild (Lambert et al. 1996). These numbers are deplorable enough, but even worse is what the authors fail to note: membership in a union does mean employment. This systematic exclusion from production has resulted in a mediated reality of African American invisibility. As the *Philadelphia Inquirer* reported in the spring of 1996, "Of 64 situation comedies that aired on the six networks, only 12 had racially mixed casts. The remaining 52 were segregated with 40 featuring all white casts" (Storm 1996: A1). And on those occasions when people of color are depicted, it is often in a stereotypical manner.

For African Americans, it has meant the transference of the already existing stereotypes from literature and vaudeville to film. The one-dimensional, derogatory characterizations included such types as the mammy, the large, dark-skinned asexual woman who happily serves her White employers or slave masters; the threatening, brutish Black man with an uncontrollable penchant for violence, usually represented as the rapist of White women; the Jezebel, the promiscuous, highly sexual seductress; the Tom, the "the hearty, stoic, generous, and selfless individual who, though enslaved, insulted, and harassed," remains faithful to his/her oppressors; and the Coon, the "unreliable, lazy subhuman . . . good for nothing more than eating watermelon, stealing chickens, shooting craps, or butchering the English language" (Bogle 1989: 5, 8). So evident in films of the past, they have been maintained through history, and continue to plague contemporary screens.

Racial intolerance has remained such an intransigent and ingrained aspect of American society that racist depictions, such as the depiction of peoples of color in the popular film *Ghost* (1990), are not noticed and rarely have impact upon the success or failure of a commercial feature.[3] The tradition established by overtly racist films such as Griffith's *Birth of a Nation* (1915) and *Gone With the Wind* (1939) is maintained today with critically acclaimed, box-office bonanzas such as the sci-fi action film *Independence Day* (1997), with its sole African American female character sexualized by her occupation as a stripper.

Another type of representation frequently profitable for the Hollywood industry has been the stereotypical depiction of Black Africans. Rather than providing images of the African continent as one containing centuries-old and diverse cultures, these creators of popular culture usually opt for what Maynard (1974) describes as a "monolithic jungle and savage dark continent" (iv). This homogenized vision of Africa, populated by primitive, infantile subservient figures and brutish, vicious cannibals who lust after White flesh, is evident in films such as the continually recurring *King Solomon's Mines* (1937, 1950, 1959, 1987), *Congo* (1995), and *Danger Zone* (1996). One cannot, of course, fail to mention the highly lucrative Tarzan productions.

Academics have recently debated the value and use of image studies, arguing that the issue of positive versus negative images no longer has currency. But one should not underestimate the power the media have in influencing attitudes, beliefs, and even public policy. As K. Sue Jewell demonstrates, the stereotypes of African American women in mass media have been used to justify African American women's limited access to societal resources and institutions (1993).

Though there have been some representations that counter the old stereotypes, they are usually few and far between. The racist depictions still persist, though often in new forms and guises. In this era, a period marked by resurgent and what Piliawski (1984) describes as "respectable racism," Hollywood has found renewed interest in the plight of the racially oppressed. By turning its cameras toward feature films in which the narratives revolve around the injustices of racial prejudice, inequality, and discrimination, Hollywood producers have regenerated what filmmaker Julie Dash describes as the "victim-misery syndrome, where Black people have to be miserable victims waiting for a White savior to come along" (as quoted by Harris 1986: 18). Examples include Alan Parker's *Mississippi Burning* (1988), Joel Schumacher's *A Time to Kill* (1996), and *Ghosts of Mississippi* (1996), directed by Rob Reiner.

These films are typical, contradictory Hollywood texts, on one level denouncing and condemning racist practices, while at the same time reaffirming the strengthened conservative values of the contemporary American political climate. Within the context of this chapter, the descriptive term "Hollywood" as used by Roffman and Purdy (1981), refers to "more than just a film made in a studio in Southern California. Rather, it implies a whole style of film, a particular approach to film narrative, a peculiar set of cultural and social values" (1).

The films of the Hollywood/dominant cinema tradition present their ideologies within a formulaic structure that, with the dominance of the Hollywood studios, has resulted in the creation of a prevailing film language. Capable of masking their own construction, the films of the dominant cinema, as argued by Ryan and Kellner (1988), "help instill ideology by creating the illusion that what happens on the screen is a neutral recording of events, rather than a construct operating from a certain point of view. . . . The formal conventions occlude this positioning by erasing the signs of cinematic artificiality"(1).[4] This conventionalized form of media construction results in a cinema that presents itself, and its ideology, as natural.

But the African American press and African American–produced media in general have historically provided opposition—serving as an advocacy tool in the African American struggle for civil and human rights. Beginning in 1827 with *Freedom's Journal*, the antislavery newspaper started by Samuel Cornish and John Russwurm, and continuing today in more than 3,000 publications, the African American press remains active toward social change. As mass communications expanded to include the aural and visual mediums of radio, motion pictures, and television, so too have the efforts of African Americans.

To counter the racist, sexist, class-biased, and homophobic media, contemporary African American women have chosen to work in the mediums of film and video to give voice to a discourse based in their reality, from their perspective. As documentary filmmaker Michelle Parkerson (1987) states:

Traditionally used to mutilate and stereotype, mass media [have] been killing women and people of color for some time. But the independent film community, particularly Black independent film and video makers create with an understanding that film and video no longer serve as mere entertainment in these dangerous times. We use film and video to validate our herstory and experiences, where before there was only distortion (12).

In their efforts such as of a counter-cinema, film and video makers like Anderson, Cobb, and Phipps actively challenge the Hollywood conventions, in form as well as content. Rather than fictionalizing the history and concerns of the community, these artist/activist choose to remain grounded in the reality of people's lives and lived experience with documentary, and they do so fully aware of the ideological underpinnings of traditional documentary form as well.

Madeline Anderson

The thing I want to do most in film is record the Black experience.

Madeline Anderson is a pioneer of African American cinema and television, and one of the most important media producers/directors of the 1970s. Julie Dash, director of the groundbreaking film *Daughters of the Dust,* considers Anderson a major influence. Anderson's awards include her selection as Woman of the Year in 1976 at the Sojourner Truth Festival of the Arts; an Indie Award for Lifelong Achievements and Contributor to the Art of Film from the Association of Independent Film and Video Makers in 1985; and induction into the Miller Gallery of Greats in 1991 and the Black Filmmakers Hall of Fame in 1992. Like most Americans, Anderson grew up with the movies, but her exposure inspired her to become a filmmaker: "I went [to the movies] every Saturday with my brother and our friends. We packed a lunch and stayed all day. . . . The films we saw didn't reflect who we were. Even then I wanted to see us in films."

While attending New York University as a psychology major, Anderson was introduced to filmmaking by working as an apprentice with renowned documentarians Richard Leacock and D. A. Pennebaker.[5] Her first film was produced in 1961, *Integration Report 1,* a short film about the year of the nation's first civil rights sit-ins. Wanting to learn more about the technical aspects of film production, Anderson began to work

Madeline Anderson, a pivotal and influential figure of contemporary documen-tary filmmaking and African American cinema. (Courtesy Madeline Anderson)

on films by others. From 1962 to 1964 she worked as an assistant direc-tor and assistant editor on Clarke's film *The Cool World*,[6] and with WNET in New York from 1964 to 1969, Anderson applied her talents as a writer, associate producer, editor, and director. While with WNET, a PBS station, Anderson also worked on the program *Black Journal*, a groundbreaking series that investigated and presented controversial is-sues from varied perspectives. The program received an Emmy in 1969. She left WNET in 1969 to work on her most acclaimed film, *I Am Some-body*.

Produced, directed, and edited by Anderson, *I Am Somebody* docu-ments the strike of African American hospital workers against the hos-pitals of Charleston, South Carolina, in 1969. Because of pay inequity, inhumane treatment, and the lack of grievance procedures, African American women began to organize and formed a union, Local 1119B. When 12 women were fired from their jobs, 400 others went on a strike that was to last more than 100 days. The movement for a living wage and respect on the job expanded into a large-scale civil rights protest.

Rallies and daily marches were held and a boycott ensued, costing the local economy upwards of $15 million in revenue loss. Hundreds of National Guard troops and state police were called in, and as expected, many people were arrested, more than one thousand in fact, including Ralph Abernathy. The Southern Christian Leadership Conference arrived, as did the chair of the Organizing Committee of Hospital and Nursing Home Employees, Coretta Scott King. In addition, as Philip Foner (1980) notes, "[T]he national heads of nine civil rights organizations and five elected Black officials issued a joint statement in support of the strike. It was the first time Black leaders had come together on a single issue since King's death" (442). An important document of the civil rights movement, Anderson's film gives testimony to the movement as a grassroots struggle and highlights the often forgotten contributions of women to the struggle.

According to Foner, in 1969, "Charleston was a most unlikely site for a major unionizing drive among Black hospital workers. A booming tourist trade and convention business attested the city's appeal, but life was harsh for its working class, especially for the Black workers. Charleston was one of the few large Southern cities that had not been touched by the Civil Rights Movement" (440). Anderson deftly depicts this in the opening of the film. The images introducing the city are like picturesque postcards: scenic landscapes, tour boats to Fort Sumter, old southern mansions, and horse-drawn buggies. This tourist "gaze" is abruptly interrupted when, the narrator explains, "Those who came in the spring of 1969 saw Charleston as it really was if you're poor and Black." Anderson immediately cuts to a shot of African American feet marching for economic and social justice. It is important to note that those in protest move from left to right, while in the shot that precedes it, the horse-drawn buggy moves right to left. By juxtaposing these shots, Anderson, with this powerful imagery, creates a metaphor for the events—movement away from tradition and its racist discrimination. But it will be a long and tedious process, and this is underscored by the music, a subdued, slow-paced instrumental of the civil rights anthem "We Shall Overcome."

An important aspect of *I Am Somebody* is the focus it places on strike participants. Several known leaders of the civil rights movement are presented in the film: Ralph Abernathy, Coretta Scott King, and Andrew Young, all in leadership roles. Yet, it is the average citizens who are interviewed: striking hospital workers, high school students, and townspeople supportive of the cause. Rather than being shown as powerless victims, those interviewed give testimony to their experiences, frustrations, and anger. Anderson provides a space where they can be heard.

The film presents varying aspects of the protest, yet throughout we are made aware of the constant danger posed by the Charleston power structure. The sequences of speeches, press conferences, and interviews are all punctuated by shots that powerfully communicate the intensity of events and the threat of potential violence. Rather than speaking with individual protestors, police officers are shown communicating with the protestors by broadcasting orders through bullhorns. Their menacing presence is enhanced by that of the military, called in to help "maintain order." Rifles drawn, the soldiers dominate the frame as they do the protestors, presenting an intimidating force against the unarmed men, women, and children. Charleston is depicted as it was—a city under siege. At one point in the film, the potential for violence is realized when the picketers are subjected to brutal truncheon blows from the police. Shot in cinema verité style, the sequence cinematically mirrors the mayhem and confusion, recorded by a handheld camera within the fray.

Because *I Am Somebody* documents a social protest organized by African American women, it speaks directly to not only issues of racism but sexism as well. The majority of the hospital workers, like others in the service industry, were women, African American women. The protest, which initially was a fight for a living wage and respect on the job, began when the African American women became increasingly angry because the efforts of their labor resulted in less pay than that earned by White men, African American men, and White women. Anderson includes in the film an excerpt from a speech delivered by Coretta Scott King at the Morris Brown A.M.E. Church. In her inspiring address, she stated, "[T]he Black working woman is the most discriminated against of all working women."

In the film, many women speak of the sacrifice required for them to remain on the picket lines, and much of that sacrifice involved the private sphere. Financial hardship ensued, as did strained relationships with their families. In a telling interview of a striking hospital worker and her husband, the woman speaks of decreased time spent with her children and the difficulty of completing household chores while participating in the public protest. And though her husband supports her efforts for social and economic justice, he does so unenthusiastically.

Anderson provides viewers with a woman's perspective through her use of camera and editing and with the structuring voice that carries the audience through the film. Rather than using the traditional documentary "voice-of-god" approach, when an omnipotent, unseen male narrator explains and interprets the images, the film is narrated, in the first person by a woman participant. Thus we get a personalized approach, revealing details, thoughts, doubts, fears, and frustrations. This narration does more than just lead us through the film, for as the consciousness of the narrator is raised, so is ours. In making the film, Anderson wanted to document the movement. She felt it important to record the Black experience because after all, as she puts it:

> If we don't do it, no one else will. Whenever any kind of exciting event happened, that would help the younger people know their heritage, and get a sense of the struggle, I would attempt to film it. So when the hospital workers started to form their own union in South Carolina, it was a very exciting thing. Here were Black women saying, "We want a union . . . we don't want to be treated like dirt anymore; we want to be treated like human beings." Also there was something else historically important about it: it was the first time in a long time that the civil rights movement and labor had formed an alliance, and that was exciting. So for those reasons I thought this had to be recorded. (Franklin 1975: 6)

Anderson did more than just record the strike for posterity. At the film's close, reflecting on the events that had transpired, the narrator says, "If I didn't learn but one thing, that if you are willing to stand up and fight for yourself, others will be ready to fight for you." The film remains relevant to us today, decades later, because it also serves as a testimony to the power of collective action. But the film must do more than just speak to collective action. As Kleinhans (1984) notes, "[R]adical film/video-makers today, if they are to make genuinely liberating work, films and tapes that contribute to fundamental change must examine their own taken-for-granted ideas and behavior, about society, about politics, and about their medium and its techniques" (318).

Many documentaries borrow a convention from the classical Hollywood narrative style, the focus on a single protagonist. This is an extremely problematic approach to narrative when films attempt to present a progressive ideology. Typically, in a Hollywood-style film, the protagonist is a single individual with a goal or desire. A conflict occurs when the antagonist, usually another individual, possessing an opposing goal, intervenes. Rather than constructing stories where the social fabric and culture serve as catalysts, events take place because of individual action. This results in the reduction of the wider social and cultural causes to individual problems, thereby making the issues lose their social significance. Filmmakers such as the Soviet director Sergei Eisenstein avoided this pitfall in the 1920s. In films such as *Strike, Potemkin,* and *October,* he constructed narratives in which the Soviet masses are the protagonists. And as Kleinhans notes, in most documentaries "emphasis is on the individual rather than collective" (325).

I Am Somebody does not follow traditional form because, even though it has a single narrator, it never focuses on an individual woman. Anderson presents several participants to carry us through the narrative. The memory presented by the narration is a collective memory. The narrator is never identified and so to us, she could be one of the women presented but she could also be Everywoman.

After completion of the film, which garnered many national and international awards, Anderson remained dedicated to effecting social change through media. In the early 1970s she became an important contributor to the Children's Television Network as the supervising editor and an in-house film producer and director for both *Sesame Street* and *The Electric Company.* In 1975, she formed her own company, Onyx Productions, and turned out a number of works, among them the television series *Infinity Factory.* The program, targeted for inner-city children ages 8–12, instructed them on how to use math and problem solving during everyday events. Broadcast over 256 PBS stations, it was the first nationally broadcast television series produced by an African American woman. In addition to her work as a film and video artist, Anderson served as part of the founding management team for WHMM in Washington, D.C., the only PBS affiliate owned by African Americans, and as a board member on the New York Film Council and on the board of Women Make Movies, a national distribution company. And, when not working as the associate director of the Office of Black Ministry in the Diocese of Brooklyn, New York, or teaching and lecturing around the country, Anderson continues to develop, produce, and direct film and television.

Portia Cobb

> As an artist, my method is to re-invent and problem solve.

Equally talented in the mediums of film and video, artist Portia Cobb has taken her experience in film production to the medium of video, doing what she calls "translating and transferring some of the aesthetic principles discovered in filmmaking, to the video medium." By taking optical printing techniques (e.g., re-photography, stop-motion, and repetition) from film to video, Cobb thinks of her work as "testing and pushing formal visual conventions by layering, reprocessing, and reinventing." She began producing experimental videos in 1989 while living in the San Francisco Bay area. Since then, she has received national and international acclaim. Her works have been exhibited/screened in cities around the world, including Atlanta, Chicago, Oakland, New York, Los Angeles, Toronto, Milan, and Paris.

Rather than producing conventional documentaries, Cobb explores the possibilities and distinct aesthetic form of the video medium. Her works, frequently nonlinear, are what she describes as *mediations*. This is an apt term, for her work demonstrates a knowledge and self-awareness about the codes of documentary film and video. Through self-reflexivity, Cobb provides a treatise on not only her subject matter but the process of mediation itself. One example of this mediation is her video *No Justice, No Peace*, produced in 1992.

On March 3, 1991, a citizen of Los Angeles County, Rodney King, was brutally beaten by members of a police force sworn to preserve and protect. The assault and blatant disregard of civil and human rights shocked the nation, and indeed the world. But perhaps what I should say is that the attack shocked White America and those who viewed the country as one where there is, indeed, justice and liberty for all. But for the African American community, it appeared that the police were conducting business as usual, for police brutality and harassment is a long-standing and endemic practice in minority communities. Despite the prevalence of police brutality across the United States,[7] no government agency keeps national records of the demonstrated routine dismissal of the constitutional rights of American citizens. Given the fact that such incidents occur all too frequently, what was it about the Rodney King assault that created such a national uproar? It was the video. George Holliday captured the

Innovative artist of mixed-media forms and media
educator, Portia Cobb. (Courtesy Portia Cobb)

brutalization on a home video camera. The television news industry was
provided with violent, dramatic footage. What bleeds, leads. The beating
became the nation's most talked about news story, and the video was
broadcast over, and over, and over again. Portia Cobb examined the beating of King and the media's treatment of it in the video *No Justice, No
Peace: Young Black Men Immediate.*

An experimental documentary, the video utilizes interviews, intertitles,
news footage, and symbolic images to observe, analyze, and critique the
media's treatment. The sound track is equally complex, consisting of
overlapping dialogue spoken by Cobb herself, and calls into question the
sounds and images broadcast into the homes of America.

It opens with Holliday's footage. We hear the voice-over in a monot-
one delivery repeat over and over, "56 times in 81 seconds," the number of blows inflicted on King by the police. These words accompanying the familiar footage, do not underscore the image but, rather, help

elicit a stronger reaction to the unmerciful violence, making it possible for the familiar images to evoke once more the feelings of shock and anger. We are introduced to the theme of the piece, the mediation of the beating, by a phrase introduced at the end of the narrator's looping voice-over, "56 times in 81 seconds . . . on video," and the whisper, "television."

Cobb intercuts the academy leader, the strip of film that usually provides the countdown to the start of a motion picture, but here the numbers are backward and upside down. Clearly, something is wrong with this picture. One of the most effective sequences of the video occurs when we watch the King beating again, this time with a television broadcaster's commentary informing the image. Rather than describing the sickening violence committed or inhumane treatment, he describes the statements made by the police justifying their actions: that after two hits from the stun guns, King was trying to get up from the ground and posed a threat to the officers. When we are shown the video footage of Reginald Denny being beaten by African American youths during the rebellion that followed the acquittal of the Los Angeles police officers, we also hear commentary by a broadcast journalist. But the descriptions of events differ. Looking down on the scene from a helicopter, the journalist exclaims in a highly emotional and agitated state, "This is attempted murder . . . there is no police presence here . . . where are the police?" Cobb then cuts once again to the King-beating footage, repeating the preceding commentary ("there is no police presence here"), followed by silence as the brutality continues. Perhaps this is what defines police presence in the African American community. The juxtaposition makes clear the different treatment attributed to race. In the King beating, the victim was African American and the police White; in the Denny beating, the victim was White and the attackers African American. My point here is not to diminish the assault on Denny, for it too was vicious, but Cobb makes the racism of the news media clear.

Media bias, stereotyping, and its effects on self-worth and identity are shown very effectively in one shot—that of an African American boy watching television. Using superimposition, Cobb shows us the boy, screen right, looking left at a television. Superimposed on that image, screen left, is a larger close up of his face. And on top of that is the television set itself, placed "in his head," where his forehead would be. The image on the television set is an incarcerated African American man.

Through this layering, with one shot, the video maker deftly communicates the influence of racist media depictions. Television does, as Bernard Shaw, news anchor for CNN states, "have a responsibility for the white fear of Black men"—the quote with which the video closes.

Even as Cobb comments on mediated reality, she also informs us that she is aware that by constructing the video, she too is mediating reality. This is most apparent during the interviews. Cobb presents five young African American men who, given their ages, are likely to be victims of brutality. Asked to speak of the experience of Black men in America, they theorize about causes of racism, describe their reactions to the King beating, recount their own experiences with police harassment, and tell of the power of television in the formation of racist ideology and self-esteem. As varied as the participants themselves, the interviews are similar in that Cobb uses electronic effects such as polarization and skipped-frame advance as self-reflexive techniques, reminding us that we are not watching privileged and objective truths.

No Justice, No Peace is an effective educational tool for media literacy. Cobb expands her role as a media educator and activist beyond the confines of the screen to the University of Wisconsin-Madison, where she is a member of the School of Fine Arts faculty. She also serves the community as the artistic director of the University of Wisconsin Community Media Project (CMP). The CMP is an outreach program that offers film and video production workshops for city residents, free of charge. The workshops teach creative, critical, practical, and social skills, and much of their success has been with the youth. In 1991, the CMP started a program to work with at-risk youth. Teens who have learned to operate video and 16mm film cameras conceptualize and create their own projects, under leadership provided by Cobb. The result? Three broadcast-length documentaries that have won national awards. As artists, the young people have used the video medium to celebrate their culture, to record their dreams and aspirations, and to create video poetry. But they also use the medium for advocacy. The video *Signs of the Times* for example, produced by children ages 7–18 residing in the Mid-town Housing Association, examines the availability of alcohol in their community and the prevalence of billboards advertising alcoholic beverages. They have presented their work at schools, universities, and conferences; attended film festivals; and represented Milwaukee and Wisconsin at a nationally broadcast youth forum.

Cyrille Phipps and Not Channel Zero—
the Revolution Televised

The camcorder is revolutionary.

Media artist Cyrille Phipps has been instrumental in providing a televised voice of the African American community to the city of New York through her productions, media education, and workshops. A graduate of Syracuse University's School of Visual and Performing Arts, she has been recognized by the New York Foundation for the Arts, the National Black Programming Association, and the Black Filmmakers Hall of Fame. She is cofounder of Black Planet Productions, a collective of camcorder activists who produced *Not Channel Zero* (NCZ), a grassroots alternative media news and cultural show for public-access cable in New York. Their program has been cablecast in Arizona, Maryland, Connecticut, Colorado, and California as well. As a collective effort, *Not Channel Zero* challenges the social relations of production, rejecting the hierarchical structure of the mainstream media industries. Its aim: to educate the public about issues ignored by the mainstream media that affect the African American community. It was founded in 1989 by three experienced media producers: videographer Tom Poole; Cyrille Phipps, a media educator in New York high schools; and George Sosa, a video instructor at Rise and Shine Productions. Other members include Jacqueline Dolly, Joan Baker, Mark Albert, Donna Golden, Art Jones, Michele McKenzie, Tracey Williamson, Donna Murch, and Nzingha Clarke. *Not Channel Zero*'s Ten Point Plan:

1. To provide a forum for the education of the African American community, promoting a cultural connection among all people of the African Diaspora.
2. To promote political, social, and economic empowerment.
3. To act as a forum to discuss issues and evaluate problems.
4. To locate and provide resources that will develop problem solving techniques.
5. To acknowledge the cultural contributions of Africans in the United States and abroad.
6. To provide a provocative alternative to mainstream media.
7. To reflect the concerns of our community and provide an outlet for their grievances.

8. To celebrate and honor the memory of our African ancestors.
9. To act as a creative venue for emerging artists.
10. To provide a positive and respectful analysis of the African American community.

Using cameras as weapons to wage a revolution, *Not Channel Zero* attacks issues as wide ranging as the Clarence Thomas hearings, protest against the Gulf War, sexism against African American women, and homophobia in the African American community. In the video *Doing What It Takes: Black Folks Getting and Staying Healthy*, they target the health-care crisis experienced in the African American community.

According to Reed, Darity, and Roberson (1990), Blacks not only do not live as long as whites, they do not live as healthily.[8] African Americans suffer preventable and chronic diseases at a greater rate than most of the other races in the United States. Hypertension, or high blood pressure, is 30 percent higher in African Americans than in whites; its complications, congestive heart failure, stroke, and end-stage renal distress, are also more common. African Americans have the highest cancer incident rates and the highest cancer mortality rates; infant mortality rates outpace those in most third world countries; and the rate of AIDS is more than three times that of whites (Reed, Darity, & Roberson 1990; Bong 1993; Blocker 1993). As noted in the video, the health issue is complex, often tied to high under- and unemployment and the lack of health insurance. When access to the health-care system is provided, African Americans who seek adequate health care often experience institutional racism from the system. In addition, high rates of poverty make it difficult to maintain proper nutrition. Blocker states, "In general, Black Americans living in or near poverty consume diets that are marginal in vitamins A, D, E, B-complex, C, [and the minerals] calcium, magnesium, iron and zinc. . . . The diets are also low in foods that are good sources of carbohydrates and dietary fiber" (269).

Like *Not Channel Zero*'s other works, *Doing What It Takes* presents an innovative media news/cultural affairs format that incorporates the information and analysis of most public affairs programs, but it does so without the staid, static studio atmosphere and without the usual cast of "experts." Though the documentary includes medical and health professionals, the experts focused upon in this video are those with lived experience: the community. The form in which the people and issues are presented is described as the music-video approach: fast, hip, and highly stylized. According to cofounder Cyrille Phipps, "NCZ gives us an opportunity to be creative, and there is not much being done by people of color from a purely grassroots perspective" (as quoted by Parris [1992], p. 40).

Once introduced to the subject matter, the people of Brooklyn lead us through the issue. The video contains no authoritative narration, no added music to try to affect the audience's thinking process with heightened emotion, and no intertitles to explain and interpret the sounds and images. It effectively presents various arguments about holistic health care and the medical establishment by allowing the community to share its knowledge and opinions, while leaving audience members to come to their own conclusions. Rather than being talked at, the audience is talked to. Through editing and use of direct address, several of the participants speak to the camera; the video is a conversation. And like the work of Cobb, the video is also self-reflexive in that the audience is permitted to hear the questions asked. We are aware of the process of construction.

In only 30 minutes *Doing What It Takes* covers a wide range of topics: nutrition and diet, self-medication with the use of herbs and home remedies, meditation, overuse of drugs by the established medical system, institutionalized health care, and lifestyle. *Not Channel Zero* takes the issue beyond the personal by including discussion on the politics of health care: the lack of health insurance and access; poverty; the need for information and education; dependence on a capitalist medical system driven not by care but by profit; and the proliferation of fast food establishments in African American neighborhoods, coupled with the shortage of grocery and health food stores. As stated in the video, health care, like all crises affecting the African American community is an issue of empowerment. In order to take control of our lives, we must take care of our bodies.

Phipps expanded her efforts in the field of democratic media in 1992, by working as co-distribution coordinator for Paper Tiger Television, another noncommercial video collective that challenged the ideology of "mainstream" media. She continued in the position, and with *Not Channel Zero*, until 1995, when she became the executive producer for Dyke TV. Currently, Phipps works for the Education and Outreach Department of Manhattan Neighborhood Network, the largest public-access facility in the United States.

*

Madeline Anderson, Portia Cobb, and Cyrille Phipps are talented artists who use their chosen media in creative and challenging ways in developing innovative and unique artistic visions. But, as I have argued, they are also media activists, working toward progressive change. As producers and directors of documentary film and video, they observe the culture and create records of life within a racist, sexist, classist, and homophobic society. But they do more. As an important part of the ongoing civil rights movement, these women, and many other media producers, work to forge a society where the individual humanity of all is recognized. Human rights are not only recognized but respected, ensured, and celebrated.

NOTES

1. A regular contributor to the antislavery newspaper *Liberator,* Maria W. Stewart is considered the first African American woman journalist. Mary Ann Shadd Cary, founder of the *Provincial Freeman*, was the first woman of the African diaspora to edit a newspaper in North America. Ida B. Wells-Barnett, as an editor, writer, and activist, led the crusade against lynching in the late 1890s and early 1900s.

2. For more information on employment discrimination in the film and television industry, see Cripps 1993, Rhines 1996, and Bielby and Bielby 1989).

3. Despite the prominent role for Whoopi Goldberg in the film as Oda Mae Brown, a role that won her the Academy Award for Best Supporting Actress, *Ghost* is problematic in its treatment of people of color. They are used as comic relief, and their beliefs in non-Christian spirituality are presented as superstitious and silly. Further, Goldberg's character, like that of Eddie Murphy in his early films, is isolated from the African American community and placed in the White community to solve a White couple's problems.

4. Among the many conventions utilized within the classical Hollywood style are linear plot with events linked by means of causality, a style of "invisible editing," and viewer/subject identification.

5. Richard Leacock and D. A. Pennebaker are filmmakers who took advantage of technological advances such as smaller cameras and faster film stocks in the 1960s. They, along with filmmakers Robert Drew and Albert Maylses, helped to innovate a style of documentary called cinema verité in the 1960s. An "observational style," verité films record events as they happen, without staging, interviews, and added narration or music.

6. *The Cool World* is a fictional feature shot in Harlem in 1964 using many nonprofessional actors. It is often called as one of the first fictional films to utilize the formal style of cinema verité to add verisimilitude to its drama. Consid-

ered controversial during its release, the film focused on Black male homosexuality.

7. Examples of brutality exist all across the nation. In June of 1996, Amnesty International released a 72-page document detailing brutality in the New York City Police Department, the results of an investigation. In 1997, the ACLU filed a lawsuit on behalf of 27 plaintiffs against Pittsburgh, Philadelphia, Tampa, Indianapolis, Detroit, and Atlanta. These cities and many more have several cases of brutality now pending in court.

8. The authors quote life expectancy statistics as provided by the 1984 U.S. Census: white males, 72; white females, 78.9; Black males, 65.1; and Black females, 73.8 (p. 7).

FILMOGRAPHY

Madeline Anderson
  Integration Report (1961)
  Malcolm X: Nationalist or Humanist (1966)
  I Am Somebody (1969)
  Walls Came Tumbling Down (1975)

Portia Cobb
  Species in Danger Ed! (1989)
  Who Are You? An Oakland Story (1990)
  No Justice . . . No Peace! (1992)
  Drive-by Shoot (1993)
  Who's In Control? (1994)
  Don't Hurry Back . . . (1997)
  Paul in the Window (1997)

Cyrille Phipps
  Mumia Abu Jamal: Giving Face to the Death Penalty (1995)
  Dreaming Ourselves: Healing Darkness (1995)
  Sacred Lies, Civil Truths (1993)
  Not Channel Zero (1990–1995)

Produced by Phipps
  Black Womyn, Sexual Politics, and the Revolution
  "Our House": Gays and Lesbians in the Hood
  NCZ Goes to War
  The Session
  In Your Own Back Yard

The Media Wilder Pseudo Graduates
The Summer of '91
The Crown Heights Affair
X & ½: The Legacy of Malcolm X
Doing What It Takes: Black Folks Getting and Staying Healthy

Distribution Information

I Am Somebody is available through First Run Icarus Films, 153 Waverly Place, New York, NY 10014. (212) 727–1711

No Justice . . . No Peace is distributed by Third World Newsreel, 335 West 38th Street, 5th Floor, New York, NY 10018. (212)947–9277.

Doing What It Takes is distributed by Third World Newsreel, 335 West 38th Street, 5th Floor, New York, NY 10018. (212) 947–9277.

REFERENCES

Bielby, W. T., and Bielby, D. D. (1989). *The 1989 Hollywood Writer's Report: Unequal Access, Unequal Pay*. West Hollywood, Calif.: Writers Guild of America West.

Blocker, D. E. (1993). "Nutritional concerns of Black Americans." In I. L. Livingstone (ed.). *Handbook of Black American Health*. Westport, Conn.: Greenwood Press. Pp. 269–81.

Bogle, T. (1989). *Toms, Coons, Mulattos, Mammies, and Bucks: An Interpretive History or Blacks in American Films* (2nd ed.). New York: Continuum.

Bong, K. M. (1993) "Cancer and Black Americans." In I. L. Livingstone (ed.). *Handbook of Black American Health*. Westport, Conn.: Greenwood Press. Pp. 77–93.

Cripps, T. (1993). *Slow Fade to Black* (2nd ed.). New York: Oxford University Press.

Fiske, J. (1987). *Television Culture*. New York: Routledge.

Foner, Philip S. (1980). *Women and the American Labor Movement*. New York: Free Press.

Franklin, O. (1975). "Madeline Anderson." *On Black Film: A Film and Lecture Series*. Philadelphia: Annenberg School of Communication, University of Pennsylvania.

Gibson, Gloria. (1994). "Recall and recollect: Excavating the life history of Eloyce King Patrick Gist." *Black Film Review*, 8, 2: 20–21.

Harris, K. (1986). "New images." *Independent*, 9(10): 16–20.

Horowitz, J. (March 1989). "Hollywood's dirty little secret." *Premiere,* pp. 56, 59–60, 62.

Jewell, K. Sue (1993). *From Mammy to Miss America and Beyond: Cultural Images and the Shaping of U.S. Social Policy.* New York: Routledge.

Kleinhans, C. (1984). "Forms, politics, makers, and contexts: Basic issues for a theory of radical political documentary." In *Show Us Life.* T. Waugh, ed. Metuchen, N.J.: Scarecrow. Pp. 318–42.

Lambert, P., L. Wright, K. Brailsford, J. Dodd, B. Cortina, N. Sales, R. Aria, and S. McFarland. (March 18, 1996). "What's wrong with this picture?" *People Magazine,* 45, 11: 42–52.

Maynard, R. A. (1974). *Africa on Film: Myth and Reality.* Rochelle Park, N.J.: Hayden.

Parkerson, M. (1987). "Answering the void." *Independent,* 10, 3: 12–13.

Parris, L. (June/July 1992). "Not Channel Zero: The revolution televised. *American Visions,* pp. 40–43.

Piliawsky, M. (1984). "Racial equity in the United States: From institutionalized racism to respectable racism." *Phylon,* 14, 2: 135–43.

Reed, W. L., W. Darity, and N. Roberson. (1990). *Health and Medical Care of African Americans.* Westport, Conn.: Auburn House.

Rhines J. (1996). *Black Film/White Money.* New Brunswick: Rutgers University Press.

Roffman, P., and J. Purdy. (1981). *The Hollywood Social Problem Film.* Bloomington: Indiana University Press.

Ryan, M., and D. Kellner. (1988). *Camera Politica.* Bloomington: Indiana University Press.

Storm, J. (1996). "Segregated Situation on Television Comedies," Philadelphia Inquirer, 14 April, A1.

Streitmatter, R. (1994). *Raising Her Voice: African American Women Journalists Who Changed History.* Lexington: University of Kentucky Press.

Waugh, T.(1984). "Why documentary filmmakers keep trying to change the world, or why people changing the world keep making documentaries." In *Show Us Life.* Metuchen, N.J.: Scarecrow. Pp. xi–xxvii.

Chapter Sixteen

"Workers Just Like Anyone Else"
Organizing Workfare Unions in New York City

Vanessa Tait

Fifty-two-year-old Edriss Anderson, mother of four and grandmother of seven, paces herself as she travels the winding paths of New York City's Central Park picking up litter, emptying trash cans, and sweeping up debris. According to the mayor's office, the park is cleaner than it has been in years, and thanks to the hard work of Edriss and some 6,000 other welfare recipients assigned to the Parks Department by the city's Work Experience Program (WEP), New Yorkers can once again point to their vast urban oasis with pride. But unlike "regular" unionized park jobs that pay about $10 an hour and come with health, vacation, sick leave, and retirement benefits, all Edriss receives in exchange for her twenty-two hours of labor a week is the continued receipt of her $176 welfare check and $55 in food stamps every two weeks.

Edriss says what bothers her most is the constant sense that she is not considered a real worker. In the eyes of many of those who lounge on the grassy slopes near the Metropolitan Museum where she is often assigned, she is merely another lazy, unemployable welfare recipient who should be forced to work in exchange for public assistance paid for by their tax dollars. Her supervisors have given her no training in handling the potentially infectious or hazardous materials littering the park, and she lacks basic protective gear like gloves. "They treat us bad. There's no other way to look at it but modern-day slavery," she says. "They're not paying you wages, they don't care if you get hurt, and they threaten to cut off your benefits if you complain. . . . We need our own union."[1]

WEP workers sometimes face discrimination from paid city workers who, laboring side by side with them, refuse to share restrooms or safety equipment. To signify her status, Edriss and her fellow "WEPs" are required to wear special orange vests—"like a chain gang," as one WEP worker put it.

Across the country, workfare workers like Edriss are organizing to demand safe jobs and dignified work at a living wage. New York City is home to the nation's largest mandatory workfare program, run by a municipal government aggressively pushing workfare as a solution to joblessness and so-called welfare dependency. Using terms such as "slavery" and "indentured servitude" to describe their situation, WEP workers are contesting the dominant conservative discourse around welfare reform and, at the same time, are reshaping notions of who is a worker. Both owners of capital and trade unionists have long defined workers as those who work for wages, and that concept has been enshrined in federal and state labor laws. The relationship of welfare and work, particularly as it is expressed in workfare programs, presents a serious challenge to that notion.

Whereas past welfare organizing tactics focused on enrolling those who were eligible for welfare or pushing for increases in the level of benefits, this new wave of organizing focuses on demanding honest work at fair wages, as well as union representation. In New York City, community-based antipoverty organizations—the Association of Community Organizations for Reform Now and WEP Workers Together!—have taken the lead in organizing workfare unions. African American women are key players in these multiracial and multiethnic campaigns. The role of organized labor in New York City has been contradictory, with some unions supporting these independent campaigns and other key unions delaying action or running ineffective campaigns. While the AFL-CIO has rhetorically welcomed workfare workers into its ranks, few local AFL-CIO unions have as yet actually organized workfare workers.

In the 1960s, Black women led a movement for welfare rights that vastly expanded access to public assistance and sought to honor unwaged work caring for children and home. Thirty years later, African American women like Edriss continue this tradition of activism, this time as part of a diverse coalition of workers—employed and unemployed, waged and unwaged—who are forcing a reexamination of welfare as a labor issue.

Disrupting the System: The National Welfare Rights Organization and Direct Action

The roots of welfare-rights organizing lie in the civil rights and Black Power movements, as well as in activists' involvement in the federal government's antipoverty programs and the welfare rights movement. By the mid–1960s, civil rights activists were looking northward, at unemployment, underemployment, and poverty rampant among African Americans in urban areas. Signifying increasing concerns with economic and racial inequality, more than a quarter million people turned out for the 1963 March on Washington for Jobs and Freedom. Around the same time, rebellions against racism and poverty in dozens of cities across the country linked the issues of class and racial equality, pushing them to the top of the national agenda.

The Johnson administration's "War on Poverty" program, launched in 1964, was intended to pacify the inner cities, but ironically, helped to boost local involvement and control over antipoverty programs in many localities. "Community action programs" founded under federal auspices provided the vehicle through which neighborhoods organized to demand government services. Welfare was central in these demands. For the first time since the 1930s, tens of thousands of poor people demanded public assistance at a level sufficient to bring a family out of poverty. Between 1960 and 1968, the number of people receiving public assistance nearly doubled, from 745,000 families to 1.5 million. The numbers doubled again by 1972, when 3 million families received relief.[2] Local welfare rights groups nationwide made similar demands, such as the right to earn additional income without a reduction in benefits, day care for working mothers, medical benefits, and higher grant levels.

As a consequence of this activity, the National Welfare Rights Organization (NWRO) was founded in 1966 by 100 representatives from 75 welfare rights groups across the country. George A. Wiley, an African American and former Congress of Racial Equality (CORE) associate national director, was elected executive director of NWRO, which sought to promote a multiracial, broad-based movement of the poor around the issue of welfare rights. The blueprint for such a campaign came from an essay by white leftists Francis Fox Piven and Richard Cloward, "A Strategy to End Poverty," which argued that activists should inform poor people of their legal right to welfare, and mobilize disruptive protests by which the poor would demand the economic relief owed to them by the government. During the late 1960s, tens of thousands of NWRO activists jammed into welfare offices and confronted authorities with demonstrations, picketing and sit-ins, demanding a just welfare system and a guaranteed minimum national income. Thousands more benefited from NWRO-assisted resolutions to their individual grievances, which often relied on direct-action tactics similar to those used by activists in the civil rights movement.[3]

While the focus of the NWRO was on benefits payments, the question of work always hovered in the background. But, note Piven and Cloward, "It was not clear how activists could, as a practical, day-to-day matter of organizing, mount an attack on poverty by attacking its main cause—underemployment and unemployment."[4] Instead, NWRO organized poor people to claim their moral and legal right to a sufficient income and welfare benefits due them from the state, largely skirting the issue of employment.

NWRO's strategists thought benefit campaigns would bring greater numbers of recipients into a national network, with the goal of ultimately achieving passage of a "guaranteed national income" in Congress. If such a measure had been passed, it would have amounted to a pay raise for NWRO's members, the majority of whom were single mothers working in the home, and who sometimes pointed to the value of this unwaged work. Using the language of welfare rights, NWRO members made arguments similar to those of waged workers. For instance, Johnnie Tillmon, a mother of six from Watts, California, and first chair of NWRO, spoke of the productive, socially important work welfare mothers performed: "If I were President, I would solve this so-called welfare crisis in a minute and go a long way toward liberating every woman. I'd just issue a proclamation that women's work is *real* work. . . . I'd start paying women a living wage for doing the work we are already doing—child raising and housekeeping. And the welfare crisis would be over. Just like that."[5] In voicing demands of this nature to the state, Tillmon and other welfare mothers reframed the debate about welfare to acknowledge the value of women's unwaged work. NWRO was, in effect, their union, though their workplaces were scattered and they had no visible employer.

Moreover, NWRO's structural resemblance to a labor union was striking. Wiley envisioned a "national union of welfare recipients,"[6] and NWRO's structure closely mirrored a labor union model. This union of the poor, like any workplace union, was run by its members and attempted to bargain collectively on behalf of all welfare recipients. Paying dues and officially becoming a member were usually required before NWRO activists or organizers would assist an individual or a group with a grievance. Like a labor union, recipients themselves elected their peers to national, state, and local policy-making bodies whose responsibility it was to set the movement's agenda. Paid staff hired as organizers contributed their technical skills but were ultimately subordinate to the rank-and-file leadership. Still, while NWRO had internal organizational difficulties, it stopped short of the narrow contractual focus and bureaucratic rigidity that had come to define AFL-CIO trade unionism in the post war era, instead reflecting the dynamism characteristic of movement organizing in the 1960s. And especially in its early days, NWRO exhibited an admirable willingness to experiment with new organizing models.

Although NWRO's stated desire was to be a broad-based multiracial coalition, its actual membership was almost entirely African American and female, and its rank-and-file leaders were strongly influenced by the Black Power movement and the emerging feminist movement. Organizers attempted to broaden NWRO's base to include men on relief and non–African American women, but several internal and external factors worked against this goal. While Wiley and most of the paid staff favored a coalition-based organization that grew by reaching out to new constituencies, Black women in the elected leadership of NWRO, who finally had an organization of their own, worked to keep its strategies focused on bringing improvements to the lives of inner-city welfare mothers instead of investing in new programs to reach others. While nationally whites accounted for half of all Aid to Families with Dependent Children (AFDC) recipients, NWRO activists concentrated their work in urban areas where a majority of welfare recipients were African American.

In addition, a deep ambivalence about welfare led many middle-class Black leaders to keep their distance from the movement, with some viewing it as composed of "vocal, out-of-the-closet recipients," and therefore "non-respectable."[7] Other stigmas associated with welfare organizing were strong:

> Few chose to join or become aligned with the protest of poor women. . . .
> Poor whites remained largely uninvolved, perceiving NWRO as a militant
> Black movement. Poor men, in general, rejected identification with a movement dominated by women. Others on welfare, the aged, blind, and disabled—or the "deserving" poor—appear to have seen few gains from such
> an association with these "undeserving" women. . . .[8]

Even though NWRO's main constituency was unemployed African American women, few unions and Black or women's organizations allied themselves with the movement. Nonetheless, NWRO persisted for nearly a decade, from 1966 until 1975, and obtained benefits for tens of thousands of recipients who probably would not have received them otherwise. NWRO's leaders organized to demand economic justice—in the form of more income, food, and shelter for themselves and their families—from a society that had stereotyped them as unemployable and morally unworthy.

The Second Wave: Women's Welfare
Rights in the 1970s

Various explanations have been advanced for NWRO's demise in the mid-1970s. Piven and Cloward believe the shift away from mass protest and toward institution building and electoral activity inhibited NWRO's ability to effectively make change—that, in their words, "organization prevented organizing."[9] Wiley blamed NWRO's inability to resolve conflicts among its leadership about whom to organize, and failure at building coalitions to broaden its base as the cause of its downfall.[10] Others suggest that Wiley's resignation in 1973—under pressure from the rank-and-file female leadership—unintentionally ended what support NWRO had enjoyed (mostly from churches and foundations), which led to an insurmountable financial crisis. But others refuse to equate demise with failure, viewing many of the changes NWRO achieved as profoundly important. While NWRO didn't achieve its stated goals of serious disruption of the welfare system or national guaranteed income legislation, it left a legacy of increased benefit levels for millions of recipients, improvements to public housing programs, and nutrition and health programs for mothers with infants and poor children (such as the Women Infants Children program, or WIC)—a legacy that has now come under heavy attack from today's antiwelfare conservatives.

Overlapping with NWRO's demise, a new generation of welfare rights organizations grew up in the early 1970s. Feminisms of various kinds became the dominant ideological influences; rather than aiming for a broad-based poor people's movement, these new activists focused on welfare specifically as a concern of women, and ties between welfare rights and women's organizations expanded.

The National Black Feminist Organization and the Coalition of 100 Black Women began participating in NWRO-sponsored actions in the early 1970s. Liberal feminist groups like the National Organization for Women and the Women's Equity Action League incorporated critiques of poverty into their agendas throughout the 1970s and '80s.[11] One of the largest second-wave welfare rights groups was New York City's Downtown Welfare Advocate Center. Led primarily by white feminists, it used a consciousness raising model to organize and advocated for better employment opportunities and child care.[12] But these efforts were small compared to the scale upon which NWRO had mobilized and were no match for the conservative backlash against welfare and workers' rights launched in the 1980s.

The Third Wave: Workfare in the 1990s

Welfare and union activists in the 1990s are confronted with a new set of challenges: sustained right-wing attacks on entitlement programs, downsizing state and federal governments, and the vast expansion of workfare programs. In absolute numbers, more people receive welfare in the 1990s and greater racial and gender diversity exists among welfare recipients than at any other time in the past two decades. Nationally, 42.5 percent of welfare recipients are white, 34 percent are African American, 19.2 percent Latina or Latino, and 4.3 percent are classified as "other."[13] Workfare organizers are consciously building on this diversity in formulating their ideologies and movement-building practices in terms of multiculturalism and unity between all working people. While this chapter analyzes workfare organizing in New York City, similar strategies are being pursued in other cities as well.

Government programs to put unemployed people to work are not new. Throughout recent U.S. history, such policies have alternated between "workfare" (mandatory, usually punitive, nonwage work programs targeted at the "undeserving poor") and "fair work" (voluntary training or job-creation programs like the depression-era Works Progress Administration, usually intended for men and those seen as "deserving" real wages).[14] The dramatic "reforms" of 1996 transformed AFDC (and renamed it Temporary Assistance for Needy Families, or TANF) from an entitlement program to a workfare-based program with a five-year lifetime limit on benefits. States, rather than the federal government, now administer welfare benefits. If deemed "able-bodied," an adult recipient must work after 2 years on the program; adults without children are required to work 20 hours a week to qualify for food stamps. Twenty-five percent of the heads of single-parent families are required to work 20 hours a week by the end of 1997, 50 percent by the end of 2002. Seventy-five percent of the heads of two-parent families must work 35 hours a week by 1997, 90 percent by 2002. There are no entitlement programs for child-care for parents on workfare.[15]

To some, workfare makes sense: why not require welfare recipients to "give back" something to the community in exchange for benefits, especially if the goal is to prepare them for paid jobs? But the reality is that workfare doesn't work; neither the welfare recipient nor the public gains. Not only do assignments almost never lead to permanent employment, but communities are economically damaged by workfare, which displaces paid workers, depresses wages, and leads to lower labor standards. Workers do not receive wages for their labor; their compensation is mostly in the form of food stamps or rent vouchers, the rest in cash welfare benefits—the combination of which puts them, on average, far below the federal poverty line. Workfare does benefit employers (mostly public but increasingly private) who reap the benefits of a subminimum-wage workforce coerced into labor by welfare requirements. Tens of thousands of workfare workers nationwide receive only their welfare benefits for the same jobs that, until recently, cities, counties and private corporations paid real wages to their employees to perform. Not only do they not receive actual wages, they cannot file grievances or exercise other employment rights. In this massive process of job restructuring, welfare recipients replace waged workers, who often end up on the welfare rolls themselves.

Nowhere is this more apparent than in New York City, where the steady upward growth of workfare assignments has almost matched the decline of unionized city positions. In 1995, conservative mayor Rudolph Giuliani decided to create the largest workfare program in the nation, the Work Experience Program (WEP). Upwards of 120,000 workfare workers rotated through 37,000 positions in the 1996 fiscal year; the number of workfare jobs is expected to climb to more than 100,000 positions by the year 2000.[16] Giuliani's strategy for balancing the city's budget has been to slash the municipal workforce by 22,000 since 1995 through restructuring, early retirements, and attrition. Part-time WEP workers have filled the majority of these jobs, and now account for three-fourths of the labor force of the city's Parks Department, and a third of the Sanitation Department.[17] Other large beneficiaries of workfare labor include the city's welfare agency itself and the housing authority, where WEP workers do maintenance and clerical tasks, and public hospitals, where they perform housekeeping and dietary jobs. Often, WEP workers staff entire workplaces, with just one or two "regular" salaried city employees as their supervisors. While using workfare workers to replace laid-off city employees is technically illegal, the law is in practice routinely violated.[18]

It is easy to see why: workfare results in tremendous salary savings in an era of municipal cost cutting. The average New York City clerical worker's hourly wage is $12.32, not including benefits. The nationally set minimum wage is $5.15, yet a WEP worker costs the city even less—an average of only $1.80 an hour for a 20-hour work week (based on a $577 monthly welfare check, of which one-quarter is paid by the city, the rest by state and federal funds).[19] For the city's conservative officials, "welfare reform" in the form of federal workfare requirements could not have come at a better time, since it requires the majority of welfare recipients to be on workfare by 2002. With New York City's current welfare caseload at approximately 419,000 adults, the number of workfare participants could eventually far outstrip the total number of public employees in the city (currently about 200,000).[20]

Stories of workers who were once employed at union wages and benefits but who now labor as unpaid WEP workers are surprisingly common. For instance, Hattie Hargrove, a 50-year-old custodial worker with the Long Island County Department of Social Services, was laid off from her union-wage job in 1992. She looked for a job—unsuccessfully—until her unemployment benefits ran out, then went on AFDC. She was given a workfare assignment that landed her back at her old job, performing exactly the same duties for the same supervisor. But under WEP, all she "makes" is a $53.50 welfare check and $263 in food stamps. Besides wanting her union pay rate back, Hargrove said, "I would feel better because I'd be getting a paycheck and people wouldn't look down at me like I was crazy anymore."[21]

The first people put on WEP were single adults on "Home Relief"— New York's name for general assistance welfare—and were primarily male. But as the program has expanded, TANF recipients like Hattie, who constitute about 55 percent of all New York City welfare recipients and are mostly single mothers, have flooded into the program. Data on the gender and race of workfare participants in New York City are not available, but advocates say it closely mirrors the city's welfare recipient population, which is less white than the national recipient population: 52 percent Latina or Latino, 34 percent African American, 13 percent white, with 1 percent classified as "other," and almost evenly split between men and women.[22]

New York City's huge workfare program is also the site of the nation's most intensive workfare organizing, and this racial, ethnic, and gender breakdown is closely reflected in the makeup of third-wave, community-based workfare organizations, where a majority of activists are people of color. Being forced to labor under workfare has, paradoxically, handed these workers a new way to look at welfare rights organizing: rather than limiting their demands to benefits increases, they now see themselves as workers entitled to the same high wages and good conditions as "real" city workers. Labor has become the primary lens through which many on welfare see themselves.

Take Alicia Portes, for example. A Puerto Rican immigrant and single mother with two children, ages 5 and 6, she was laid off from her job as a cashier for a convenience store in 1995 and has since become dependent on a monthly welfare check of $523, plus about $150 in food stamps. She was assigned to work 26 hours a week as a WEP custodian in a city-owned building. As required by law, her welfare benefits, divided by the number of hours she is forced to work, equal the minimum wage, but she is quick to point out that the worker in the position before her—who was not a WEP worker—made about $14 a hour, nearly three times what she gets in benefits. And, that employee was provided with health and safety equipment and training, tuition reimbursement, Social Security benefits, unemployment compensation, sick leave, vacation and retirement, and the protection of a union contract. "The skin on my hands is peeling off from exposure to all these cleaning chemicals," said Portes, "but they keep ignoring my requests for decent gloves. They think we're expendable just because we're WEPs."[23]

Other workers say they are denied back braces when assigned heavy lifting; protective equipment when cleaning up used needles or other hazardous refuse in the parks; or warm coats and boots when shoveling snow or working outdoors in the winter. Workers have been required to climb dangerously high—higher than union contracts allow—to trim park trees. Refusing a particular workfare assignment or resisting participation in the program altogether opens one up to being "sanctioned" by the workfare authorities, resulting in lost benefits. When a WEP worker believes an assignment is dangerous, she or he is legally allowed to refuse to work but, if sanctioned, must go through a hearing process that can be long and arduous.

Parents with children over 3 years old who are on workfare are handed a list of child-care centers—most of them full—and told to report for work. Eric Mayer, a young African American father with a 6-year-old daughter, said TANF allows him to get job training at a local community college—at least for six months. "Soon, I'll be on workfare and I'm worried about never getting a permanent job. After you use up your eligibility, they kick you off and you're back in the same situation." Nine thousand welfare recipients studying at city universities have been forced out of classrooms and into WEP assignments, and tens of thousands more have been forced to leave adult literacy, ESL, GED, or job-training programs—programs that, statistically, give welfare recipients a much better chance of getting a job than workfare.[24]

As for getting on-the-job training or a new career, WEP workers say there are several problems with the system. Workfare actually has the effect of reducing job openings, since employers have a ready supply of "free" labor in the form of WEP workers to fill jobs. "Why should they actually hire anyone?" asked Pat Simmons, a 49-year-old African American woman on a WEP assignment at Bellevue Hospital, where she changes beds and transports patients. Of her two-year long work experience there, she said, "We all but work for free."[25] Of the more than 123,000 welfare recipients who have passed through the workfare program since 1994, only a few hundred have been hired by the city.

Workfare also establishes a two-tier employment system, undermining possibilities for solidarity between paid workers and workfare workers. WEP worker Brenda Stewart was a clerk in the social services department for two years, but because she was on a workfare assignment rather than "regular staff," the department did not allow her to apply for permanent positions. "They don't consider us workers," said Stewart, a Black woman. "As soon as they hear the word 'WEP' a stigmatism is placed on that worker. I've seen where people, as soon as they found out I was on welfare, they felt they didn't have to treat me in a certain way, because now, I'm just a WEP instead of a worker."[26] Other workers say they are denied rest or lunch breaks, or even the use of sanitary facilities, by non-WEP workers who supervise them. Some also say a practice of "racial steering" is used by some WEP supervisors to discriminate against workers of color in job assignments.

Portes said she would happily take the custodial job she is now forced to do as a WEP worker, if she were accorded the dignity and respect of a paycheck, benefits, and union protection. "I don't disagree with the welfare-to-work idea," says Portes. "Of course, I'd love to work and be self-sufficient, but that's a far cry from this virtual slavery."

Poor Workers, Trade Unions, and Movements for Economic Justice

Even while recognizing that welfare recipients exist in relation to the employed workforce, most trade unions have historically kept an arm's length from welfare rights activity. They have most often viewed those on welfare not as unemployed or unpaid workers but as a social problem that threatens their own members' pocketbooks (as taxpayers) or their jobs (when brought in as strike breakers by employers). "To white working-class people, and even to many Black workers," wrote Piven and Cloward in 1968, "it appears that the welfare recipient is enjoying a free ride on their hard-earned tax dollars, meanwhile, scorning the value of work and the self-esteem of workers."[27]

Contributing to these beliefs is a long history of employers exploiting racial, ethnic, gender, and class differences among workers to increase their own profits and maintain labor control, as well as ample evidence of racial, ethnic, and gender discrimination within trade unions themselves.[28] African American women and other women of color have been active participants and leaders in working-class movements, though their efforts have often been met with discriminatory responses in the white- and male-dominated labor movement. The emergence of industrial unionism in the late 1930s, with its aim of organizing unskilled workers without regard to race and gender, was a major blow to the exclusionism of the long-dominant AFL craft-based unions. The half million Black workers who joined CIO-affiliated unions, write Korstad and Lichtenstein, were "in the vanguard of efforts to transform race relations" as they built the beginnings of a powerful "labor-based civil rights movement."[29] It is situations like these, when demands for social equality have come to inhabit trade union institutions and take them past immediate concerns for "bread-and-butter" issues, that the U.S. labor movement may be its most effective. The twin effects of anticommunism and bureaucratization in the postwar years, Korstad and Lichtenstein note, led to a decline in Black activism within unions. A more routinized system of labor relations with the goal of maintaining "labor peace" took the place of a social movement unionism aiming for more sweeping economic and social change. As a result, movements for racial and gender justice would remain largely separate from trade union organizing for two decades.

In the late 1960s, questions of diversity and social equality reemerged within the union movement. Within particular unions, rank-and-file caucuses formed, such as the Dodge Revolutionary Union Movement (in existence from 1968 to 1973 and affiliated with the League of Revolutionary Black Workers) in the United Auto Workers. Reformers founded umbrella groups like the Coalition of Black Trade Unionists in 1972, and the Coalition of Labor Union Women in 1974, to fight for equality within AFL-CIO unions and to argue for greater organizing efforts in industries that employed women and people of color. A few unions, such as the Hospital Workers Local 1199 in New York City, consciously organized around issues of racial justice.[30]

These and subsequent efforts have had some success. While diversification within the trade union movement has progressed considerably since the 1960s, it varies widely by locality, union, and industry. For instance, the biggest growth in union membership in the past two decades was among public employees, many of whom are African American and/or female, but large numbers still remain in nonunion workplaces, such as domestic work and private-sector clerical and service jobs. Still, Black women more often join unions than their white counterparts. But even though female membership in trade unions has skyrocketed in the past three decades, women are still seriously underrepresented in union leadership positions.[31]

While women of color have been historically underrepresented in the labor movement, they have been overrepresented in the low-wage labor force, often shuttling back and forth from welfare to minimum-wage jobs. Economist Julianne Malveaux estimates that women of color, the majority of them low-paid, represent at least 20 percent of the U.S. labor force. Moreover, almost half of all women who receive public assistance—in the form of food stamps, welfare or housing grants—also have some sort of low-wage job at the same time. Those who have only a low-wage job are generally worse off than if they received only welfare benefits. Many work in service industries—like food service, retail sales, home health care, or domestic work—where union representation is rare, benefits unheard of, and wages extremely low. Although all women suffer discrimination in the labor market, Black women are "doubly disadvantaged" by their race and their gender; Malveaux notes that African American women's unemployment levels are twice those of white women, and they are laid off more quickly during economic downturns.[32] Improving the economic conditions of poor women requires pushing for union wages coupled with employer- or state-paid child care for workers employed outside the home, and adequate welfare payments to parents who work inside the home. Progressive welfare and paid-work policies are complementary: both are necessary to provide people the means to live in dignity above the poverty line, and neither can be won without grassroots organizing.

Low-wage workers—the majority of whom are women and people of color—have had to contend with a peculiar problem: while they are generally pro-union, most unions have been uninterested in organizing them, preferring instead to concentrate their efforts in industries where they already have a presence. In the absence of union assistance, movement organizations with working-class agendas, like NWRO, have often provided an institutional framework for poor workers' struggles. In the 1990s, some unions began to aggressively organize low-wage workers, using social movement tactics that incorporated demands for social as well as economic change. At the same time, community-based organizations conducted their own independent, sometimes highly successful union campaigns, drawing on previous traditions of poor peoples' labor organizing.

Organizing in the Streets versus Lobbying in the Legislature

Organized labor in New York City has spoken out against Giuliani's workfare programs, which it sees as a misguided and punitive social policy, and as taking jobs from its members. But the rhetoric has, for the most part, not been matched with action. The leaders of the unions representing the vast majority of city employees and that are therefore the most directly affected by workfare—AFSCME District Council 37 (120,000 members) and the Transport Workers Union (31,000 members)—have sat on the sidelines, doing little to protect their own members from displacement, and even less to help workfare workers. Under threat of downsizing and layoffs, both unions were on the defensive, agreeing to the city's demands in its use of WEP workers. In addition, AFSCME District Council 37 Executive Director Stanley Hill is a close ally of Republican Mayor Giuliani and lent his support to the city's workfare program.[33]

In the summer of 1996, tired of waiting for help from established unions, workfare workers invented their own, WEP Workers Together! (WWT), with the assistance of neighborhood antipoverty community organizations (the Urban Justice Center, Community Voices Heard, and the Fifth Avenue Committee).[34] Using direct actions like pickets, sit-ins, work slowdowns, and public demonstrations, WEP workers began demanding better conditions, grievance rights, and benefits like day care and health insurance. For instance, WWT staged a takeover of the parks commissioner's office after he refused to meet with WEP workers about the denial of warm clothing, gloves, rest breaks, and sanitary facilities in the parks. Echoing NWRO's welfare office occupations in the 1960s, twenty-five workers marched into his office followed by television news cameras and shut it down. After being threatened with arrest, the workers succeeded in getting most of their demands. In another action, WWT held a "baby-in" on June 16, 1997, in which parents brought their children to a sit-in at the welfare office to demand day care.

Shortly after WWT's founding in 1996, the Association of Community Organizations for Reform Now (ACORN), which has a long history of organizing poor workers,[35] launched a WEP organizing campaign using similar tactics but focusing specifically on collecting signatures authorizing ACORN to bargain for the workers. ACORN's campaign, like WWT's, was run from the bottom up, with WEP workers themselves making the decisions about how the drive was conducted. ACORN organized more than thirty demonstrations in Manhattan, the Bronx, Brooklyn, and Queens during the first half of 1997, and has also filed collective grievances—one on behalf of nearly 1000 workfare workers in June 1997—as a way of bringing workers together to support one another as well as winning real protections. WEP workers have also blocked trucks from leaving sanitation garages in order to force meetings with welfare officials. Demands for real pay instead of welfare benefits are also on the agenda: hundreds of workfare workers descended on a welfare office in Manhattan's Union Square in April 1997 chanting, "A day's work for a day's pay."[36]

While there were tensions between WWT and ACORN initially, an agreement was reached to work cooperatively. ACORN launched a campaign to collect thousands of authorization cards for a union representation election, while WWT focused on smaller-scale projects like training workfare workers in representational skills and organizing the city's nonprofits and religious institutions in a "pledge of resistance" against workfare. Some of the city's more progressive unions played supportive roles, such as Communications Workers of America Local 1180 (representing some 10,000 white-collar city workers), which helped organize a WEP coalition of more than 60 nonprofit and union groups. A few union leaders came out in public support, such as CWA's Arthur Cheliotes, who recognized that WEP not only exploits workfare workers but "violates every right the labor movement fought for, every basic right we've won." New York Jobs with Justice, a community-labor coalition including some local AFL-CIO unions, contributed to the public debate against workfare by holding a "workers rights' tribunal," aimed at pressuring governments and corporations to reject workfare. "Embarrassment is our primary tool," said chair Dominic Chan. "We want to tell them this is unacceptable."[37]

In June 1997, ACORN announced it had the signatures of upwards of 13,000 WEP workers—more than a third of all workfare workers in New York City, the percentage required to call for an election under labor law—supporting ACORN as their collective bargaining agent. When the city refused to accept the signatures, ACORN said it would run its own union election. In October 1997, with the help of Jobs with Justice, ACORN held a legally nonbinding election in which community and religious leaders set up and monitored polling sites in low-income neighborhoods and at WEP work sites across the city for the three-day vote. The result: 16,989 workers voted for ACORN representation; 207 voted for no representation.[38] Although WEP workers are not legally entitled to bargain collectively under state or federal labor law, ACORN felt the process would put political pressure on city officials to voluntarily recognize the workers as city employees.

Just after ACORN announced its achievement of some 13,000 authorization cards in June 1997, AFSCME District Council 37 said it too would begin a union drive among workfare workers by asking them to sign up as AFSCME members. Attempts to coordinate the two competing union drives were unsuccessful. Sources in the community-based organizations said that while they wanted AFSCME and other AFL-CIO unions' cooperation in organizing, they were cautious of unions "poaching" workfare union members from workplaces they had been organizing without giving those workers real representation.

AFSCME's strategy also differed sharply from that of ACORN and WWT. Council 37 Director Stanley Hill said pushing for the legal right of workfare workers to unionize at the legislative level was higher on his agenda than actually organizing WEP workers at the workplace, and said publicly, "We have the power to do that more than ACORN does."[39] During the summer of 1997, New York's Republican-controlled state government rejected AFSCME's legal reforms, and the union's strategy was reduced to hoping for a more sympathetic Democratic administration in the future. This reliance on the legal process distinguished AFSCME's more bureaucratic approach from that of the community-based organizations. The community organizations—particularly ACORN—have focused on creating strong workplace organizing committees in order to win immediate workplace gains and prepare the ground for the longer-term struggle, as well as building political power through public confrontations with city officials. While not discounting the importance of legal rights for WEP workers, ACORN and WWT believed those rights were more likely to be won if workfare workers organized themselves on the job and in the streets. By summer 1998, AFSCME organizers had gathered thousands of authorization cards from workfare workers, but those cards remained useless because of the unwillingness of AFSCME's leadership to bring political pressure on Mayor Giuliani to recognize WEP workers as workers.

The sheer size of the WEP workforce means a union of these workers could potentially be among the city's largest and most powerful. With up to 2 million welfare recipients expected to be forced onto workfare nationally, organizing campaigns have begun in other cities. Among the most significant are ACORN's workfare projects in Los Angeles and Milwaukee, and the General Assistance Rights Union's POWER (People Organized to Win Employment Rights) in San Francisco. The AFL-CIO went on record encouraging its affiliates to organize workfare workers in February 1997. Actual organizing, however, is up to local unions, which vary widely in their attitudes toward workfare workers. In Philadelphia, a coalition that included the Kensington Welfare Rights Union, an AFSCME affiliate, and the Teamsters issued a joint call for that city's mayor to investigate "why city-subsidized shelters are being used to recruit homeless individuals to break a strike and eventually throw striking workers into the ranks of the homeless" during the 1997 UPS strike.[40] Members of San Francisco's POWER have tried to build coalitions between unions and community groups, but differences in organizing styles and objectives are still a major obstacle, and it remains to be seen if cooperative organizing will ever take place. In mid–1998, ACORN and the Communications Workers of America launched an innovative project in New Jersey in which they will jointly organize workfare workers.

The Ideological Battleground: Forced Labor or Free Choice?

While financially strapped municipalities have, up to now, employed the majority of workfare workers, corporations are becoming increasingly interested in what they accurately perceive to be a plentiful source of cheap labor. The Clinton administration has promised generous tax subsidies to private employers who hire welfare recipients. Given restraints on public funding, CEOs are looking forward to the pool of newly available low-cost labor, acknowledging that the private sector is "the only potential source for as many as 2 million jobs that will need to be found in the next 5 years."[41]

For conservatives, welfare has always been about the regulation of labor; the object is not the elimination of poverty but the use and discipline of low-wage workers. Doing away with entitlements and instituting punitive workfare programs are based on the notion that welfare recipients are unemployed not because of lack of jobs but because they personally lack motivation, skills, or a work ethic. Racial and gender stereotypes are rife within the lexicon of welfare revisionists. Conservative discourse presents poor people as "naturally" deficient in the characteristics that make for a responsible citizen and good worker; being poor is seen as a moral condition rather than a result of lack of job or income brought about by structural problems in the U.S. economy. The language surrounding welfare policy slips "easily, unreflectively, into a language of family, race, and culture rather than inequality, power and exploitation."[42] Poverty is individualized as a pathology, obscuring its origins in social and economic inequalities.

Influential neoconservatives of the 1980s, such as best-selling author George Gilder, claimed that a "welfare culture" fostered by public assistance exerted "a constant, seductive, erosive pressure on the marriages and work habits of the poor." Right-wing journalist William Tucker asserted that public assistance created a gigantic, self-perpetuating underclass, built on "dysfunctional" single-parent families. African Americans, he declared, "have been especially susceptible to the negative incentives of welfare," which, in the absence of marriage, cause people to "breed as fast as humanly possible." Policies that keep women at home to support male workers, argued Tucker, should be the goal of welfare reform.[43] The Reagan and Bush administrations drew on this type of ideology throughout the 1980s, using welfare as a "coded" issue that "activate[d] white Americans' negative views of Blacks without explicitly raising the 'race card.'"[44]

Other conservatives were less interested in imagined pathologies and more concerned with their pocketbooks; they said workers were simply no longer willing to perform entry-level work. In the mid–1960s, claimed *National Review* writer Ed Rubenstein, African American men in particular "lost interest in work," and "dropped out" of the labor force to collect welfare instead. In this unlikely scenario of big business-as-victim, corporations "began to flee the inner cities because of a declining pool of willing workers." But, with entitlements to welfare ended, "such 'dead-end jobs' probably won't be sniffed at." Gilder, too, worried about the "increasing reluctance of the poor to perform low-wage labor" and the "increase in the independence of Black women, secured by both welfare and jobs."[45] The fear that welfare gives workers greater leverage in the job market—because they have a "safety net" to fall back into should working conditions or wages become unacceptable—accounts for much of the right-wing distaste for welfare, matched only by its desire to resurrect the "traditional" heterosexual nuclear family of wage-earning husband and dependent wife through social and economic policy.

This kind of racially and sexually charged rhetoric is an attempt to blame poor people for larger economic problems. It bears little resemblance to the real lives of most welfare recipients, the majority of whom are independent single mothers working a "double shift" on workfare and at home. They often have extensive work experience in the unstable, low-wage labor market, and suffer not from a missing work ethic but from an economy that doesn't provide either the jobs or support systems like child care that they need in order to work. New York City will average just 91,000 job openings each year, while 320,000 city residents are officially unemployed and another 419,000 receive public assistance.[46]

With the safety net itself full of holes and giving way to universal requirements for workfare, activists are creating a counterdiscourse about
welfare by explicitly recasting welfare struggles in terms of social equality, and civil and economic rights. Their emphasis is on the commonalities that join low-wage workers and welfare recipients, connections that
ring true across gender and racial divisions. In response to the mayor's
campaign to bring nonprofits on board as workfare employers, sixty-
eight New York churches, synagogues, and nonprofit organizations came
together to denounce workfare, using the language of abolitionism. With
signs directed at the mayor—"Rudy, We Will Not Be Your Slave Dri-
vers"—clergy and nonprofit leaders called workfare "unjust" and
"evil."[47]

Such arguments don't sit well with New York City's business establishment, including the *Wall Street Journal*, which editorialized that this
imagery of workfare slavery was "easeful debasement of both language
and history." Poor people can't get jobs, opined the *Journal,* because they
don't have the "right attitude. They can't get to work on time, they don't
wear the appropriate clothes, they won't treat customers courteously."
Besides, it is all a matter of free choice, according to *Times* op-ed writer
Robert A. Sirico, who wrote that "workfare is not a ball and chain"—
welfare recipients are free to simply refuse their benefits if they don't want
to work. In other words, in the absence of jobs, they can choose to live
on the streets, without food, housing, or medical care. Echoing the "culture of poverty" arguments, Sirico wrote, "If we are looking for the ball
and chain, we need look no further than unchecked subsidies for doing
nothing but staying poor."[48]

Workfare workers are also using state and federal labor laws to protect their rights. A group of WEP workers won a New York State
Supreme Court suit (*Brukhman v. Hammons*) that argued they were entitled to the same wages paid to unionized city employees. That decision,
currently under appeal by the city, could throw a wrench into the program by reducing the number of hours required to "work off" benefits
since the city would have to figure hours at a higher wage. In Maryland,
a community-labor coalition persuaded the governor to issue an executive order making it a crime to use tax credits to hire welfare recipients to
cut payroll costs. A broad coalition of civil rights, women's, community,
religious, and labor groups successfully pressured President Clinton in
May 1997 to protect workfare workers under federal employment laws
such as the Fair Labor Standards Act and the Occupational Safety and

Health Act. Some community activists are also looking for guarantees for freedom from poverty and forced labor contained in the Universal Declaration of Human Rights, the United Nations Child Rights Convention, and even the U.S. Constitution's 13th Amendment, which states, "Neither slavery nor involuntary servitude . . . shall exist within the United States. . . ."[49]

Conservatives have opposed these measures, which both individually and collectively enhance the power of workers and undermine the abilities of employers (in both the public and private sectors) to divide workers by race, gender, or welfare status. Extending employment rights to workfare workers, said one businessman, potentially "sucks people onto welfare" by providing *better* benefits than those accorded to other low-income workers who are not on welfare.[50] The logical outcome of workfare organizing is to enable people to leave welfare through the creation of living-wage jobs; those jobs would also have the effect, through "free market competition," of bringing up the wages and benefits of other poor workers.

Labor Rights as a Framework for Poor People's Organizing

The large-scale reemergence of workfare programs is opening up new possibilities for organizing welfare recipients by tying workers' rights to welfare rights. Historically, movements for labor rights have been separate from poor people's organizing. With the advent of near-universal workfare requirements in the 1990s, the issue of labor rights has moved to the center of the welfare debate. NWRO attempted to collectively bargain for welfare recipients within the context of the civil rights and Black Power movements. Current welfare rights activists sense the possibilities of deep and lasting change if they can organize themselves to demand economic justice within the context of the labor movement.

In New York City, the chorus of voices supporting workfare organizing has grown to include many individual trade unions. But community-based antipoverty organizations were the first to help workfare workers organize, recognizing that wages were not the only criterion for being a worker. Workfare workers have brought with them previous experiences in feminist, civil rights, Black power, and union movements, and have shaped community-based workfare unions to suit their needs, from using direct action tactics to win immediate goals, to making ethical arguments to change public opinion. Unlike many trade unions that rely on contractual protections in the absence of rank-and-file activity, workfare unionists have been forced by lack of legal protections to mobilize in a more aggressive and directly political way. Similar to the way in which demands for social equality can sometimes inhabit union institutions, so too can labor consciousness reside comfortably within the structures of community organizing.

Workfare workers are demanding that the labor they perform be regularized as permanent, living-wage employment. Through a combination of grassroots organizing, media publicity, and legal strategies, they may actually win these rights. But the process of organizing for their labor rights is also changing the way welfare recipients see themselves: as workers joining together for equal pay for equal work, and for a safe working environment, rather than as unemployable or discarded people who must argue for a handout because the economy has no place for them. "We're workers just like anyone else. . . . I'm doing the same work as other people were doing beside me," noted Brenda Stewart. She sees her fight as one alongside union workers: "We expect the city to create some new jobs. We don't want to move from one position to another, moving a union worker out to put a WEP worker in. We want real job creation and all the benefits afforded to any other worker because we are workers."[51] On a larger level, Stewart and other workfare workers are arguing for an economy based on social and economic justice rather than exploitation.

Workfare organizing in New York City is multiracial and is equally shared by women and men. It is directly about jobs, and just as directly about values of diversity and democracy. While the dynamics of NWRO were influenced by the Black power and feminist movements, workfare organizing takes place within the context of multiracial organizing and coalition building in the 1990s. The goal is to achieve racial and gender justice along with grassroots economic power. In this, workfare organizing bears similarities to other local movements emerging primarily from communities of color led by a new generation of activists that has intentionally chosen not to privilege class, race, or gender, instead seeing them as simultaneously constructing one another. On the level of social theory, "metalanguages" of race and gender have given way to an acknowledgment of the tensions between class, race, gender, and sexuality, and the effort to create new ways of thinking about interlocking oppressions.[52]

The acknowledgment of women's unpaid work in the home by NWRO activists initiated a reconceptualization of the relationship between work and welfare. However, today's workfare activists are realistic about the political climate in which most parents on welfare, at least for the foreseeable future, will not be able to avoid labor outside the home. Most activists, like their predecessors in NWRO, still believe that unwaged work in the home should "count" as work and entitle parents to welfare. Others believe this is problematic because it opens the way for the state to interfere in, and therefore make intrusive moral judgments about, parenting. But both sides agree that a large part of the solution lies in the provision of universally available child care for all parents who work outside the home, and in organizing to transform the social and economic conditions that keep single-parent families in poverty.[53] Workfare workers' call for state-paid child care and real, living-wage jobs acknowledges the "double shift" parents work, and serves to transform welfare rights demands about individual entitlements into broad-based social policy changes.

Workfare activists are also transforming the ideology surrounding welfare away from racist and sexist notions about poor workers and toward the goals of fair wages and job creation. Conservative discourse on welfare has long been highly racialized and oriented around notions of individual or collective cultural failure. With workfare on the rise, conservatives are making the same arguments in a different form: the state should force unwilling workers to pay a debt to the taxpayers who support them. By insisting that people on public assistance are workers within an exploitative capitalist economy, workfare activists radically redefine welfare in terms of economic justice: the right to a decent job at livable wages.

This changing definition of work has enormous implications for how the labor movement as a whole sees itself. Because of the threat workfare poses to union jobs, trade unions are being forced to face a sector of the labor force that lies outside the waged workplace. If trade unions choose to vigorously pursue workfare organizing, it will push them toward a broader notion of who "workers" are. Trade unions, however, are only one part of the labor movement. Another was built by low-waged or unwaged workers outside "mainstream" labor, in the form of economic justice organizations (like NWRO and ACORN), which have long recognized the relationship of waged to unwaged workers, and that the politics of race, ethnicity, and gender are central to class-based movements. Workfare organizing provides an opportunity to reconnect movements for racial and gender justice with unionism. It gives trade unions a chance to look beyond the confines of their own institutions and members and, joining forces with independent community-based unions, economic justice organizations, and antipoverty activists, to contribute to a more diverse, inclusive, and ultimately more powerful labor movement.

NOTES

Thanks to the workfare workers who allowed me to interview them in the course of researching this chapter, which is dedicated to their courage, intelligence, and perseverance. In-person and telephone interviews were conducted with twelve workfare workers and seven paid staff organizers between October 1996 and August 1998. In some cases, I have changed workers' names in deference to their requests for confidentiality. For readings of this article in draft, I am grateful to Craig Alderson, Dana Frank, Virginia Rodriguez-Jones, and Kimberly Springer.

1. Edriss Anderson, WEP worker, interview by author, New York City, June 3, 1997.

2. Francis Fox Piven and Richard Cloward, *Poor People's Movements: Why They Succeed, How They Fail* (New York: Vintage, 1979), 273–75.

3. See ibid.; Guida West, *The National Welfare Rights Movement: The Social Protest of Poor Women* (New York: Praeger, 1981); Nick and Mary Lynn Kotz's biography of George Wiley, *A Passion for Equality* (New York: Norton, 1977); and Jacqueline Pope's book about the NWRO-affilated Brooklyn Welfare Action Council, *Biting the Hand That Feeds Them: Organizing Women on Welfare at the Grass Roots Level* (New York: Praeger, 1989). Piven and Cloward's "A Strategy to End Poverty" was initially a mimeographed essay circulated among activists; it was later published in *The Nation*, May 2, 1966.

4. Piven and Cloward, *Poor People's Movements*, 277.

5. Johnnie Tillmon, "Insights of a Welfare Mother: A Conversation with Johnnie Tillman," *Journal of Social Issues* (January-February 1971): 23.

6. Piven and Cloward, *Poor People's Movements*, 287.

7. Pope, *Biting the Hand*, 8.

8. West, *National Welfare Rights Movement*, 3–4.

9. Piven and Cloward, *Poor People's Movements*, 316.

10. Katz and Katz, *Passion for Justice*, 289–94.

11. Mimi Abramovitz, *Under Attack, Fighting Back: Women and Welfare in the United States* (New York: Monthly Review Press, 1996), 131.

12. Megan H. Morrissey, "The Downtown Welfare Advocate Center: A Case Study of a Welfare Rights Organization," *Social Service Review* 64, no. 2 (June 1990): 189–207.

13. Committee on Ways and Means, U.S. House of Representatives, *1996 Green Book*, "Table 8–25: Historical Trends in AFDC Enrollments and Average Payments, 1970–2001" (Washington, D.C.: Government Printing Office, 1996), 467; U.S. Department of Commerce, Bureau of the Census, *Current Population Survey, 1989–94* (Washington, D.C.: Government Printing Office, 1995).

14. Nancy E. Rose, *Workfare or Fair Work: Women, Welfare, and Government Work Programs* (New Brunswick: Rutgers University Press, 1995).

15. Personal Responsibility and Work Opportunity Reconciliation Act of 1996, PL 104–193 (HR 3734), in *Congressional Record*, July 31, 1996.

16. Liz Krueger, Liz Accles, and Laura Wernick, *Workfare: The Real Deal II* (New York: Community Food Resource Center, rev. ed., July 1997), 3–4; Charles Tilly, *Workfare's Impact on the New York City Labor Market: Lower Wages and Worker Displacement*, Working Paper 92 (New York: Russell Sage Foundation, 1996).

17. Melissa Healy, "N.Y. 'Workfare' Not So Fair After All, Some Say," *Los Angeles Times*, July 5, 1997.

18. Krueger et al., *Workfare*, 13.

19. Annette Fuentes, "Slaves of New York," *In These Times* (December 23, 1996): 14–17.

20. David Firestone, "New York Braces for Surge in Workfare Effort," *New York Times*, August 13, 1996; City of New York, Office of the Mayor, "Mayor's Management Report," February 13, 1997.

21. Healy, "N.Y. 'Workfare' Not So Fair."

22. Bureau of the Census, *Current Population Survey, 1989–94*.

23. Alicia Portes, WEP worker, interview by author, New York City, June 14, 1997.

24. Eric Mayer, WEP worker, interview by author, New York City, June 8, 1997; Krueger et al., *Workfare*, 8.

25. Joe Sexton, "Discontented Workfare Laborers Murmur 'Union,'" *New York Times*, September 27, 1996.

26. Brenda Stewart, WWT activist, presentation at WEP Forum, New York City, May 28, 1997.

27. Piven and Cloward, "Workers and Welfare," 141–50.

28. See for instance, Philip S. Foner and Ronald L. Lewis, eds., *Black Workers: A Documentary History from Colonial Times to the Present* (Philadelphia: Temple University Press, 1989); Dana Frank, *Purchasing Power: Consumer Organizing, Gender, and the Seattle Labor Movement, 1919–1929* (Cambridge: Cambridge University Press, 1994); David Gordon, Richard Edwards, and Michael Reich, *Segmented Work, Divided Workers: The Historical Transformation of Labor in the United States* (Cambridge: Cambridge University Press, 1982); Dolores Janiewski, *Sisterhood Denied: Race, Gender, and Class in a New South Community* (Philadelphia: Temple University Press, 1985); David R.

Roediger, *The Wages of Whiteness: Race and the Making of the American Working Class* (New York: Verso, 1991); Joe Trotter, *Black Milwaukee: The Making of an Industrial Proletariat* (Philadelphia: Temple University Press, 1985).

29. Robert Korstad and Nelson Lichtenstein, "Opportunities Found and Lost: Labor, Radicals, and the Early Civil Rights Movement," *Journal of American History* 75, no. 3 (December 1988): 786–812.

30. On DRUM, see Dan Georgakas and Marvin Surkin, *Detroit: I Do Mind Dying: A Study in Urban Revolution* (New York: St. Martin's, 1975), and James A. Geschwender, *Class, Race and Worker Insurgency: The League of Revolutionary Black Workers* (Cambridge: Cambridge University Press, 1977). For a history of Local 1199, see Leon Fink and Brian Greenberg, *Upheaval in the Quiet Zone: A History of the Hospital Workers Union 1199* (Urbana: University of Illinois Press, 1989).

31. For numbers of African American women in unions, see Louise L. Hornor, ed., *Black Americans: A Statistical Sourcebook* (Palo Alto, Calif.: Information Publications, 1997), 231., "Table 6.21, Union Membership." For data on women in union leadership, see Ruth Milkman, "Women Workers, Feminism, and the Labor Movement since the 1960s," in *Women, Work and Protest* (New York: Routledge, 1985).

32. Julianne Malveaux, "The Political Economy of Black Women," in *Race, Politics, and Economic Development: Community Perspectives,* edited by James Jennings (London: Verso, 1992), 33–52; Julianne Malveaux, "The GOP's War Against Poor Women: Welfare Reform Proposals are Based on Myths, Not Realities," *Black Enterprise* (February 1995): 32; for the relationship between low-wage employment and welfare, see Kathryn Edin and Laura Lein, *Making Ends Meet: How Single Mothers Survive Welfare and Low-Wage Work* (New York: Russell Sage, 1997).

33. Fuentes, "Slaves of New York," 16–17; E. Assata Wright, "The Fight to Unionize Workfare Workers: Divided They Fall?" *Village Voice*, January 28, 1997; David Firestone, "Labor Leader Drops Demand on Workfare," *New York Times,* September 28, 1996; Joyce Purnick, "On Workfare, Fig Leaves and Silence," *New York Times,* September 30, 1996. Hill reversed his position in April 1998, after the mayor laid off nearly 1000 city workers at a city hospital that was heavily staffed by WEP workers. "AFSCME" is the acronym of the American Federation of State, County and Municipal Employees.

34. Heidi Dorow, WWT organizer, interview by author, New York City, June 9, 1997; Arthur Poland, WWT activist, interview by author, New York City, June 9, 1997.

35. Many of NWRO's activists went on to work with ACORN. For an excellent history, see Gary Delgado, *Organizing the Movement: The Roots and Growth of ACORN* (Philadelphia: Temple University Press, 1986).

36. Milagros Silva, ACORN lead organizer, interview by author, New York City, June 11, 1997, and by phone August 6, 1998; Martin Gonzalez, ACORN activist, presentation at WEP Forum, New York City, May 28, 1997. See also "Bronx Up Close: Anger in Workfare Ranks," *New York Times,* June 1, 1997, and "Looking for the Union Label" *Newsday,* April 20, 1997. A third, smaller group, Workfareness, is also attempting to organize workfare workers in New York City.

37. Arthur Cheliotes, CWA Local 1180 president, presentation at WEP Forum, New York City, May 28, 1997; Dominic Chan, chair of New York City Jobs with Justice, interview by author, New York City, June 2, 1997; quote from Chan in Steven Greenhouse, "Union Friends Unite to Bash Foes," *New York Times,* November 22, 1996.

38. "United Stance/Workfare Employees Vote Overwhelmingly to Unionize," *Newsday,* October 24, 1997.

39. Stanley Hill, executive director of AFSCME District Council 37, interview by author, New York City, June 2, 1997; Hill quote from Steven Greenhouse, "Petitions Seek Vote on Union for Workfare: Organizing Groups Says It Has 13,000 Signatures," *New York Times,* July 3, 1997; see also "Organizing Workfare Workers: AFSCME's Road Map" (Washington, D.C.: AFSCME, n.d.) for an outline of the union's organizing strategies.

40. Kensington Welfare Rights Union, "Press Release: Homeless Residents of City Shelter Used to Cross Teamsters' Picketline," August 13, 1997.

41. Daniel Roth, "Workfare," *Forbes,* November 4, 1996.

42. Michael B. Katz, *The Undeserving Poor: From the War on Poverty to the War on Welfare* (New York: Pantheon, 1989), 8. Welfare "stigma" not only steers debates over social policies but can also deeply affect welfare recipients' views of their current lives and possible futures; see, for instance, Robin L. Jarrett, "Welfare Stigma Among Low-Income African American Single Mothers," in *Family Relations* 45, no. 5 (October 1996): 368–74.

43. George Gilder, *Wealth and Poverty* (Toronto: Bantam, 1981), 148; William Tucker, "All in the Family," *National Review,* March 6, 1995.

44. Martin Gilens, "'Race Coding' and White Opposition to Welfare," *American Political Science Review* 90, no. 3 (September 1996): 593–604.

45. Ed Rubenstein, "Right Data," *National Review* 48, no. 24 (December 23, 1996): 14; Gilder, *Wealth and Poverty,* 143, 150.

46. Krueger et al., *Workfare,* 1.

47. Steven Greenhouse, "Nonprofit and Religious Groups Vow to Fight Workfare Program," *New York Times,* July 24, 1997.

48. "Slaves of New York," editorial, *Wall Street Journal,* July 31, 1997; Robert A. Sirico, "Work Is Moral and So Is Workfare," *New York Times,* July 27, 1997.

49. Jon Jeter, "Maryland Shields Jobs from Welfare Law," *Washington Post,* May 4, 1997; Cynthia Cheski, "Reforming Welfare," *Human Rights* 21, no. 4 (fall 1994): 10–11, 42.

50. Healy, "N.Y. 'Workfare' Not So Fair."

51. Stewart, WEP Forum, May 28, 1997.

52. Evelyn Brooks Higginbotham, "African-American Women's History and the Metalanguage of Race," *Signs* (winter 1992): 251–74.

53. For a review of this debate, see Felicia Kornbluh, "Feminists and the Welfare Debate: Too Little? Too Late?" *Dollars & Sense,* no. 208 (November-December 1996): 24–29, and Theresa Funiciello, "The Work of Women (and the Mistakes of Workfare Organizing)," *Third Force* 5, no. 5 (November/December 1997): 22–5, 38–40. For historical perspectives, see Gwendolyn Mink, *The Wages of Motherhood: Inequality in the Welfare State, 1917–1942* (Ithaca: Cornell University Press, 1995), and Dorothy Roberts, "The Value of Black Mothers' Work," *Radical America* 26, no. 1 (August 1996): 9–15.

Epilogue
African American Women's Activism in the Global Arena

Loretta J. Ross

When I was contacted by Kimberly Springer to write the epilogue for this book, I was preparing to go to South Africa to attend the 8th World Conference of the International Cross-Cultural Black Women's Studies Institute, held in August 1998 in Johannesburg. The Institute, convened by an international network of activists and scholars under the leadership of Dr. Andree Nicola McLaughlin of Medgar Evers College in New York City, provides a forum for cross-cultural study and organizing by Black women and serves as a systematic vehicle for broadening practical knowledge of women's experiences globally. It is committed to empowering women to exchange information, identify resources, and build global links in our various struggles for self-determination and autonomy.

I thought it would be a fitting conclusion to this volume to examine African American women's activism in the international arena. Because of my involvement in other world conferences for women beginning in 1980, I attempted to observe and analyze African American women's participation in the conference, and to better understand the tasks that lie before us as African American women.

This epilogue does not attempt to offer a comprehensive analysis of all that occurred at the conference, which was decidedly a positive experience, but instead to take a global snapshot of our efficacy in connecting our local issues to a global analysis, and to discern the many international parallels that can inform our activism in the United States.

The conference did not disappoint. It became a metaphor for the status of African American women's activism. It brought together more than 400 women of African descent from 35 countries. Other than women from the continent itself, the second-largest delegation was composed of women from the United States, perhaps nearly a third of the participants. Symbolically, we came in our mud cloth, kente, and cowrie shells—but we were also in our Western suits and heels.

World Conferences and African American Women

The 1998 South Africa conference was significant in its timing. Global forums bringing together Black women are still extremely rare, even though impressive strides were made in the organizing of African American women during the World Decade for Women (1976–1985), which was declared by the United Nations in 1975 to examine the status and progress of women in their quest for equality around the world.

The decade was marked by three World Conferences for Women—in Mexico City (1975), Copenhagen (1980), and Nairobi (1985)—and the National Conference for Women in Houston in 1977. The goal of the first world conference was to develop a global "Plan of Action" to improve the status of women; the mid-decade conference assessed progress on the plan; and the end-decade conference in Nairobi presented a plan of action for women to be implemented until the year 2000. The goal of the Houston conference was to create a U.S. version of the World Plan for American women.

The decade was particularly significant for African American women because it sparked many opportunities for organizing locally, nationally, and internationally. Many impressive advances were made during the decade, not the least of which was the tripling of the actual number of women-of-color organizations in the United States from approximately 300 to nearly 1,000.[1]

A sizable base of support for Black feminism did not emerge until the late 1980s. bell hooks's groundbreaking 1981 book, *Ain't I a Woman,* laid out the ideological framework for this embryonic movement when she wrote, "Only a few Black women have rekindled the spirit of feminist struggle that stirred the hearts and minds of our nineteenth century sisters. We, Black women who advocate feminist ideology, are pioneers. We are clearing a path for ourselves and our sisters."[2] Alice Walker, writing in 1978, called on Black women to reevaluate their relationship to the women's movement: "[T]o the extent that Black women disassociate themselves from the women's movement, they abandon their responsibilities to women throughout the world. This is a serious abdication from and misuse of radical Black herstorical tradition: Harriet Tubman, Sojourner Truth, Ida B. Wells, and Fannie Lou Hamer would not have liked it."[3]

The 1985 Nairobi conference was the watershed event of the decade for African American women. Because the conference was in Africa, more than 1,100 African American women attended, among the nearly 20,000 women. This was the largest number of women to ever come together at a global women's rights conference and certainly the largest number of Black women ever to attend an international conference.

African American women came to Nairobi excellently prepared to participate in the global discussions of the day. Preparatory conferences sponsored *by* Black women *for* Black women in the five years between Copenhagen and Nairobi helped familiarize attendees with the history of the decade and the workings of the United Nations, and catalyzed the development of strategies to have an effective impact on the governmental and nongovernmental conferences in Nairobi.

The Nairobi conference signaled the massive entry of African American women into the international women's movement, both locally and globally. After Nairobi, organizing by Black women literally exploded. Some of it was in response in the increasing repression promoted by the Reagan administration through welfare cutbacks and punitive reproductive health policies. But mostly, this impressive amount of organizing may be attributed to a broader acceptance of Black feminism, an idea whose time had finally come among activist women. Although many Black women still rejected the word *feminism* for themselves, they strongly identified with feminist causes, particularly the movements for reproductive freedom and to end violence against women.

The Fourth World Conference for women was held in Beijing, China, in 1995. At first glance, for African American women, it appeared to live up to the budding promise of the Nairobi conference ten years earlier. Hundreds of African American women attended the conference; a daily caucus for about 300–400 African American women was organized. Unfortunately, in my judgment, our agency as African American women was less effective in Beijing than in Nairobi. A number of explanations are possible.

First, the autonomous wave of preparatory conferences organized by Black women did not precede Beijing, as had been done for Nairobi. Thus, many more African American women came to Nairobi unprepared to understand and enter the debate on the Beijing Platform for Action. For example, many participants tried to reopen discussion on closed, agreed-upon paragraphs in the platform. They, incorrectly, did not focus on the remaining "bracketed" paragraphs that were the subject of the negotiations in Beijing. This is not to say that there were not sophisticated African American women leaders who represented us excellently throughout the official conference, but the opportunity to deploy the richness of hundreds of voices was lost as valuable time was spent introducing many women to the Platform for Action for the first time in Beijing. For this lapse, we have only ourselves to blame because although many of us participated in preparatory conferences sponsored by the United Nations and a few nongovernmental organizations, these were mostly attended by women of color already in the existing informal network, rather than by the "new" activists who showed up in Beijing. No specific and open preparatory meetings for African American women were sponsored by any national Black women's organization. Only the National Council of Negro Women sponsored pre-Beijing trainings for its members.

A second explanation may be in the diffusion of the visible activism by Black women, which I will address later in this chapter.

The Cross-Cultural Institute itself was an outcome of the decade, sponsoring its first conference in 1987, two years after Nairobi. In 1998, African American women came to South Africa with all of our triumphs and contradictions as we explored the conference theme: Women's Empowerment: Self-Help, Technology and Sustainable Development. The conference identified key areas of African American women's activism in the global arena: (1) global economics and sustainable development; (2) the impact of technology on women's lives; and (3) confronting white supremacist and patriarchal oppression as Black women.

Conference Highlights

Presentations, workshops, and discussions at the conference reconceptualized the intersection of gender, class, and race, reflecting the polyvocality of multiple social locations for African American women.[4] The participants from the United States were largely academics, independent scholars, and activists who are writing and rethinking the African American experience from a feminist perspective.

The speakers recognized that global economic, political, and social decisions are as often based on race and gender as profit, acknowledging the racial and economic restructuring taking place due to forces of globalization and wars. Welfare, exile labor, and sweatshops go hand in hand as economic decision makers recalculate how to use or, more important, not use our labor in the global economy as we compete with other unskilled or semiskilled workers around the world. A challenge for the African American women was to explicate the dialectic between our agency and the social, political, and economic hierarchies.

We discussed how neoliberals collaborate with conservative fundamentalists to create an atmosphere even more toxic to African American women. Unchecked market forces worldwide demand—even force—budgetary cuts away from social spending on education, child care, health care, food, and shelter.

The debt crisis of the United States, which was created in the first place by excessive militarism, is the excuse used by neoliberals like Bill Clinton and right-wing conservatives like Newt Gingrich to destroy our welfare system for helping poor women and children. The Orwellian-named 1992 Personal Responsibility Act, better known as welfare reform, was based on ideological attacks on the nature of social welfare itself, arguing against the distribution of benefits and burdens throughout society to move toward social justice.

As the conference participants discussed, welfare reform and the prison industrial complex is the U.S. version of structural adjustment policies that dramatically reshape our workforce. Welfare reform forces many poor women to work at low or no-pay jobs that are dangerous and have no child-care or health-care benefits. These ills of privatization and globalization turn us into new slaves in the marketplace. Subminimum-wage jobs at McDonald's or picking up trash in public parks cannot lift anyone out of poverty. Prisoners are paid as little as four cents an hour for jobs previously held by unionized workers. This provides a captive set of low-cost workers for our corporations while displacing workers who made more money and had benefits like health insurance and union protection.

The conference participants also grappled with the lack of a universal concept of social justice. Many framed their ideas in human rights language, seeking the establishment of societies in which human rights are respected and enforced, and the world's resources are equitably distributed in ways that acknowledge that freedom, justice, and equality are not individual issues of autonomy but collective needs for Black women worldwide.

We are living in a world in which we are denied not only our human rights, but also the right to *know* our human rights. Human rights are the language of people's power against the tyranny and neglect of their governments. They have the power to create a new worldwide movement of poor people and to generate a whole new generation of activists who can construct a new value system, social identity, and laws finally worthy of our human dignity.

Speakers affirmed the promising potential of the human rights umbrella to unite all social justice movements—women, civil rights, youth, environmental, gay and lesbian, the elderly—all working for the human rights of their own constituencies. African American women can engage in many struggles under one movement, healing our fragmented selves seemingly trapped by the obvious limits of identity politics. Human rights theory, law, and enforcement appeal to African American women who feel they experience more than one kind of oppression. As one speaker said, "We have less in life so we need more of law."

It was also uplifting to see so many women identify positively with the word *Black*. I met women who appeared Asian, Native, or even European who overwhelmingly affirmed their blackness and solidarity with women more obviously of African descent. For them, Black was more a political identity than a biological destiny. In addition to the women from the Americas and Africa, Black women from Russia, India, Hawai'i, Israel, Samoa, Australia, New Zealand (self-described as Aotearoa), and Europe loudly demanded their inclusion in the African diaspora. The many languages of the simultaneous translation provided a wonderfully blended symphony that made speeches in Portuguese as accessible as those in French, Spanish, or English. The normative nature of our diversity was powerfully transcendent.

The conference also spanned the generations. In particular, many "older" women were an outstanding feature of the conference. An International Council of Elders presided over the conference in an affirming spirit of continuity and linkages to the past, while many young women attended from schools and universities in the United States. A special parallel conference on the "Girl Child" was offered in conjunction with the institute.

Another remarkable feature of the institute was the lack of endless debate about the word *feminism*, perhaps due to the influence of the elders who themselves were legendary activists in the women's movement. People like Gloria Joseph and Vinie Burrows added substantial maturity to the discussion of this often inflammatory debate among women of African descent. Instead, the South Africa 1998 conference recognized that there is no one right way to be an activist or a feminist and, alternatively, spoke of the many "feminisms" that Black women embrace as a praxis for empowerment.

This was a significant change from 1985, when at the Nairobi World Conference, the word *feminism* was hotly contested terrain, with women of African descent in varying degrees either embracing or rejecting the word based on their own perceptions and realities. The stereotype of a "feminist status quo" dominated Nairobi because of myths and stereotypes about the ideology and practitioners of feminism. For example, as late as 1984, a panel of African American feminists was nearly booed off the stage at a National Black United Front Convention when the women declared their support for the Nairobi conference. The women were called "man-haters," "lesbians," and "mindless followers" of white women for daring to participate in this international conference. Two full decades after the 1960s, participation in a world conference on women was still equated by some Black nationalists with abandoning the struggle against racism.

The institute also bravely addressed the class tensions among the participants. Because the conference reached out and incorporated a large number of poor women from Africa, the class differences between them and the African American women who could afford to attend this conference were sometimes painful. Although many African American women define ourselves as "poor," knowing the fluid nature of our class status in the United States, we also feel our privilege acutely when we buy the arts and crafts of our sisters on the continent, knowing we may spend more money on souvenirs than they are likely to earn in a month. We know we are not responsible for their poverty, but it's hard to remember that in the face of it. Similarly, women from the rural areas called attention to the urban biases among some of the presenters.

Religion and Self-Help

The conference also produced its share of contradictions. The theme of women's empowerment was woven throughout the conference and provided an opportunity to examine the different and nuanced meanings of this word among Black women. It was interesting to note that several African American speakers moved the discussion on empowerment away from externalized boundaries imposed by oppressive forces like racism, sexism, classism, and homophobia into internalized concepts like self-esteem and self-help. Some of the speakers passionately spoke about realizing personal power in the face of external threats.

While many of the speakers offered scathing critiques of macroeconomic structural adjustment policies that beggar Black women worldwide, whether through welfare reform instituted by neoliberals, or debt crises manipulated by the International Monetary Fund or the World Bank, some unfortunately turned their analyses into shallow justifications of microcredit enterprises, as if petty capitalism can turn the tide of our oppression. A majority of the conference participants seemed skeptical about the likelihood of microenterprises and microcredit programs dramatically improving the economic conditions of women, whether in the developing or developed world. As one participant quipped, "This is a Republican solution to a Democratic problem."

While on the one hand this was a liberating process, the claiming of personal power and triumph over the forces that would dehumanize us, it was also a bittersweet proclamation. Too often, the speakers interpreted the self-help theme in a way that would have delighted racist Republicans. The ideological hand of the religious right was felt because although they were infrequent, cries for Black women to stop "depending on the welfare system" and pull themselves out of poverty through microenterprise were a sad reminder not only that the right wing has poisoned the political well when it comes to white folks, but that African Americans are also vulnerable to believing the lies told about us—that we are morally crippled by our alleged overdependence on welfare and other forms of public support.

The role of religion in the conference highlighted other strange contrasts. The conference was opened with a prayer by a Black South African Catholic priest, and the conference agenda itself dealt with issues such as abortion, lesbianism, independent religious institutions for women, women's sexuality, and other topics that surely would anger the Catholic hierarchy. That African American women's organizations in the United States are under pressure from Catholic funders not to address those same issues was mentioned at the conference. African American women discussed the recent decision of the Catholic Church's Campaign for Human Development (CHD) to "require grantees" to assure that none of CHD's funds will be used to support organizations that "promote or support abortion, euthanasia, the death penalty, or any affront to human life and dignity." This is an important divide-and-conquer strategy because many antipoverty African American women's organizations supported by CHD now have to either not work with their prochoice allies or refuse to accept much-needed funding.

At one point in the middle of a plenary session on women and technology, a participant from the United States successfully demanded that the entire conference should join her in a prayer/chant ritual that included speaking in tongues and singing Christian anthems. Most of us looked on in shock as religious fervor hijacked the plenary. It seemed anti-Christian to interrupt this epiphany, but most of us questioned whether Black women's activism had descended into new forms of religious rituals instead of a political mandate and plan of action.

This was not a phenomenon particular to being in Africa. I have been to African American women's conferences in the United States that felt more like a revival meeting or mass spiritual therapy through rituals than a pragmatic and visionary strategy to lift ourselves out of poverty and oppression. I attribute some of this trend to the success of the religious right and its penetration of the African American community.

When a few conference presenters were romantically extolling the virtues of self-help, castigating Black women for not seizing their "opportunities," I felt we had entered a twilight zone where victim blaming had triumphed. For hundreds of years lies have been told by white supremacists about African American women. A large measure of our activism has been in resistance to these lies with all of our souls. Yet, the more we embrace the beliefs and programs of the neoliberals and the conservatives, the more we become victims believing the lies instead of resisting them.

Perhaps many African American women are confused because the religious right does not use open racism to promote its agenda. Because this bigotry is exotically disguised, it can be difficult for most people to identify and challenge. This furtive racism is particularly oblique because the religious right uses classic misdirection plays—maybe a page out of

Promise Keepers' founder Bill McCartney's playbook—fake to the Left and move to the right. The religious right takes advantage of the fact that its allies on the far right have succeeded in limiting the definition of racism to its overt expression, such as gutter epithets, while denying its overt operation.

A large sign of the religious right's success at misdirection is its attempt to cloak itself in the moral mantle of the civil rights movement. Its cynical manipulation of civil rights imagery and so-called civil rights leaders like Alveda Celeste King, niece of Dr. Martin Luther King, Jr., serves both to discredit the civil rights movement and to disguise its true anti–human rights agenda. This corrupt and bankrupt appropriation of the civil rights language and symbols pits, for example, African Americans against gays and lesbians. The tactic furthers the agenda of the religious right, while betraying the moral authority of the civil rights movement.

The impact of the religious right and its ability to hide its racism are exposed in how it has repackaged its social agenda. The religious right often takes advantage of desperate people's needs to recruit them to a larger, more ominous social agenda. Beginning with the Christian Coalition's laughable one-million-dollar offer in 1997 to help rebuild burned Black churches, the coalition has flanked itself with a half dozen Black and Latino ministers to launch the Samaritan Project to bridge the racial and ideological gap between people of color and white evangelicals to "provide a faith-based alternative to the welfare state." In addition to attacking welfare as a symbol of moral degeneracy, its agenda includes promoting abstinence-based sex education, lobbying for school vouchers to undermine public schools, and seeking government grants to provide drug rehabilitation through religious indoctrination. The religious right is, of course, opposed to arts funding for gay and lesbian groups but heavily involved in promoting school prayer, opposing abortion, and supporting censorship campaigns.

In the end, with time and repetition many of the supporters of these themes are not white or particularly conservative. More than 700 right-wing conservative think tanks and foundations have changed America's social agenda and lead in the dismantling of the welfare state. They have launched campaigns to promote the English Only movement and to support anti-immigration and anti–affirmative action legislation; circulated theories of alleged Black genetic inferiority (remember *The Bell Curve?*); led damaging welfare and tort reform; and funded campus-based battles against multiculturalism, women's studies, and African American studies.

Addressing the role of religion in the organizing and mobilizing of African American women is a serious issue, one too important to be left to the machinations of the religious right. Spirituality is extremely important—but should not be used to ritualize us away from critical discussions of our agency in addressing the key issues and becoming inoculated against the blandishments of the Right.

Professional Victims

The conference also had its share of what I call "professional victims" from the African American women's movement. Nearly drowning out legitimate discussions of race, class, language, and heterosexist privileges were the voices of a few women who constantly whined about being left out, perfecting *the politics of complaint*. They were usually self-righteous—claiming that their oppression is so unique that not even other Black women experience it. When seeking power and recognition, they profess to speak for all Black women. When held accountable, they claim they can't be used as a representative token and mouthpiece for the race.

Some were careerists, seeking financial security through "working for the movement." Others were Black Junior Leaguers, apparently blind to the class contradictions in which they are mired. Often they are used to thwart their more radical sisters. To a longtime observer of African American women in the women's movement, it was obvious that most of them had sharpened their politics of complaint on white women, using race more as a weapon for their own advancement than in any true solidarity with other Black women. They had become so accustomed to the victim role that they located their power and self-esteem in what is essentially a powerless posture. Victims can be survivors, but survivors must become victors to progress toward full human rights and dignity. As Dr. King said, "Hate is too great a burden for people moving on toward their date with destiny."

We may never successfully build and strengthen the African American women's movement if we are perpetually preoccupied with the peccadilloes of white women. Even with the best will in the world, white women will never represent the authenticity, authority, and uniqueness of the African American women's experiences. We must do that ourselves without letting anger at white racism distract from our mission. Our lives are shaped by race, class, and gender, but I believe there is more to African

American women than the symbiosis of our oppression. Moreover, strident self-righteousness toward other African American women serves only to distance us from other women we need. We have to acknowledge that African American women have class and identity crises among ourselves that are even more crippling than the racism we experience at the hands of white women in the movement.

More damaging perhaps is the way such political posturing can derail a discussion. One conference plenary session was interrupted by a woman who felt she was silenced because she was not allowed to give an impromptu speech during a question-and-answer session. In fact, she was using her time to personally attack the speakers, not ask a question or rebut their political views.

Is the Movement Growing or Not?

I am concerned about what I perceive is both a decline in the visible activism of African American women and a structural and ideological diffusion that may be disguising our activism. In the late 1980s, a proliferation of African American women's organizations was cause for celebration and joy to many of us who had been operating within the women's movement without an identifiable constituency in the 1960s and 1970s. We believed that the organizations and institutions we were creating both nationally and locally would sustain themselves and our burgeoning Black women's movement. We may have been prematurely optimistic.

We have had our successes in the 1990s. The spontaneous response to the Clarence Thomas/Anita Hill debacle aroused 1,600 women to purchase an advertisement in the *New York Times* in November of 1991 to express their outrage at the racist and sexist attacks against Anita Hill during Thomas's Supreme Court confirmation hearings. "African American Women in Defense of Ourselves" supported Hill's right to make public Thomas's sexual misconduct and challenge his fitness to assume Thurgood Marshall's seat on the court.

More recently, the Million Woman March was a vibrant and moving testament to the eagerness of African American women to find their voices and assert their dignity in the midst of a white supremacist construct.

While Black women's culture is *in vogue* and Black women's literary contributions have never been more warmly received by the publishing industry (largely due to the economic success of Toni Morrison, Alice Walker, Octavia Butler, and Terry McMillan), the actual leadership and agency of African American women is more contested than ever.

Many of the Black women's organizations founded in the 1980s folded in the 1990s. Those remaining have often been reduced to a shadow of their former strength. At one time, the National Black Women's Health Project drew 2,000 women to its founding conference in 1983. The voices of national Black women's organizations are strangely muted, missing that vibrant "in-your-face" activism that energized us in the 1980s.

A 1990s retrenchment occurred—partly because of attacks from the right but also because of the slow development of strong Black women's organizations, as well as class, age, and leadership tensions. Example: in 1989, I was part of a team with Donna Brazile that developed and distributed a quarter of a million *We Remember* brochures to protest the Bush administration's attempt to recriminalize abortion (see chapter 3 of this volume). Similarly, the National Black Women's Health Project sent thirteen busloads of Black women to march for abortion rights in 1989. Women of color, especially Latinas, organized on a range of issues.

Now the events drawing the largest crowds of Black women are beauty and hair shows and megachurches. Many of the strongest women-of-color organizations have splintered into rival groups, competing against one another for members and funding. Many younger activists are blaming the feminist generation before them for not showing them how they can have it all: be successful career women and mothers at the same time. They often claim that our only legacy to them is identity politics, through which they often microdivide themselves or, even more bizarrely, deny their continuing race, class, or gender oppression.

Perhaps this is a maturation process that is creating the space for many diverse and sometimes opposing voices, another polyvocality, as Rose Brewer calls it. But it also may be that we expected too much unity among African American women too soon. We may have been lulled and then distracted by Clinton's presidency. Without an easily identified opponent, we became susceptible to our own contradictions and overtures by the Right.

I have also noticed a tendency of African American women to be overlooked when the term *women of color* is used. This is not only in the hostile and traditionally discriminatory arenas of employment in the corporate sector but also in the practices of our white-dominated feminist institutions that seem to prefer to hire or work with any woman of color who does not confront them directly on their race and class privileges. Jobs in the women's movement, grants from women's foundations, positions as leaders are more often than not awarded to women who are more assimilated or less threatening to the white women in charge.

I don't blame the women of color who are used in this way; often they are chosen for their youth and inexperience to avoid accountability. Instead, I blame the white supremacist construct that rears its ugly head in feminist settings that should be hostile to it. This fosters interracial hostility and competition among women of color. Beset already by specters of competitive victimhood, this lack of feminist ethics and feminist leadership to address the specifics of racism in the movement is problematic and difficult for African American women to name and identify. When we do, we are made to appear to be attacking other women of color rather than the white power hierarchy. At one time such practices would have been loudly critiqued by assertive African American women. Now there seems to be a new conspiracy of silence about the manifestations of anti-Black racism in the women's movement.

This is sharp irony indeed because it was African American women who helped birth the term *women of color* at the National Women's Conference in Houston in 1977 when the Black Women's Agenda was transformed into a more inclusive Women of Color Agenda for inclusion in the National Women's Plan of Action.

This cynical manipulation accompanies a corruption of feminism by which it has become more esoteric than accessible. Feminism has always been about choices—the power to make choices that make sense. Confusion over the range of choices for some privileged women wars against the limited nature of choices for other women.

Activism for the Future

In summary, I believe the chapters in this book highlight the important advances African American women's activism has made in the recent past. But we have yet to collectively tackle some of our most difficult issues. Issues such as class, homophobia, religion, and privilege *among* African American women often feel like reopening Pandora's Box. For those of you reading this book, it may sound like I'm preaching to the choir, but believe me, the choir is not all singing the same song.

This book is about women who work to self-determine their own fate, against all odds, who rise to come together with their sisters in struggle, learning to trust and lean on one another for strength. Audre Lorde perhaps expressed it best:

> For Black women, learning to consciously extend ourselves to each other and to call upon each other's strengths is a life-saving strategy. In the best of circumstances surrounding our lives, it requires an enormous amount of mutual, consistent support for us to be emotionally able to look straight into the face of the powers aligned against us and still do our work with joy. It takes determination and practice.[5]

There will be many more international conferences for African American women. An international women's health conference is planned for Canada in the year 2000, and the next World Conference of the International Cross-Cultural Black Women's Studies Institute will most likely be held in Brazil in 2001. We will have many more opportunities to sharpen our activism, develop our Black feminist theory, and practice our politics in these settings. It is hoped that by documenting our successes and our sorrows that we can embrace the 21st century with a new commitment to ourselves and our sisters that will let our activism showcase that it is "Still Lifting, Still Climbing."

NOTES

1. National Women's Conference Committee, *A Decade of Achievement 1977–1987: A Report on a Survey Based on the National Plan of Action for Women* (NWCCenter, P.O. Box 455, Beaver Dam, WI 53918, May 1988), 54.

2. bell hooks, *Ain't I a Woman: Black Women and Feminism* (Boston: South End Press, 1981), 196.

3. Alice Walker, "One Child of One's Own: A Meaningful Digression Within the Work(s)—An Excerpt," in Gloria T. Hull, Patricia Bell Scott, and Barbara Smith, *All the Women Are White, All the Blacks Are Men, But Some of Us Are Brave: Black Women's Studies* (Old Westbury, N.Y.: Feminist Press, 1982), 42.

4. Rose M. Brewer, "Theorizing Race, Class and Gender: The New Scholarship of Black Feminist Intellectuals and Black Women's Labor," in *Theorizing Black Feminisms: The Visionary Pragmatism of Black Women,"* ed. Stanlie M. James and Abena P. A. Busia (London: Routledge, 1993), 13.

5. Audre Lorde, *A Burst of Light* (Ithaca, New York: Firebrand Books, 1988), 123.

Index